Quiet Water

NEW JERSEY AND
EASTERN PENNSYLVANIA

AMC's Canoe and Kayak Guide to the
Best Ponds, Lakes, and Easy Rivers

KATHY KENLEY

Appalachian Mountain Club Books
Boston, Massachusetts

The AMC is a nonprofit organization and sales of AMC books fund our mission of protecting the Northeast outdoors. If you appreciate our efforts and would like to make a donation to the AMC, contact us at Appalachian Mountain Club, 5 Joy Street, Boston, MA 02108.

http://www.outdoors.org/publications/books/

Distributed by The Globe Pequot Press, Guilford, Connecticut.

Front cover photograph © Ariel Skelley and Photolibrary
Back cover photograph © Kathy Kenley
All interior photographs © Kathy Kenley
Book design by Eric Edstam

Maps by Ken Dumas, © Appalachian Mountain Club

Library of Congress Cataloging-in-Publication Data

Kenley, Kathy.
  Quiet water New Jersey & eastern Pennsylvania : AMC's canoe and kayak guide to the best ponds, lakes, and easy rivers / Kathy Kenley.
      p. cm.
  Includes bibliographical references.
  ISBN 978-1-934028-34-6
  1. Canoes and canoeing--New Jersey--Guidebooks. 2. Canoes and canoeing--Pennsylvania--Guidebooks. 3. New Jersey--Guidebooks. 4. Pennsylvania--Guidebooks. I. Appalachian Mountain Club. II. Title.
  GV776.N5K465 2010
  797.1220974--dc22
                        2009045906

The paper used in this publication meets the minimum requirements of the American National Standard for Information Sciences-Permanence of Paper for Printed Library Materials, ANSI Z39.48-1984. ∞

Outdoor recreation activities by their very nature are potentially hazardous. This book is not a substitute for good personal judgment and training in outdoor skills. Due to changes in conditions, use of the information in this book is at the sole risk of the user. The author and the Appalachian Mountain Club assume no liability for accidents happening to, or injuries sustained by, readers who engage in the activities described in this book.

Interior pages contain 30% post-consumer recycled fiber.
Cover contains 10% post-consumer recycled fiber.
Printed in the United States of America,
using vegetable-based inks.

FSC
Mixed Sources
Product group from well-managed forests, controlled sources and recycled wood or fiber
Cert no. SCS-COC-002464
www.fsc.org
©1996 Forest Stewardship Council

10 9 8 7 6 5 4 3 2 1   10 11 12 13 14 15 16

LOCATOR MAP

Contents

SECTION 1: NORTHERN NEW JERSEY

SECTION 2: CENTRAL NEW JERSEY

SECTION 3: SOUTHERN NEW JERSEY

SECTION 4: EASTERN PENNSYLVANIA

NATURE ESSAYS

At-a-Glance Trip Planner

#	Trip	Page	Location	Area	Estimated Time
NORTHERN NEW JERSEY					
1	High Point State Park—Steeny Kill Lake and Sawmill Pond	2	Colesville	30 acres; 20 acres	1.0 hour; 0.5 hour
2	Wawayanda State Park	7	Vernon	255 acres	2.5–3.0 hours
3	Green Turtle Pond	11	West Milford	40 acres	1.0–1.5 hours
4	Monksville Reservoir	14	West Milford	505 acres	4.0 hours
5	Pompton Lake	18	Pompton Lakes	204 acres	2.0–2.5 hours
6	Splitrock Reservoir	21	Rockaway	625 acres	4.0–5.0 hours
7	Lake Hopatcong and Lake Musconetcong	27	Landing	2685 acres; 326 acres	to 15 hours; 2.5 hours
8	Cranberry Lake	32	Cranberry Lake	180 acres	2.0–2.5 hours
9	Kittatinny Valley State Park—Lake Aeroflex and Twin Lakes	35	Newton	117 acres; 29 acres	2 hours; 1 hour
10	Paulin's Kill Lake and Paulin's Kill River	38	Newton	174 acres	2.0–2.5 hours

Hiking Trails	Swimming	Motor Boats	Permit Required	Trip Highlights
Y	Y	electric only	N	Quaint scenic lakes in NJ's highest elevations
Y	Y	electric only	N*	Islands, beautiful scenery, abundant waterfowl and wildlife
N	N	electric only	N	A hidden gem with islands surrounded by steep hills
Y	N	10 horse-power limit	N	Raptors, swans, beavers, rock faces and a drowned forest
N	N	electric only	N	Waterfowl, lush mountains, islands
Y	N	electric only	N	Spectacular! Maine-like rock islands, clear water, remote, beavers, abundant bird life
N	Y/N	unlimited; electric only	N*/N	Largest lake in NJ and a smaller lake with pretty scenery
Y	N	unlimited horsepower	N	Nice lake tucked into Allamuchy Mountain on the west
Y	N	electric only	N	Deepest glacial lake in NJ, beavers, raptors
Y	N	electric only	N	Abundant wildlife, scenic setting, very pretty river

Hiking Trails	Swimming	Motor Boats	Permit Required	Trip Highlights
Y	Y	electric only	N	Large lake with islands, dozens of swan, waterfowl
Y	Y	N	N	Remote, pristine mountain lake high in the Kittatinny Mountains
Y	N	electric only	N	Crystal clear waters, great fishing, abundant bird life
N	N	electric only	N	Wildflowers and butterflies, marsh-grass islands, near Delaware Water Gap
N	N	unlimited horsepower for part of trip .	N	Bountiful and diverse bird life, marshlands, migratory stopover, falcons
Y	N	electric only	N	Pretty lake, quiet respite, and abundant waterfowl in the middle of town
Y	N	electric only	N	Hawks, osprey, nesting eagles, ducks, deer, coyotes, good fishing
Y	Y	electric only	N*	Serpentine lake, a few islands, lots of bird life
Y	Y	10 horse-power limit	Y	Eagles, osprey, hawks, tall wooded hillside, rock faces, scenic
Y	N	electric only	N	Miles of historic waterway surrounded by a scenic greenway
N	N	electric only	N	Large, long scenic lake with abundant wildlife near town
N	N	electric only	N	Excellent fishing and easy paddling in town
N	N	electric only	N	Miles of shoreline, pleasant paddle, waterfowl, next to ocean
Y	N	electric only	N	Long lake with plentiful waterfowl, bird life, and turtles
Y	N	electric only	N	Nice lake in a large park on the outskirts of Trenton

Hiking Trails	Swimming	Motor Boats	Permit Required	Trip Highlights
N	N	electric only	Y	Remote, abundant waterfowl, raptors, pine and oak forests
N	N	electric only	Y	Waterfowl, herons, good fishing
Y	N	electric only	N*	Nesting osprey, cormorants, drowned forests, eagles
Y	N	electric only	N	Islands, waterfowl, freshwater marshes, scenic, close to town
N	N	electric only	N	Marsh and wading birds, wetlands, islands, close to town
N	N	electric only	N	Waterfowl, birds, hawks, quails, foxes
Y	N	electric only	N	Turtles, beavers, scenic waterway, abundant bird life
Y	N	electric only	N	Two nice lakes close to town, waterfowl, turtles
Y	N	electric only	N	Easy paddle with pleasant scenery in town
Y	Y	electric only	N	Cedar bogs, marsh birds and wildflowers, frogs, turtles
N	Y	electric only	N	Drowned cedar forest, osprey, wild cranberry, remote
N	Y	electric only	N	Freshwater pineland marshes, waterfowl, wild blueberry bushes
Y	N	electric only	N	Ospreys, eagles, wild iris, cedar bogs, herons and egrets
N	N	unlimited horsepower, but rare	N	Eagles, osprey, tea-colored water, cedar bogs, wading birds, river otter, beavers
N	N	electric only; unlimited horsepower, but rare	N	Shore birds, saltwater marshes, wading birds, osprey

Hiking Trails	Swimming	Motor Boats	Permit Required	Trip Highlights
N	N	electric only	N	Ducks, geese, swans, migratory stopover, wetlands
Y	Y	electric only	N*	Nice lake with lakeside cabins, plenty of bird life
N	N	electric only	N	Beavers abound, plentiful waterfowl, raptors, freshwater marshes
N	N	unlimited horsepower, but sparse	N	Brackish marshes, diverse and abundant waterfowl, migration stopover, muskrats
N	Y	electric only	N	Pretty lake, wildlife, easy paddle
N	N	electric only	N	Cedar swamps, islands, song birds, carnivorous plants,
Y	Y	electric only	N	Hardwood forest and swamps, turtles, wading birds
Y	Y	electric only	N*	Eagles, osprey, islands, nationally-ranked scenic river
N	N	unlimited horsepower in small section	N	Premier migratory stopover, plentiful bird life, falcons, hawks, brackish marshes
Y	N	10 horsepower limit	Y	Huge lake with islands, hawks, raptors, wildlife, good fishing
N	N	electric only	N	Brackish water marsh, marsh and wading birds, swan, osprey
Y	Y	electric only	N	Very remote, raptors, white cedar wetlands, plentiful bird life
Y	Y	electric only	Y	High mountain lake, islands, plentiful bird life, waterfalls, gorges
N	N	N; electric only	Y	Raptors, waterfowl, marshes, islands

Hiking Trails	Swimming	Motor Boats	Permit Required	Trip Highlights
Y	Y	electric only	Y	Remote, wooded hillsides, raptors, waterfowl
Y	N	electric only	Y	Birds of prey, woodland birds, long mountain range
Y	Y	unlimited horsepower with no-wake zones	Y	Steep wooded cliffs, rock faces, clear water, waterfall, beaver, otter, birds galore
N	N	electric only	Y	View of Kittatinny Ridge, glacial wetlands, tanagers, near Delaware Water Gap
Y	Y	electric only	Y	Aquatic mammals, woodland birds, good fishing
Y	N	electric only	Y	Bluebirds, butterflies, waterfowl, quiet
Y	Y	20 horse-power limit with no-wake zones	Y	Osprey, waterfowl, beaver, view of Haycock Mountain
Y	N	electric only	Y**	Pastoral landscape interspersed with wooded hillsides, waterfowl
Y	Y	unlimited horsepower with no-wake zones	Y	Steep wooded hillsides, long coves, abundant waterfowl and bird life
Y	N	N	Y	Premier migratory bird stopover, wild turkey and pheasant
N	N	electric only	Y	Nesting egrets, birds of prey, quiet and scenic
Y	Y	electric only	Y	Beavers, islands, beautiful wooded Highlands park
Y	N	unlimited, but rare	Y	Pretty river, historic and scenic canal, waterfowl
Y	N	electric only	Y**	Pleasant paddling on nice lake near town
Y	N	electric only	Y**	Song and woodland birds, turtles, and wildflowers in town

NOTES

* Small fee required to enter the park or launch
** Bucks County parks require a county permit

Hiking Trails	Swimming	Motor Boats	Permit Required	Trip Highlights
Y	N	electric only	Y	Eagles, forested rolling hillsides, deer, good fishing
Y	N	electric only	Y	Quiet rural lake with easy paddling, dragonflies
Y	Y	electric only	Y	Rocky shores, forested hillsides, mergansers, woodpeckers, scenic
Y	N	electric only	Y	Remote, clean water, mountains, osprey, eagles, view of Rocky Knob
N	N	electric only	Y	Hidden rural gem, deer, raccoons, egrets
Y	Y	20 horse-power limit	Y	Two large islands, bald eagles, diverse bird life, migratory stopover
Y	N	electric only	N	Raptors, waterfowl, quiet, scenic wooded hillsides
Y	N	unlimited horsepower; unlimited horsepower in small section	Y	Petroglyphs, eagles, osprey; Wonderland of rock islands, abundant waterfowl, major migratory route
Y	Y	electric only	Y	Large island, shore birds, waterfowl, raptors
Y	N	electric only	N*	Quiet, rock cliffs, serpentine shape, eagles, waterfowl, migratory stopover
Y	N	10 horse-power limit	Y	Scenic waterway with views of Boathouse Row and Philadelphia Art Museum

Preface

This book is more of an upgrade rather than a revision of the second edition of *Quiet Water New Jersey*, published in 2004, because it covers 28 new sites in eastern Pennsylvania. Most Pennsylvania sites are in the Highlands region, the southeastern part of the state that roughly forms a semicircle from a little south of Scranton on I-80 to Harrisburg and a little west of I-81 south to Maryland; the remainder are located within a short distance of the Highlands region.

In addition to covering lakes, ponds, and reservoirs, this edition also includes a few slow-moving rivers and extends lake information to describe inflowing streams where they can be paddled for some distance upstream. A few small sites in New Jersey were removed because they have a large daily fee or deteriorated conditions, and to make room for exciting sites that opened to the public since the previous edition, and to include two slow-moving rivers.

I love the adventure of exploration, of finding gems that surprise and excite the senses and widen my experiences. Although I had paddled a number of sites in Pennsylvania over the years, the addition of the eastern Pennsylvania area made this particularly exciting and rewarding as I investigated many sites I had never known about or paddled. As I drove through different geographic and environmental areas, each turn of the road was a refreshing change of scenery or a revisit to areas not seen in a long time. Even a few Pennsylvania paddling friends who accompanied me on some trips were pleasantly surprised at new sites to add to their repertoire not far from home. I hope you, too, will enjoy exploring these sites and all they offer.

Acknowledgments

First and foremost, I would like to thank AMC for the opportunity to write this book and make the large revision to include eastern Pennsylvania and enjoy paddling many new sites in the process. My thanks go to Dan Eisner, editor, for his guidance and kind words along the way, and to Beth Kruzi, the editor for the first edition of this book. A special note of thanks goes to Heather Stephenson, publisher; Athena Lakri, production manager; and other members of the staff involved in the publishing of this book for their understanding and compassion in working with me on deadline extensions due to a serious injury during the summer I worked on this book. A note of thanks also goes to Jill Cooley, intern, who checked all the eye-boggling numbers of GPS coordinates, a new addition to this revision, and Eric Pavlack, the canoeing/kayaking chair of AMC's Delaware Valley Chapter, who provided input for the Pennsylvania sites.

Many people I met during this adventure helped me by supplying information about various sites and their surroundings. The list would be too long to singly name and thank all the park rangers, birders, and naturalists who gave their assistance. I met many local kayakers, canoeists, and anglers who extended their time and gave me insider information about their favorite places.

I am deeply indebted to many friends; first and foremost is Susan Williams, who spent many hours assisting with Pennsylvania boating regulations and Pennsylvania header and campground information, as well as accompanying me on numerous kayak–camping trips in both Pennsylvania, where she resides, and New Jersey; Vince Lewonski, who supplied information on different lakes and rivers in both states and accompaniment on several trips; Steven Miller, who provided insight into many rivers and bodies of water in Pennsylvania; and Deena Kaestner, who helped with assembling some headers and compiling campground information in the appendix. I extend appreciation to my kayaking friends who accompanied me on different trips and made them more enjoyable, and helped with information and suggestions on their favorite local sites. Thanks also go to Gayle Jackson, Nancy Eberly, and Bob Yellen, who provided photographs for sites where inclement or poor weather conditions prevented good photographic opportunities when I visited them.

Thanks also go to the many people who assisted in so many ways with the first edition of this book, including Professor Jack Connor, Professor Mike Hozik, Bill Bell, Karen Roseman, Linda Burdett, and Gerald Marcus.

Finally, warm love and appreciation go to my mother, who encouraged my interest in nature from an early age instead of making me play with dolls. Thanks, Mom.

Introduction

Most kids have an attraction to water, as evidenced by the number of puddles they'll go out of their way to jump in. Some of us never outgrow this attraction.

Something intangible, almost spiritual, happens when I place my boat in the water. Sitting quietly for a moment, I let the water's soothing bob realign my soul. I dip my paddle over the side and the little splash starts my transport on a magic liquid carpet ride. I watch an ospreys hunt for fish or listen to the symphony of avian songs that makes me feel one with nature.

Other than some canoe experiences I had as a child in the Pocono Mountains of Pennsylvania, my paddling adventures began in my late teens when I stumbled across a small, old kayak at a garage sale. It was light enough to load and unload myself and, more important, it fit on the roof of my small car without extending past the bumpers—well, at least not too far. A strange sense of freedom came with that first boat, a freedom rimmed with both the excitement of adventure and the peacefulness of solitude. Whenever I opened local county maps, my eyes zoomed in on every splotch of blue—the search was on for the magic blue liquid.

Among my favorite places are quiet lakes, marshes, ponds, and slow-moving streams, where I can sit on the water and drink in the scenery and wildlife with all my senses. Seeing which animals live in this little cove or what might be found around the back of that island tweaks my curiosity. With each new site, I discover different habitats and learn the links between ecosystems—their similarities and their differences. As a naturalist, my binoculars, camera, field guides, and a journal usually accompany me.

One tactic I occasionally employ is to combine biking and paddling. I lock my bike to a tree on the downstream take-out of a waterway or the opposite end of the lake, then go to the put-in and start paddling. At the end of the trip, I lock up the boat, bike to my vehicle, and drive back to pick up the boat. The bike rides range from 15 to 40 minutes, and it's a great way to see an area's land and water views, plus get an upper and lower body workout on the same outing. A few such trips are included in this book, although it is not necessary to take a bike along to enjoy these waters.

WHY QUIET WATERS?

When the opportunity to prepare this book for AMC arose, I gladly accepted it to seek out new sites and visit those I hadn't paddled in years. Available books only covered the many rivers that dissect the area, but none mentioned the hundreds of lakes, ponds, and reservoirs available to paddlers. Open skies over large bodies of water draw a different variety of wildlife, like ospreys, eagles, ducks, and certain hawks, which do not frequent narrow streams or rivers. These quiet waters offer their own special ambiance, one suited to those who enjoy the tranquility of nature or want a respite, however brief, from hectic city life.

Livery services are necessary for most trips down a river and are not conducive to picking up and paddling whenever you please, particularly if you prefer going solo or like the option of a last-minute paddle after work. Slow-moving rivers where no livery is required provide a different experience than lakes, yet are easy and safe for newcomers. Quiet waters also are ideal for families taking children out for the first time, when a trip may need to end earlier than planned. Novices can gain experience on the calm and unthreatening environment of lakes and ponds. As an experienced paddler, I visit small, local ponds a few times each spring just to loosen up the paddling muscles, check out my equipment, and practice different strokes and maneuvers before venturing out on longer paddles—a practice many experienced paddlers observe.

THE SELECTION PROCESS

What's the recipe for a book such as this? Take quite a few weeks poring over detailed county and topographical maps, thousands of road miles, lots of water miles, tons of photographs, a dozen small notepads, lots of camp food, and mix well. My culinary skills did not improve, but my repertoire of paddling sites escalated tenfold. Along the way I learned how to put my minivan into "squeeze gear" on narrow roads and teased it into becoming four-wheel drive for short distances. Some absolutely delightful gems in the area are covered in this book, and I encourage all readers to visit them. If you don't, you'll be missing some of the best paddling adventures in the Northeast.

How did I make selections for this book? My main focus was to provide information on the better sites available in eastern Pennsylvania and New Jersey to assist those getting started and increase the repertoire of more experienced paddlers. After consulting with my regular paddling buddies, I also made it a goal to have a wide enough geographic selection to provide a location within 30 minutes of anyone, from the beginner who wishes to get out frequently for experience, to a parent initiating a child into the sport, to someone who simply cannot travel longer distances or wants to get in a quick paddle after work. To that end, a number of sites have been included that may seem less than ideal for the more experienced paddler or someone out for a day on wilderness waters, but they provide a convenient place to paddle for those living or working nearby. Where lake density was thick, I tried to choose the best body of water, not necessarily the biggest or the most popular.

If you're out for the quietest paddling, select sites offering only boating, fishing, and possibly camping; swimming, picnicking, and recreational facilities tend to draw large crowds, particularly in July and August. If the whole family is out for the day, and you are the only one who paddles, you will want sites that provide additional recreational activities for the family to enjoy. What each of us looks for on any given day is different—some days it's a long, silent paddle; other days we just need something big enough to float our boat. The At-a-Glance Trip Planner will help guide you to the sites that meet your needs.

SAFETY

The single most important piece of safety equipment is the personal flotation device (PFD), also called a life jacket or life vest, with a waterproof whistle attached. The PFD should always be worn, because even the most experienced paddlers can find themselves on the wrong side of the waterline or in a difficult situation. Some lakes and reservoirs require that a PFD be worn at all times or be readily accessible within 30 seconds. Don the vest immediately if fog, inclement weather, or other hazardous conditions arise. Non-swimmers and children should always wear a PFD, with straps secured tightly enough to prevent the vest from slipping off. Children should not wear an adult PFD, as they can easily slip out of it; make sure they have a child's vest that fits properly.

Unless you have a propensity for a particular color or feel you must make a fashion statement, select a yellow or orange PFD, particularly for children or non-swimmers. Light colors are seen more readily against a dark water surface, facilitating a quicker rescue. PFDs also add a bit of warmth on chilly days. Small children riding in a canoe or in the front compartment of a tandem

A father makes sure his daughter's vest is fastened and snugged properly.

(two-person) kayak should be warned not to lean over the side, stand up, or move about suddenly.

Motorboats over ten horsepower are loud and can be unsettling to novice paddlers as they zip by throwing large wakes. If caught unexpectedly, turn the bow of your boat into the wake as quickly as possible to prevent swamping. Most waters listed in this book permit only slow-moving electric motorboats, and there are a few sites that allow only manually powered boats. A very small number that permit limited (usually 20 horsepower) or unlimited motorboats have paddler-friendly no-wake zones. Fortunately, many lakes ban personal watercraft altogether, and more than one lake ban their use on weekends during the summer. Many bodies of water are located within or adjacent to prime hunting areas. Check with your state Fish and Game official or local sporting goods store for specific hunting seasons, particularly in spring and fall.

If you paddle solo, let someone know where you are going, especially if you live alone. In big-boat arenas, it's called a float plan. Recently, a very experienced friend who lives alone went kayaking down a local river swollen with recent rains. He hit a submerged log, quickly found himself inspecting the river bottom, and surfaced with his head just inches from a fat overhanging tree limb. "I could have been knocked unconscious and nobody would have known where I was!" he exclaimed. "And the water was cold—I could have gone hypothermic." We discussed the incident among our circle of paddling friends, promising to send an email or call someone whenever we go out alone, and let them know when we return.

WHAT TO BRING

Always bring the following ten items with you:

1. PFD with whistle.
2. Hat. It not only shields your eyes from the damaging effects of the sun, but also helps retain body heat when the air is chilly and offers a degree of protection from overheating when the sun is broiling.
3. Proper footwear, such as neoprene socks or booties, or closed-toe water shoes to protect against sharp rocks, glass, or shells.
4. Whistle. This should be attached to your vest. Trying to shout for help is extremely difficult, especially if it's windy. Whistle sounds carry a long way.
5. Water and food. Dehydration can have devastating effects on the body. Make sure you have enough fluids and some food to re-energize. One quart of fluid is sufficient for a short trip, but carry two quarts or more for longer trips.
6. Dry bag securely fastened to the boat to carry food, first aid kit, dry clothes, map, and other essentials for your trip. Trash bags and plastic grocery bags are not waterproof. Invest in a dry bag.
7. Rope throw bag. This is a valuable rescue device that can be thrown to a swimmer in trouble or used to tow another boat to shore. The rope can also be used to tie up your boat to a tree if you stop for lunch on a windy day.
8. Knife. This preferably should be clipped to your PFD so that it's easily accessible. It has many uses, particularly if you enjoy camping while paddling.
9. First-aid kit. Carry at least a few bandages, first-aid ointment, gauze pads, and tape. Insect repellent in summer is also a good addition.
10. Sun protection. Absolutely have a high SPF sunblock. I prefer the spray containers so I can apply it to my back if I'm out alone. Sunblock specifically made for lips is also a good idea.

My personal additions to the above are a paddle float, bilge pump, and waterproof VHF radio when out on large lakes, bays, or oceans where a swim to shore would be daunting, if not impossible. On large bodies of water, a chart and compass should be added. Self- and assisted-rescue skills are extremely important.

PADDLING AT NIGHT

Full-moon paddles are becoming increasingly popular, but paddling at night requires extra equipment and safety precautions. Never, ever paddle a site for the first time at night before becoming familiar with it during daylight. Even if you paddle with people who are very familiar with the site, there is a risk of becoming separated. Plan where on the water you'll be paddling at night, take note of compass directions, and, best of all, log the launch coordinates into your GPS and mark it as a waypoint. Having a GPS won't save you, but knowing how to use one will. If possible, paddle with others and always let someone know where you will be, when you plan to start out, and when they can expect a call letting them know you're safely back to the launch.

Equipment for night paddling, in addition to the previously listed 10 items, should include, at a minimum, a map of the body of water, compass, waterproof flashlight, headlamp, and extra clothes. The map should have a north indicator and GPS coordinates noted for the launch and any other landmarks you deem important. Make sure the map is in a waterproof map case—zip-top bags don't always keep things dry and readable. Headlamps with different light intensity levels are essential. The low-level intensity allows you to read the map without blinding your vision or those around you. The high-level is useful when you're coming close to land or the launch to see any logs or obstructions.

Inland rules-of-the-road for manually powered vessels require an all-around light or handheld flashlight that can be "shown in sufficient time to avoid collision." A light on a stanchion is available that attaches to your boat by a strong suction cup. Your handheld waterproof flashlight should be readily accessible. In additional, reflective tape can be attached to your hat, vest front and back, the back side of your paddle, and even along both sides of your bow to make you visible to other boaters. Chemical glow sticks are fun to use, but they do not provide enough light to read a map. Position any light on your body or boat so it does not interfere with your vision or that of your buddies.

Carry additional charged batteries for your GPS in a waterproof container. Extra clothes and a poncho are musts. Not only can it become cold quickly, but you should have them in case of emergency. Additional equipment, such as a VHF radio, could be useful on some waters. Much depends on the type of waters you'll be paddling on. If possible, go with a group of paddlers who are experienced at night paddling to become familiar with the particular tips and risks involved.

HYPOTHERMIA

Water robs the body of heat 25 times faster than air, potentially causing a condition called hypothermia, or subnormal body temperature. Drowning may occur when extended immersion in cold water cools the body to such a degree that a person becomes physically and mentally incapacitated. Symptoms of hypothermia include slurred speech, loss of coordination, confusion, apathy, and irrational behavior. All symptoms become more critical when you are paddling solo. Prime conditions for hypothermia exist in spring and early summer, when water temperatures are cold but warm air lulls us into wearing less-than-adequate clothing for coldwater immersion. Roll up your long-sleeved shirt if you must, but don't take it off. A PFD not only adds a small amount of insulation, but also will keep you afloat should you lose consciousness. Change into warm, dry clothes as soon as practical, and drink warm liquids. Pick up a pamphlet on hypothermia from your local hospital or American Red Cross chapter to learn more.

EQUIPMENT

Any book on paddling must have sections on equipment, technique, and safety. For those of you who are experienced paddlers, please take a moment to review these sections. For those just starting to paddle, I offer only preliminary tips and advice, as numerous books detail equipment, paddling techniques, and boat styles far more completely than I can in an abbreviated format.

The first two pieces of equipment are a boat and a paddle. If you're old enough, you remember a time when there were only two types of sneakers: Converse high-tops or regular. Today sneaker designs exist for every sport and then some. The same is true for kayaks, canoes, and paddles. Styles are available for whitewater, rodeo, sea, surf, touring, and racing, which can set even the most experienced paddler's head spinning when reviewing all the models on the market. Don't let it overwhelm you. Since your main interest is paddling quiet waters, you'll want a boat that is stable and that tracks well. If you intend to camp or carry extensive camera equipment, make sure the volume of the boat is large enough to carry the desired gear. Your best bet is to rent a boat a few times until you get the feel of paddling and are comfortable. Renting a different boat each time also allows you to experience different designs and models.

Outfitters and paddle shops gladly recommend boat models and paddles they feel will best suit your needs and your physical characteristics such as height and weight. When you're ready to buy, find a boat that handles well for your current skill level—you can always upgrade later. Dealers located near a lake usually let you test paddle different models for little or no fee. Paddle festivals held in late spring through early fall offer a great opportunity to try out a number of boats and different types of paddles. Some rental operations offer end-of-season sales on used boats—a great way to pick up a boat inexpensively. Most of all, make sure you're comfortable in the boat.

Materials also vary. Roto-molded plastic is the least expensive and best for beginners, as it takes quite a bit of abuse. Fiberglass increases the cost tremendously and, although the boat will move faster than its plastic counterpart, is more susceptible to damage from rocks or gravelly bottoms. Roto-mold boats are slightly heavier than their fiberglass counterparts and occupy the heavier side of the spectrum. Kevlar increases the cost but decreases weight substantially. Carbon fiber is the lightest and most expensive but is more susceptible to damage.

Always take at least two quarts of water if you intend to paddle for any length of time. The heat of a summer's day or the dry west winds of fall can rob your body of moisture and bring on dehydration. And how about a small journal? Not only is it a log for sites paddled, but also a reference for wildlife observations and friends you've paddled with or met along the way.

If you plan to visit sites where you have to carry your boat any distance, wheeled carts and canoe yokes are available. The carts are compact and fold up to store in the bottom of your boat or can be lashed on the rear deck. Wash all your gear with clean, fresh water at the end of a trip and dry thoroughly to prevent corrosion and mold.

TECHNIQUE

Unlike downriver or ocean paddling, quiet water paddling requires no special skills. However, knowing how to hold a paddle correctly and properly execute the basic forward, backward, sideway (draw), and turning strokes will make for a more enjoyable day and lessen the risk of injury. It's always better to learn correct technique initially than to correct sloppy habits later.

If you can, find the time to take a quick lesson. Most outfitters offer private and group instruction for beginning and experienced paddlers. A half-hour to one-hour lesson is all you need to start off in the right direction. Expand your technique repertoire as time and money permit—it is money well spent. Novices should stay with smaller ponds before tackling large lakes, where wind and waves could challenge them beyond their capabilities. Most lakes are usually glasslike in the early morning hours, but as an old salt once told me, "As the sun comes up, so does the wind." That adage holds true for the ocean as well as the lake down the street. Winds tend to die down in late afternoon or early evening. Early morning and late afternoon are also prime times to observe wildlife.

Braces and self-rescue techniques should be learned prior to venturing out to the middle of a large lake or reservoir. Take a few minutes to review these skills at the beginning and periodically throughout your paddling season. You may never need them, but if a squall arises suddenly or a large boat passes dangerously close, you will be prepared. Increasing your skill level will not only make you feel more comfortable with your boat, but will instill a level of confidence in case less-than-ideal conditions arise—and they eventually will.

Basic navigation skills come in handy on larger lakes, where rainstorms or fog can obscure the shoreline suddenly. (Most prevalent in early morning and late afternoon during spring and fall, fog is due to a marked difference between land and air temperatures.) Always bring a waterproof compass on large bodies of water and know how to use it properly. A GPS is a wonderful tool, but if your batteries die, a regular compass is an excellent backup.

TAKING THE CHILDREN ALONG

Paddling with children is rewarding but requires special considerations. In addition to wearing a PFD, children must understand the importance of proper movement while in a boat, such as moving slowly without sudden moves, sitting and staying low in the boat, and knowing the proper procedure for entering and exiting the boat. Plan on shorter trips initially. Long paddles may require you to land occasionally and let them romp around a bit, even if the space is small, depending on the child's normal activity level. Most children are so excited to be going out in a boat that they sit quietly and absorb the sights and sounds—at least the first few times out.

Try to include them in the adventure. Play games that involve spotting specific turtles or birds. Ask their opinion on which way to go, or what they think about the scenery in a particular cove. Inexpensive binoculars will help engage them in nature observations. Having some equipment to call their own, and being responsible for it, will help make them feel part of the trip. Very young children may want to bring along a special toy, perhaps a small one that won't get ruined if it gets wet.

Kids eat—often! Be sure to pack enough snacks and drinks for the paddle as well as for the trip home. Pack an extra sweater or jacket for them, even in summer, as a light breeze over cool mountain waters or in dense shade near shore can be chilly for those not paddling. A change of clothes kept in the car will be handy if they accidentally trip and fall into the water getting in or out of the boat.

Kids between the ages of 8 and 10 want to paddle. They don't just want to hold a paddle; they want to be part of the actual process. Child-sized canoe and kayak paddles are available, and if you want to keep the peace and avert mutiny, buy one. Keeping kids in a tandem kayak while they're learning techniques only works for a short time. Once they get the hang of it, they'll want their own kayak. In canoes, you'll be able to stretch this out a little longer by teaching them both bow and stern techniques before they can adequately handle their own boat. Enjoy the experience of sharing this wonderful world with children.

WILDLIFE

It's a well-known practice of wildlife photographers, birders, and other serious nature observers: Once you are in an area of abundant wildlife, sit still. Let them come to you, and you have a better chance of closer observation for longer periods of time. Dawn and dusk are the best times to spot deer, raccoons, otters, and other mammals that come to drink water. Look for animal tracks near tiny openings around the lakes they frequent, get into position ahead of time, and then wait quietly and patiently for their arrival.

Do not feed wildlife and never attempt to touch or approach wild animals. Raccoons, bears, skunks, foxes, and coyotes are potential visitors to your campsite and may be encountered while hiking, particularly in the mountainous northern regions. Raccoons and bears have been known to open coolers and rummage through food containers. Keep food tightly packed and stored in your vehicle or away from the campsite—never in your tent. Clean all cooking implements immediately after use, and place garbage where animals cannot smell it or gain access to it.

Any wild animal can harbor diseases such as rabies. Never approach or chase after an animal. You can disrupt its daily routine and frighten it into defending itself or its territory. In addition, never get between a wild animal and its young. If you accidentally find yourself in this situation, lower your eyes and back away slowly. Should you be bitten or scratched, seek medical attention immediately.

New Jersey and Pennsylvania, along with other Mid-Atlantic and New England states, are home to *Ixodes scapularis*, the deer tick that carries the bacteria responsible for Lyme disease. This tick normally crawls around on the body for three or more hours before settling on a spot. It takes another hour or two before burrowing deep into the skin. While you do have plenty of time before a tick can do damage, it is wise to check yourself often if you brush past foliage while loading or unloading your boat. Always do a thorough check for ticks at the end of the day.

Tick kits, available at most outdoor and sporting goods stores, contain a small magnifying glass, specialized tweezers, and instructions on proper removal, as well as common signs and symptoms of Lyme disease. A bull's-eye rash, the most obvious sign, often develops within a day or two around the bite, but not everyone is lucky enough to develop that symptom. Lyme disease is easily treated if detected early.

CAMPING

There's nothing like paddling and then heading to a campground for the night and paddling the next day to make a perfect getaway weekend. Be respectful of campgrounds and leave your site as clean as, or cleaner than, you found it. Keep noise to a minimum and observe the rules for quiet hours. If you have a dog you'd like to bring along, make sure the campground accepts pets and always pick up after them. Prevent the spread of invasive pests and diseases, such as gypsy moth and borers, by leaving your firewood at home and purchasing what you need from a supplier near where you will be camping.

Kayak- or canoe-camping, such as for Round Valley (see Trip 19), is an exciting adventure, but requires pre-planning. Always test-fit what you intend to bring, and make sure everything fits in dry bags and the dry bags fit in your boat. Pack all the essentials first, and then add personal amenities and extras as room permits. A boat loaded with camping equipment will handle differently than when empty, and weight distribution becomes important. If you pack all the heavy items in the bow, the nose will want to dive if you encounter wind waves. If the heavy items are all in the stern, steering can become an issue, as the bow will ride high in the water. It's worth the time and effort to do a test paddle with all your equipment on a nice day and redistribute equipment if necessary before your first boat-camping trip. Mother Nature can be unpredictable.

Local paddling groups are a wonderful resource for information and some even offer a boat-packing demo day to go over the essentials of camping from your boat and how to pack for best fit and boat handling. A list of area paddling groups can be found in Appendix C.

FISHING, CRABBING, AND PERMITS

Catching your own dinner, whether camping overnight or returning home, is a rewarding experience. If you are camping, bring along some add-water-and-heat meals—just in case the fish are not biting that day. Break-apart rods that come in two or three sections are relatively inexpensive and stow compactly in even the smallest boat. Rod-holders are available for canoes and kayaks.

In New Jersey, be advised that anyone between the ages of 16 and 69 must display a valid New Jersey fishing license to fish in fresh waters. Licenses may be obtained from most county or municipal offices, or agents such as sporting

goods stores and bait shops. For complete information, visit www.njfishand
wildlife.com.

In Pennsylvania, a current fishing license is required of persons age 16 and
over to fish or angle for any species of fish. Licenses may be obtained from
license-issuing agents, county treasurer offices, and most bait shops and sporting goods stores. You can also obtain a license online immediately by visiting www.theoutdoorshop.state.pa.us. Visit www.fish.state.pa.us for complete
information.

Blue crabs, at their peak in August, can be caught in brackish coastal regions
from late June through September. Crabbing requires no license, but current
New Jersey law requires a legal minimum size of 4.5 inches across the body,
tip to tip.

WHAT TO EXPECT IN NEW JERSEY

New Jersey lies in the highly populated Northeast corridor between two major cities: Philadelphia and New York City. Let's not kid ourselves. We cannot
expect to find as many remote areas per square mile as in Maine or Montana
within our borders, but we do have many beautiful bodies of water to paddle,
some of which are quite isolated. I have discovered many lakes in more "remote"
regions that are extremely crowded and unappealing—houses line the shores
down to the water's edge, while motorboats and personal watercraft roil the
waters like a storm. In contrast, some lakes and ponds within highly populated
towns proved a very lovely surprise, with dense woods surrounding some or all
of the lake and private houses set well back from its banks—a pleasant oasis in
the midst of a large urban setting.

What mountains we do have in the northwestern quadrant of the state are
small, with 1,804-foot High Point Mountain in High Point State Park (Trip 1)
being the greatest elevation in the state. Yet in these mountains are delightful,
pristine lakes beset with islands and interesting coves. In the flat coastal plain of
southern New Jersey, Apple Pie Hill rises meekly to a whopping 183 feet above
sea level. If it weren't for the damming of rivers in this region, I doubt there
would be any lakes deep enough to paddle.

Since more than half the state is a low-lying coastal plain bordering the
Atlantic Ocean and Delaware Bay, you'll find a number of sites in tidal saltwater
and brackish marshes carefully chosen for their minimal current. Although
first-timers have paddled these waters with no problem, I strongly advise gain-
ing some experience on other waters first. It is equally important to know tide
schedules. Starting your trip against the current while you are still fresh and
letting it help you on the way back is best. Make your first trips short, until you

get the feel of tidal currents for that particular waterway. These habitats contain extensive wildlife, making them well worth the effort.

WHAT TO EXPECT IN EASTERN PENNSYLVANIA

In and around Philadelphia along the Delaware River and northeast to Morrisville, across from Trenton, New Jersey, is the most densely populated area of eastern Pennsylvania. Some mid- to large-sized cities like Harrisburg, Reading, and Allentown are found along major rivers, such as the Susquehanna and Schuylkill rivers. The best part about the state is that you don't have to travel far outside populated areas to find lakes in very rural and remote areas. This is due in part to the more rugged landscape created by the Appalachian Mountains. As in New Jersey, most Pennsylvania lakes and ponds have been dammed to some degree, increasing their holding capacity and acreage for recreational use, irrigation, or water storage to augment local reservoirs.

Within the rolling hills of the piedmont that occupies the land approximately east of I-81 south of Harrisburg and south of I-78 from Harrisburg to Easton, you will find numerous bodies of water like Octoraro Reservoir (Trip 79) and French Creek State Park (Trip 66) tucked into beautiful valleys surrounded by rich farmlands, small suburban towns, or densely forested lands. In the Appalachian Highlands and Ridge and Valley provinces to the west and north of the piedmont, there's the much more rugged landscape of higher mountains with zigzag roads that lead to lakes like Beltzville State Park (Trip 57) and C. F. Walker Lake (Trip 54). I hope you enjoy getting out and discovering the diversity of lakes and landscapes in eastern Pennsylvania.

How to Use This Book

Each section includes a description of the lake and surrounding area, directions for getting there along with GPS coordinates, a basic map showing roads and launch areas, a map of the lake including features like islands and inlet streams, and what you can expect to see. Hiking trails around the lake, within the park, or in the immediate vicinity have been added in this edition. Be advised that trails shown are reasonably accurate, but you should procure a detailed trail map from the park or purchase one from a company that specializes in trails for that area.

GPS coordinates are usually for the launch, but there are a few instances where the unimproved road to the launch is not marked well on the main road or is easily passed. For those few instances when the GPS coordinates are given for the entry road to the launch, simply follow the road to the launch. GPSs are wonderful tools, but if you've used one enough, you know that often your screen shows you in the middle of a big green blotch because most unimproved roads are not displayed.

Times shown are based on the average paddler traveling around the whole body of water, including all coves and inlets, at a casual pace with time to observe wildlife—usually around 2.5 MPH. If you're a newcomer, don't let high times deter you. You don't have to paddle the whole lake on one outing. For a few of the larger lakes, you'll find the paddling broken into suggested sections, sometimes from different launch sites around the lake, to provide several days of pleasant paddling experiences.

Campgrounds come and campgrounds go. For that reason, call well ahead of time for reservations with sufficient time allowed if you need to find another campground nearby. For up-to-date information, it is best to purchase a campground guide or search the Internet for campgrounds near your intended destination. Suggested books and resources are listed in Appendixes B and C.

Maps and directions in this book are for near-site use only. Complement a large state map with county maps for finer detail, which becomes important in urban areas. County maps are also handy in backcountry areas, where route signs may not be displayed at reasonable intervals or properly indicated at critical junctions.

Backcountry roads also have a habit of changing names at every little hamlet and junction to further confuse matters. A topographic map book, such as that produced by DeLorme and others, not only shows topographic features, but many unimproved roads not indicated on county maps. Topographic maps of individual quadrangles are the best for exploring remote areas. They show almost all unimproved roads and trails, one of which may provide the only access to a new pond (for map sources, see the Appendix C).

In the Take Note section of the header, you'll find useful information on motorboat power allowed on the lake, whether any special permits are required, and any potentially dangerous conditions like unmarked dams or high wind potentials. The majority of sites allow only electric motorboats and a few allow only manually powered boats, but there are a few sites where motorboats of higher horsepower are permitted. Fortunately, most of those sites have paddler-friendly no-wake zones, which are noted on the lake map.

In New Jersey, various state parks, particularly those with recreational facilities, charge an entrance fee from Memorial Day through Labor Day. A few of these have a separate fee to use the boat ramp, but often the boat ramps are free. For an additional fee, you can buy a permit from any state park office that allows unlimited access to state parks. In Pennsylvania, state parks are free, except that some charge a small fee if they have a swimming pool.

This book can never be complete. Lands around lakes and ponds are bought and sold continually, voiding or allowing public access. New housing developments and roads that spring up may render a site much less desirable or change accessibility. Contacts made during the compilation of this book will help keep me posted on changes in specific areas. With your help, future editions will include additional paddling sites and updated information on current ones. Your opinions and thoughts about these sites are important. Perhaps you know of a good lake I missed, notice some inaccuracy in this edition, or discover changes to existing sites. If so, please pass them along to me: Kathy Kenley, c/o AMC Books, 5 Joy Street, Boston, MA 02108. Enjoy the adventure—now, get out and paddle!

Stewardship and Conservation

The more often you get out to enjoy the waters, the more you will appreciate our precious ecosystems and understand the need to help protect them. Numerous community organizations, college clubs, and paddling clubs host cleanups of various waterways. They are usually well advertised and paddlers can join in the effort—and it's a great way to meet other paddlers. On an individual level, my friends and I often carry a trash bag with us to remove carelessly discarded refuse. It may be a small effort, but it makes the waters cleaner for everyone and safer for wildlife. It's a good idea to carry a trash bag or two in your vehicle anyway, as many sites lack refuse containers, having a carry-in, carry-out policy instead.

Local Audubon Society chapters acquire and maintain wildlife sanctuaries that protect wildlife and natural habitats, and have educational centers that foster environmental awareness. Many of their on-premises programs and community-sponsored events are perfect for the younger generation. The Nature Conservancy places its emphasis on the identification and preservation of ecologically important areas and endangered species. Look to the Sierra Club for involvement with environmental concerns and to join organized hikes sponsored around the state.

The New York–New Jersey Trail Conference, based in Manhattan, maintains more than 1,000 miles of trails in two states and monitors 7,600 acres of National Park Service lands that are part of the Appalachian Trail system. Its water-resistant trail maps are conveniently sized for backpacking or paddling. The goals of both the New Jersey Division of Fish and Wildlife and the Pennsylvania Fish and Boat Commission are to protect habitats necessary to maintain and enhance species diversity and wildlife distribution, while at the same time balancing commercial and recreational interests.

THE AMC'S CONSERVATION EFFORTS

The Appalachian Mountain Club is working to protect rivers, lakes, and watersheds in the New Jersey and Pennsylvania Highlands. The AMC supported the efforts to designate the Musconetcong River in the Highlands region of New Jersey as a National Wild and Scenic River. The Musconetcong River was designated Wild and Scenic the day after Christmas in 2006.

The AMC has also advocated for water conservation in the Pennsylvania Highlands, supporting the "Buffers 100" campaign to create 100-foot buffers next to waterways throughout Pennsylvania. By establishing buffers of least 100 feet on either side of every stream in the Commonwealth, communities and waterways will be protected from erosion, pollution, flooding, and drought. To highlight the importance of water quantity and quality, AMC recently developed a Pennsylvania Highlands Water Resources brochure. Waterways in the Pennsylvania Highlands, besides providing recreational opportunities, supply the majority of drinking water to southeastern Pennsylvania and southern New Jersey.

Visit AMC's website, www.outdoors.org, for more information.

LEAVE NO TRACE

The Appalachian Mountain Club is a national educational partner of the Leave No Trace Center for Outdoor Ethics. The Center is an international nonprofit organization dedicated to responsible enjoyment and active stewardship of the outdoors by all people worldwide. The organization teaches children and adults vital skills to minimize their impacts when they are outdoors. Leave No Trace is the most widely accepted outdoor ethics program used today on public lands across the nation by all types of outdoor recreationists. Leave No Trace unites five federal land management agencies—the United States Forest Service, National Park Service, Bureau of Land Management, the Army Corps of Engineers, and the United States Fish and Wildlife Service—with manufacturers, outdoor retailers, user groups, educators, organizations such as the AMC, and individuals.

The Leave No Trace ethic is guided by these seven principles:

Plan ahead and prepare. Know the terrain and any regulations applicable to the area you're planning to visit, and be prepared for extreme weather or other emergencies. This will enhance your enjoyment and ensure that you've chosen an appropriate destination. Small groups have less impact on resources and the experience of other backcountry visitors.

Travel and camp on durable surfaces. Travel and camp on established trails and campsites, rock, gravel, dry grasses, or snow. Good campsites are found, not made. Camp at least 200 feet from lakes and streams, and focus activities on areas where vegetation is absent. In pristine areas, disperse use to prevent the creation of campsites and trails.

Dispose of waste properly. Pack it in, pack it out. Inspect your camp for trash or food scraps. Deposit solid human waste in catholes dug 6 to 8 inches deep, at least 200 feet from water, camp, and trails. Pack out toilet paper and hygiene products. To wash yourself or your dishes, carry water 200 feet away from streams or lakes and use small amounts of biodegradable soap. Scatter strained dishwater.

Leave what you find. Cultural or historic artifacts, as well as natural objects such as plants or rocks, should be left as found.

Minimize campfire impacts. Cook on a stove. Use established fire rings, fire pans, or mound fires. If a campfire is built, keep it small and use dead sticks found on the ground.

Respect wildlife. Observe wildlife from a distance. Feeding wildlife alters their natural behavior. Protect wildlife from your food by storing rations and trash securely.

Be considerate of other visitors. Be courteous, respect the quality of other visitors' backcountry experience, and let nature's sounds prevail.

The AMC is a national provider of the Leave No Trace Master Educator course. The AMC offers this five-day course, designed especially for outdoor professionals and land managers, as well as the shorter two-day Leave No Trace Trainer course, at locations throughout the Northeast.

For Leave No Trace information and materials, contact Leave No Trace Center for Outdoor Ethics at 800-332-4100, or visit www.lnt.org.

1 | NORTHERN NEW JERSEY

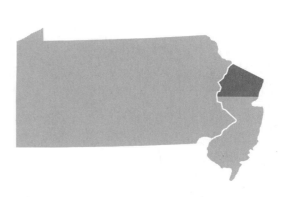

Northern New Jersey includes most of the state's largest natural lakes and natural or artificial reservoirs tucked in valleys between the mountains that comprise part of the Appalachian Ridge and Valley region and the Piedmont Plateau. Creeks and streams along the western edge of the state drain into the Delaware River. From the central and eastern portions of the state, they drain into the Hudson River or the Atlantic Ocean.

The Appalachian Trail traverses the crest of the Kittatinny Ridge in the northwest corner of the state, where black bears, coyotes, and bobcats are seen frequently. Limestone, shale, siltstone, sandstone, and gneiss compose most of the rock types here, along with smaller amounts of quartzite and schist. Volcanic activity during continental rifting around 200 million years ago left behind the durable basalt of the Watchung and Orange mountains and the dramatic columnar diabase cliffs of the Palisades. Basalt and diabase are gray to black rocks formed by the cooling of lava from volcanic activities. The geologically recent ice age that ended about 15,000 years ago carved out numerous glacial lakes, such as Hopatcong and Swartswood, which are now fed by winter snowmelts and natural runoff. Glaciers once deeply gouged the valley now occupied by Lake Aeroflex in Kittatinny Valley State Park. A paddle on this lake can be found in Trip 9.

The most notable geologic feature in northern New Jersey and northeastern Pennsylvania is the Delaware Water Gap, with Mount Tamany on the New Jersey side and Mount Minsi on the Pennsylvania side. The Appalachian Ridge that the Delaware River bisects is called Blue Mountain in Pennsylvania and Kittatinny Ridge in New Jersey. A portion of the Appalachian Trail travels through these mountains and across the gap.

Population density on New Jersey's northeastern side, across the Hudson River from New York City, is the highest in the state. Cities such as Newark, Jersey City, and Patterson meld together as one and extend their urban sprawl farther west each year. Conservation of undisturbed lands in and around this vicinity is most critical for wildlife habitat preservation. A prime example of this is Hackensack Meadows (Trip 15), where you will find an extraordinary diversity of species in the marshlands.

1 | High Point State Park—Steeny Kill Lake and Sawmill Pond

Enjoy raptors, mountain bog and marsh plants, and miles of forested mountains surrounding these remote lakes in the highest elevations in New Jersey.

Location: Colesville, NJ
Maps: *New Jersey Atlas and Gazetteer*, Map 19; USGS Port Jervis South
Area: Steeny Kill Lake: 30 acres; Sawmill Pond: 20 acres
Time: Steeny Kill Lake: about 1.0 hour; Sawmill Pond: 0.5 hour
Conditions: Both lakes: depth average 4 feet
Development: Remote
Information: High Point State Park, 1480 Route 23, Sussex, NJ 07461; 973-875-4800; $5 weekdays in-season, $10 weekends in-season. Fees apply only for access to the recreational site at Marcia Lake. Access to the launches is free.
Camping: On-site at Sawmill Lake; call the park office for reservations. Pleasant Acres Farm Campground, 10 minutes southeast. See Appendix A.
Take Note: Electric motorboats only (rare)

GETTING THERE

To the park office: Drive north on Route 23 out of Colesville for about 2.6 miles to the park office located on the left side of the road. *GPS coordinates*: 41°18.342′ N, 74°40.247′ W.

To Steeny Kill Lake: Proceed another 1.5 miles north of the park office on Route 23 (1.0 mile north of the entrance to Sawmill Lake) to the marked entrance road for the boat launch. You'll find parking for about ten cars. *GPS coordinates for the entrance road to the launch*: 41°19.386′ N, 74°40.695′ W.

To Sawmill Pond: Proceed 0.5 mile on Route 23 past the park office to the marked entrance road on the left leading to the pond; turn left and follow the main road 1.8 miles to the parking area and launch on your left. You'll find parking for about six cars. *GPS coordinates*: 41°17.579′ N, 74°41.366′ W.

WHAT YOU'LL SEE

On the drive along Route 23 to High Point State Park in the extreme northwest corner of the state, be prepared for some steep hills in this mountainous area in the Appalachian Ridge and Valley region. As you can guess by the park's name, you will find within its 15,827 acres the highest elevation in the state, a spot marked by a 220-foot gray stone monument. High Point Mountain rises 1,804 feet above sea level—not much by "real" mountain standards, but it's ours. High Point Mountain is part of the Appalachian Trail, a continuous footpath that starts at Springer Mountain in Georgia and passes through this park on the way to its northern terminus at Mount Katahdin in Maine—a distance of more than 2,000 miles.

At the visitor center, pick up maps and pamphlets that show hiking trails, campgrounds, roads to the two lakes, and directions to the High Point monument. Wildlife, artifact, and geological exhibits in the center will give you a flavor of the area. A swimming beach and small playground are located on Lake Marcia, which is not open to boating. These lakes are small, but the scenery and hiking at this famous park are worth the trip.

Steeny Kill Lake

At 30 acres, Steeny Kill Lake is the larger of the two small lakes. Hickory, beech, and red maple prevail in the more open areas on the south shore. I personally prefer Steeny Kill Lake to Sawmill Pond—not because it's larger, but because it has an irregular shoreline with more nooks and crannies to explore. With only two camping cabins, which are set back from the lakeshore, it also offers a more remote setting. Black bear, bobcat, deer, coyote, groundhog, and fox are among the wildlife species found in the park's hardwood and conifer forests.

HIGH POINT STATE PARK

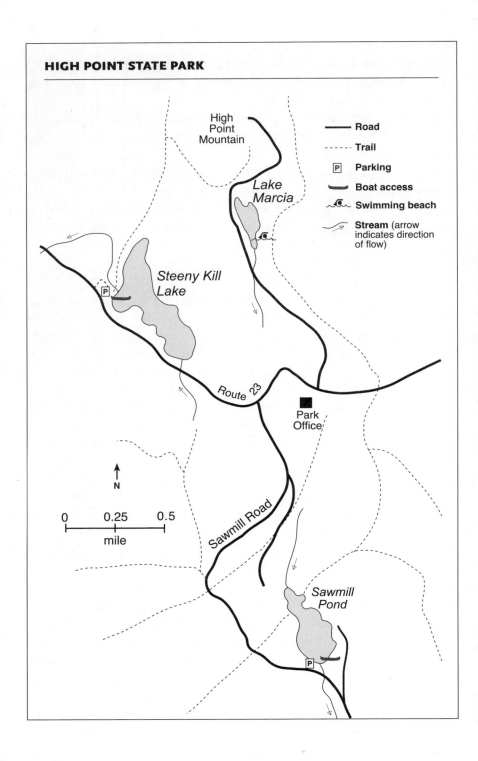

High Point Mountain

Lake Marcia

Steeny Kill Lake

Route 23

Park Office

Sawmill Road

Sawmill Pond

Road

Trail

P **Parking**

Boat access

Swimming beach

Stream (arrow indicates direction of flow)

N

0   0.25   0.5
mile

Canoeists enjoy exploring Steeny Kill Lake on a sunny day high in the mountains.

If you enjoy birding, keep alert for Cooper's and red-shouldered hawks, which are often seen here. Bog and wood turtles inhabit the swampy southern end of the lake. Bog and swamp flowers are prolific and add sparks of color around the lake. Depending on the month, a few species will be in bloom at any given time from May through October, including wild yellow and blue iris. Wild blueberry and blackberry bushes can be seen a foot or two back from the lake's edge. If you like to fish, perch, sunfish, pickerel, bass, and trout are stocked by the Division of Fish and Game at both lakes.

Sawmill Pond

Sawmill Pond lies at the bottom of a depression on the south side of High Point Mountain. The small, 20-acre pond is roughly elliptical, with a few coves on the eastern and southern shores. Tall pine, oak, and hickory dominate the woods around the lake while white racemes of sweet pepperbush scent the air. Pond lilies, bog algae, and marsh grasses fill most of the northern tip by late summer and provide food for foraging waterfowl. You might hear the *whomping* sound of a beaver's tail at the south end of the pond where Big Flat Brook exits the lake on a sinuous path to the Delaware River.

BOWFIN (*AMIA CALVA*)

As the only extant (still living) representative of the family *Amiidae*, bowfins date back to the early Jurassic about 100 million years ago when dinosaurs roamed the earth. A bony gular (throat) plate located between the jaws on the underside is a distinctive characteristic of this olive-colored fish with a long, low dorsal fin and partially lobed caudal fin (tail). Males have a black spot ringed with yellow or orange at the upper base of the tail; females have a similar spot, but no ring. Hard plates in the mouth wreak havoc on anglers' hooks and their sharp teeth can cut through line—and fingers—readily. Like gars, bowfins have a modified air bladder that enables them to breathe surface air and thus tolerate stagnant, oxygen-depleted waters.

Although the majority of the extinct forms were marine, modern bowfins are restricted to the sluggish-moving streams and backwaters of eastern North America, the same environment as bass and crappie. Bowfins are known to inhabit Wawayanda Lake in northern New Jersey (Trip 2) and Lake Marburg in Codorus State Park in Pennsylvania (Trip 75). Voracious feeders, they have decimated local game fish populations on occasion. Their primary diet consists of crustaceans, insects, larvae, and small fish. Adults attain lengths of 18 to 42 inches and can reach weights up to 20 pounds. While considered poor tasting, they are sought after by anglers for the feisty fight they provide. Use the same bait and tackle to catch them as you would a bass.

Bowfins breed during spring after an elaborate ritual during which they construct bowl-shaped nests by tearing out weeds in a shallow area. Once a

female is attracted to the nest, spawning commences. Males guard the eggs and fry for several weeks and may mate with several females during that time, thus having eggs in various stages of development. Young are equipped with an adhesive organ on their snout that enables them to hold on to weeds and remain at the nest site. Rapid growth rate allows them to reach lengths up to 9 inches in their first year.

Although rustic tent sites and a few cabins ring the shoreline, you will barely be aware of them because most campers will be there for the serenity. I ended my day at Sawmill Pond. Before retiring, I paddled out to the middle of the lake, sat under a quarter moon, and watched the stars while a chorus of frogs filled the night air. At one point, coyotes howled back and forth in the distance for about a half hour. It was August, and the Perseid meteor showers graced me with two shooting stars—the end of a perfect day.

More than 50 miles of trails provide hiking opportunities from easy to difficult and from 0.5 to 18.0 miles. Trails are too numerous to mention in this guide. For detailed trail maps, stop at the park office.

No other trip is close, but an option would be to camp at Wawayanda State Park, 55 minutes west, and paddle that lake the next day. See Trip 2.

2 | Wawayanda State Park

Enjoy islands and beautiful scenery while exploring the interesting, highly irregular shoreline of this mountain lake.

Location: Vernon (Sussex), NJ
Maps: *New Jersey Atlas and Gazetteer*, Map 20; USGS Wawayanda
Area: 255 acres
Time: 2.5–3.0 hours
Conditions: Depth average 30 feet
Development: Remote
Information: Wawayanda State Park, 885 Warwick Turnpike, Hewitt, NJ 07421; 973-853-4468; $5 weekdays in-season, $10 weekends in-season.

Camping: On-site group camping (7 to 15 people); call the park office for reservations. Beaver Hill Campground is 30 minutes southwest. See Appendix A.

Take Note: Electric motorboats only

GETTING THERE

To the visitor center: Drive south 0.2 mile on Route 23 from Route 171 to the Clinton Road Exit. Drive north on Clinton Road about 7.0 miles until you come to the T-junction at Route 513 (Warwick Turnpike). Turn left (north) onto Route 513 and drive 2.3 miles to the park entrance on your left. Stop at the visitor center to pick up a map and other useful pamphlets. *GPS coordinates:* 41°11.870′ N, 74°23.845′ W.

To the boat launch: From the visitor center, continue 1.9 miles to the turnoff for the recreation area. The road to the boat launch will be on your left. There's a nice sand and grass launch for cartop boats only. You'll find parking for 100 cars. *GPS coordinates:* 41°11.289′ N, 74°25.573′ W.

WHAT YOU'LL SEE

Nestled in the vast mountains of Wawayanda State Park, this large mountain lake will provide hours of exciting paddling. Picnic grounds, a sandy bathing beach, and a playground are located at the park's recreation area on the north end of the lake. Boat rentals and launches are also on the north end of the lake, but separated from the recreation area.

Numerous deep coves and half a dozen islands provide plenty of adventurous exploring and opportunities for wildlife observations. The two largest islands have a few spots to land for lunch or a break. Other places to stop for a break are scattered around the lake, but most are on the eastern shoreline. Most boaters do not venture past the large island in the middle of the lake, making the southern end a more peaceful experience.

Wawayanda Lake is a good place to try your luck at fishing. Depths range from just a few feet close to shore to about 90 feet in the center of the northern half of the lake. Trout, largemouth bass, catfish, yellow perch, and large sunfish swim beneath the surface, and any one of them would taste delicious cooked over a campfire at day's end. One interesting and uncommon fish with a long history on earth, the bowfin, also can be found in the lake. Along with gars and sturgeons, they are among the few freshwater fish that were alive at the same time as the dinosaurs.

Around the lake, wood and bog turtles inhabit swampy areas and sun themselves on logs at the water's edge. Raccoons, opossums, deer, rabbits, black

WAWAYANDA STATE PARK

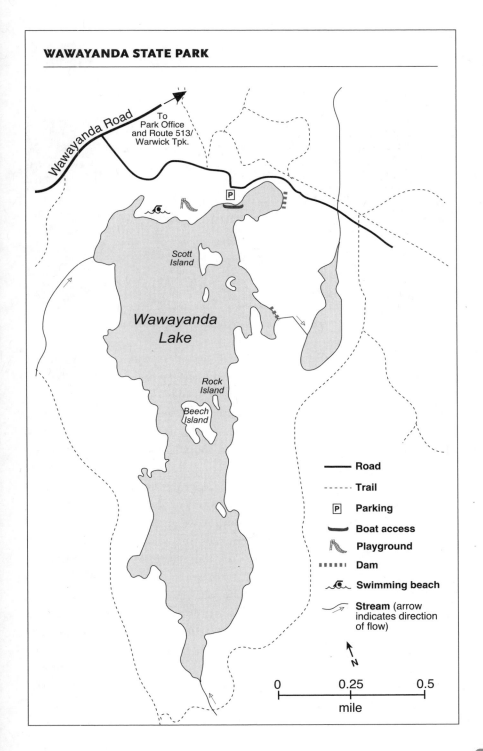

To Park Office and Route 513/ Warwick Tpk.

Wawayanda Road

Scott Island

Wawayanda Lake

Rock Island

Beech Island

— Road

---- Trail

P Parking

Boat access

Playground

Dam

Swimming beach

Stream (arrow indicates direction of flow)

N

0   0.25   0.5

mile

A paddler heads out on a quiet afternoon to explore the lake and enjoy the wildlife.

bears, and skunks might be seen close to the water, along with coyotes and foxes. Throughout the park, birdlife is bountiful. Look for red-shouldered hawks, great blue herons, vultures, eagles, warblers, orioles, and various songbirds. Start out early in the morning or late afternoon for the most peaceful paddling. Those are also the best times to enjoy bird activity and look for other wildlife. Look closely in the long, shallow inlets and you might be lucky enough to see a river otter.

Paddle left after leaving the launch to explore the first cove. Tall stands of wetland grasses on the east end support a variety of wrens. Return to the lake and start exploring, perhaps circling around those islands right in front of you. Continue paddling down the east shoreline, venturing in and out of coves and inlets until you reach Beech Island, which is the largest island in the middle of the lake. There's a smaller island off the northeast tip that has plenty of passage room. Head into the southern half of the lake and drink in the views while looking for river otters, kingfishers, hawks, and other wildlife. Hemlocks, pines, and a good diversity of hardwood species create magnificent foliage displays in fall. On your return trip up the western shoreline, notice the many areas that rise sharply to a height of 15 to 20 feet, creating a different topography than the eastern shoreline. Birdlife is abundant around the stream inlet in the northwest corner of the lake, your last stop before returning to the launch.

Hiking and biking trails meander for more than 40 miles throughout 12,000 acres of Atlantic white cedar swamps and hardwood forests, not including a 19.6-mile stretch of the Appalachian Trail that runs along the western boundary. Twenty marked trails, some designated hiking only, range from 0.4 to 6.0 miles in length, and from easy to difficult. Pick up a detailed map at the visitor center.

Both Green Turtle Pond and Monksville Reservoir are approximately 30 minutes southeast. See Trips 3 and 4.

3 | Green Turtle Pond

The pond offers waterfowl, eagles, hawks, foxes, turtles, and an enticing island.

Location: West Milford, NJ
Maps: *New Jersey Atlas and Gazetteer*, Map 20; USGS Greenwood Lake
Area: 40 acres
Time: 1.0–1.5 hours
Conditions: Depth average 13 feet
Development: Remote
Information: North Jersey District Water Supply Commission, 1 F. A. Orechio Drive, Wanaque, NJ 07465; 973-836-3600.
Camping: Wawayanda State Park, 25 minutes northwest. See Appendix A.
Take Note: Electric motorboats only

GETTING THERE

Starting on Greenwood Lake Turnpike in West Milford, drive south for 0.8 mile on Route 511, then turn left onto Awosting Road. Be careful here—this is a hairpin turn. Drive 0.6 mile on Awosting Road to the wildlife management area entrance. A large sign is at the entrance, but it sits back from the road partially hidden by trees. The best bet is to look for two stone pillars, one on each side of the road, about 500 feet before the entrance. Each pillar is approximately three feet square and five feet high. Once partially blacktopped, the steep road leading down to the lake is now extremely potholed. Parking is available for twelve to fifteen cars. *GPS coordinates*: 41°08.938′ N, 74°19.739′ W.

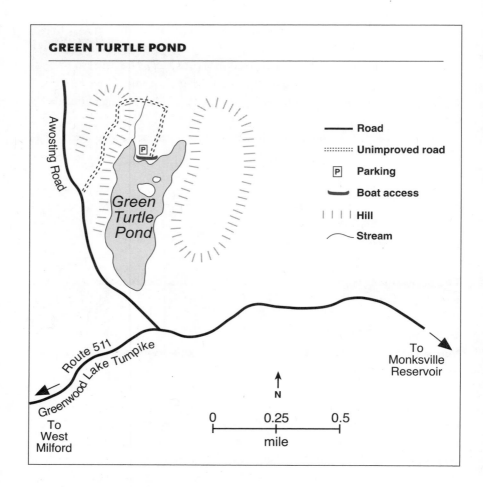

GREEN TURTLE POND

Awosting Road

Green Turtle Pond

P

Route 511
Greenwood Lake Turnpike

To
West
Milford

To
Monksville
Reservoir

Road
Unimproved road
P Parking
Boat access
| | | | Hill
Stream

N

0   0.25   0.5
mile

WHAT YOU'LL SEE

Don't miss this little gem! Driving down the steep, tree-tunneled, potholed road to the lake for the first time, I came around the last bend and slammed on the brakes. An island jutted out of the water a couple of hundred yards off the sunlit dirt-and-stone ramp ahead. I couldn't wait to get my kayak into the water. There's something about exploring islands that has always held a special fascination for me. Islands not only provide more shoreline to explore, but also visually break up a lake's surface, creating a feeling of adventure and exploration. At the sound of my car creeping toward the ramp, a female mallard, 10 feet away, quickly escorted her brood toward dense shrubs farther along the edge; I had disturbed their tranquil swim.

Tucked in a valley with steep mountains on three sides, this is the perfect place to visit on windy days because the mountains block the wind from most

Members of a local paddling club come to this hidden gem to practice their skills.

directions. On either side of the ramp, aquatic plants and grasses lie at the feet of cedar, sassafras, white birch, and red maple. Turkey vultures soar on warm thermals of air along the steep mountainside on the northern edge of the lake. Only one other boat was on the lake that first day—an electric outboard with two anglers fishing by the island. We nodded in recognition, but exchanged no words as we maintained the perfect quiet of the lake. The island has a few small, shallow areas where you can land your boat, although the landings are usually moss-covered low rocks and gravel at the island's edge. Larger rocks or fallen tree limbs at the landing provide a perfect spot to sun yourself while enjoying lunch. Keep your eyes peeled for eagles.

Several narrow animal paths lead to the lake, and you can usually spot a number of deer, especially in the morning and late afternoon. Two dead trees on the island showed evidence of recent woodpecker activity; perhaps one had nested there earlier that summer. The rocky outcroppings on the lake's western edge may harbor timber rattlesnakes or northern copperheads, both of which are poisonous. Exercise caution if you decide to head into the woods.

One of my visits was in late summer and, in addition to another perfectly tranquil day of paddling, I found the shallow areas around the launch site carpeted with tall, bright red cardinal flowers. It's a love–hate relationship. I love the cardinal flower for its shape and vibrant color, but alas, it comes into bloom in late August, signaling the start of the end of summer and the warm paddling weather. Still, I enjoyed the lovely, vibrant, sunlit blossoms that contrasted sharply against the dark cedar trees. There are no formal swimming beaches, picnic tables, or facilities of any kind—just the dirt-and-stone ramp leading to a pristine environment.

While I found no hiking trails around the lake itself, the pond lies minutes from Long Pond Ironworks State Park and a number of hiking trails. Monksville Reservoir is only 12 minutes away; see Trip 4 for details on hiking.

For another paddle, try Monksville Reservoir, only 10 minutes east. See Trip 4. Or camp at Wawayanda State Park, 25 minutes northwest, and paddle there the next day. See Trip 2.

4 | Monksville Reservoir

Enjoy raptors, bouldered shorelines, rock faces, and pretty scenery at this reservoir.

Location: West Milford, NJ
Maps: *New Jersey Atlas and Gazetteer*, Map 20; USGS Greenwood Lake and Wanaque
Area: 505 acres
Time: 4.0 hours
Conditions: Depth average 43 feet
Development: Rural
Information: Long Pond Ironworks State Park, c/o Ringwood State Park, 1304 Sloatsburg Road, Ringwood, NJ 07456; 201-962-7031.
Take Note: Motorboats limited to 10 horsepower

GETTING THERE

Two boat ramps are located at the reservoir. From I-287, take Exit 55 toward Wanaque and drive north 3.8 miles on Ringwood Avenue/Route 511 and continue straight 5.6 miles on Greenwood Lake Turnpike/Route 511. The south launch will be on your left. You'll find parking for about 40 cars. *GPS coordinates*: 41°07.615′ N, 74°18.058′ W.

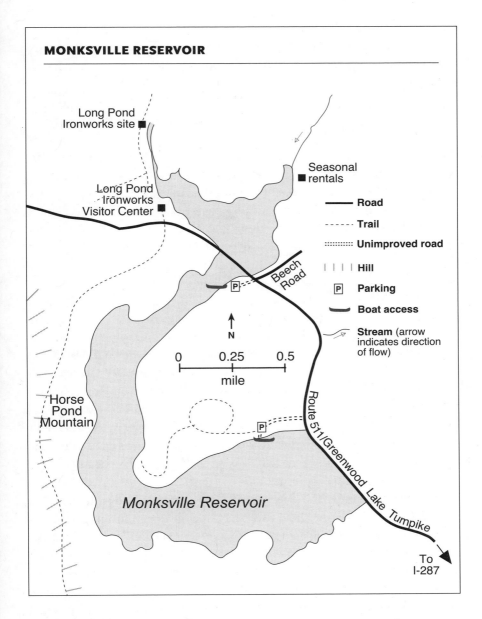

MONKSVILLE RESERVOIR

Long Pond Ironworks site ■

Seasonal rentals ■

Long Pond Ironworks Visitor Center ■

Beech Road

P

━━━ **Road**

- - - - **Trail**

⋯⋯⋯ **Unimproved road**

| | | | **Hill**

P **Parking**

⬋ **Boat access**

⤳ **Stream** (arrow indicates direction of flow)

N

| 0 | 0.25 | 0.5 |

mile

Horse Pond Mountain

P

Route 511/Greenwood Lake Turnpike

Monksville Reservoir

To I-287

To get to the north launch, continue an additional 0.65 mile north on Greenwood Lake Turnpike/Route 511. The north launch will be on your left. You'll find parking for about 100 cars. *GPS coordinates*: 41°08.197′ N, 74°18.145′ W.

Seasonal boat rentals are available on Beech Road, directly across the road from the north launch. *GPS coordinates*: 41°08.224′ N, 74°18.071′ W.

WHAT YOU'LL SEE

For a nice, long paddle and some great scenery, visit the 505-acre Monksville Reservoir, which encircles Long Pond Ironworks State Park like a giant horseshoe. Both launch sites have well-maintained portable toilets, and a grassy picnic area can be found on Beech Road next to the boat rental concession.

Huge boulders and interesting rock faces line the shores south of the Greenwood Lake Turnpike bridge. White birches seem particularly abundant around the lake, contrasting sharply against dark evergreens and lush forest. Ducks, geese, and other waterfowl can be found around the lake in the protected coves. This reservoir has a good population of cormorants and gulls in summer. Eagles, several species of hawks, and vultures frequent the skies over the lake, and a variety of woodland birds will be seen all along the shores throughout your paddle. Large coves in the southern half provide interesting pockets of scenery and wildlife. Along the western side, Horse Pond Mountain rises sharply to a height of 400 feet with some impressive rock faces.

Of all the fish that inhabit these waters, big muskellunge are the most sought after by anglers. As of this writing, the state record muskie, 42 pounds and 13 ounces, was caught here in 1998. Prehistoric-looking snapping turtles inhabit the lake, but are seen rarely as they spend most of their time underwater (unlike other turtles, which like to bask in the sun). Very few places are available to land for a break because of the bouldered shoreline and steep dropoffs. Your best options are the two launches and the grassy area around the Beech Road boat rental concession. The only detriments to the scenery are two sets of power lines, one of which bisects the lake; the other is at the southern end by the dam. Sometimes you can't escape all the signs of civilization. Stay focused on the scenic mountains and plentiful wildlife.

After passing under the Greenwood Lake Turnpike bridge, the scenery changes. That's what I like about paddling under bridges; I just might be surprised by a totally different environment on the other side. To the left, a large field of drowned trees sticks out of shallow waters, inviting you to weave in and out of the maze looking for turtles sunning themselves on low stumps, peering into the clear waters looking for fish, or watching swans and geese weave through the maze. The drowned trees, now silvered with age, provide a pleasant contrast to the deep greens of summer trees or autumn colors. Dense clumps of aquatic grasses along the edges create perfect nursery grounds for large lake fish. Bird-watching here is also quite different, as warblers and finches visibly flit about and pileated woodpeckers nest in cavities of dead trees. On the east side, you can rent canoes at a small boat shed on a large, open, grassy area. A small dock invites you to pull up, stop for lunch, and stretch your legs.

A paddler explores the rock-strewn edges of this reservoir, which is nestled against Horse Pond Mountain in the background.

For the hiker, the 2.5-mile circular Monks Trail starts at the west end of the north launch parking lot by the yellow gate with a triple white blaze. In addition to offering views of Monksville Reservoir, the trail passes some remnants of an abandoned iron mine. Horse Pond Trail is a 6.0-mile, moderately challenging hike up to Horse Pond Mountain and along the ridge with spectacular views of the reservoir. The parking lot for the trailhead is 0.9 mile north on Greenwood Lake Turnpike from the north launch, on the left side. Visit www.nynjtc.org for detailed hiking information. The Long Pond Ironworks visitor center is on your right immediately after crossing the reservoir on Greenwood Lake Turnpike. A 2.5-mile, out-and-back trail leads you past a variety of ruins from the old ironworks village. Pick up maps and information for that and other trails at the visitor center.

For additional trips nearby, visit Green Turtle Pond, 10 minutes west, and Wawayanda State Park, 30 minutes northwest. See Trips 3 and 2.

5 | Pompton Lake

Abundant waterfowl, a couple of islands, and lush mountain backdrops offer you a pleasant paddling experience.

Location: Pompton Lakes, NJ
Maps: *New Jersey Atlas and Gazetteer*, Map 26; USGS Wanaque and Pompton Plains
Area: 204 acres
Time: 2.0–2.5 hours
Conditions: Depth average 40 feet
Development: Suburban
Information: New Jersey Division of Fish and Wildlife, Northern Region Office, 26 Route 173 West, Hampton, NJ 08827; 973-383-0918.
Camping: Mahlon Dickerson Reservation, 33 minutes west. See Appendix A.
Take Note: Motorboats to 10 horsepower

GETTING THERE

While there are a few launches around the lake, the two described below are the most user-friendly. The north launch is most commonly used by paddlers.

North launch: From I-287 north near Oakland, take Exit 58 toward Pompton Lakes, which will put you on Skyline Drive. Drive 350 feet and stay right to continue on West Oakland Avenue and drive 0.6 mile to the parking lot and launch on your left. When you enter the parking lot, you'll see a narrow, one-car bridge that leads to the launch. Unload your boat and gear, and then leave your car in the parking lot. You'll find parking for about 25 cars. *GPS coordinates:* 41°01.442′ N, 74°15.505′ W.

From south of Exit 57 off I-287 toward Ringwood/Skyline Drive: At the end of the ramp, turn right onto West Oakland Avenue and drive 0.4 mile to the parking lot and launch on your left.

Central launch: From I-287 south, take Exit 53 toward Route 694/Route 511/Pompton Lakes. Turn right onto Hamburg Turnpike at the end of the ramp and drive 0.9 mile, then turn left onto Wanaque Avenue and drive 0.4 mile. Turn right at Colfax Avenue and drive 250 feet, then turn right at Lakeside Avenue and drive 0.7 mile to the small park and launch on your right. Unload your boat and equipment, and then drive to the marked and designated boat parking areas

POMPTON LAKE

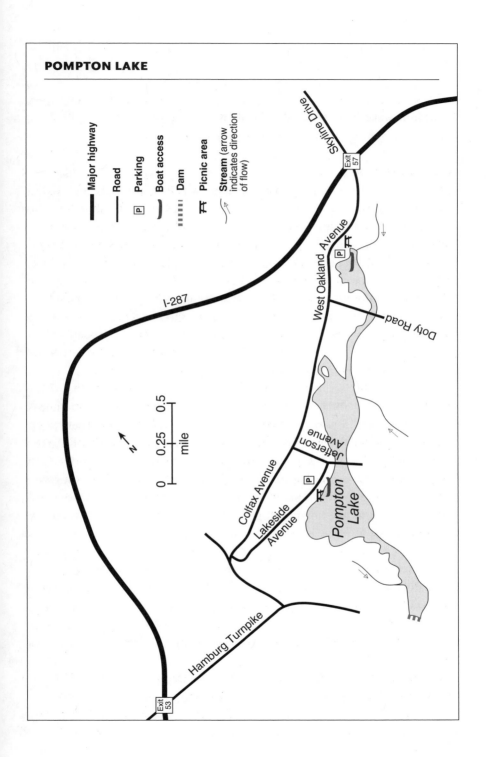

Major highway
Road
Parking
Boat access
Dam
Picnic area
Stream (arrow indicates direction of flow)

Skyline Drive
Exit 57
West Oakland Avenue
Doty Road
I-287
Jefferson Avenue
Colfax Avenue
Lakeside Avenue
Pompton Lake
Hamburg Turnpike
Exit 53

0   0.25   0.5
mile

N

on Grant Avenue and Schuyler Avenue one-half block north. There's parking for about fifteen cars. *GPS coordinates*: 41°00.398′ N, 74°16.621′ W.

From I-287 north, follow directions to the north launch, but drive 1.3 miles on West Oakland Avenue, and continue straight on Colfax Avenue for 0.7 mile. Turn left onto Jefferson Avenue and drive 0.3 mile, then turn right at Lakeside Avenue and drive 0.1 mile to the parking lot on your right.

WHAT YOU'LL SEE

The majority of lakeside property on Pompton Lake is privately owned, but most of the houses are on large properties set back from the shoreline and screened by trees, providing pleasant paddling conditions. Small parks and uninhabited shorelines break up the residential shoreline nicely. Ramapo Mountains to the north and east offer a magnificent green backdrop around the lake and town. In addition to conifers and hardwoods lining the shores, scattered willows drape long, delicate branches that shimmer and rustle with the slightest breeze. A few islands, lots of coves, a few bridges to paddle under, and some narrow passageways provide interest throughout the paddle. Abundant ducks, geese, and swans forage among vegetation in shallow waters while egrets and herons search for food along the shores.

The north launch, although farthest from the extreme southern end of the lake, is the prettiest and best of the launches. There's a quaint observation deck next to the launch, a portable toilet, and a small, unmarked trail that travels for a short distance through the woods to the north and about 0.2 mile to the south. What you're launching into here is really Potash Lake that connects to Pompton Lake through a channel about 130 feet wide. Only a few houses are found along Potash Lake, located on the west side approaching Doty Road bridge. Woods bordered by marsh reeds and some wildflowers consume the rest of the lakeside.

As you paddle under the Doty Road bridge and enter into the northern terminus of Pompton Lake, you'll travel a few hundred yards down the channel before the lake opens up. Take time to explore all the coves in this section; some are actually islands tucked tightly against the mainland or that lead to pretty and remote hideaways. One island is near the midline of the lake right before the Lakeside Avenue bridge. As a note, the straight-line distance between the bridges is 1.0 mile.

On the west (right) side of the lake, a few hundred yards south of the Lakeside Avenue bridge, is the central launch. It's a picturesque but small and pleasant park with restrooms and a gazebo that would provide an ideal lunch stop. This is the largest area of the lake. Paddle along the western shoreline and enjoy the quiet scenery. As you funnel into the southern narrow area, look for Terhune Memorial Park on the east shore. It's a quaint park with shaded picnic tables and restrooms—an excellent spot for a lunch break if you haven't already stopped. The park is large enough to provide a good opportunity to walk around and stretch your legs. An island on the west side not far from the dam is fun to explore. White buoys warn you of the dam. When you see them, turn around and start heading back to the launch, exploring any lakeshores you did not already pass.

This is a long lake. You may want to launch from the north end one time and explore the areas down to the Lakeside Avenue bridge, then use the central launch just south of that bridge to paddle the southern part the next time. If you fish, cast your lines for carp, bass, pike, perch, and trout—all found in these waters.

For additional trips nearby, visit Splitrock Reservoir, 35 minutes southwest, or Monksville Reservoir and Green Turtle Pond, both 25 minutes north. See Trips 6, 4, and 3.

---

6 | Splitrock Reservoir

Maine-like geographic features, eagles, hawks, abundant wildlife, beavers, deer, islands galore, and clear water will entice you to return time and again to this large lake.

Location: Rockaway, NJ
Maps: *New Jersey Atlas and Gazetteer*, Map 25; USGS Boonton
Area: 625 acres
Time: 4.0–5.0 hours
Conditions: Depth average 20-plus feet
Development: Remote/rural
Information: New Jersey Division of Fish and Wildlife, Bureau of Land Management, PO Box 400, Trenton, NJ 08625; 609-984-0547.
Camping: Mahlon Dickerson Reservation, 30 minutes west. See Appendix A.
Take Note: Electric motorboats only

GETTING THERE
From I-80 east, take Exit 37 for Route 513. Turn left onto Route 513 North/ Green Pond Road and drive 6.4 miles. Turn right onto Upper Hibernia Road

and drive 0.3 mile to the T-intersection, then turn right to stay on Upper Hibernia Road and drive 0.7 mile. Turn left onto Split Rock Road and drive 1.2 miles to the parking lot on your left shortly after crossing over the dam. The launch is a 60-yard carry from the parking lot down a hill, which is steep for the last 10 yards. The path is wide and covered with wood chips. There's parking for about 60 cars. *GPS coordinates for the launch path entrance in the parking lot*: 40°57.764′ N, 74°27.443′ W.

From I-80 west, take Exit 37 for Rockaway/Route 513 and turn left onto Hibernia Avenue. After crossing under Route 80, Hibernia Avenue becomes Green Pond Road. Continue as above.

WHAT YOU'LL SEE

I found the paddling heaven of New Jersey! This is the author's #1 choice for the state. When I first visited this site in 2000, it wasn't open to the public but plans were in place. From what I saw then from the dirt road, it was beautiful. It is now open to the public and draws paddlers from near and far. The beauty laid out in front of you from the launch is only a taste of the banquet you'll experience. Be sure to look at the interpretive kiosk near the pit toilet at the head of the launch path. One panel provides an overview for the hiker, another tells the history of the Cobb Furnace and ruins, and another shows information for anglers. To the east, Farny State Park has two tracts of land that come close to the reservoir. Another 1,500 acres of land around the lake are owned by Jersey City, but protected by the Division of Fish and Wildlife under the Green Acres Program.

While this may be one of the best of sites, it has the worst launch. Perhaps that will change in the future. The launch is down a rather steep, 60-yard, wood-chipped path with large rocks at the entry. A small area on the left side has a gravel bottom about 10 inches below the surface, but you still have to plan on getting wet up to midcalf or knee unless you're adept at launching from rocks—and then it can wreak havoc on all but plastic boats. Wear a dry suit, wetsuit, or tall waterproof paddling boots when the water is cold so you don't chill or risk hypothermia.

A landscape of huge boulders along the shores and a wonderland of rock islands in the north end will look more like Maine than New Jersey. Wildlife abounds here. Ospreys, eagles, and hawks fly high over the water, blue herons are common, blue jays fill the air with their raucous calls, cormorants stick their thin necks and heads above the surface, kingfishers dart back and forth along some banks, deer come to the edge to drink, and beavers are active. Add to that a large diversity of woodland and songbirds, wildflowers, and land mammals for a spectacular wildlife adventure. During spring and fall migration, the lake

SPLITROCK RESERVOIR

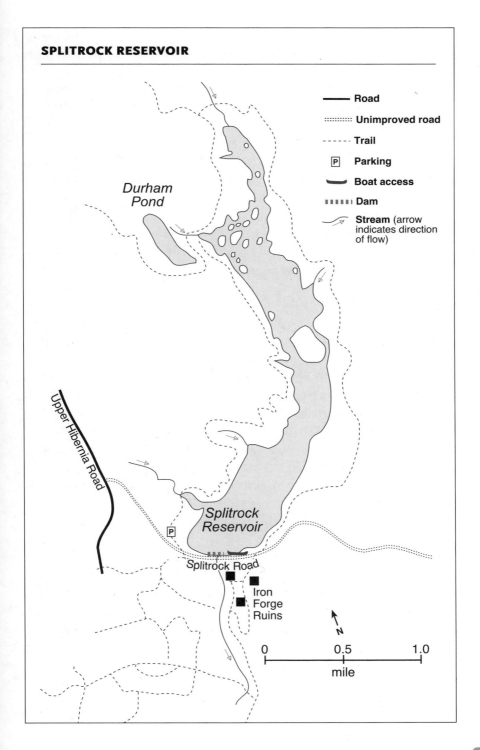

Road
Unimproved road
Trail
P Parking
Boat access
Dam
Stream (arrow indicates direction of flow)

Durham Pond

Upper Hibernia Road

Splitrock Reservoir

Splitrock Road

Iron Forge Ruins

N

0   0.5   1.0
mile

AMC AND THE HIGHLANDS CONSERVATION ACT

The Highlands Conservation Act (HCA), enacted in 2004, enables federal and state funding assistance to the Highlands region, 3.5 million acres in Connecticut, New York, New Jersey, and Pennsylvania, for permanent land acquisitions to protect and conserve wildlife and valuable natural, cultural, and recreational resources. Lands considered for appropriation must have high conservation value, such as significant watersheds and aquifers; areas with a high density and variety of flora and fauna; rich agricultural lands; significant recreational or cultural resources; rare habitats; and dense forest lands. Assistance of up to $10 million per year from the federal government is set aside for those states to help purchase lands. The HCA also requires a non-federal match that can come from states or local entities in any of the Highlands' states.

The Appalachian Highlands itself comprises a wide swath of land, sometimes up to 300 miles in width, from Newfoundland to Alabama, and dominates the landscape of the eastern seaboard along the eastern edge of the Appalachian Mountains typified by ridges, hills, and valleys for a length of 2,000 miles. Within the four states covered in the HCA, the Highlands cuts across western Connecticut, across the lower Hudson Valley and northern New Jersey, then across southeastern Pennsylvania.

Responsibility for determining the resources and lands significant for appropriation falls on the shoulders of the USDA Forest Service (USFS). The USFS has conducted Highlands studies in the four states, working with the Appalachian Mountain Club, Rutgers University, United States Geological Survey, University of Connecticut, Penn State, State University of New York–Syracuse, and Yale University's School of Forestry, to name a few. Between them, they have the difficult job of delicately balancing protection of these resources with recreational opportunities for the public.

What makes these lands so significant? The Highlands' most important geographic identifier is the Reading Prong, which stretches from near Reading, Pennsylvania, through northern New Jersey and southern New York, reaching its northern terminus in Connecticut. The Reading Prong is part of the Precambrian basement, which is discontinuously exposed in the north-central Appalachians. The rocks that make up the prong consist of diverse gneiss rocks. According to the USFS, these rocks are "hard crystalline rocks that rise above the terrain formed from softer materials to the east and west.

The bedrock geology is complex and includes sedimentary, igneous, and metamorphic rocks that are used to discriminate among the Highlands' ecological subdivisions." The geologic makeup of the rocks determines the type of soils created by erosion, and if and how water, whether from rainfall or snow melt, is held or run off. That in turn determines the types of habitats that develop and the diversity of flora and fauna species that can thrive in those habitats. Some wildlife species require large corridors of connected lands to live, reproduce, and thrive. By the same token, be they carnivores or omnivores, their food source must also be protected. Rare plants require very specific environments in order to thrive. Some avian species require specific types of forests or specific types of berries or insects. Water is our most important resource, and watershed health must be preserved. Without it, nothing can live. It's a chain where every link is critical and must be protected by sensible stewardship.

Conserving and protecting these lands from development and overuse preserves and enhances the health of the land and ensures greater biodiversity and clean water for generations to come. The AMC, along with other organizations, disseminates information and develops programs to inform the public of the importance and reasoning behind land use, management, and conservation of lands covered by the HCA.

Trips in this book will take you paddling on waters within this region. A few suggestions are Wawayanda State Park, Trip 2, Splitrock Reservoir, Trip 6, and Merrill Creek Reservoir, Trip 17, in New Jersey, and Nockamixon State Park, Trip 61, and Marsh Creek State Park, Trip 70, in Pennsylvania.

provides an excellent stopover for food and rest. Loons, wood ducks, mergansers, you name it, they stop here during their journey. Beneath the surface, smallmouth and largemouth bass, catfish, crappie, pickerel, and sunfish are sought after by anglers.

The lake is a little more than 3.0 miles long and averages 0.2 mile across. It's bent slightly in the middle with a very large island about midway, so you won't be able to see the whole lake at any one point. The southern half below the island has many picturesque rugged boulder faces and numerous inlets to explore. Around every corner, something different sparks your interest, some new birds are spotted, and the lakeshore changes. Paddle to the north end of the lake along the western shoreline, where you'll find a number of pretty coves. Great blue heron seem to be everywhere here. If you spot one and have

The author explores a prominent rock face across from the launch at Splitrock Reservoir.

a camera, paddle quietly toward them and just drift once you get near to allow you to get as close as possible.

After passing the large island along the eastern shore, you'll see numerous rock islands ahead of you. Some are tiny, with only tufts of grass in the cracks; others are large enough that saplings and shrubs have been able to take root, creating mini-habitats. On one trip there, my friend and I saw paddlers on two of the islands having a lunch break. Each group of two had an island all to their own and a few hundred feet apart. Paddling up the narrow northwest arm, look for beaver activity. Tree stumps with conical ends are telltale signs that beaver downed them. The last time I visited, my friend and I came upon a large beaver lodge nestled against the rocky shore, and signs of a new lodge were on the eastern shore a few hundred feet away.

Heading back to the launch along the eastern shore, enjoy paddling through the passage between the island and the mainland. It's here where you'll find the greatest abundance of turtles basking on the many limbs sticking out of the water. Here, as elsewhere on the water, look into the clear water to see fish swimming around. On the two trips I took here, there were a dozen or so other paddlers on the water plus a few people fishing from boats. Yet the reservoir is so large that my friend and I felt like we had the place almost to ourselves—a feeling of solitude. Only at the launch and two places along our paddle did we come in direct contact with other paddlers; the rest were specs scattered around the water.

Note: Park only in the designated parking lot. The only other legal parking is 0.4 mile east of the dam that's used for hikers to enter the Four Birds Trail. Do not park anywhere else, because you may be ticketed.

Hiking opportunities abound here. A 13.8-mile loop trail around the lake connects Split Rock Loop North on the east side of the lake with part of the Four Birds Trail on the west side. A wonderful interactive map can be found at f.vanderburgh.home.att.net. Wait 5 seconds and a new screen appears, then click on B Trail Map of SR. Deer, wild turkey, and black bear might be spotted along your hike, as well as a plethora of woodland and songbirds. Trails are moderate, but rocky. Bring appropriate footwear.

For an additional paddle nearby, visit Pompton Lake, 35 minutes northeast, or Lakes Hopatcong and Musconetcong, 35 minutes southwest. See Trips 5 and 7.

---

7 | Lake Hopatcong and Lake Musconetcong

At Lake Hopatcong, enjoy paddling the largest lake in the state. Lake Musconetcong offers quiet scenery, swans, and waterfowl.

Location: Landing, NJ
Maps: *New Jersey Atlas and Gazetteer*, Map 24; USGS Stanhope and Dover
Area: Lake Hopatcong: 2,685 acres; Lake Musconetcong: 326 acres
Time: Lake Hopatcong: variable up to 15 hours; Lake Musconetcong: 2.0–2.5 hours
Conditions: Lake Hopatcong: depth average 18 feet; Lake Musconetcong: depth average 5 feet
Development: Suburban
Information: Hopatcong State Park, PO Box 8519, Landing, NJ 07850; 973-398-7010; $6 weekdays, $10 weekends in-season.

Lee's County Park Marina, 433 Howard Boulevard, Mount Arlington, NJ 07856; 973-398-5199; $5 cartop launch fee.

Lake Musconetcong, New Jersey Division of Fish and Wildlife, Northern Region Office, 26 Route 173 West, Hampton, NJ, 08827; 973-383-0918.

Camping: Mahlon Dickerson Reservation is 25 minutes north, and Panther Lake Camping Resort is 15 minutes northwest. See Appendix A.

Take Note: Lake Hopatcong: unlimited horsepower; Lake Musconetcong: electric motorboats only

GETTING THERE

To Lake Hopatcong State Park: Drive north 1.2 miles on Route 631 (Landing Road) from Exit 28 off I-80. At the junction of Routes 631 and 607, Route 631 turns left. Stay to your right and drive 0.4 mile north on Route 607. The park entrance will be on your right. The state park is so popular that signs leading to it are everywhere. You'll find parking for more than 300 cars, but remember, the parking lot is also used for beach visitors. *GPS coordinates*: 40°55.058′ N, 74°39.810′ W.

To Lee's County Park access to Lake Hopatcong: Take Exit 30 (Mount Arlington) from I-80 and drive north 3.6 miles on Route 615 (Howard Boulevard) to the entrance of Lee's County Park on the left. You'll find parking for 100 cars. *GPS coordinates*: 40°55.952′ N, 74°37.881′ W.

To Lake Musconetcong: From I-80, take Exit 27 toward Netcong. Drive 0.2 mile on Route 183/Lackawanna Place. At the rotary, take the second exit for Route 183/Ledgewood Avenue and drive 0.4 mile. Turn right onto Allen Street and drive 300 feet, then turn slightly left onto Dell Avenue and drive 150 feet to the parking lot and launch on your left. If you are coming from Lake Hopatcong State Park, drive 0.4 mile south on Route 607/Lakeside Boulevard from the park entrance, turn right onto Route 631 south (Center Street) and drive 2.2 miles (it will become Allen Street after 1.65 miles). Make a sharp right turn onto Dell Avenue. The parking lot and launch will be 50 feet ahead on your left. There's parking for about fifteen cars. *GPS coordinates*: 40°54.050′ N, 74°42.193′ W.

WHAT YOU'LL SEE

Lake Hopatcong

Lake Hopatcong is the largest natural lake in the state, covering 2,685 acres and more than 40 miles of shoreline. Summer weekends can be a veritable zoo, with fishing tournaments, sailing regattas, and other boaters zipping around the water. Why, then, is it included in a book about *quiet* waters? Because I feel at some point you should paddle it simply to feel and absorb its expansiveness. Also, I understand from local paddlers that during the week, even in August, it's pretty quiet, so try to visit during the week, and preferably in September or October after tourist season.

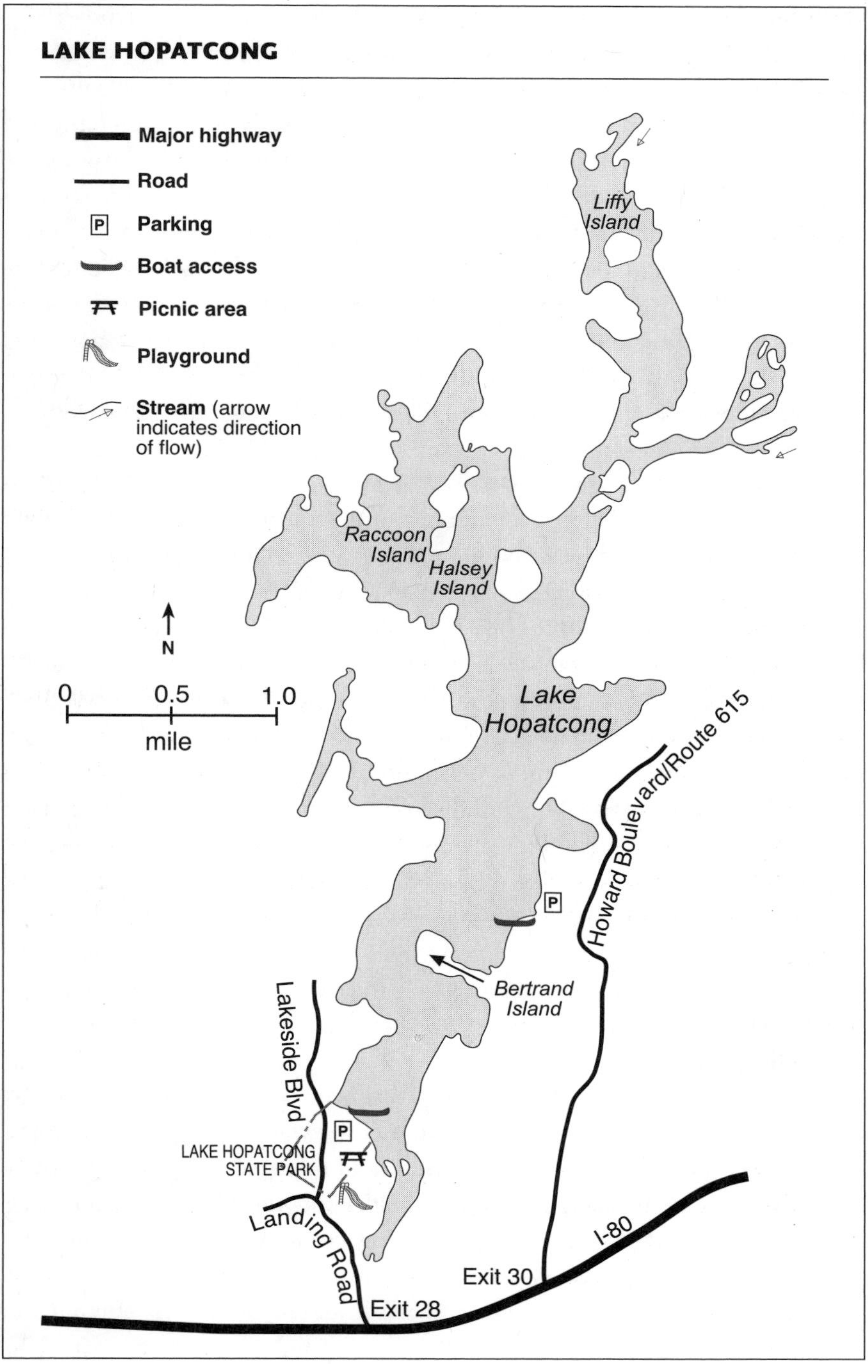

LAKE HOPATCONG

— Major highway

— Road

P Parking

⌣ Boat access

🏛 Picnic area

🎠 Playground

↝ **Stream** (arrow indicates direction of flow)

Liffy Island

Raccoon Island

Halsey Island

↑
N

0   0.5   1.0
|——————|——————|
mile

Lake Hopatcong

Howard Boulevard/Route 615

P

Bertrand Island

Lakeside Blvd

P
🏛
LAKE HOPATCONG
STATE PARK
🎠

Landing Road

Exit 30

I-80

Exit 28

Local historians (www.hopatcong.org) believe the name Hopatcong is derived from the Lenni-Lenape word "hapakonoesson," meaning pipestone. A glacial lake left by the last ice age 10,000 years ago, winter snows now refurbish the waters that are cold even in summer. It was actually two lakes connected by a stream. In the creation of the Morris Canal, which functioned from 1831 until 1924, the dam that was built across the lower and much larger lake to supply water to the canal raised the water level 12 feet and connected the two lakes. Public access to the lake is provided through Lake Hopatcong State Park on Route 631 on the southwest end of the lake. A public beach and restrooms are next to the launch. An alternate public access to the lake is through Lee's County Park, a third of the way up the lake on the eastern side.

Lake Hopatcong boasts trophy-size rainbow and brown trout, hybrid bass, crappie, walleye, pickerel, largemouth and smallmouth bass, perch, sunfish, and other species. The numerous coves peppering the entire shoreline are prime habitat for bass. Gulls, ospreys, cormorants, and waterfowl are found around the lake, and chickadees, pewees, and kingbirds can be seen along the lakeshores.

From the state park launch, you can plan a trip of approximately 5.0 miles to explore the southern end of the lake up to Bertrand Island and back. Bertrand Island was the site of a large amusement park, which closed in 1983. Paddle farther north on the lake as you desire, but be mindful of the return trip.

Starting your trip from Lee's County Park, you can paddle north to Halsey Island and back for a trip of about 4.5 miles. If you paddle from the island into the northeast arm of the lake, it will be around 9 to 10 miles round-trip. That arm has more than a mile of uninhabited lakeshore on the west side and includes Liffy Island. Because that area is uninhabited, wildlife is more abundant and varied. Liffy Island sits close enough to the edge of the lake that its narrow passage may become clogged with waterlilies and algae by late summer.

The most important thing to consider is the wind and your ability to handle potentially windy conditions. This is true of any large lake. Even if it's flat-calm when you launch, the wind can come up an hour or two after you start out. Check the hourly weather forecast the night before and in the morning. In summer, the prevailing winds are south to southwest. In fall, the prevailing winds are northwest. May and September are a toss-up for wind direction as we change seasons. While you can never predict Mother Nature, it's best to start your trip into the wind in order to have an easy return trip. Ever notice how flat and calm a lake, river, or ocean is in early morning and early evening? Those are the best times to paddle.

The park offers a few informal and very short trails, one of which begins at the historic Morris Canal Locktender's House on the north side of the parking

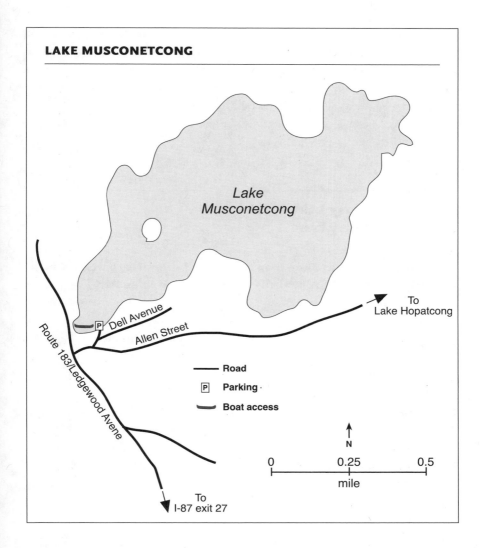

LAKE MUSCONETCONG

Lake
Musconetcong

Route 183/Ledgewood Avene

Dell Avenue

P Parking

Allen Street

To
Lake Hopatcong

Road

Boat access

N

| 0 | 0.25 | 0.5 |
mile

To
I-87 exit 27

lot and passes around to the north side of the dam. A short white-blazed trail
starts from the southeast corner of the parking lot and traverses through the
picnic-tabled hill and back to the parking area.

Lake Musconetcong

Musconetcong is an American Indian word for "rapidly running river." It is
minutes away from the southern end of Lake Hopatcong and part of Hopatcong State Park. Though far smaller than Lake Hopatcong at only 328 acres,
this lake is surrounded by quaint towns and is more scenic and relaxing. Far
fewer houses line the shores here, and there is quite a bit of shoreline without

residences. A small island in the middle of the lake not far from the launch is fun to explore, and I found my trip here very pleasant and relaxing. Because this lake is so shallow, waterlilies and aquatic grasses claim about a quarter of the lake by late summer. I've always seen swans, geese, and ducks on the lake and a variety of birds around the lakeshore.

Cranberry Lake is 15 minutes west and Kittatinny Valley State Park is 20 minutes north. See Trips 8 and 9.

8 | Cranberry Lake Park— Cranberry Lake

This pleasant lake has more than six miles of shoreline, parts of which are within the pristine Allamuchy Mountains and State Park.

Location: Cranberry Lake (Sussex), NJ
Maps: *New Jersey Atlas and Gazetteer*, Map 24; USGS Stanhope
Area: 180 acres
Time: 2.0–2.5 hours
Conditions: Depth average 8 feet
Information: New Jersey Division of Fish and Wildlife, Northern Region Office, 26 Route 173 West, Hampton, NJ 08827; 973-383-0918.
Development: Rural
Camping: Panther Lake Camping Resort, 2 minutes north. See Appendix A.
Take Note: Unlimited horsepower

GETTING THERE
From Route 607, drive 3.2 miles north on Route 206, turn left onto South Shore Road, and drive 0.2 mile. A Cranberry Lake Park sign will be on your right. The right turn onto the gravel road is a sharp hairpin turn that goes up a short but steep embankment. At the top of the embankment, turn right to get to the launch. You'll find parking for about twenty cars. *GPS coordinates*: 40°57.117′ N, 74°44.206′ W.

WHAT YOU'LL SEE
The 180-acre Cranberry Lake is almost cut in half by a long, narrow peninsula barely attached on its western side, giving more shoreline to explore. Cranberry

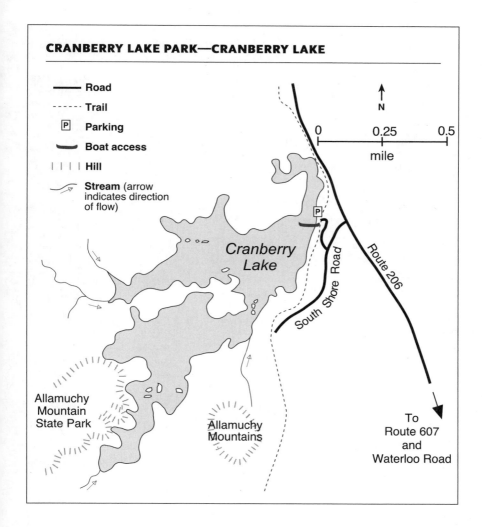

CRANBERRY LAKE PARK—CRANBERRY LAKE

Legend:
- Road
- Trail
- P Parking
- Boat access
- Hill
- Stream (arrow indicates direction of flow)

N

0   0.25   0.5
mile

Cranberry Lake

South Shore Road

Route 206

Allamuchy Mountain State Park

Allamuchy Mountains

To Route 607 and Waterloo Road

Lake Park on the east side of the lake provides a public boat launch. Allamuchy State Park borders the southern end, offering remote and pristine coves and inlets to explore where mountains rise sharply from the lake.

Saving the best for last, start your trip to the right of the launch and paddle around to the northeastern tip of the lake, pass under a quaint footbridge, and into an area of rocky small coves with a small island in the middle. Paddle back out to the lake and along the northern shore, where you'll find a few islands to explore. Most of the houses on the lake are modest and tasteful with a few mansion-type residences. The long spit of land that almost bisects the lake has a number of islands around its eastern tip that are fun to circumnavigate. Once

Paddling under the picturesque wooden bridge over Cranberry Lake will provide a closer look at the rock-faced cliffs.

around the peninsula and into the southwest half of the lake, you'll see the Allamuchy Mountains ahead of you. Continue paddling along the north shore, enjoying the view ahead, until you're past the residential area.

The area ahead is very remote and pretty, where mountains rise sharply around you. Allamuchy Mountain State Park grips the southern end of Cranberry Lake with tenacious fingers, cradling quiet coves that beg you to stop paddling, close your eyes, and breathe in the fresh mountain air of this tranquil hideaway. Stop, sit, and enjoy the sights and sounds of nature. A few small islands at the entrance add interest. Because the area is shallow, it is best visited before pond lilies and duckweed take over the surface by the end of July. The excessive surface vegetation is usually gone by the end of September, just in time for you to visit during the fall foliage display. Head back to the launch along the southern shore, but turn around to catch a last glimpse of the mountains before you leave.

For the hiker, a trail leads off from the south end of the parking lot and traverses the eastern side of the Allamuchy Mountains to the restored nineteenth-century canal town of Waterloo Village. It's a moderate hike of about 4.5 miles round-trip that crosses a few streams and passes Jefferson Lake before reaching a hiker's parking lot on Waterloo Road, 0.7 miles east of Waterloo Village. Alternately, you can visit the restored village and park nearby for a hike. From

Route 206 at the Cranberry Lake launch, drive south 2.1 miles, then turn right onto Waterloo Road and drive 1.1 miles to the hiker's parking lot or continue another 0.7 mile to the village.

For another paddle the same day, visit Kittatinny Valley State Park, 15 minutes north, or Lakes Hopatcong and Musconetcong, 15 minutes east. See Trips 9 and 7.

 ## 9 | Kittatinny Valley State Park— Lake Aeroflex and Twin Lakes

Enjoy paddling the deepest glacial lake in the state as you watch raptors soar above abundant waterfowl.

Location: Newton, NJ
Maps: *New Jersey Atlas and Gazetteer*, Map 24; USGS Newton East and Newton West
Area: Lake Aeroflex: 117 acres; Twin Lakes: 29 acres
Time: Lake Aeroflex: 1.5–2.0 hours; Twin Lakes: less than an hour
Conditions: Lake Aeroflex: depth average 40 feet; Twin Lakes: depth average 5 feet
Development: Rural
Information: Kittatinny Valley State Park, PO Box 621, Andover, NJ 07821-0621; 973-786-6445.
Camping: Columbia Valley Campground, 10 minutes south. See Appendix A. Swartswood State Forest, 30 minutes west. See Appendix A.
Take Note: Electric motorboats only

GETTING THERE
To Lake Aeroflex: Take Exit 25 off I-80; drive north about 7.0 miles on Route 206 to Andover, where Routes 517 and 613 intersect. Continue north 0.7 mile on Route 206 to Route 669 (Limecrest Road); turn right onto Limecrest Road and drive 1.1 miles to the New Jersey State Park Northern Regional Office entrance on the left. The boat ramp and parking are within 200 feet of the entrance. The regional park office, which covers all state parks in the northern part of the state, is located next to the launch and has park and trail maps for this and other parks. You'll find parking for about 30 cars. *GPS coordinates:* 41°00.571′ N, 74°44.040′ W.

To Twin Lakes and the Kittatinny Valley State Park office: From Route 669, drive north 0.9 mile on Route 206, turn right onto Goodale Road and drive 0.6 mile to the fenced entrance on the left. Drive across the parking area to the short and bumpy gravel road leading to the launch. You'll find parking for about 25 cars. *GPS coordinates*: 41°00.740′ N, 74°44.875′ W.

To Kittatinny Valley State Park office: Drive an additional 0.4 mile north on Goodale Road. Turn right at the park office entrance road and drive 0.4 mile. The parking lot will be on your right and the park office on your left. *GPS coordinates*: 41°01.088′ N, 74°44.222′ W.

WHAT YOU'LL SEE

Four bodies of water reside within Kittatinny Valley State Park, two of which provide pleasant paddling opportunities. Situated just outside the mountainous Appalachian Ridge and Valley region, the land here starts giving way to the gentle rolling hills of the Piedmont Plateau. Note: If you view Lake Aeroflex on Google Earth, it's now called New Wawayanda Lake, although most Web references and maps still note it as Lake Aeroflex. Clean restrooms and picnic tables are available at both the regional park office at the Lake Aeroflex launch and at the park office on the west side of the lake.

Lake Aeroflex

Aeroflex-Andover airport sits on the south side of Lake Aeroflex. Normally I would stay away from airports, but this is a very small, local airport with infrequent activity. Besides, somehow a small plane taking off or landing lends an air of adventure to the setting.

At 110 feet in depth and with a profile shaped like a U, Lake Aeroflex is the deepest natural glacial lake in the state. Its long and narrow 117 acres parallel Limecrest Road (Route 669) on the northwest side of the quiet town of Andover. Ducks and geese are abundant on the shallower western shores and at the north end of the lake, where clumps of aquatic grasses provide for ideal foraging. Trees along the eastern shore between the lake and Limecrest Road afford visual and auditory screening from the sparse road traffic. If you fish, cast your line for trout, which is stocked seasonally. Perch, sunfish, and catfish can also be caught.

Toward the north end of the lake, it will first appear that you're near the end. But paddle closer and you'll see the 200-foot passage into a quarter-mile long area where waterfowl, marsh birds, and songbirds abound. Because it is shallower than the larger section of the lake, bog and painted turtles frequently sun themselves along the banks, and snapping turtles hide in the sediment on

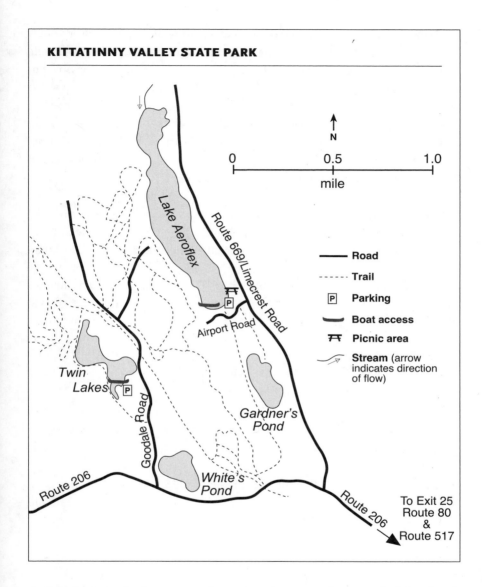

KITTATINNY VALLEY STATE PARK

Lake Aeroflex

Route 669/Limecrest Road

Airport Road

Twin Lakes

Goodale Road

Gardner's Pond

White's Pond

Route 206

Route 206

To Exit 25
Route 80
&
Route 517

0   0.5   1.0
mile

N

—— Road

----- Trail

P   Parking

Boat access

Picnic area

Stream (arrow indicates direction of flow)

the lake bottom. At the very northern tip, where a creek enters the lake, there's a small island at the entrance. When water levels permit, a paddle up the creek for a little more than a quarter-mile will reward you with beaver, muskrat, and other wildlife.

Twin Lakes

Twin Lakes provides quaint paddling waters. Two bodies of water connected by a narrow neck not far from the launch site give this lake an hourglass shape.

Although much smaller in size than Lake Aeroflex, the very shallow waters harbor a different variety of waterfowl and wading birds. About a quarter-mile from the launch, you can choose to go right or left. The right side leads you to waters where short hills rise steeply from the shore. This is a great place to watch for belted kingfishers that build nests in cavities along the steep embankments a few feet above the water's surface. I spotted three in the short time I paddled that section, along with numerous frogs and spotted turtles. The brightly colored northern red salamander hides under logs on shore. This lake always seems to have a large colony of mute swans gracing the waters.

The park offers numerous hiking opportunities. An easy 2-mile, self-guided nature trail starts from the parking lot at the park office on the west side of Lake Aeroflex. A criss-cross of interconnecting trails provides quite a few miles to explore that are too numerous and close to depict here. Pick up a detailed map at either of the park offices.

Paulin's Kill Lake and Swartswood State Park are both within 30 minutes to the west. See Trips 10 and 11. Cranberry Lake is 20 minutes south. See Trip 8.

---

10 | Paulin's Kill Lake and Paulin's Kill River

Abundant wildlife in the quiet north half of the lake and a scenic trip up the river are yours to enjoy for the day.

Location: Newton, NJ
Maps: *New Jersey Atlas and Gazetteer*, Map 23; USGS Newton West
Area: 174 acres
Time: 2.0–2.5 hours
Conditions: Depth average 8 feet
Development: Suburban/rural
Information: Paulin's Kill Wildlife Management Area, Northern Regional Office, 26 Route 173 West, Hampton, NJ 08827; 973-383-0918.
Camping: Swartswood State Park, 15 minutes west. See Appendix A.
Take Note: Electric motorboats only

GETTING THERE
From Route 206 in Ross Corner, drive 2.1 miles on Route 206 South, then turn right onto Halsey-Myrtle Grove Road and drive 1.6 miles. Turn left at Spirol

PAULIN'S KILL LAKE AND PAULIN'S KILL RIVER

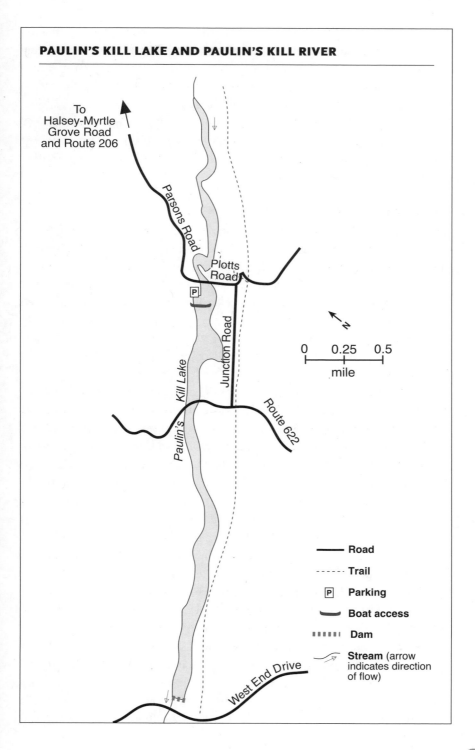

To Halsey-Myrtle Grove Road and Route 206

Parsons Road

Plotts Road

P

Junction Road

Paulin's Kill Lake

Route 622

West End Drive

N

| 0 | 0.25 | 0.5 |
mile

─────── Road

------- Trail

P Parking

Boat access

▪▪▪▪▪▪ Dam

Stream (arrow indicates direction of flow)

Road and drive 1.8 miles, then turn right onto Parsons Road and drive 0.4 mile. Immediately after turning onto Parsons Road, you will go under a very narrow abandoned railroad trestle that is little more than one car width. You'll find parking for about fifteen cars. *GPS coordinates*: 41°04.970′ N, 74°46.966′ W.

The grassy launch into the small arm of the lake can become overgrown with tall brush and shrubs if unused for a long time. If it becomes too difficult, there is a clearing on the south side of Parsons Road, 100 yards from the east side of the bridge. There is space for three cars to unload boats and gear, then park in the lot mentioned above.

WHAT YOU'LL SEE

Paulin's Kill Lake is unique due to its extremely long and narrow shape. A private community gobbled up the land on the southern half of the lake. Most of the homes sit back from the shoreline, but their docks are prominent features. Only a few private properties adjoin the lake in the northern section above the Route 622 bridge, where the New Jersey Division of Fish and Wildlife acquired a large parcel of land through the Green Acres Program. This is a great location on days with high winds when you want to get a good workout, because its narrow width offers protection from all but the windiest conditions. No facilities are available here, but there are plenty of shrubs and trees.

After launching, head down the northern edge of the lake, where you'll immediately pass a dense stand of hemlocks and pines before passing into an area of mixed-hardwood forest. Steep banks for almost a mile are prime locations for kingfishers to make their nests. Blue jays, blue herons, hawks, kingbirds, and swifts are among the many species of birds found here. In the middle of the lake, look for graceful swans that live here year-round. Once you pass under the Route 622 bridge, you'll start seeing residences, but there are long stretches of woods that are pleasing to the eyes with large trees overhanging the banks. It is only in the western mile of the lake where residences become denser and you'll see docks sticking out into the lake. Low concrete structures on both sides of the lake right before the West End Drive bridge signifies the dam. Stay 50 to 100 feet away from the dam when you cross over to the eastern side of the lake.

On your return trip from the dam, residences thin out quickly and become sparse for the rest of the paddle. There's a small cove right past the Route 622 bridge where waterfowl forage in the shallower waters. There's another larger cove a little farther up with a small island in the middle. The water around the island is shallow, which means you might bottom out if water levels are low. Continue paddling up the south side where you'll find a large area of dense waterlilies and aquatic grasses. Look here for waterfowl, swallows, darners, dragonflies, and butterflies. At this point you can return to the launch on the other side of the spit of land to your left. However, in front of you is the Parsons Road bridge that leads into Paulin's Kill River. It's pretty low, so you may have to "kiss the deck" to get under it or do a short portage to the other side, but the trip up the river is spectacular.

After passing under (or over) the bridge, you'll feel like you're in no-man's land. There will be no signs of civilization for a mile, and even after that it will be very sparse for another mile where the river becomes too difficult to continue because of downed trees and shallow areas. Bird-watching here is excellent, and you might even spot a curved-billed ibis or gallenule in late summer. Freshwater marshlands right past the bridge sport a variety of wildflowers and flowering aquatic plants. Upstream, mixed-hardwood forests border the river. These diverse environments provide a wide variety of habitats for wildlife. The American bittern has been sighted here often along the shores within a few hundred feet of the bridge.

For the hiker, part of the 30-mile long Paulin's Kill Valley Trail traverses the entire length of the southern side of the lake and passes an old telegraph station and numerous remains of structures and equipment of the now-defunct railroad. To reach the trail, drive east on Parson's Road from the launch. As you approach the railroad trestle tunnel, there will be a parking lot on the north (left) side of the road. Park there, walk out to Junction Road, then cross the road and walk directly into the woods on the other side for 140 feet to pick up the trail. For a map of the entire trail, visit www.libertygap.org.

Swartswood State Park is 15 minutes west and Kittatinny Valley State Park is 20 minutes southeast. See Trips 11 and 9.

 ## 11 | Swartswood State Park—Swartswood Lake and Little Swartswood Lake

---

Enjoy a huge swan population, good bird-watching, and an island to explore on this large lake.

Location: Swartswood, NJ
Maps: *New Jersey Atlas and Gazetteer*, Map 23; USGS Newton West
Area: Swartswood Lake: 494 acres; Little Swartswood Lake: 75 acres
Time: Swartswood Lake: 2.5–3.0 hours; Little Swartswood Lake: about 1.0 hour

Conditions: Swartswood Lake: depth average 25 feet; Little Swartswood Lake: depth average 20 feet

Development: Rural

Information: Swartswood State Park, PO Box 123, Swartswood, NJ 07887-0123; 973-383-5230; $5 weekdays, $10 weekends in-season for the recreation area only—boat launches are free.

Camping: On-site; call the park office for reservations.

Take Note: Electric motorboats only

GETTING THERE

To the park entrance for the recreation center: From the junction of Routes 94 and 206 in Newton, drive 1.8 miles on Route 94 South, turn right onto Anderson Hill Road and drive 0.8 mile. (Note: Anderson Hill Road makes a right-hand turn after 0.3 mile.) Make a hairpin left turn onto Route 622/Newton-Swartswood Road and drive 2.7 miles. Turn left onto Swartswood East Side Road and drive 0.7 mile to the park entrance on your right. The swimming beach, playground, and picnic areas are also located there and you can pick up a map at the entrance booth. *GPS coordinates:* 41°04.417′ N, 74°49.129′ W.

To the cartop east launch: Follow as above and continue 1.0 mile past the park entrance to the east launch on the right. It is a U-shaped driveway with a grass and dirt launch. You'll find parking for about fifteen cars. *GPS coordinates:* 41°04.060′ N, 74°50.054′ W.

To the cartop west launch: Follow as above to the park entrance and continue 2.4 miles. Turn right onto Pond Brook Road and drive 0.8 mile to West Shore Drive. Turn right and drive 0.8 mile to the launch entrance on your right. This is a pretty spot tucked in the woods and a nice spot for a picnic before or after your paddle. Parking is available for about eight cars. *GPS coordinates:* 41°03.774′ N, 74°51.166′ W.

WHAT YOU'LL SEE

The 2,472-acre Swartswood State Park was established as the first state park in 1914, and offers camping, picnicking, playgrounds, and swimming. Boat rentals are available in-season at the park's recreation center. The park fee applies for entrance to the recreation area only.

Neither lake lies completely within the park's boundaries, so you will find private property with modest homes around part of Little Swartswood Lake and more than half of Swartswood Lake. Many of the houses sit back 50 to 100 feet from the lakeshore with a privacy screen of trees and do not detract from the overall setting.

SWARTSWOOD STATE PARK

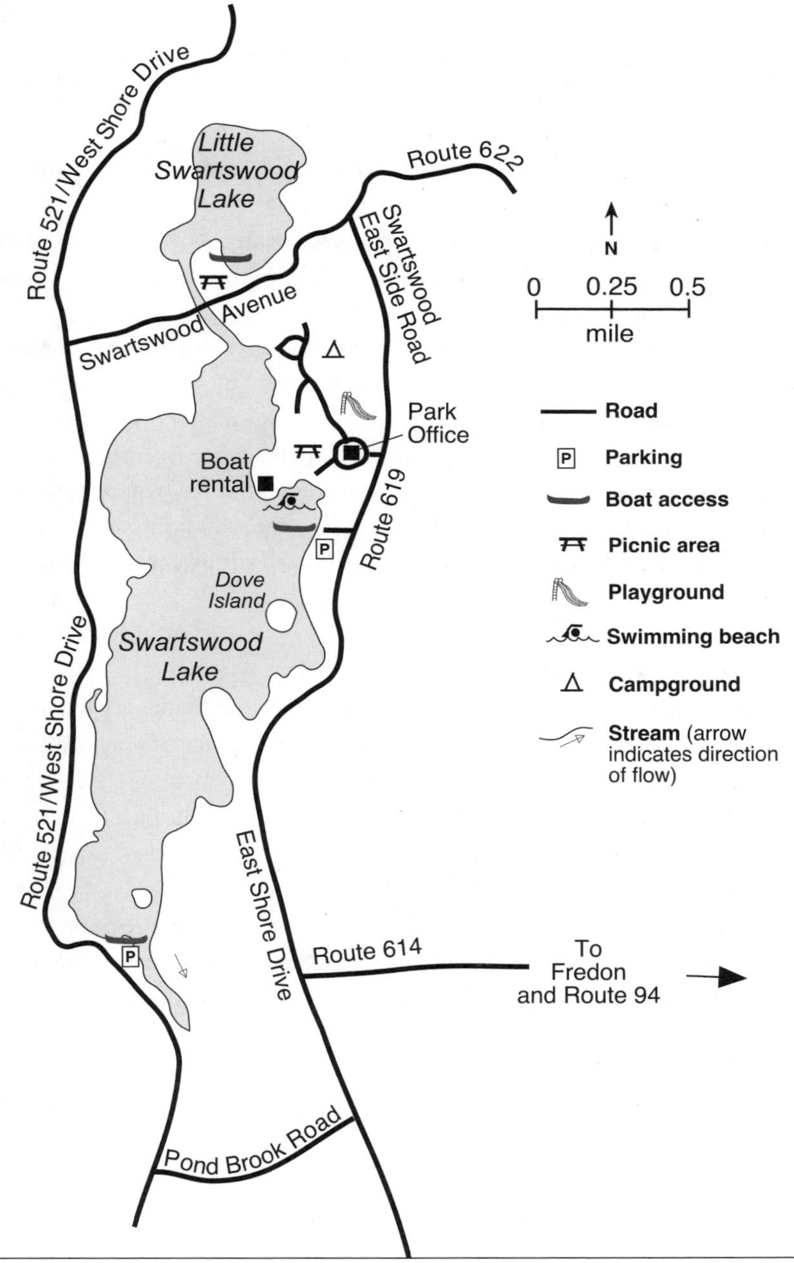

Little Swartswood Lake

Route 521/West Shore Drive

Route 622

Swartswood East Side Road

Swartswood Avenue

△

Park Office

Boat rental

Route 619

Dove Island

Swartswood Lake

Route 521/West Shore Drive

East Shore Drive

P

Route 614

To Fredon and Route 94

Pond Brook Road

N

| 0 | 0.25 | 0.5 |

mile

— **Road**

P **Parking**

⌣ **Boat access**

🪑 **Picnic area**

🎠 **Playground**

🏊 **Swimming beach**

△ **Campground**

🌊 **Stream** (arrow indicates direction of flow)

Swartswood Lake

Swartswood Lake gives you almost 500 acres in which to paddle. Hours can be spent exploring the numerous coves and peninsulas along the perimeter. Start your paddle by heading left from the east launch along the bend and then out to circumnavigate Dove Island. I'm sure you'll agree that you've never seen so many mute swans in one location. Continue to paddle up the east side of the lake, crossing over to avoid the noisy beach area if it's a summer weekend, then paddle into the quiet northern cove to enjoy bird-watching. Rocks along the shoreline add texture to the landscape, and in the shallow areas near shore, ducks, geese, and swans can be found foraging.

The western side of the lake is relatively quiet, even though there are clusters of houses in many sections. Plenty of wooded shorelines will provide you with pleasant paddling.

According to locals, fishing is good in both lakes, with walleye and brown trout the best catches. Mountain laurel and mulberry bushes grow in the shade of pine, oak, ash, birch, and hickory trees. Birding is excellent—watch carefully as you might catch a glimpse of the colorful scarlet tanager. Butterflies, essential to the pollination process of many botanical species, dance from wildflower to wildflower along the sunny shores. If you're like me, you'll finish your exploratory paddle, then head to the middle of the lake to simply sit and drink in the scenery and wildlife.

Little Swartswood Lake

This smaller lake is ideal if it's a windy day and you're introducing a youngster to paddling, because the winds will not whip up the surface as much. While the average depth is 20 feet, there's a 40-foot swath around most of the lake that is very shallow. Pond lilies and duckweed start to take over the lake by the end of July, providing great foraging for ducks, geese, and swans. More than half of the lakeshore is uninhabited and bordered by trees and dense shrubs.

The hiker can enjoy all or part of the 5.7 miles of trails in the park that lead through upland forests and bogs. Trails range from easy to slightly difficult, and from 0.6 to 2.8 miles in length. The Duck Pond Multi-Use Trail includes a bird blind for excellent birdlife viewing.

For another paddle nearby, visit Paulin's Kill Lake, 15 minutes east, or Catfish Pond, 35 minutes southwest. See Trips 10 and 12.

12 | **Appalachian Mountain Club's Mohican Outdoor Center—Catfish Pond**

Abundant wildlife around a remote and scenic lake in the rugged Kittatinny Mountains along the Appalachian Trail is yours to enjoy for the day.

Location: Millbrook, NJ
Maps: *New Jersey Atlas and Gazetteer*, Map 23; USGS Bushkill
Area: 31 acres
Time: 1.0 hour
Conditions: Depth average 10-plus feet
Development: Remote
Information: Mohican Outdoor Center, 50 Camp Road, Blairstown, NJ 07825; 908-362-5670.
Camping: On-site; call the office for reservations; 908-362-5670, 9 A.M. to 5 P.M., 7 days/week.
Take Note: Manually propelled boats only

GETTING THERE

From I-80, take Exit 4C if coming from the west, or 4-A-B-C if coming from the east. Merge onto Route 94 toward Blairstown and drive 7.9 miles, then turn left onto Mohican Road and drive 3.2 miles. Turn left onto Gaisler Road and drive 0.5 mile, then turn right onto Camp Road and drive 0.6 mile, then continue straight on Camp Mohican Road for 0.6 mile to the public parking lot on your left. Stop at the center on your left 0.1 mile before the parking lot if you wish to procure a camping site. Once at the parking lot where you will park after unloading, continue straight past the "Authorized Vehicles Only" sign, and drive 300 yards (0.15 mile) to the unloading area and launch on your left. You'll find parking for 40 cars in the parking lot. *GPS coordinates for the parking lot*: 41°02.133' N, 74°59.984' W. *GPS coordinates for the launch*: 41°02.211' N, 74°59.838' W.

Note: It's a very narrow, single-lane dirt road to the launch. Only one car at a time can enter the road beyond the sign. Unload your equipment, drive back to the parking lot, and then walk back to the launch. Allow plenty of extra time to get on the water if there is more than one car because of the long walk from the parking lot.

AMC'S MOHICAN OUTDOOR CENTER—CATFISH POND

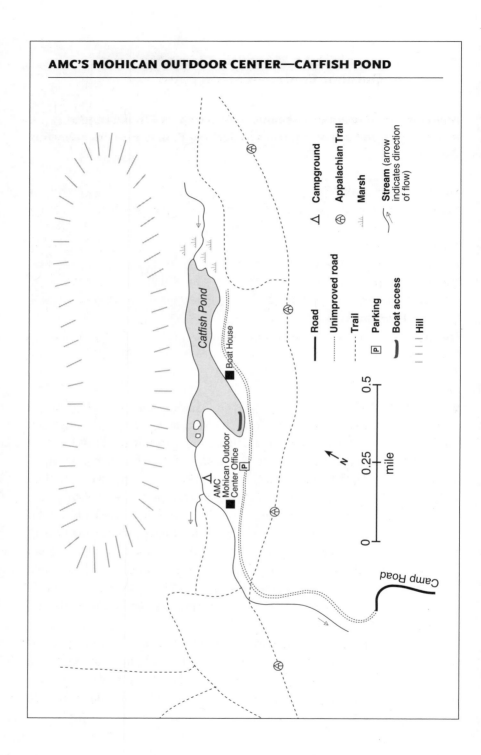

Legend:
— Road
⋯⋯ Unimproved road
⋯ Trail
P Parking
) Boat access
||| Hill

△ Campground
⊕ Appalachian Trail
⩘ Marsh
Stream (arrow indicates direction of flow)

Catfish Pond
Boat House
AMC Mohican Outdoor Center Office
Camp Road

0   0.25   0.5
mile

N

Catfish Pond sits nestled high in the mountains along the Appalachian Trail just west of the Kittatinny Ridge.

WHAT YOU'LL SEE

Looking like a long-sleeved mitt, Catfish Pond sits atop the Kittatinny Mountain ridge within the 15,000-acre Delaware Water Gap National Recreation Area at the Appalachian Mountain Club's Mohican Outdoor Center. Camping, hiking, boating, and boat rentals, as well as lodging, are offered at the center in this rugged and pristine environment. Across from the launch, the mountains rise 120 to 150 feet above the lake, and quite sharply at the eastern end. Rock faces and cliffs peek here and there between the trees, adding texture to the landscape. The forest is primarily hardwoods, with conifers along the lakeshore and in small pockets on the mountain. At the northeast end of the lake, where the mountains rise quite steeply, coniferous trees are more prevalent.

Paddle left from the launch to explore the end of the cove where ducks forage among waterlilies and shallow grasses. Continue to paddle the shoreline counterclockwise, dipping your paddle quietly as you near the tip of the peninsula, where you might spot a great blue heron. Around the peninsula is a narrower cove with three small islands just off the southern shore. Paddle softly between the islands and the shore to get a glimpse of birds and land mammals seeking refuge in more secluded areas. As you travel along the north side, look up to catch a glimpse of raptors flying overhead while enjoying the scenic mountains and shoreline. By the way, over the top of that mountain and down in the next valley is the Delaware River, only 1.1 mile west.

The north end of the lake has an area of saplings interspersed with scrub-shrub where a small creek enters the lake. You can't paddle up the creek any distance, but you can nudge the nose of your boat in a few places to get close-up views of the different vegetation and wildlife flowers growing in that marshy area. Paddling back along the south shore, perhaps just sit, look, and listen for a minute to the sounds and sights around you. Around the bend you'll find a small swimming beach, which might make a refreshing stop on a hot day. About a tenth of a mile beyond that is the center's boat rental concession. Beyond that is one of the center's rustic lodges with a picturesque deck overlooking the lake. Enjoy paddling along the rest of lake to the launch.

The hiker will be thrilled with the number and diversity of trails here, the most notable of which is the Appalachian Trail. Trails range from 2.4 to 7.5 miles, and most are rated moderate. Trails traverse over footbridges and past small waterfalls, old mines, and swamp areas. Spectacular views of the lake, Lower Yards Creek Reservoir, and mountains are seen on many of the trails. The terrain is rugged and can be wet in swamp areas—wear appropriate footwear. Stop at the center on the way in for detailed trail maps and also check out the activities and workshops they offer.

Other trips nearby include Columbia Lake, 25 minute southwest, and Swartswood State Park, 30 minutes east. See Trips 14 and 11.

---

13 | White Lake

Crystal-clear waters will entice you to peer for fish in this unique marl lake where abundant birdlife can be found.

Location: Squires Corner, NJ
Maps: *New Jersey Atlas and Gazetteer*, Map 23; USGS Flatbrookville and Blairstown
Area: 70 acres
Time: 2.0 hours
Conditions: Depth average 22 feet
Development: Rural

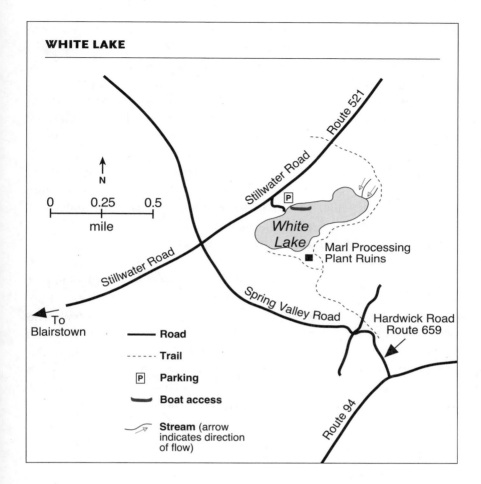

WHITE LAKE

Route 521

Stillwater Road

N

0   0.25   0.5
mile

Stillwater Road

White Lake

P

Marl Processing
Plant Ruins

Stillwater Road

Spring Valley Road

To
Blairstown

Hardwick Road
Route 659

Route 94

Road

Trail

P   Parking

Boat access

Stream (arrow
indicates direction
of flow)

Information: New Jersey Division of Fish and Wildlife, Northern Region
Office, 26 Route 173 West, Hampton, NJ 08827; 973-383-0918.
Camping: Triplebrook Family Camping Resort, 25 minutes south. See
Appendix A.
Take Note: Electric motorboats only (rare)

GETTING THERE:

White's Lake Natural Resource Area is located about 5.0 miles north of Blairstown along the east side of Route 521 (Stillwater Road), 0.4 mile north of the
Route 659 junction. A few houses at that junction compose the blink-and-
you'll-miss-it town of Squires Corner. A large reserve area sign is displayed
prominently at the entrance to the gravel road leading to the lake and parking

area visible from Route 521. You'll find parking for about twenty cars. *GPS coordinates*: 41°00.044′ N, 74°54.989′ W.

WHAT YOU'LL SEE

White Lake is totally enclosed by the 665-acre White Lake Wildlife Management Area in the rural countryside of western Warren County. Vegetation between the wide launch area of the lake and the road consists primarily of tall grasses, shrubs, saplings, and a few trees. At the launch, thick stands of phragmites backed by shrubs and trees provide ample screening from the road. In recent years, thick posts have blocked the sand launch access. Because of this, you'll rarely see anything other than canoes, kayaks, and rowboats on this lake. The first thing you'll notice is the absolutely crystal clear water for which this lake is known. White streaks on the bottom of the lake are marl, prehistoric deposits of aquatic shells.

Immediately to the left (north) of the launch, you'll find an open, shallow cover where waterfowl seek refuge on windy days or forage in the shallow grasses just offshore. Dense woods surround more than half of the oval-shaped lake, with red maple, willow, and other water-loving trees more common close to the water's edge. Large swaths of pines and hemlocks intersperse with hardwood forests to create colorful contrasts in fall foliage and prevent the landscape from looking stark when deciduous trees are bare. On the west end, a few farm fields with modest shoreline trees and vegetation offer a more open environment for different species of birds than found elsewhere around the lake. It is here where hawks can be spotted in the skies searching for small mammals such as field mice, moles, squirrels, and small rabbits.

Wild carrot, butterfly-weed, thistle, purple loosestrife, goldenrod, and tall yellow daisy bushes color grassy borders and attract a multitude of butterflies to dine on their nectar. Dragonflies, choosy about their habitat, are attracted to the clear, clean water. They are carnivorous and feed on bees and butterflies, found in abundance here. On the lake, painted and spotted turtles bask on fallen logs, primarily along the southern shorelines—and some of them are huge. Great blue herons and an occasional great white heron are also found along with ducks, swans, and geese. In cooler weather, loons have been spotted on the lake. Those who like to fish can cast a line for bass, trout, perch, and sunfish. This lake has depths to 40 feet, but the edges are quite shallow. Paddle carefully if you find downed trees along the shore.

If you feel like taking a hike after your paddle, there's a wonderful 3-mile easy trail that passes tall stone ruins from the old marl-collecting factory that was active in the late 1800s. The trail is planned to eventually connect to the 27-mile-long Paulin's Kill Valley Trail. To view the ruins and hike the trail, exit the parking lot and turn left. Drive 0.4 mile to the junction with Spring Valley Road, turn left and drive 0.75 mile to the dirt parking area on your left. The trail head is at the northeast corner of the parking area.

For an additional paddle the same day, visit Appalachian Mountain Club's Mohican Outdoor Center, 20 minutes northwest, or Cranberry Lake, 30 minutes east. See Trips 12 and 8.

14 | Columbia Lake

Colorful wildflowers and marsh grasses, abundant wildlife, and a paddle up a scenic river are yours to enjoy at this lake.

Location: Polkville, NJ
Maps: *New Jersey Atlas and Gazetteer*, Map 22; USGS Portland
Area: 55 acres
Time: 1.5 hours
Conditions: Depth data unavailable. Estimated average depth is 4 feet (I couldn't touch bottom with my paddle in most locations).
Development: Rural
Information: New Jersey Division of Fish and Wildlife, Northern Region Office, 26 Route 173 West, Hampton, NJ 08827; 973-383-0918.
Camping: Camp Taylor Campground, 8 minutes north. See Appendix A.
Take Note: Electric motorboats only; very short portages if you travel up the Paulin's Kill River

GETTING THERE

Take I-80 to Exit 4, drive north 0.25 mile on Route 94, turn right, and drive 0.3 mile on Warrington Road. After crossing over a small bridge where Paulin's Kill Creek flows into the lake, turn right onto the dirt road (there will be a small sign for Columbia Lake), and drive about 0.6 mile to the end. Because the dirt road parallels private property, it may appear to be part of a driveway, but it isn't. You'll find parking for fifteen cars. *GPS coordinates*: 40°55.863' N, 75°04.551' W.

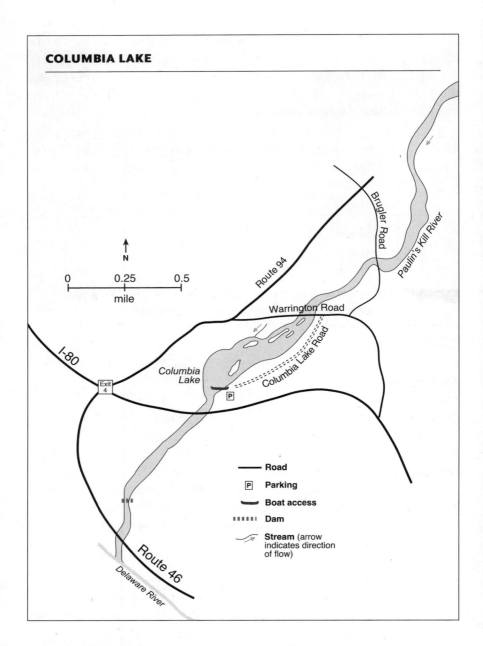

COLUMBIA LAKE

0   0.25   0.5
mile

N

I-80

Exit 4

Route 94

Brugler Road

Paulin's Kill River

Warrington Road

Columbia Lake Road

Columbia Lake

P

Route 46

Delaware River

— Road

P Parking

Boat access

Dam

Stream (arrow indicates direction of flow)

WHAT YOU'LL SEE

From the I-80 ramps, you get a magnificent view of the Delaware River Water Gap. Once a continuous east–west mountain ridge holding back a large inland sea, erosion worked on a weak spot, gradually etching its way through until the waters started to escape. Once the outflow started, erosion accelerated, eventu-

Looking down the southern end of Columbia Lake, keep your eyes peeled for darners and butterflies.

ally creating a channel that would later become part of the Delaware River. At the Delaware River Water Gap, Mount Tammany is on the New Jersey side and Mount Minsi on the Pennsylvania side.

Long, narrow, and somewhat shallow, Columbia Lake is a fine place for bird-watching around the marsh island and adjacent wetlands. The only drawback is the proximity to noisy I-80, but once you're on the water, you're in another world. Pond lily islands and hammocks offer abundant shelter for waterfowl and provide an interesting trip as you weave in and out of the serpentine maze. A superb variety of colorful wildflowers and marsh grasses can be found in and around the marshy hammocks and adjacent wetlands.

The launch area can be dense with lily pads by late summer, but people fish here often and keep a channel open into the lake. Paddle left after leaving the launch and pass around and under the I-80 bridge. Ahead is a long, narrow section of the lake that usually stays clear as the Paulin's Kill River channels into the dam at the other end. Birdlife is abundant along the shores, and deer, foxes, and raccoons may be seen lakeside. The old pump house next to the dam is quite picturesque. You won't be able to land there because a line of white buoys warns of the sluiceway danger. After enjoying this section of the lake, paddle back under I-80 to explore the northern section of the lake and perhaps paddle up the Paulin's Kill River for a mile or so.

Once north of the launch, it will look like a maze of lily pad islands and some hammocks, but there are distinct water trails where you can detect channels of flow. Enjoy the wildflowers and birdlife as you weave your way in and around the water trails, making your way to the Warrington Road bridge. The lake ends a little north of the bridge, but beautiful paddling awaits you on the other side, where you can paddle up the Paulin's Kill River more than two miles, depending on water levels and downfalls. Getting under this bridge is a "kiss the deck" maneuver, but you can portage it without too much difficulty if water levels are too high.

Once into the river, you're far enough away from I-80 that you won't hear anything except the sounds of nature and a car or two. The scenery is beautiful with the river bordered by long stretches of woodlands with a few farmlands interspersed. Wildlife is abundant along the whole trip. About three-quarters of a mile north of the bridge will be an area you may need to portage over or slog through. It's the remnants of a long-abandoned railroad. You can usually paddle upstream for another 1.5 to 2.0 miles before turning around and lazily paddling with the current back to the launch.

Other sites nearby include Minsi Lake, Pennsylvania, 20 minutes southwest, and the Appalachian Mountain Club's Mohican Outdoor Center, 25 minutes northeast. See Trips 58 and 12.

15 | Hackensack River and Meadowlands

Observe wading and marsh birds, peregrine falcons, ospreys, and more as you paddle through brackish tidal marshes.

Location: Secaucus, NJ
Maps: *New Jersey Atlas and Gazetteer*, 32; USGS Weehawkin and Jersey City
Area: 1.5-mile section of the Hackensack River, about 950 acres of Meadowlands
Time: 3.0–4.0 hours for suggested route
Conditions: Depth average 30 feet in the river, 3 to 5 feet in the meadowlands
Development: Urban
Information: Hackensack Riverkeeper Inc. in residence at Fairleigh Dickinson University, 1000 River Road–T090C, Teaneck, NJ 07666; 201-692-8440; www.hackensackriverkeeper.org.

Take Note: Motorboats on the river (but not in the meadowlands); tidal influence; winds

Outfitters: The Paddling Center at Laurel Hill Park; www.hackensackriverkeeper.org

GETTING THERE

From I-95/New Jersey Turnpike south, drive north on I-95 North. Where it splits for the eastern and the western spurs, take the eastern spur for Route 46/I-80/Lincoln Tunnel. Take Exit 15X (built for the Secaucus Train Station), merging onto Seaview Drive, and drive 2.3 miles. Turn left at New County Road and drive 0.7 mile to the entrance for the parking lot and launch. You'll pass the Welcome to Laurel Hill Park sign on the way in. Parking is available for 30 cars. *GPS coordinates*: 40°45.830′ N, 74°05.200′ W.

From I-95/New Jersey Turnpike north, follow the same directions as above, except that it's a 2.5-mile drive on Seaview Drive.

WHAT YOU'LL SEE

You're probably thinking, "Secaucus? This is supposed to be a book on good, quiet paddling sites." You may think it is crazy to suggest paddling anywhere in this highly industrialized, overly populated, and cacophonous area. For those living nearby, the Hackensack River and Meadowlands offer one of the few spots to paddle within a reasonable distance—and it's a wildlife haven and beautiful paddle to boot. Paddlers are starting to come here from far away to visit this magnificent estuary. It also helps us realize how important it is to protect such precious environments, both for the wildlife and for public enjoyment. The Hackensack River is a few hundred yards wide here and, with nothing but open salt marshes all around, can churn up pretty well on a windy day. Keep alert to changes in weather and observe the same caution as you would on a large lake.

The Hackensack Riverkeeper Canoe Project's main goal is to have Hackensack Meadowlands designated as a National Wildlife Refuge to protect it from further development. The organization maintains a base of operation in a small trailer next to the boat ramp, where they rent canoes, offer guided paddles, run eco-cruises, organize river cleanups, and distribute literature to foster public awareness of this valuable environment. It is open on weekends, 9 A.M. to 6 P.M., from the last weekend in April until the last weekend in October. If you are new to paddling, I suggest you take one of their guided paddles your first time here.

From the boat launch, head downstream (left) and across the river to the end of the marshes a little more than halfway between the launch and the railroad bridge. Hug the edge of the tall grasses, which is technically Sawmill Creek, for the deepest water—it becomes very shallow quickly toward the mud flats. You can circle around a number of small grass islands if the water level permits, but don't hang out there because you may get stuck. Sit, look, and listen to the amazing amount of wildlife found here. As you head around the corner to your right (north), numerous small coves and niches are fun to explore for more wildlife viewing.

Across from the western end of Straight Ditch, you'll see an opening under I-95 that leads to more mudflats, and you'll see the yellow "Do Not Enter" sign. Obey it. Paddle around slowly to the wide opening into K Ditch, and then turn left (west). Paddle quietly as you pass numerous channels and narrow passages so you don't disturb foraging birds. When you see I-95 ahead of you (again, with a "Do Not Enter" sign), turn right at the next wide opening, which will be Kingsland Creek. Paddle down the creek to the river, then cross to the other side and back down to the launch.

More than 50 species of birds are known to nest in the marshlands and adjacent scrub-shrub and lowland woods. During spring and fall migrations, more than 150 species are known to utilize those areas as a stopover to rest and feed before continuing their journeys. Some stay to grace the state with their presence throughout the warmer months, and a few become year-round residents in this rich estuarine environment where the Hackensack River winds through the marshes. Birds frequently seen here include ospreys, harriers, egrets, herons, yellowlegs, stilts and semipalmated sandpipers, least and Forster's terns, red-winged blackbirds, marsh wrens, and black skimmers, to name a few. The variety of prey, from insects, shellfish, and small fish to snails, frogs, and small mammals, is a testament to the health of the restored wetlands.

Watch the forked-tailed terns as they hunt for prey, hover in place 20 to 40 feet above the water, then plunge straight down for the catch. Scan the mudflats carefully for the occasional avocet, and the grassy shallows for the common moorhen or stilt. Look carefully at the edges of marsh grass for yellow- and black-crowned night herons, a delightful find. One of my favorite treats is to spot the curve-billed white ibis foraging in the mudflats for snails. They are often seen foraging alongside snowy egrets, whose yellow feet are often referred to as "golden slippers" and stand out against their black legs.

When the peaty marsh ground is exposed, listen for clicking sounds, and then look for the red-jointed fiddler crabs making the noise. Periwinkles (small snails) crawl around the peat. The diamondback terrapin, *Malaclemys terrapin*, is the only turtle in the continental United States that is found solely in brackish saltwater environments. Aside from habitat, concentric rings or ridges on its

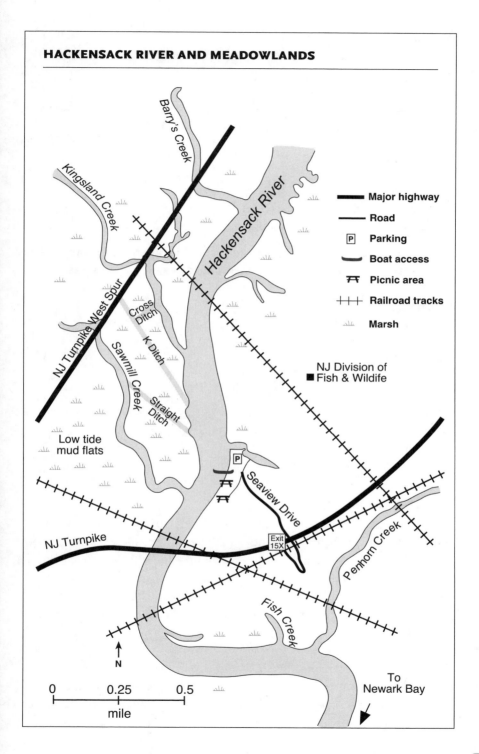

HACKENSACK RIVER AND MEADOWLANDS

Legend:
- ▬▬ Major highway
- ── Road
- P Parking
- Boat access
- 🞪 Picnic area
- +++ Railroad tracks
- Marsh

NJ Division of
Fish & Wildife

Barry's Creek

Kingsland Creek

Hackensack River

NJ Turnpike West Spur

Cross Ditch

K Ditch

Sawmill Creek

Straight Ditch

Low tide
mud flats

Seaview Drive

Exit 15X

NJ Turnpike

Penhorn Creek

Fish Creek

N

0   0.25   0.5
mile

To
Newark Bay

shell and a spotted head and limbs confirm this reptile's identification. It's rare here, but they have been spotted. Look carefully at the grassy corners for the gnawed, telltale sign of muskrat activity, then see if you can find their mounded house about 15 feet or so back from the water.

For another paddle nearby, visit Pompton Lake, 40 minutes northwest, or Weequahic Lake, 25 minutes southwest. See Trips 5 and 16.

16 | Weequahic Lake

Swans, geese, and a variety of ducks grace this quiet lake in the middle of a highly urbanized area for a peaceful getaway if you live nearby.

Location: Newark, NJ
Maps: *New Jersey Atlas and Gazetteer*, Map 32; USGS Elizabeth
Area: 80 acres
Time: 2.0 hours
Conditions: Depth average 5 feet
Development: Urban
Information: New Jersey Division of Fish and Wildlife, Central Region (Assunpink WMA), 386 Clarksburg-Robbinsville Road, Robbinsville, NJ 08691; 609-259-2132.
Take Note: Cartop boats only

GETTING THERE
From the junction of Routes 27 and 28 in Elizabeth, drive 0.5 mile on Route 27 North/Broad Street, then slight right onto Route 27 North/Newark Avenue and drive 2.1 miles. Turn left onto Meeker Avenue and drive 0.3 mile, then turn left onto Weequahic Park Drive and drive 450 feet to the parking area and launch. Parking will be on your left and the floating dock launch on your right. You'll find parking for twenty cars. *GPS coordinates*: 40°42.338′ N, 74°11.865′ W.

WHAT YOU'LL SEE
Weequahic Park (pronounced WEE qua) is a welcome respite in the midst of a highly industrialized and urban area. The park offers an 80-acre lake, multiuse trails, playing fields, playground, clean restrooms, and shady picnic areas. For paddlers living in the surrounding highly developed areas, it offers the oppor-

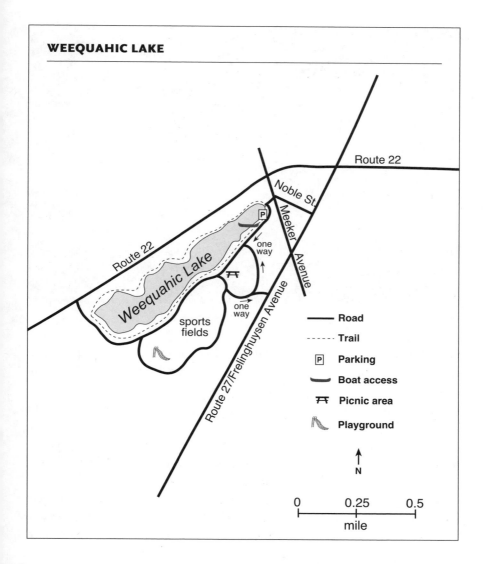

WEEQUAHIC LAKE

Route 22

Noble St

Meeker Avenue

Route 22

Weequahic Lake

one way

one way

sports fields

Route 27/Frelinghuysen Avenue

Road

Trail

P Parking

Boat access

Picnic area

Playground

N

0   0.25   0.5

mile

tunity to get on the water after work for an hour or two of peace and relaxation or spend a weekend morning on nearby waters. The lake is dredged and cleaned every few years, ensuring good water quality. Water levels here remain constant, even in the driest of years, because the lake is fed by springs instead of being a dammed section of a river like most lakes.

The irregular shoreline provides a pleasant paddle as you explore numerous coves and niches around the lake. Large trees hug the shores, overhanging the water's edge in many places. Here and there, clusters of willow trees grace the water's edge with their hanging limbs that move softly with any whisper of

Mute swans enjoy the quiet lakeside in the middle of a large city.

breeze. Modest hills on the north and west sides add interest to the topography as you paddle along the lake. A local angler I talked with proudly displayed the large carp he had caught earlier saying, "There's lots o' big carp in these waters. Can catch one 'bout every day I come here." Bass, sunfish, and catfish can also be caught here.

Swans, ducks, and Canada geese are everywhere. Cormorants are common on the water and egrets stalk shallow shores. There's a nice population of birds that enjoy the refuge of the park, and I think you'll be surprised at the diversity of species and quantity of birds flitting about the water's edge or along the mul- tiuse trail. On a visit there in the summer of 2009, I spoke with a park attendant who told me about a pair of nesting swans about 10 feet back from the shoreline between the two playing fields on the south side. Difficult to see from the trail, the nest was easily visible from the water. What a treat for the locals, and what a statement it makes for how the city has upgraded the park and kept the lake clean. It's still an ongoing project, with better launch facilities planned and an aeration system to keep the late summer plankton blooms down. Still, if you're local to the area, it's a quick and easy place to get on the water and enjoy nature while paddling in pleasant surroundings.

A well-maintained, rustic-red, rubberized, 2.2-mile trail encircles the lake. Most of the trail winds through shady trees and offers nice views of the lake along the way.

Another nearby paddle is Hackensack River and Hackensack Meadows, 20 minutes northeast. See Trip 15. If you want to get farther away from the industrialized setting, visit Farrington Lake, 40 minutes southwest, or Round Valley Reservoir, 45 minutes west. See Trips 21 and 19.

17 | Merrill Creek Reservoir

Look for eagles, hawks, more eagles, ospreys, deer, foxes, and maybe a black bear at this reservoir.

Location: Stewartsville, NJ
Maps: *New Jersey Atlas and Gazetteer*, Map 28; USGS Bloomsbury
Area: 650 acres
Time: 3.0–4.0 hours
Conditions: Depth average 60 feet; crystal clear water
Development: Rural
Information: Merrill Creek Reservoir Visitor Center, 34 Merrill Creek Road, Washington, NJ 07882; 908-454-1213. No fees are charged, but during the summer you must sign in at the kiosk by the boat ramp.
Camping: Delaware River Family Campground, 25 minutes north. See Appendix A. Spruce Run Recreation Area, 30 minutes southeast. See Appendix A.
Take Note: Electric motorboats only; cold water; winds; closed on a few holidays (refer to website); black bear; best seasons are spring and fall during bird migration; minimum length requirement for kayaks and canoes: 9 feet and 12 feet, respectively.

GETTING THERE

Take Exit 3 from I-78, following signs for Route 22. Drive west 0.8 mile on Route 22 and exit onto Uniontown Road toward Port Warren (northeast). Drive north about 1.6 miles, turn right (north) onto Route 57 north and drive 3.1 miles to Montana Road. Turn left onto Montana Road and drive 2.0 miles. At the Y intersection, turn left onto Richline Road, drive 0.3 mile, then turn left onto Merrill Creek Road and drive 0.3 mile. At the Y-junction, turn right to go to the visitor center or stay straight to proceed to the ramp. Signs at the entrance will direct you to the visitor center and the boat launch.

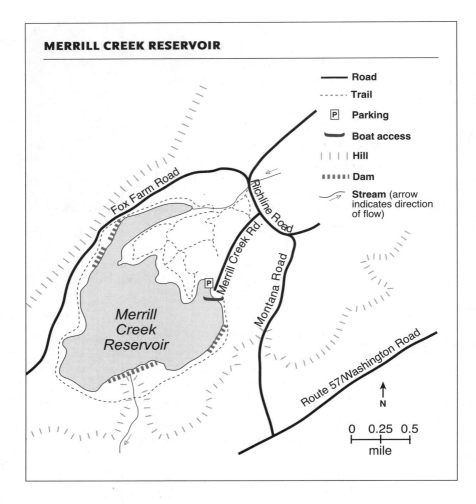

MERRILL CREEK RESERVOIR

Legend:
- Road
- Trail
- P Parking
- Boat access
- Hill
- Dam
- Stream (arrow indicates direction of flow)

Fox Farm Road

Richline Road

Merrill Creek Rd.

Montana Road

Merrill Creek Reservoir

Route 57/Washington Road

N

0   0.25   0.5
mile

From the north, at the junction of Routes 31 and 57 in Washington, drive south on Route 57 for 6.4 miles to Montana Road. Turn right onto Montana Road and continue as above. You will find parking for about 60 cars. *GPS coordinates for the launch*: 40°44.578′ N, 75°05.231′ W. *GPS coordinates for the visitor center*: 40°44.335′ N, 75°05.465′ W.

WHAT YOU'LL SEE

A 290-acre environmental preserve and an additional 2,000 acres of woods and fields surround Merrill Creek Reservoir's 650 acres. Eagle- and hawk-watching are very popular and there's an official HawkWatch and count held during the month of November each year. The reservoir's main purpose is water supply for the Delaware River, with water being pumped up from the river in spring

Paddle along the shoreline of Merrill Creek Reservoir to study the weather drowned trees.

when levels are high and released back to the river in summer to utility companies downstream when energy use is high. The pipeline from the river is 3.5 miles long.

Lights on two towers flash when winds exceed 25 MPH for five seconds or more, and all boats must head back to the launch. Yes, that means you. Positioned atop a mountain where vigorous winds can prevail, the warning lights provide an excellent safety measure for boaters.

The perimeter of the lake has many areas of silvery-gray, weathered drowned trees, remnants from when the area was flooded to create the reservoir in 1988. Those areas provide good conditions for smallmouth and largemouth bass, a favorite among anglers. Three species of trout, muskies, yellow and white perch, chain pickerel, crappies, and sunfish all reside under the surface. Closer to the woods, some of those tall dead trees also provide nesting sites for woodpeckers and sheltered areas for mergansers, wood ducks, loons, and other waterfowl. Our turtle friends can be found basking just above water level on the many limbs jutting from the water.

The list of bird species found here, either as migrants during spring and fall or as summertime residents, is staggering. Ospreys and eagles abound everywhere and at least one pair of eagles has nested right by the water since 2000. The eagle nest is along the western shoreline. White buoys mark a "stay clear" area so as not to disturb the nest. Orioles, tanagers, kingfishers, and other birds also nest here, and you should be able to spot some of them on your paddle or hike. Terrestrial wildlife includes black bears, deer, foxes, raccoons, wild turkeys, pheasants, and coyotes. Around grassy lakeshore areas, look for muskrat.

Most of the shoreline is smooth, but with enough coves and interesting features to keep you coming back for more, especially with all the raptors and hiking opportunities. Head to your right from the launch to circle the lake counterclockwise. After paddling past a drowned-tree area and into a few coves, you'll come to the long arm in the northwest corner where ducks and geese are plentiful. Continue your paddle around to the southern end, passing one of the dikes, then lily-dip down the long, densely tree-studded shoreline. Along the southern shore is another dike. I tend to use the opportunity when paddling past dikes to look skyward for the big birds: ospreys, hawks, and eagles. Between the south dike and the east dike is a long section of drowned trees that is very picturesque, both above water and in the crystal-clear depths below. If you have a waterproof camera, dip it in the water and take some pictures. Continue paddling up the eastern shoreline and back to the ramp.

The hiking enthusiast will be thrilled with the seven trails available. The longest is a 5.5-mile perimeter trail that provides access to the entire shoreline and takes you through a variety of habitats. There are a few rocky areas, but this trail is considered easy. Six other trails range from 0.3 to 1.7 miles in length. Eagle Trail is the shortest and offers a wildlife observation blind. Stop at the visitor center for a detailed trail map and to ask about current trail conditions.

Spruce Run Reservoir is 35 minutes southeast. See Trip 18.

2 | CENTRAL NEW JERSEY

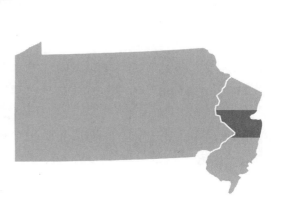

Northwest of an imaginary line running approximately from Trenton on the Delaware River, to New Brunswick and Perth Amboy near the Atlantic Ocean, start the rolling hills of the Piedmont Plateau, which grade into the higher mountains of northwestern New Jersey. Southeast of that line, the rolling hills gently flatten and give way to the low-lying coastal plain. Valleys become natural holding basins for rainwater and small streams. Dark soil, rich with minerals on which horse and agricultural farms flourish in the northern area, gradually gives way to the gravel and sand of the coastal plain. Slightly cooler weather in the hills creates the southern extent of northern birds, such as the bobolink, which rarely make it south of Trenton during the summer. Barrier islands rim the Atlantic Ocean like a necklace and help protect developed coastal areas from pounding ocean waves.

The Delaware and Raritan Canal connects the Delaware River with the Raritan River, which flows into Raritan Bay on the Atlantic Ocean. This historic route once provided essential passage for the transportation of coal and other cargo from Pennsylvania to New York City and other towns along the eastern seaboard between 1834 and 1932. Mules plodded along the towpaths beside the canal, pulling barges laden with goods on a two-day journey from Bordentown to New Brunswick. Many historically designated bridge-tenders' houses and hand-laid cobblestone spillways along the canal offer a glimpse of the era before railroads replaced water as an economic and efficient mode of transportation. The canal and towpath are now part of the National Recreational Trail System. Trip 20 guides you along parts of this great canal system.

18 | Spruce Run Reservoir

A huge body of water with dozens of coves to explore and lots of wildlife to observe will provide you with hours of paddling pleasure.

Location: Clinton, NJ
Maps: *New Jersey Atlas and Gazetteer*, Map 29; USGS High Bridge
Area: 1,300 acres
Time: 5.0–5.5 hours
Conditions: Depth average 26 feet
Development: Rural
Information: Spruce Run State Park, One Van Syckel's Corner Road, Clinton, NJ 08809; 908-638-8572; $5 weekdays in-season, $10 weekends in-season.
Camping: On-site; call the park office for reservations.
Take Note: Motorboats to 10 horsepower; winds

GETTING THERE
From the east: Take Exit 17 off I-78 for Route 31/Clinton/Flemington. Drive 3.1 miles on Route 31 North, turn left onto Van Syckel's Corner Road and drive 1.5 miles to the park entrance on your left.

From the west: Take Exit 12 off I-78 for Route 173/Norton. Turn left onto Mechlin Corner Road/Route 635 and drive 1.1 miles, then turn right onto Van Syckel's Corner Road and drive 1.9 miles to the park entrance on your right.

The park office is right behind the entrance booth. The road to the boat launch is the first left after the entrance booth. Turn left and drive 1.2 miles to the boat launch area. There will be signs for the sand cartop launch on the west side of the parking lot. Clean restrooms are available. You'll find parking for 100 cars. *GPS coordinates*: 40°39.646′ N, 74°55.493′ W.

SPRUCE RUN RESERVOIR

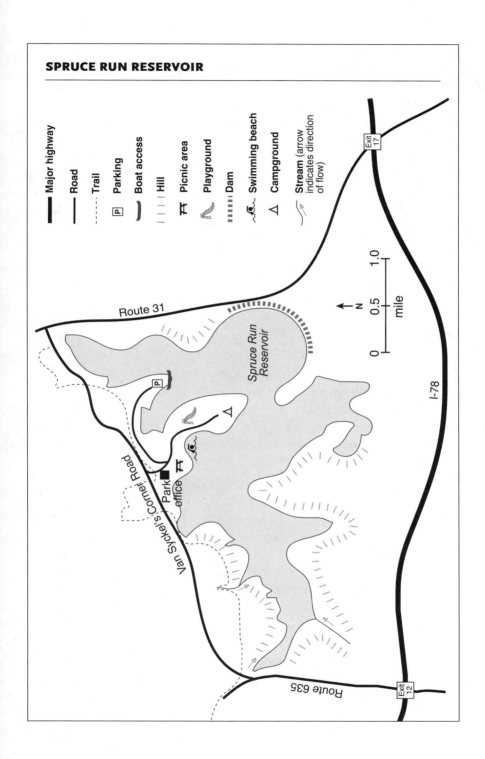

Legend:
- Major highway
- Road
- Trail
- P Parking
-) Boat access
- Hill
- Picnic area
- Playground
- Dam
- Swimming beach
- △ Campground
- Stream (arrow indicates direction of flow)

Route 31

Spruce Run Reservoir

Van Syckel's Corner Road

Park office

Route 635

Exit 17

Exit 12

I-78

N

0   0.5   1.0
mile

WHAT YOU'LL SEE

A 1,193-acre section of the Clinton Wildlife Management Area and the 2,012-acre Spruce Run State Park surround most of the 1,290-acre reservoir, offering thousands of acres of forest and undisturbed habitat for wildlife viewing and paddling. Built in 1965 for the Elizabethtown Water Company, the reservoir's highly irregular outline resembles an amoeba on steroids. Recreational facilities at the park include a swimming beach, ball fields, concession stands, and small boat rentals. Campsites are available, inviting you to spend a few rewarding days. Make reservations ahead of time to ensure availability.

With 15 miles of shoreline, you could spend a few afternoons paddling in and out of all the little coves, nooks, and crannies. I found the most picturesque paddling to the south and southwest, where coves and peninsulas are most abundant and give you a better chance for solitude on crowded summer weekends. As with Round Valley and Merrill Creek Reservoirs, Spruce Run has a warning tower that flashes red when winds increase to warn boaters to get off the water.

Because of the vast habitat provided by the adjacent wildlife management area, the reservoir has an enormous diversity of birdlife and small mammals. Eagles, hawks, harriers, vultures, and ospreys fly overhead, and it's fairly common to see an osprey plunge for prey if you're on the water for a few hours. Along tree- and shrub-lined shores you'll find bobolinks, warblers, pewees, towhees, scarlet tanagers, and a variety of songbirds flitting about the branches overhanging the waters and in and around stands of phragmites and cattails. Willows are abundant along some shores, creating a softness to the landscape at the slightest breeze.

The big attraction at Spruce Run for the paddler is its size and convoluted shape. At any one place on the water, you can only see about one-quarter to one-third of the reservoir. It's the adventurous element of what's around the next corner that will keep you exploring happily for hours; every turn brings something new into view. The combination of shoreline features, from long sandy beaches and open grasslands to shrublands and wooded hillsides, are responsible for the diversity of wildlife visible from your boat.

Turn left after leaving the launch and head around into the northeastern arm of the lake. It's a pretty arm to explore, far away from the recreational areas and open areas that the sailors prefer. After exploring, paddle along the eastern edge until you're near the dam, then head over to the peninsula on the west side of the dam. The large cove to the south has numerous smaller coves and crannies to explore before continuing your travel along the southern shoreline.

One of the best places for a peaceful paddle is in the western quarter of the lake. Because it's farthest from the boat launch and sailing center, and more shallow, it gets the least boat traffic. A few small streams enter the reservoir at the far western corner, and you can paddle upstream for a short way if water levels are high. Numerous sandy beaches invite you to stop for a break and lunch. Look for beaver lodges all along the shores here; a number have been seen over the years. Head back toward the launch along the northern shoreline, past wooded shores interspersed with small grass or scrub-shrub environments. Past the swimming beach to the south is the campground peninsula. Perhaps you'll see a waterfront site to reserve for your next trip here. Round the peninsula and explore the last cove where the cartop launch is located.

For the hiker, the Highlands Millennium Trail (teal diamond), which will eventually connect the Delaware River to the Hudson River, is approximately 0.9 mile (one way) within the park boundaries. An interesting segment of that trail immediately outside the park boundaries takes you through the Union Furnace Nature Area and on to restored furnace buildings. To pick up the trail, exit Spruce Run State Park and turn right on Van Syckel's Corner Road. Drive 0.9 mile to the parking area on your right. The furnace building will be directly across the road. The nature area is an additional 0.45 mile west, with a large parking lot on your right and the marked entrance directly across the road.

Additional trips nearby include Round Valley Reservoir, 15 minutes southeast, and Merrill Creek Reservoir, 35 minutes northwest. See Trips 19 and 17.

19 | Round Valley Recreation Area

Enjoy eagles, ospreys, vast open waters, and wilderness campsites accessible only by foot or boat at the state's largest reservoir.

Location: Lebanon, NJ
Maps: *New Jersey Atlas and Gazetteer*, Map 35; USGS Califon and Flemington
Area: 2,350 acres
Time: 4.0–4.5 hours
Conditions: Depth average 60 feet
Development: Rural
Information: Round Valley Recreation Area, Box 45D, Lebanon Stanton Road, Lebanon, NJ 08833; 908-236-6355; $5 weekdays in-season, $10 weekends in-season for the day-use recreation area—the boat launch area is free.

Camping: On-site wilderness campsites; call the park office for reservations. Spruce Run State Park is 15 minutes northwest. Mountainview Campground is 30 minutes west. See Appendix A.

Take Note: Motorboats to 10 horsepower; dry suits required from November 1 until May 15 (posted sign); New Jersey boat ramp maintenance permit required. See Appendix D

GETTING THERE

From the east, take I-78 west to Exit 20 toward Lebanon/Round Valley Recreation Area. It will merge into Route 639 south (Cokesbury Road). Drive 0.3 mile to the T-intersection at Main Street. Turn left and drive 0.1 mile to Route 629 (Cherry Street). Turn right and drive 1.4 miles to the boat launch entrance road on the left. You'll find parking for more than 100 cars. *GPS coordinates*: 40°37.900′ N, 74°50.923′ W.

From the west, take I-78 east to Exit 18 (Lebanon/Route 22 east). Follow Route 22 east for 1.6 miles, veer right onto Main Street, drive 0.6 mile to Route 629 (Cherry Street), and continue as above. Large signs are posted all along the roads for a 5.0-mile radius around the reservoir, making it impossible to miss.

Continue another 0.9 mile past the boat launch entrance to reach the small recreational lake (boating prohibited) that features a beach, picnic grove, and a playground. A fee is charged in-season.

WHAT YOU'LL SEE

At 2,350 acres, Round Valley Reservoir is the state's largest reservoir and its second largest body of freshwater, surpassed only by Lake Hopatcong. It opened in 1972 as a backup to nearby Spruce Run. The launch is open 24 hours a day, 365 days a year. Stay 200 feet away from the dam towers and 100 feet away from the dams themselves. Impressive to look at, the reservoir is a little more than 2.5 miles long and 1.5 miles wide—that's a lot of water to paddle.

Surrounded by rolling hills 120 to 200 feet high, pockets of hemlocks and pines are interspersed within dominant mixed-oak and hardwood forests. Other than two concrete dams on the north and west sides, the scenery is delightful. Crystal clear water allows you to see large fish to a depth of 20 to 25 feet on calm days. As with Merrill Creek and Spruce Run, a red warning light flashes from a tower when winds blow 25 MPH for five seconds or more, requiring all boats to head back to the launch. If you're in the middle of the reservoir when that happens, you might want to head to the closest land before working your way back to the launch.

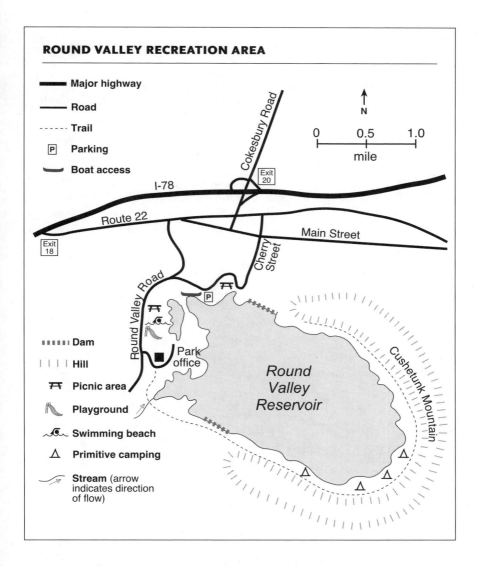

ROUND VALLEY RECREATION AREA

Legend:
- ━━━ Major highway
- ━━━ Road
- ----- Trail
- P Parking
- ⌣ Boat access
- ▐▐▐▐▐ Dam
- | | | | Hill
- ⊓ Picnic area
- Playground
- Swimming beach
- △ Primitive camping
- Stream (arrow indicates direction of flow)

Cokesbury Road

Exit 20

I-78

Route 22

Exit 18

Main Street

Cherry Street

Round Valley Road

Park office

Round Valley Reservoir

Cushetunk Mountain

0   0.5   1.0
mile

N

Leaving behind the busy launch area, paddle straight out to the peninsula beyond the day-use impoundment and notice the pink granite boulders and interesting rock faces. Once around the small peninsula, drink in the expanse of the wide-open waters. Around the peninsula are a few large coves that break up the shoreline. Along the sand and rock beaches there, remnants of fallen trees and broken limbs give you a feeling of wilderness. Beyond the last cove you'll see the western dam. Remember to pass 100 feet away from it as you head to the eastern end of the lake. The rest of the lake's shoreline is relatively straight, but with enough boulders and fallen trees to remain pleasant and interesting.

OSPREY

For years, the osprey population suffered decline due in large part to pesticides and habitat destruction. Now, with the help of artificial nesting sites and a ban on DDT, they are making a tremendous comeback. Known also as "fish hawks," they are the only raptor whose front talons turn backward and the only one that plunges feet-first into the water. Spines on its toes enable it to hold on to slippery fish, its main prey. They are also known to take an occasional small rodent or crustacean when fishing is extremely poor. Ospreys favor open streams, rivers, and lakes, nesting in treetops found near water. Brown above and white below, their most distinguishing field marks are their broad, black cheek patch and black wrist patches. A female osprey's wingspan averages 4 to 4.5 feet. Male wingspans are slightly smaller.

Females choose partners based on nest location, and the pair generally mates for life. Both adults help build the large stick nest that measures 3 to 5 feet in diameter. While males and females may winter in different locations, they return to their nest within a few days of each other. Ospreys arrive in southern New Jersey around the end of March and in northern New Jersey a week or two later. Courtship flights, graceful touch-and-go aerial maneuvers,

may be seen the first week or two after their arrival as mating pairs are made or renewed. Part of the mating ritual entails the male catching fish for the female, to prove he will be, or still is, a good provider. From pairing to egg-laying, females are fed by the male. Both adults assist in repairing the old nest, shoring up walls with fresh twigs and lining the bottom with mucky sod. While both will bring in twigs, more often than not the female does the arranging.

When not out hunting, the male can be found on his roost about a hundred yards away and within visual contact of the nest. At a hint of danger, such as human intrusion or blackbird mobbing, the female emits a high-pitched *eep, eep, eep* sound, a signal for the male to come flying to the rescue. As the female nears egg-laying time, she stays closer to the nest, leaving infrequently to stretch her wings. Once the eggs (two to four) are laid, she hunkers down in the nest, with only the top of her head visible to a careful observer. She incubates the eggs most of the time, but does trade off periodically with the male. After catching a fish, the male eats the head and neck area, and then brings the remainder to the nest and takes over incubation while the female feeds. After she has eaten and preened, she takes over incubation and the male returns to his proximal roost.

Young hatch about 5 weeks after the eggs are laid, but it will take an additional 7 to 8 weeks until they are ready to leave the nest. Even then, the parents must provide food for the first few weeks until the young can hunt well enough on their own: catching fish through the warped air–water interface evidently requires practice, practice, and more practice. By mid-October, ospreys start heading south to their favorite wintering ground. Mating pairs usually split for the duration, only to meet again the following spring when the courtship ritual must be observed before actual mating takes place.

Hawks and vultures circle in the thermals of air above the lake; warblers, kingfishers, blue jays, finches, and other songbirds flit in and about the trees along the water. It is not uncommon to see ospreys, or even an eagle, plunge for fish. If you see them in the sky, keep track of them during your paddle and you might see one of them catch prey. Along the shores around the lake you're likely to see deer, wild turkeys, raccoons, skunks, and squirrels.

Weekends in July and August can become crazed with anglers. Round Valley is noted for its trout fishing, producing the state record for lake trout and brown trout, and is the only lake in New Jersey with a population of reproducing

After a family paddle, a mother pulls her boat on shore while the father makes sure his daughter is on firm ground.

lake trout. Other species include largemouth and smallmouth bass, brown and rainbow trout, yellow and white perch, and large sunfish. While the average depth is 60 feet, the reservoir is up to 175 feet deep in the middle. If you fish, bring plenty of line.

The eastern end of the reservoir tends to have the least motorboat traffic. Although there are numerous sand beaches around the perimeter to land for lunch or to stretch your legs, the southwest to southeast shoreline is rimmed with beach—an excellent place to plan a stop and view of the entire lake and surrounding countryside. Paddling back to the launch, a hill rises rather steeply and impressively at the point of land right before the north dam. Again, remember to stay at least 100 feet from the dam structure when you pass. Before exiting your boat at the launch, take a few minutes to turn around and look at the large body of water you just paddled.

A note about fog: While you can get fog or foglike mist anytime and on any lake, in early summer and early fall the water and air temperatures are vastly different, making fog more likely. Be aware of where you are on the lake at all times when paddling during those seasons, as well as early morning and early evening the rest of the year.

Three marked trails, accessible from the south parking lot of the day-use area, pass through hemlock valleys and hardwood highlands around the lake.

The 9.0-mile, out-and-back Cushetunk Trail is moderate-difficult and provides accesses to the wilderness campsites area.

For another paddle nearby, visit Spruce Run State Park, 15 minutes northwest. See Trip 18.

---

20 | Delaware and Raritan Canal

You'll find waterfowl, birds, and a beautiful greenway along this historic waterway.

Location: South Bound Brook to Griggstown, NJ
Maps: *New Jersey Atlas and Gazetteer*, Maps 36 & 37; USGS Bound Brook and Monmouth Junction
Area: The canal length between lock portages varies from 2.6 to 10.0 miles
Time: 2.0–3.0 hours
Conditions: Depth average 10 feet
Development: Rural
Information: Delaware & Raritan Canal Park Main Office, 145 Mapleton Road, Princeton, NJ 08540; 609-924-5705.
Take Note: Electric motorboats only

GETTING THERE

Numerous designated parking lots with boat access are found next to the towpath along the canal. I have listed only two, chosen for their historical settings and scenic waters. Other launch locations are shown on the map. For a downloadable, detailed map of all lock locations and distances between the locks, visit www.dandrcanal.com.

To reach the canal at East Millstone: From Route 206, drive east for 3.6 miles on Route 514 (Amwell Road). After passing over the Millstone River, look for the parking lot on the left just prior to the canal bridge. Launch directly into the canal. Parking is available for eight cars. *GPS coordinates*: 40°30.202′ N, 74°34.980′ W.

To reach the canal at Blackwells Mills: Follow the above directions and continue on Route 514 across the canal, turn right onto Canal Road and drive 2.2 miles to Blackwells Mills Road. Turn right and cross over the canal. Leave your car in the large parking lot down the hill (west) from the canal and launch from the west side of the canal on either side of Blackwells Mills Road. Parking for about 25 cars and portable toilets are available. *GPS coordinates for the launch*: 40°28.525' N, 74°34.329' W. Note: There's room for only one car at a time to unload at the canal. *GPS coordinates for the parking lot*: 40° 28.515' N, 74°34.363' W.

WHAT YOU'LL SEE

In my opinion, fall is the best time to paddle the canal, when the brilliant foliage of various tree species lines the banks and sprinkles the water with colorful fallen leaves. Ask anyone who paddles the Delaware and Raritan Canal, and they'll tell you they think it more a long, narrow lake than a river. Overflow culverts drain excess water from the canal into nearby waterways such as the Raritan and Millstone rivers, thus retaining a very slow flow rate throughout the canal's length. In times of insufficient rain, water is pumped into the canal from these same nearby rivers. The canal parallels the Millstone River all the way from Princeton, New Jersey, to the north side of the lock at Zarephath, where it joins the Raritan River to continue its journey to Raritan Bay and the Atlantic Ocean.

Quaint villages along the canal, such as Griggstown, Amwell, and Blackwells Mills, have retained their nineteenth-century architecture, transporting you back in time as you glide past historic houses and under turn-of-the-century thick wooden bridges. You may have to "kiss the deck" and duck a bit when passing under one or more of the old, low wooden bridges than span the canal, especially in times of high water after heavy rains. Nesting swallows will flit about as you pass under the canal bridges. Keep your eye out for anglers who may be fishing from the bridge. Monofilament fishing line is hard to see. The canal is the perfect place to paddle on chilly, windy days because of the dense cover of trees lining the canal on both sides for most of its length.

Trees burst with color in autumn when maple, sycamore, beech, sassafras, and hickory display their finery before the onset of winter. Small, shallow coves along the way are good spots to find ducks and geese with their young because of the cover afforded by overhanging shrubs and small trees. Turtles, ducks, geese, and songbirds make their homes all along the canal. Kingfishers and blue herons are common along densely wooded shorelines. While paddling the canal, you may spook a blue heron that will fly off a hundred feet ahead of you, only to be spooked again as you come upon it a second, third, or fourth time. Eventually the heron will either fly behind you or head over to the adjacent Millstone River.

DELAWARE AND RARITAN CANAL

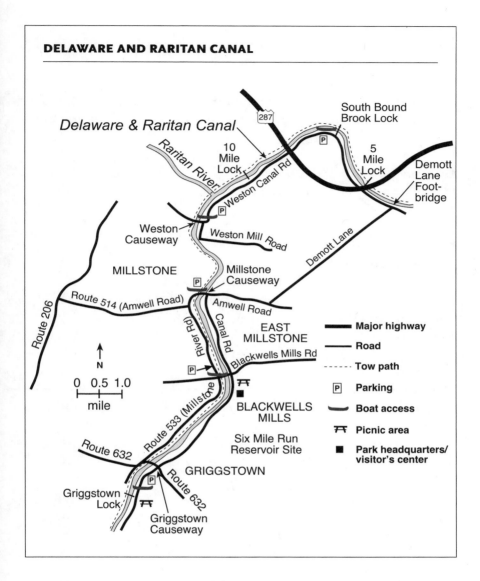

At the charming village of Blackwells Mills along the canal, you'll find a stone bridge-tender's house that serves as the canal's museum. It is open to the public and hosts several events throughout the year. Joggers, hikers, and bikers enjoy the natural earthen towpath that parallels the western side of the canal as it winds its way past miles of fields and forests between quaint rural towns.

For an additional paddle, try Farrington Lake, 25 minutes east. See Trip 21. Also try Carnegie Lake, 20 minutes south. See Trip 24.

21 | Farrington Lake

Enjoy a very scenic respite and wonderful wildlife viewing on this long lake close to the densely populated towns of New Brunswick and East Brunswick.

Location: New Brunswick, NJ
Maps: *New Jersey Atlas and Gazetteer*, Map 37; USGS New Brunswick
Area: 290 acres
Time: 2.5–3.5 hours
Conditions: Depth average 6 feet
Development: Suburban with wide areas of wooded shoreline
Information: New Jersey Division of Fish and Wildlife, Central Region (Assunpink WMA), 386 Clarksburg-Robbinsville Road, Robbinsville, NJ 08691; 609-259-2132.
Take Note: Electric motorboats only

GETTING THERE

Washington Place launch: From the junction of Routes 1 and 130, drive 1.7 miles on Route 130 South. Turn left onto Washington Place and drive 0.4 mile to the parking area and gravel launch on your right immediately after crossing the bridge. You'll find parking for fifteen cars. *GPS coordinates*: 40°26.344′ N, 74°27.986′ W.

Church Lane launch: From the junction of Routes 1 and 130, drive 1.8 miles on Route 130 South. Turn left onto Old Georges Road and drive 0.8 mile, then turn left onto Church Lane and drive 0.8 mile. Turn left onto Riva Ave and the parking area and dirt launch will be on your left. You'll find parking for about twelve cars. *GPS coordinates*: 40°25.466′ N, 74°28.608′ W.

WHAT YOU'LL SEE

Created by damming Lawrence Brook on its way to the Passaic River, this long, narrow lake is bordered on both sides by large sections of county and township parklands. Located in a suburban neighborhood on the south side of the bustling college town of New Brunswick, this lake offers a serene getaway and pleasant respite from traffic, crowds, and industry.

Goldfinch, cardinals, wrens, warblers, blue jays, and other songbirds seek refuge among the trees, while sunfish, bass, pike, pickerel, perch, and catfish

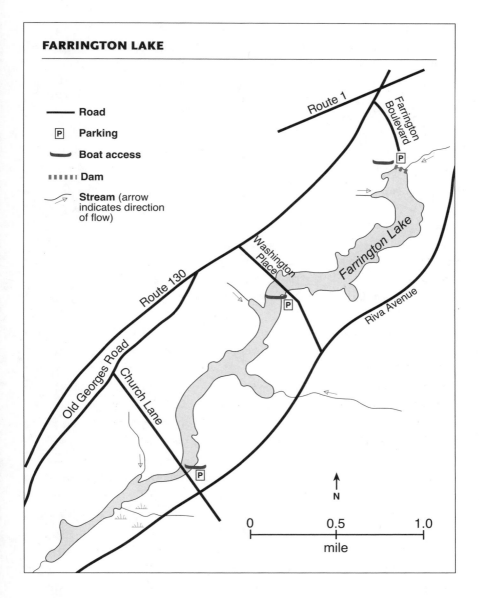

FARRINGTON LAKE

Road

P Parking

Boat access

Dam

Stream (arrow indicates direction of flow)

Route 1

Farrington Boulevard

Farrington Lake

Washington Place

Route 130

Riva Avenue

Old Georges Road

Church Lane

N

| 0 | 0.5 | 1.0 |

mile

swim in the waters alongside stocked trout and bass. Electric outboards are permitted, but most fishing is done from shore or bridges. Wildlife is abundant all along the lake. Deer, raccoons, and even wild turkeys have been spotted in areas bordered by wide swaths of woods.

The area north of the Washington Place bridge is the widest section of the lake. A paddle around the shoreline north of that bridge will yield a trip of about 3 miles. Some houses are located here, but they are set back from the lake and have a border of trees. Immediately north of the bridge are two narrow strips of land jutting into the lake that are part of a submerged, abandoned railroad. Some submerged pilings are close to the land, but they are easily avoided. The south shoreline is wooded for a half-mile above the bridge, where most of the land is part of Bicentennial Park. A large cove in the park is accessible through a 50-foot opening from the lake.

North of the park is a small section of modest residential properties followed by a quarter-mile of wooded shoreline. Exercise caution at the north end by the dam. You'll hear the sound of rushing water if lake levels are high. Two low concrete dam structures on either side of the lake signal the position of the dam, and there are white warning signs near the structures. Do not paddle past the warning markers as you cross over to the other side of the lake. Paddling south on the west side from the dam area is a three-quarter-mile stretch of North Brunswick Township Park. Here will be a good opportunity for bird-watching and wildlife viewing. Sit in your boat and simply enjoy the quiet serenity it offers. If you want to stop for a stretch, there are a few small areas to land a couple of boats.

A shoreline paddle between the Washington Place bridge south to the Church Lane bridge and back will yield a trip of a little more than 3 miles. A cove next to a small farm on the west side bordered by a wide swath of woods is excellent for bird-watching. Look for towhees, kingbirds, chickadees, and finches. Halfway between the bridges on the east side is a large cove that is excellent for waterfowl and birdlife viewing, particularly on the north side, where there's a large stand of conifers rimmed by hardwood trees.

South of the Church Lane bridge, the lake narrows and becomes shallower. Lawrence Brook enters the lake at the far southern end. A paddle along the shoreline from that bridge and up Lawrence Brook a little past the Davidson Mill Road bridge and back will yield a trip of 3 miles. Few houses will be seen along the way and the land on both sides is more wooded and wild. Two small streams enter the lake on the west side and are worth paddling into for a few hundred feet if water levels are high enough. While much smaller in size than the other two sections of the lake, it is no less rewarding as far as wildlife is concerned—and it's more remote. You can spot plenty of turtles, dragonflies, egrets, and herons among the lily pads. Beyond the Davidson Mill Road bridge, the brook becomes very shallow, but you can paddle upstream for about a quarter-mile before you need to turn around.

The Delaware and Raritan Canal is 25 minutes west and Assunpink Wildlife Management Area is 35 minutes south. See Trips 20 and 26.

22 | Shadow Lake

Enjoy great fishing and look for plenty of waterfowl and wading birds in this freshwater lake.

Location: Red Bank, NJ
Maps: *New Jersey Atlas and Gazetteer*, Map 44; USGS Long Branch West
Area: 88 acres
Time: 1.5–2.0 hours
Conditions: Depth average 15 feet
Development: Suburban
Information: New Jersey Division of Fish and Wildlife, Central Region, 386 Clarksburg-Robbinsville Road, Robbinsville, NJ 08691; 609-259-2132.
Camping: Pine Cone Resort, 30 minutes southwest. See Appendix A.
Take Note: Electric motorboats only

GETTING THERE

From southbound Garden State Parkway, take Exit 109, turn left at the end of ramp, and drive 0.3 mile east on Route 520 (Newman Springs Road). Turn left onto Half Mile Road and drive 0.6 mile. Turn left onto West Front Street and drive 0.5 mile. A sign is on the right for Stevenson Park. Turn right (Shady Oak Way) and drive 0.15 mile, where you'll see paved parking areas on both sides of the road. Immediately past them, turn right onto the dirt road that leads to the launch. Unload, and then park in the areas provided. You'll find parking for eight cars. *GPS coordinates*: 40°20.815′ N, 74°06.296′ W.

From northbound Garden State Parkway, take Exit 109. As you come down the exit ramp, stay left, watching for signs for Half Mile Road that will be straight ahead of you at the bottom of the ramp. Cross Route 520 onto Half Mile Road and proceed as above.

WHAT YOU'LL SEE

This is a wonderful place for an easy paddle after work or freshwater fishing trip. At the launch, it looks like it's only a small creek. Paddle left (east) from the launch through a narrow passage about 150 feet long. At the end of the passage, the water divides around a small island. Pass on either side of the island to enter the large part of the lake. Up until about midsummer, there's a nice shallow cove

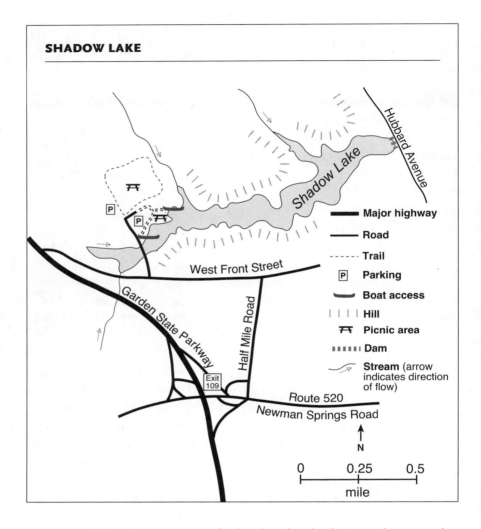

SHADOW LAKE

Shadow Lake

Hubbard Avenue

West Front Street

Garden State Parkway

Half Mile Road

Exit 109

Route 520

Newman Springs Road

— **Major highway**

— **Road**

----- **Trail**

P **Parking**

⌣ **Boat access**

| | | | **Hill**

🔏 **Picnic area**

▪▪▪▪▪ **Dam**

⌒↗ **Stream** (arrow indicates direction of flow)

N

0   0.25   0.5

mile

on your right (west) to view waterfowl and wading birds. By midsummer that cove fills in with duckweed and pond lilies, but there's still plentiful waterfowl to view there, include numerous swans. A word of warning: During breeding and brooding season, swans can be very territorial, so give them a wide berth if you see a family on the water.

Head east into the main body of the lake where numerous coves along both shores invite you to explore. The wooded area on both shores for the first 0.2 mile is Stevenson Park, where you can observe a variety of woodland birds darting in and out of the trees and across the lake. Beyond that, suburban residences are found along the shores, but most are set back from the lakeshore

Huge red-bellied turtles can be observed basking on logs at this lake.

by 50 to 100 feet with a dense cover of trees and shrubs until you approach the east end. There the residences are closer together and close to the water's edge, many with small wood docks projecting into the lake.

Shadow Lake is known for its good fishing. The times I've visited, there was always someone heading out in a canoe or kayak with fishing equipment. These trout-stocked waters also have an abundance of pan fish, carp, catfish, and largemouth bass. Egrets, herons, ducks, geese, and swans are found all over the lake, and ospreys are sometimes seen on the eastern half of the lake scanning the water for dinner. A few shallow spots along the grassy embankment at Hubbard Avenue at the far eastern end provide places to stop for a break. The small dam and spillway are on the right (south) end of the embankment bulkhead. It is obvious and well marked.

For a pleasant hike after your paddle, you can walk north from the parking lot and up a hill where a nice township park provides play areas and walking paths. Turn right onto the trail across from the park's parking lot. That trail has a few short spurs with views of the lake and benches to sit and observe wildlife.

Other paddles nearby are Deal Lake, 20 minutes south, and Manasquan Reservoir, 30 minutes south-southwest. See Trips 23 and 28.

23 | Deal Lake

This very nice lake has lots of waterfowl, numerous bridges, and miles of shoreline to enjoy in the midst of the bustling north Jersey shore.

Location: Asbury Park, NJ
Maps: *New Jersey Atlas and Gazetteer*, Map 45; USGS Asbury Park
Area: 158 acres
Time: 3.0–4.0 hours
Conditions: Depth average 5 feet
Development: Dense suburban
Information: Monmouth County Park System, 805 Newman Springs Road, Lincroft, NJ 07738; 732-842-4000.
Take Note: Unlimited motorboat horsepower, but large motorboats on this shallow lake are rarely seen

GETTING THERE

From Exit 100 of the Garden State Parkway, follow signs for Route 33 South/Bradley Beach/Ocean Grove. Drive 4.7 miles on Route 33 South, then turn left onto Route 71/Main Street and drive 1.3 miles. Turn left at Seventh Avenue. The parking lot and launch will be on your right. There's parking for about ten cars in the lot, plus street parking for another ten cars. *GPS coordinates*: 40°13.757′ N, 74°00.551′ W.

WHAT YOU'LL SEE

It looks like an octopus and, with the Atlantic Ocean only 500 feet from its head, I suppose the shape is symbolic; at the very least it's an interesting coincidence. Deal Lake interweaves its tentacles through four towns, the most notable of which is Asbury Park on the south side. Although only 158 acres in size, the lake has 7-plus miles of shoreline waiting to be paddled. The variety of native and planted tree and shrub species provide spectacular spring blooms and fall colors.

I think of the section from Main Street to Ocean Avenue as the neck and head of the octopus. Its concrete-walled shores are rimmed with houses and a few tall condominiums. Sailboats are often seen on this open part of the lake taking advantage of ocean breezes and, because it's more open, tall buildings in Asbury Park to the south fill the skyline. On the peninsula where Grassmere Avenue

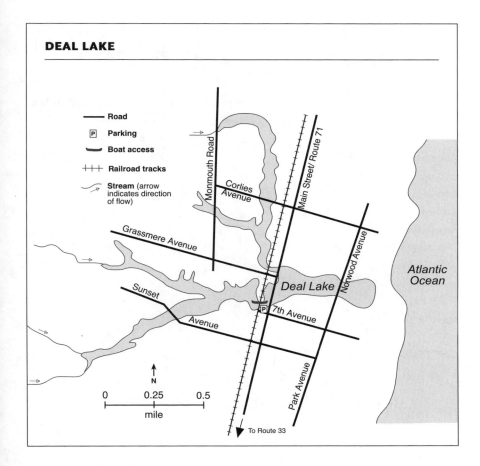

DEAL LAKE

Road
P Parking
Boat access
+++ Railroad tracks
Stream (arrow indicates direction of flow)

Monmouth Road

Corlies Avenue

Main Street/ Route 71

Grassmere Avenue

Sunset Avenue

Deal Lake

Norwood Avenue

Atlantic Ocean

P 7th Avenue

Park Avenue

N

0   0.25   0.5
|————|————|
mile

To Route 33

meets Main Street, two tentacles break off to the north, and two to the south. In this densely populated shore area, there's an eclectic mix of lakeside houses, including a few large, modern homes, a few art deco homes, older and architecturally interesting ones, and the dominant modest homes. A golf course on the north side and a few small parks offer a break in the suburban landscape.

The narrow tentacles vary in width from 50 to 250 feet, and you'll feel like you're in a quiet river instead of a lake. The sheltered condition allows for easy paddling conditions even on the windiest of days. Lush lakeshore greenery and trees not only afford privacy for homes, but also create pleasant scenery for the paddler. Paddle left from the launch under the narrow train bridge opening. Some wildflowers can be seen growing amidst the shrubs lining the railroad spit. This open area, and west to where two tentacles split off, is usually excellent for viewing ducks, geese, brants, cormorants, and blue herons. An occasional vulture or osprey may visit the wider sections along the lake.

A red-winged blackbird sits atop a lakeside bush.

The left tentacle is longest and passes under the Sunset Avenue bridge and continues for another half-mile. It's very shallow near the end with logs sticking out of the water where turtles bask beside herons stalking the shallows. Explore the other tentacle before heading back under the trestle and then under the Main Street bridge.

Ahead of you is the wide neck and head area of the octopus-shaped lake where you're likely to see small outboard fishing boats and small sailboats. A few low spots and step ledges along the wall offer an opportunity to get out and stretch your legs if you choose. Paddling a counterclockwise route, when you pass under the north side of Main Street, you'll find a fountain in the middle of the opening between it and the railroad trestle and a restaurant on the right. Yes, on hot days paddlers are fond of passing under the spray of the fountain for the evaporative-cooling effect.

Pass under the railroad trestle and enter a wide area where the two northern tentacles will split off. The southernmost tentacle is short but very scenic and passes under the Monmouth Road bridge. Residences on both sides are separated from the lake by a road edged with trees and shrubs. Explore that tentacle and then head into the northern, and last, tentacle. When you pass under the Corlies Avenue bridge, Allenhurst Train Station will be on your right, separated from the lake by a very quaint town park. You might see kayakers using this area as a launch. It is permissible to launch here, although trying to find a parking space around the train station on a weekday is almost impossible—and it's about a 75-foot carry from your car to the launch spot underneath Corlies Avenue.

Longer sections of wide swaths of trees and greenery in this section make this area very pleasant to paddle. On the north tip is a large golf course, whose open grounds provide an opportunity to spot hawks and birds that prefer a more open environment. Around the golf course, numerous shallow areas are likely spots to view egrets and ducks. As you paddle back to the launch and pass under a couple of bridges, think of how different and unique this lake is from your normal lake paddle.

For another paddle nearby, visit Manasquan Reservoir, 25 minutes southwest, or Shadow Lake, 20 minutes north. See Trips 28 and 22.

24 | Carnegie Lake

Enjoy song birds, turtles, waterfowl, and islands at this long and narrow lake.

Location: Princeton, NJ
Maps: *New Jersey Atlas and Gazetteer*, Map 42; USGS Hightstown
Area: 237 acres
Time: 3.0–3.5 hours
Conditions: Depth average 6 feet
Development: Urban/suburban
Take Note: Electric motorboats only

GETTING THERE
From the north: From the junction of Route 1 and Promenade Boulevard, turn right onto Promenade Boulevard and drive 1.3 miles to Route 27. Turn left onto Route 27 South for 2.1 miles to the parking lot entrance on your left. The parking lot is 300 yards long and has three launch areas and space for more

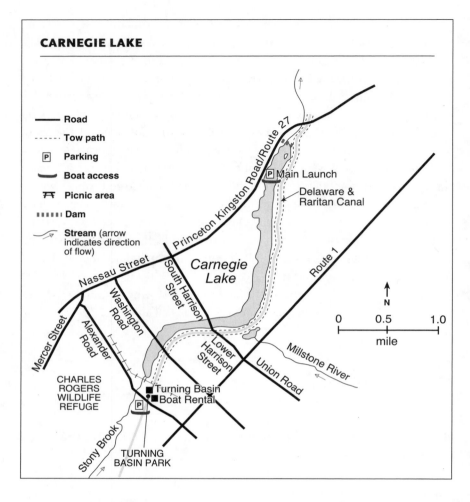

CARNEGIE LAKE

Map legend:
- Road
- Tow path
- P Parking
- Boat access
- Picnic area
- Dam
- Stream (arrow indicates direction of flow)

Princeton Kingston Road/Route 27
Main Launch
Delaware & Raritan Canal
Route 1
Nassau Street
South Harrison Street
Carnegie Lake
Washington Road
Alexander Road
Mercer Street
Lower Harrison Street
Millstone River
Union Road
CHARLES ROGERS WILDLIFE REFUGE
Turning Basin
Boat Rental
Stony Brook
TURNING BASIN PARK

N
0   0.5   1.0
mile

than 50 cars. One of the southern launches has a gravel ramp next to a floating dock. The two other launches are small, sandy beaches.

From the south: From the junction of Route 1 and Lower Harrison Street (west side)/Union Road (east side), drive west on Lower Harrison Street 1.4 miles to Route 27. Turn right (north) and drive 1.3 miles to the parking lot entrance on your right. *GPS coordinates*: 40°22.012′ N, 74°37.560′ W.

WHAT YOU'LL SEE

Carnegie Lake was formed by damming the Millstone River to create a lake for the Princeton University rowing team. Funding for the project, completed in 1906, came from a generous donation to the university by businessman and philanthropist Andrew Carnegie. Although the lake is privately owned by

Canada geese forage quietly in the grassy area next to the launch at Carnegie Lake.

Princeton University, it is open to the public for boating, fishing, and picnicking. A regional rowing regatta is held each year around the third weekend in June. With all the visitors and attendees, the lake can get frantic that weekend, although the northern half of the lake is usually not affected. The Delaware and Raritan Canal Greenway, with its beautiful towpaths, edges the eastern side of the lake. See Trip 20 for more information on the history of the canal and its towpath, along with park information.

The first thing you'll notice at the launch site are some white buoy markers used by rowing teams that start out from the boathouse at the southern end of the lake. If you visit in early morning or late afternoon, you might see a few rowers practicing in their sleek, narrow crafts. Be aware of these boats because they are not as maneuverable as canoes and kayaks. Also know that rowers generally see only where they've been and not where they're going, catching only an occasional glimpse over their shoulder to stay on track. Just as there are rules of the road defining the right of way for drivers, there are similar rules for boats. In general, the least-maneuverable boat has the right of way. In the case of a paddler and a rowing shell, the rower has the right of way.

Head left from the boat ramp and go about two-tenths of a mile, then cross over to the eastern side, staying well inside the dam safety rope—a thick, white, wire rope 50 feet in front of the dam. The steep drop down to the Millstone River is dangerous. You'll immediately find a small island to paddle around as you look for green and blue herons and listen for the splashes of frogs and turtles. As you go south along the shoreline, keep your eyes and ears attuned for the belted kingfisher. It's one of my favorite birds and I've never failed to find a number of them along the banks. Kingfishers make their burrows (nests) in steep banks of rivers and lakes. Thanks to its 2-foot banks, Carnegie Lake on this side provides an ideal environment for these birds. If you're lucky, you'll also spot scarlet tanagers and maybe even an oriole along with many other songbirds. Ducks and geese are prevalent and there's no shortage of squawks from great blue herons, particularly in the southern half of the lake.

You might also catch a glimpse of a hiker or two between the trees as they walk along the canal towpath, a narrow strip of land that runs between the canal and the lake that you can hike later in the day. Waterlilies and arrowheads can be found where the water is shallow; these are also good places to watch waterfowl feeding. Autumn comes alive with the vibrant reds, oranges, and yellows of oak, beech, gum, ash, hickory, cherry, and maple trees. In the fishing department, largemouth bass, shad, pickerel, and crappies are prized. The lake is also stocked with non-reproducing trout and tiger muskies.

About two miles down the lake will be another island, a little more toward the center of the lake. There's a magnificent cluster of river birches that graces the western shoreline here, providing a striking contrast against deep green trees. A little past the island you'll pass under the Harrison Street bridge, where barn swallows nest. Because they eat mosquitoes, I love swallows. Honeysuckle sweetly scents the air in late spring and early summer. A little more than halfway between the Harrison Street bridge and the Washington Road bridge is a third island close to the west side of the lake. The water in this part of the lake starts getting shallower with logs and branches protruding prominently along the banks. I've never failed to spot turtles and frogs here. In marshy areas you'll find cattail, purple loosestrife, and, in fall, the red cardinal flower. As you pass under the Washington Road bridge, Princeton University's striking boathouse will be on the west bank and a section of student housing next to it. The Princeton train bridge just past the student housing marks the southernmost end of the lake.

While you could turn around at the train bridge and paddle back to the launch site, you also have the option of paddling upstream into Stony Brook for 0.2 mile, passing under the train bridge and the Alexander Road bridge. Stony Brook is one of the streams that feed Carnegie Lake. I love this small section because there are turtles everywhere and birdlife increases fivefold. Don't be surprised if a deer splashes into the water right in front of you. I've experienced that treat more than once. Immediately after the Alexander Road bridge will be a take-out on your left. It can get a little muddy there, so watch your footing.

At the top of the small hill is a picnic area with benches, a water fountain, and a portable toilet.

This is Turning Basin Park, where barges being towed along the Delaware and Raritan Canal could be turned around and unloaded. Originally there were two turning basins; the remnants of one is on the north side of Alexander Road. The other was filled in to become the 9.8-acre park you're standing on. The park is only 250 feet wide between Stony Brook, where you landed, and the canal. Freshwater marshes on the south and west sides of the park provide a bountiful environment for a plethora of warblers, songbirds, and wading birds.

If you wish to rent a kayak, Princeton Canoe and Kayak is a small concession conveniently located on Alexander Road directly across from the entrance to the Turning Basin Park parking lot. See Appendix C.

Either Lake Mercer, 20 minutes south, or the Delaware and Raritan Canal at Blackwells Mills, 20 minutes north, would make a good choice for a nearby paddle. See Trips 25 and 20.

---

25 | Mercer County Park

This county park offers waterfowl, wading birds, raptors, and turtles.

Location: West Windsor, NJ
Maps: *New Jersey Atlas and Gazetteer*, Map 42; USGS Princeton
Area: 275 acres
Time: 2.5–3.0 hours
Conditions: Depth average 15 feet
Development: Urban/suburban
Information: Park ranger office, 609-443-8956; *GPS coordinates*: 40°15.753′ N, 74°38.570′ W; Mercer County Park Commission, 334 South Post Road, Princeton Junction, NJ 08550; 609-443-8974. For lake and road closure schedules, visit nj.gov/counties/mercer/commissions/park/mercer_park.html.
Take Note: Electric motorboats only

GETTING THERE
To the main marina and park office on the south side: From Route 571, drive south 3.8 miles on Route 535 (Old Trenton Road). Turn right (west) onto Paxson Avenue into the park entrance and drive 1.1 miles to the marina

entrance on your right. The park ranger office is to your left if you want to stop in for a park brochure. Stay to your right when you drive into the marina entrance. The lower-level parking lot is for big boats that need to be hauled by a trailer. After unloading your kayak or canoe, drive back up and around to the upper-level parking lot. From Route 33, drive north 3.8 miles on Route 535. Turn left (west) onto Route 602 (South Post Road) and continue as above. You'll find parking for about 100 cars. *GPS coordinates*: 40°15.933′ N, 74°38.503′ W.

To the more scenic north launch: From Route 571, drive south 1.9 miles on Route 535 (Old Trenton Road). Turn right (west) onto Village Road East and drive 2.1 miles, then turn left onto Village Road West and drive 0.2 mile. At the T-junction, turn left (south) to continue on Village Drive West and drive 0.5 mile. Turn left on South Post Road and drive 0.9 mile to the launch.

From Route 33 in Nottingham, drive north on Whitehorse Mercerville Road 0.2 mile and continue straight onto Quakerbridge Road for 3.1 miles. Turn right onto Village Road West and drive 1.8 miles, then turn right onto South Post Road and drive 0.9 mile to the launch. You'll find informal parking for about twenty cars. *GPS coordinates*: 40°16.174′ N, 74°38.484′ W.

WHAT YOU'LL SEE

Mercer County Park is a huge complex of more than 2,500 acres located midway between Princeton and Trenton. The park's miles of rolling hills sprinkled with trees and recreational areas literally have something for everyone, including golf, soccer, tennis, and, of course, boating. Set in the midst of the park is the 275-acre Lake Mercer with a marina, food and boat rental concessions, launch facilities, small nature center, and restrooms. To the right of the concrete boat ramp is a specially designated sand beach launch for canoes and kayaks. Being the major recreational facility for the densely populated Trenton area, it can become a veritable zoo on summer weekends, particularly after school lets out in mid-June. When I was at the park ranger office one summer Sunday, a man came in wanting to reserve a large picnic pavilion for the following week for 100 to 120 people. The park ranger didn't bat an eyelash at the number; they're used to large groups like that.

Most kayakers I know who use this lake as their home base launch from the north ramp. Not only is it prettier than the launch at the main office, but parking is a lot more convenient. No park activities are located on this side either, except for the rowing center. Recreational water activities, like hourly kayak and pedal-boat rentals, occur in front and to the right of the marina on the south side of the lake.

MERCER COUNTY PARK

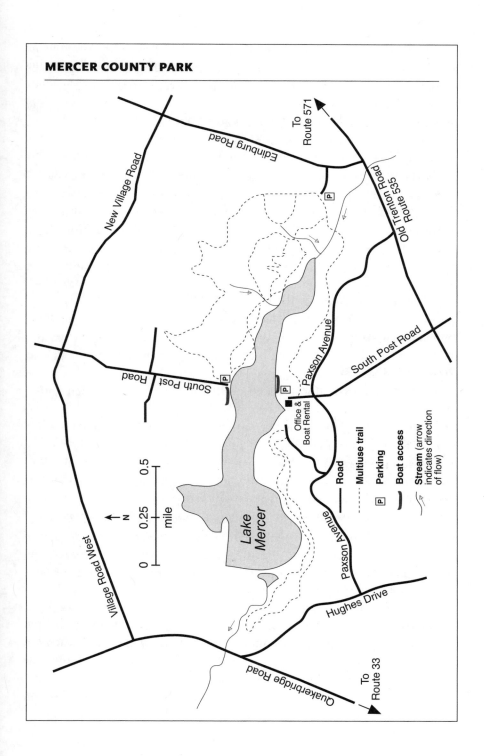

Small sailboats tend to use the more open and usually windier western area of the lake. A large portion of that area is lined with thick woods and provides a nice paddle. Ducks, Canada geese, and swans are everywhere. The only things that detract from the scenery are the tall power line towers. Water close to the shoreline can become quite shallow quickly and some areas have a lot of sunken logs and limbs—good for providing a protective environment for fish fry, not so good on gelcoats. More scenic and tranquil paddling conditions can be found on the far eastern end, where thick woods line the shores and you are beyond the rental use zone. Turtles become more plentiful. Assunpink Creek flows into the lake at the densely wooded narrow tip of the eastern end. Water levels are usually good enough to paddle upstream for a quarter-mile or so, providing a brief shaded respite on a hot summer's day. A wide variety of trees, including shagbark hickory, maples, sycamore, various oaks, tulip, and sweet gum, create a magnificent array of colors in fall. Blue jays squawk and cardinals make their *tink, tink* sound throughout the woods. The diversity of flora hosts numerous bird species in their specific habitats of upland woods, moist lowlands, or marshes. Mammals such as deer, opossums, skunks, and even pheasants and red foxes all reside in the park. In the fishing department, muskies, shad, and largemouth bass are the primary species here.

The park holds bass tournaments each year. University and high school sculling crews practice on the lake from the boathouse located across the lake from the marina. If you put in at the north launch, you're right next to the boathouse. The lake is closed to boat traffic when there's a rowing regatta. One or more roads into the park are closed, in part or in whole, for a few special events like marathon bike races and special walk-a-thons. If you go on a weekend, check the park closure schedule first.

There are a few trails, mostly multiuse; be careful on the multiuse trails, which are heavily used by very energetic young mountain bikers. The bicycle path and the short nature trail northwest of the tennis center are marked on the park map. A walking trail leads off from the kayak launch at the marina and links into the nature trail.

If you want to paddle another lake nearby, you have several options. Carnegie Lake is 20 minutes north. See Trip 24. Prospertown Lake is 30 minutes southeast. See Trip 27. Lake Assunpink is 25 minutes southeast. See Trip 26.

26 | Assunpink Wildlife Management Area—Lake Assunpink, Stone Tavern Lake, Rising Sun Lake

Look for abundant waterfowl, wading birds, and raptors at these lakes.

Location: Roosevelt, NJ

Maps: *New Jersey Atlas and Gazetteer*, Map 43; USGS Allentown and Roosevelt

Area: Assunpink: 225 acres; Stone Tavern: 52 acres; Rising Sun: 38 acres

Time: Lake Assunpink: 2.0–3.0 hours; Stone Tavern Lake: 1.0–1.5 hours; Rising Sun Lake: less than 1.0 hour

Conditions: Lake Assunpink: depth average 8 feet; Stone Tavern Lake: depth average 12 feet; Rising Sun Lake: depth average 12 feet.

Development: Rural

Information: New Jersey Division of Fish and Wildlife, Central Region (Assunpink WMA), One Eldridge Road, Robbinsville, NJ 08691; 609-259-2132.

Camping: Timberland Lake Campground, 20 minutes southeast. See Appendix A.

Take Note: Electric motorboats only; New Jersey boat ramp maintenance permit required. See Appendix D.

GETTING THERE

To Lake Assunpink: Take I-195 to Exit 11 (Hightstown/Imlaystown). Drive north 2.6 miles toward Hightstown on Imlaystown-Hightstown Road to the huge parking and launch area. The road becomes sand for the last 1.3 miles after crossing Herbert/East Branch Road. You'll find parking for about 25 cars. *GPS coordinates*: 40°12.924′ N, 74°31.028′ W.

If the parking lot is full, exit it, take the first right (Clarksburg-Robbinsville Road) onto the sand road, and drive 0.3 mile. At the fork, bear right and drive 0.15 mile to the first sand road on your right. Turn right and drive 300 feet to the small launch, or turn left at the small sand launch and drive 0.1 mile to the larger parking lot and sand launch. You'll find parking for about twenty cars. *GPS coordinates*: 40°13.020′ N, 74°31.322′ W.

To Stone Tavern Lake: From Imlaystown-Hightstown Road, drive 1.8 miles east on East Branch Road (it will make a right bend 0.5 mile into the drive). You will pass a narrow dirt road on the left (north) about 150 feet before the gray-stone entrance road, also on the left. Drive 0.4 mile to the lake; there is parking for about ten cars. *GPS coordinates*: 40°11.583′ N, 74°29.240′ W.

To Rising Sun Lake: From Imlaystown-Hightstown Road just north of I-195, drive 3.2 miles east on Route 524 (New Canton-Stone Tavern Road). Turn left (north) on Route 571 (Rising Sun Tavern Road) and drive 1.3 miles to the dirt entrance road on the left (west). You'll find parking for about four cars. *GPS coordinates*: 40°11.769′ N, 74°28.570′ W.

WHAT YOU'LL SEE

More than 6,000 acres of wildlife management area surround three lakes: 225-acre Lake Assunpink, 52-acre Stone Tavern Lake, and 38-acre Rising Sun Lake. Each lake has its own character and its own special charm. The name Assunpink comes from the Lenni-Lenape word meaning "stony creek" or "rocky place that is watery."

Lake Assunpink

With its large size and numerous coves and inlets, Lake Assunpink offers hours of paddling pleasure and is never very crowded. Anglers come here on summer weekends to cast their lines for prized bass, crappies, and chain pickerel. This lake is one of the top bass waters in central New Jersey. A number of springs seep into the lake to keep the waters a little cooler than other lakes. Because of its size and the openness of surrounding farmlands, even small breezes keep the lake wind-swept, which keeps oxygen levels high. Both of those conditions provide an optimal environment for largemouth bass. Sweet gum, pine, red maple, and oak dominate the surrounding woods behind a screen of cattails, phragmites, mulberry bushes, and joe-pye weed that border lakes. During late summer, joe-pye weed develops purplish-brown flower clusters that add a soft touch of color to swampy borders. This plant (*Eupatorium maculatum*) was used extensively by American Indians to cure renal problems, especially kidney stones, and fevers. Reputed American Indian healer Joe Pye lived in colonial New England and used this herb to cure typhoid and other fevers.

The area out from the northern shoreline can get shallow during late summer. The eastern quarter of the lake is shallow and can get particularly so during late summer. Both of those areas are the better spots for waterfowl and wading birds. I prefer to launch from the sand launch because it feels more like a kayak launch. Not only that, but there's a small island just offshore I like to circumnavigate right after I launch, simply because I love islands. Start your paddle by heading west and then north, following the impoundment dike, and then start winding your way along the northern shores to explore the many coves and inlets and watch wildlife. The eastern arm usually abounds with ducks, geese, and the occasional swan.

ASSUNPINK WILDLIFE MANAGEMENT AREA

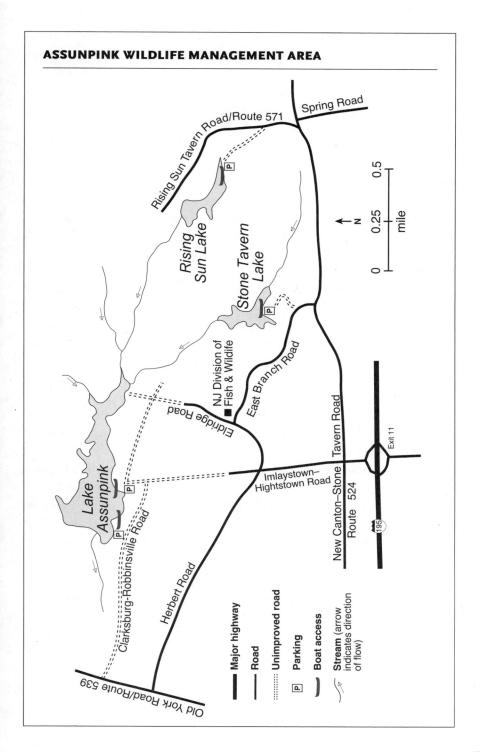

The springs that seep into the lake help keep the water relatively clear. In shallow areas you can spot fish fry and tadpoles skittering about the bottom. Because of all the farmlands in the surrounding area, a number of hawk species can be spotted. Winding your way back to the launch, you will see a few spots with small sand beaches to land on and take a break. You're not that far from the launch, but it's still neat to stop and snack along the route rather than go back to the launch and snack in your car.

Stone Tavern Lake

I love Stone Tavern Lake. It's much smaller than Lake Assunpink, but sits among woods and open fields and is much more remote and very quiet. Because the sand road leading to it is rough, be sure to drive slowly. Now and then you'll find another paddler or two on the lake, but you're more likely to have it all to yourself, particularly on weekdays. Occasionally you will see someone casting a line from shore around the launch. Glance skyward to look for one of the many red-tailed hawks that frequent the area. Wild blueberry and fragrant sweet pepperbush nudge their way into the dappled sunlight along with mountain laurel and swamp magnolia. For a small lake, it has enough coves and crannies along its two arms to make a very enjoyable and interesting paddle.

Rising Sun Lake

Rising Sun Lake, the smallest of the three, is a little gem where I've yet to encounter anyone else on the water, although I once saw someone fishing from the launch. Other than the short dike on the north end, it has an interesting shoreline edged with overhanging trees. If you like to fish, try some of the little coves around the lake.

Timberland Lake Campground is 20 minutes southeast. Stay there and dip your paddle into Prospertown Lake the next day. See Trip 27. Manasquan Reservoir is 30 minutes east. See Trip 28. The reservoir is a 25-minute drive from the campground.

27 | Prospertown Lake

Enjoy waterfowl and numerous coves to explore on this lake in the northern Pine Barrens.

Location: Prospertown, NJ
Maps: *New Jersey Atlas and Gazetteer*, Map 49; USGS Roosevelt
Area: 80 acres
Time: 2.0 hours
Conditions: Depth average 4 feet
Development: Rural
Information: New Jersey Division of Fish and Wildlife, Central Region, 386 Clarksburg-Robbinsville Road, Robbinsville, NJ 08691; 609-259-2132.
Camping: Indian Rock Campground, 15 minutes southeast. See Appendix A.
Take Note: Electric motorboats only; New Jersey boat ramp maintenance permit required. See Appendix D

GETTING THERE

Take I-195 Exit 15 toward Mount Holly and drive south on Monmouth Road 2.6 miles to the parking lot and launch on your left. You'll find parking for about 40 cars. *GPS coordinates*: 40°08.106′ N, 74°27.474′ W.

WHAT YOU'LL SEE

You'll have an enjoyable paddle at this remote yet easily accessible lake surrounded by the Prospertown Wildlife Management Area. Neither gas nor electric motors are permitted. These waters rarely become crowded, even on the hottest summer weekend. A narrow stretch of open sandy beach near the launch can get a bit busy at dusk, when local anglers come to try their luck from shore for an hour or two. Bass, catfish, pickerel, sunfish, and crappie are the sought-after species. While the water depth average is only 4 feet, there are depths to about 21 feet found closer to the side opposite the launch. The only downside to this lake is the sight of the tops of a few rides at Six Flags Great Adventure Park situated next to the lake on the northeast corner.

Head right or left from the launch and explore the irregular shoreline around the lake. Southeast of the launch across the lake is a small island, and there are two small islands close to shore on the southeast end of the lake.

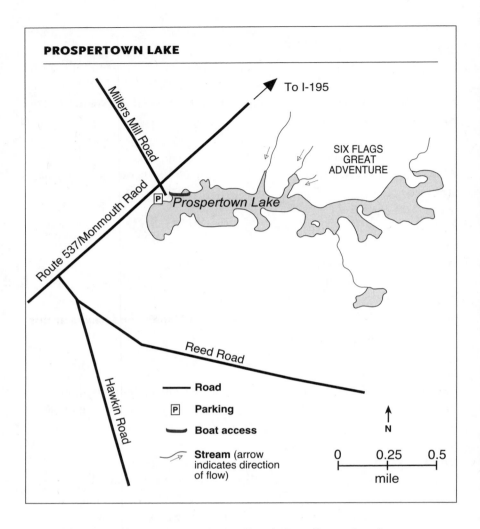

PROSPERTOWN LAKE

Millers Mill Road

To I-195

SIX FLAGS
GREAT
ADVENTURE

Route 537/Monmouth Raod

P Prospertown Lake

Reed Road

Hawkin Road

— Road

P Parking

Boat access

Stream (arrow
indicates direction
of flow)

N

0   0.25   0.5

mile

Inlets and coves of all sizes provide excellent habitat for turtles, deer, raccoons, beaver, and a variety of waterfowl. Painted and spotted turtles are a common sight on sunny shores and logs. In a few spots, small clusters of silvery-smooth, weathered dead trees close to shore provide a prime habitat for woodpeckers and roosting spots for ospreys, hawks, and vultures. Along the shoreline, blue jays, great blue herons, and a diversity of songbirds can be seen in the pristine habitat of dense beech, hickory, and hardwood forests.

Open coves on the southern shoreline are the better places to look for water-fowl. The smaller coves on the eastern end can become weedy and overrun with pond lilies by the end of summer, but they provide good foraging habitats for waterfowl. Pheasants and quails are stocked yearly by the state for hunting season, and you might catch a glimpse of one, particularly around the southern shores.

If you paddle toward the extreme northeast end, you'll find yourself entering grounds owned by Six Flags Great Adventure Park. No, you won't be permitted to land on their property; guards continually patrol that section. Though located near this popular attraction, you will usually only hear noise from the amusement park when you are close to the park. That's due in part to the prevailing southwest summer wind direction that carries the noise away from the lake.

Assunpink Wildlife Management Area is 20 minutes north and Manasquan Reservoir is 20 minutes east. See Trips 26 and 28.

28 | Manasquan Reservoir

Look for waterfowl, songbirds, ospreys, bald eagles, and hawks at this large reservoir.

Location: Farmingdale, NJ
Maps: *New Jersey Atlas and Gazetteer*, Map 50; USGS Farmingdale
Area: 720 acres
Time: 3.0–4.0 hours
Conditions: Depth average 40 feet
Development: Suburban
Information: Manasquan Reservoir Visitor Center, 311 Windeler Road, Howell, NJ 07731; 732-919-0996. Manasquan Reservoir Environmental Center, 331 Georgia Tavern Road, Howell, NJ 07731; 732-751-9453.
Camping: The Pine Cone Resort, 15 minutes west. Allaire State Park, 15 minutes east. See Appendix A.
Take Note: Electric motorboats only; winds

GETTING THERE
From Route 9 at its junction with I-195, drive north for 0.2 mile on Route 9. Turn right onto Georgia Tavern Road and drive for 0.4 mile, then turn right onto Windeler Road (there is a sign for the Manasquan Reservoir at Windeler Road). Drive 2.0 miles to the park entrance on the left and follow signs to the boat launch. You'll find parking for 60 cars. *GPS coordinates*: 40°10.323′ N, 74°12.180′ W.

To the environmental center: From the intersection of Windeler and Georgia Tavern roads, drive northeast on Georgia Tavern Road for 0.2 mile and turn right into the entrance road. *GPS coordinates*: 40°10.643′ N, 74°13.224′ W.

WHAT YOU'LL SEE

The 720-acre Manasquan Reservoir is set within a 1,204-acre park and offers hours of paddling. Outboard (electric only), kayak, and canoe rentals are available on the lower level of the visitor center next to the boat ramp. The upper level of the visitor center houses a food concession, operated only during summer months, as well as a few environmental displays and an observation deck. Horseback riding is available. Artifacts found around the area indicate that the Lenape once inhabited the area. Manasquan in Lenape means "stream of the island of women." Fishing is excellent, particularly for crappies, bass, trout, hybrid striped bass, and muskie.

Turn right from the launch to paddle past a small cove filled with dead trees bleached silvery-gray from years in the sun. Woodpeckers occasionally tap their way into the hollow core of the taller dead trees in early summer. The eastern side of the reservoir, where Timber Brook Creek enters, is open and faced with a concrete and stone embankment. Numerous shallow coves dot the wooded northern shoreline where you will likely hear and see kingfishers darting out from the trees in search of food. Listen for the *eep eep* of ospreys as you paddle along. Several pairs return year after year to nesting sites close to the reservoir's shores.

The western and southern shorelines are my personal favorites with their numerous peninsulas and coves to explore. It is along those shores that you will find areas of dead, drowned trees that provide an ideal habitat for the fish underneath and the ducks and other waterfowl on the surface. Painted turtles sun themselves on logs spring though fall. Some of these areas extend up to 400 feet into the reservoir. They are perfect for quietly meandering around to get better close-up views of waterfowl or scan the shallow waters for schools of fish. A paddle around the reservoir's shores without stopping will take you about 2 hours, but expect to spend 3 to 4 hours to allow for nature watching and exploring.

A well-maintained, 5-mile flat trail for hiking, running, and biking extends around the reservoir's perimeter. The trail has several foot bridges over marshy wetland areas where flocks of ducks paddle quietly around logs topped with basking painted turtles. Additionally, a 1.2-mile pedestrian Cove Trail starts and ends at the Manasquan Reservoir Environmental Center, taking you along

MANASQUAN RESERVOIR

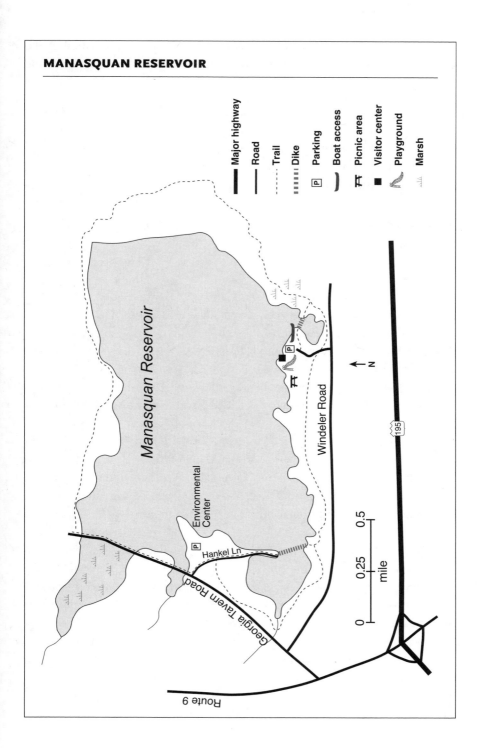

some of the shoreline and past small protected coves. The environmental center, completed in 2002, is well worth a visit.

Lakes Carasaljo and Shenandoah are 20 minutes south. See Trip 29. Forge Pond is 25 minutes southeast. See Trip 30.

29 | Lakes Carasaljo and Shenandoah

Look for waterfowl, wading birds, and freshwater marshes at these two lakes.

Location: Lakewood, NJ
Maps: *New Jersey Atlas and Gazetteer*, Map 50; USGS Lakewood
Area: Lake Carasaljo: 67 acres; Lake Shenandoah: 50 acres
Time: 1.5–2.0 hours for each lake
Conditions: Depth average in both lakes is 8 feet
Development: Urban/suburban
Information: Carasaljo Municipal Park: Lakewood Township Parks Department; Municipal Building, 231 Third Street, Lakewood, NJ 08701; 732-367-6737.

Lake Shenandoah County Park: Ocean County Department of Parks and Recreation; 700 Route 88, Lakewood, NJ; 732-506-9090.
Camping: Allaire State Park, 20 minutes northeast. Albocondo Campground, 20 minutes south. See Appendix A.
Take Note: Electric motorboats only

GETTING THERE

To Lake Carasaljo: From the junction of Routes 70 and 9, drive north 2.7 miles, turn left (west) onto Central Avenue and drive 100 feet, then turn right onto South Lake Drive. Drive 0.8 mile to the parking lot and ramp on your right. You'll find parking for about twelve cars. *GPS coordinates*: 40°05.575′ N, 74°13.695′ W.

To Lake Shenandoah public launch: From the junction of Routes 70 and 9, drive north 3.0 miles and turn right (east) onto Route 88. Drive 0.85 mile, then turn right onto Clover Street and drive 0.15 mile to the parking lot and launch on your left. You'll find parking for about 30 cars. *GPS coordinates*: 40°05.311′ N, 74°11.968′ W.

LAKES CARASALJO AND SHENANDOAH

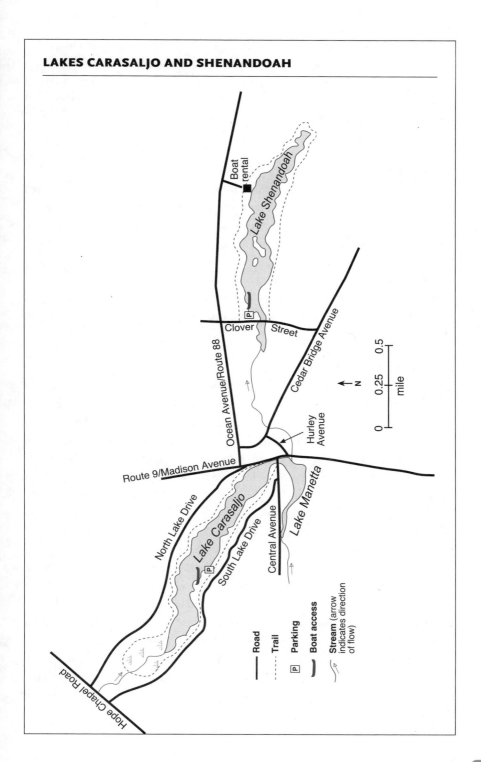

Boat rental

Lake Shenandoah

Ocean Avenue/Route 88

Clover Street

Cedar Bridge Avenue

N

0   0.25   0.5
mile

Hurley Avenue

Route 9/Madison Avenue

North Lake Drive

Lake Carasaljo

South Lake Drive

Central Avenue

Lake Manetta

Hope Chapel Road

——— Road

- - - - Trail

P Parking

) Boat access

Stream (arrow indicates direction of flow)

To Lake Shenandoah boat rental: From the junction of Route 9 and 88, drive east 1.5 miles on Route 88 and turn right into the park. There will be a large brown sign on the road. You cannot launch private boats here, but they have canoes and rowboats for rent on the water on a first-come, first-served basis. There is parking for about twenty cars. *GPS coordinates*: 40°05.301′ N, 74°11.342′ W.

WHAT YOU'LL SEE

It was a pleasure to find two nice lakes to paddle in a densely populated town that includes many industrial parks. Both lakes are fed by the South Branch Metedeconk River. Long and narrow, Lake Carasaljo is located within the 176-acre municipal park of the same name. Carasaljo derives from the names Caroline, Sara, and Josephine, daughters of businessman Joseph W. Brick, who lived here in the late 1800s. Manetta was Brick's wife, and the smaller "lake" attached to Lake Carasaljo is named after her. Lake Manetta is not actually a lake, but an arm of Lake Carasljo that cannot be launched into. However, you can paddle there.

Lake Carasaljo

Although this is a congested urban/suburban area, a narrow tree-lined swath of the park surrounds Lake Carasaljo. The far eastern end borders busy Route 9, which creates quite a bit of road noise in that area. The eastern half of the lake has the most population, but the houses are separated from the lake by a road and a border of trees. There is a nice little addition awaiting you at the south-eastern tip of the lake. Paddle south along the Route 9 embankment and under a footbridge that's part of the circular hiking trail around the lake. You may want to hike the path later. Continue and paddle under the Central Avenue bridge and enter the 18-acre Lake Manetta. No outboards of any kind are allowed here. The south shore borders a wide area of dense woods and you can usually find a spot or two of sandy beach to land your boat and take a break under the shade of overhanging trees. Watch for kingfishers darting along the tree edge. You'll usually find some ducks and geese back here too.

Head back out to Lake Carasaljo and up to the western end. Here the lake borders a wide area of woodlands and freshwater marsh. Herons, egrets, and waterfowl like it here and find feeding an easy task. Depending on water levels, you may be able to paddle up the South Branch Metedeconk River for a half-mile or more. The entrance to the river is a little left of center and should be easy to locate if you look for signs of a small current.

Bikers, joggers, and walkers make their way along a 5-mile trail that circles the lake and meanders through three areas where footpaths and footbridges traverse wetlands. You paddled beneath one of those footbridges if you went into Lake Manetta. If you wish to take an interesting short hike, drive to the parking lot off South Lake Drive just west of Lake Park Drive and start your hike there. This end of the park is woods, wetlands, and swamp, so you'll find a number of footbridges along the trails, the first of which you'll traverse as you enter the trail from the parking lot. *GPS coordinates for the parking lot*: 40°05.892′ N, 74°14.339′ W.

Lake Shenandoah

Lake Shenandoah County Park was once part of John D. Rockefeller's vacation estate, to which hemlock and unique specimens of trees were imported from all over the country. More than 140 acres of park offer biking and hiking trails, a small picnic area, fishing piers, on-site bait and tackle shop, canoe and rowboat rentals, a small coffee shop, and restrooms. Although smaller than Lake Carasaljo, this lake has far fewer houses or businesses nearby, making it more of a getaway. Wide and dense woods of pine and oak surround the lake on the south, east, west, and northeast sides. The rest of the north side has a narrow swath of trees between the lake and a sand access road. On the northwest side, tall grasses give way to dense shrubs and saplings, a perfect habitat for box turtles, painted turtles, and black racers, which are fast-moving, satiny black snakes. The most exciting part of the paddle to me is the two islands, which have a few small, sandy beach areas where you can land and take a break. This lake is also known for its good fishing, particularly for herring when they're running in May. Besides herring, you'll find pike, largemouth bass, perch, catfish, pickerel, bluegill (sunfish), eel, and many more species.

A 2-mile loop trail goes around the lake. The trail on the south side of the lake is the most interesting because it winds through the woods and has short feeder paths leading to the lake where you might find a lone angler or spot an egret or heron fishing in the shallow waters.

For additional paddles nearby, check out Manasquan Reservoir, 20 minutes north, and Forge Pond, 15 minutes east. See Trips 28 and 30, respectively. All are within a half hour of Allaire State Park if you wish to camp there. Colliers Mill is 35 minutes east and easily accessible from Albocondo Campground. See Trip 31.

30 | Forge Pond

Abundant waterfowl, shore birds, wading birds, marsh birds, and freshwater wetlands can be found here.

Location: Brick, NJ
Maps: *New Jersey Atlas and Gazetteer*, Map 50; USGS Lakewood
Area: 45 acres
Time: 1.0 hour, longer if you paddle upstream
Conditions: Depth average 5 feet
Development: Urban/suburban
Camping: Allaire State Park, 25 minutes north. Albocondo Campground, 20 minutes southwest. See Appendix A.
Take Note: Electric motorboats only
Outfitter: Jersey Paddler, 1756 Route 88 West, Brick, NJ 08724; 732-458-5777.

GETTING THERE

At the sometimes confusing and very busy junction of Routes 88 and 70, take Route 70 East and drive for 0.3 mile to the entrance on the right. Go slow as the turn-off lane is short and comes up quickly as you round the slight curve on Route 70. Parking is available for ten to twelve cars. *GPS coordinates for the entrance road*: 40°03.999′ N, 74°07.954′ W.

WHAT YOU'LL SEE

Forty-five acres are yours to enjoy in the midst of this bustling city. The serene pond area is historically where the Lenni-Lenape met and performed their ceremonial rituals up until the mid-1700s, when European settlers drove those who remained inland or to reservations. Early in the nineteenth century, a dam was built across the Metedeconk River and a forge erected on the pond to harvest and process bog ore from the marshes. Most of the ore was used to make water pipes. The dam broke in 1847, destroying the forge and surrounding homes. Forge Pond itself is the only thing that remains today of that era.

You can paddle the perimeter in less than an hour, but do take time to paddle quietly to enjoy the wildlife and venture upstream for additional treats. During the day, egrets, blue herons, songbirds, box and painted turtles, and huge snapping turtles are plentiful. A lucky treat is when a few swans visit the pond, sometimes staying for weeks before seeking other waters. An occasional water

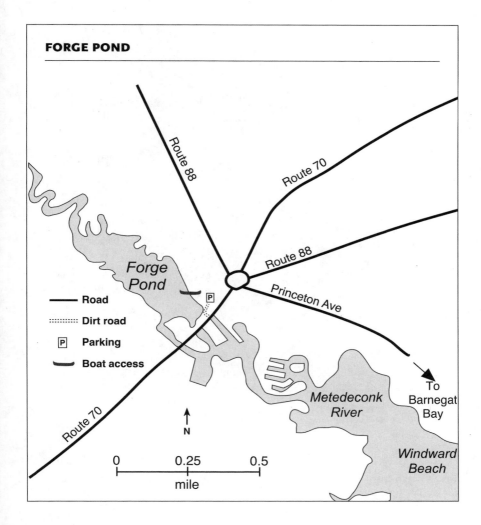

FORGE POND

Route 88

Route 70

Route 88

Forge Pond

Princeton Ave

— Road

⋯⋯ Dirt road

P Parking

⌣ Boat access

Route 70

Metedeconk River

To Barnegat Bay

Windward Beach

↑ N

0   0.25   0.5

mile

snake may be spotted slithering along the surface. In May and June, the pale pink and white blossoms of mountain laurel are sprinkled along the wooded shoreline. Paddle around the pond counterclockwise and as you get close to the south end and the launch, hug the western shoreline tightly and you'll find the entrance for the South Branch Metedeconk. You can paddle upstream for almost 2 miles and explore a number of small islands and inlets along the way for added enjoyment. This tranquil route winds through freshwater wetlands that are alive with an abundance of waterfowl, marsh birds, wading birds, ospreys, and turtles. Various wetland plants, such as marshmallow, goldenrod, cattail, red cardinal flower, and purple loosestrife, add sparks of color from spring through fall.

Kayakers from a local paddling group load their boats for a day on the water.

You can also paddle under the Route 70 bridge and enter the Metedeconk River. Turn left from the launch and continue to hug the left shore for about 0.1 mile to pass under the Route 70 bridge. There will be a very mild current as Forge Pond flows past a marina and through a half-mile channel into the Metedeconk River and then on to Barnegat Bay, about 3.5 miles east. Only electric outboards are permitted on the pond, but when you enter the Metedeconk River proper, anything goes, although most motorboaters are considerate and slow down when paddlers are in the area.

Summerfest concerts are held on Thursday nights during July and August at the Windward Beach Park located on Princeton Avenue off Route 70. The park is a 10-minute drive from Forge Pond. The more experienced paddler who is familiar with the waters can enjoy the concerts by paddling down river from Forge Pond; you will find Windward Beach Park about a mile east of the Route 70 bridge on the north side of the shoreline. You can land on the beach and enjoy the concert along with food from local vendors. Caution: Be sure you are equipped for paddling at night. Consult the section in the front matter for night paddling information and equipment.

Nearby is Jersey Paddler, a large and complete paddling store located on Route 88 on the west side of the junction of Routes 70 and 88. We call it our local "toy store" and usually cannot resist stopping in to check out all the canoes and kayaks or pick up an extra piece of equipment. See the trip header for more information.

Lakes Carasaljo and Shenandoah are 15 minutes west. See Trip 29. Manasquan Reservoir is 25 minutes northwest. See Trip 28.

31 | Colliers Mill Wildlife Management Area— Turn Mill Lake and Lake Success

Here you'll find waterfowl, song birds, pheasants, quails, hawks, and red foxes.

Location: Colliers Mill, NJ
Maps: *New Jersey Atlas and Gazetteer*, Map 49; USGS Cassville
Area: Turn Mill Lake: 100 acres; Lake Success: 40 acres
Time: Turn Mill Lake: 1.5 hours; Lake Success: about 1.0 hour
Conditions: Turn Mill Lake: depth average 5 feet; Lake Success: depth average 4 feet
Development: Rural
Information: New Jersey Division of Fish and Wildlife, Central Region (Assunpink WMA), One Eldridge Road, Robbinsville, NJ 08691; 609-259-2132.
Camping: Timberland Lake Campground, 20 minutes northeast. Indian Rock Campground, 10 minutes northeast. See Appendix A.
Take Note: Electric motorboats only

GETTING THERE
To Turn Mill Lake: From Route 70 near Whiting, drive 9.6 miles north on Route 539. Turn right onto Colliers Mill Road and drive 0.9 mile to the entrance of Colliers Mill Wildlife Management Area, which will be right in front of you. All roads are sandy and somewhat rutted. From there, turn right (south) onto

SNOWY EGRET

"Oh, dem golden slippers." Perhaps a familiar tune and words heard each New Year's Day by those living around the Philadelphia area as the unofficial theme song of the Philadelphia Mummer's Day Parade, but they also describe one of the conspicuous features of the snowy egret—its bright yellow toes. At first glance, it may be confused with the great egret, another member of the family *Ardeidae* with stark white feathers, black legs, and a long, slender neck, but the great egret, in addition to being much larger, sports a yellow beak and black toes; the snowy egret has a black beak and yellow toes. Just remember the "golden slippers" tune and it's easier.

Avid birders refer to snowy egrets as "snegs" and great egrets as "gregs," as a sort of shorthand. Members of *Ardeidae* have several things in common: long necks that fold into an "S" shape in flight, spearlike bills, and legs that trail when flying. Adult snowy egrets have shaggy head, neck, and back plumes more clearly visible when not in flight—almost like they forgot to comb their hair.

Snowy egrets typically frequent wetland environments such as salt marshes, and brackish marshes, ponds, and swamps within the Coastal Plain. While it is not unusual to spot a solitary egret, they more often tend to be found in small colonies foraging for food. They will sometimes maintain

a separate feeding territory, particularly during the mating season. If you hear a lot of low croaking and see some feathers rustling, chances are that one of them felt its territory infringed upon.

Commensal feeding, where one species gives a feeding advantage to another, is prevalent between snowy egrets and either ibis or other herons. Most egrets and herons forage in a "stalk and strike" method. Snowy egrets, while they may initially stalk, shuffle their feet in a flurry to stir up aquatic invertebrates, a favorite prey. In the process, many creatures are sent scurrying, available to be picked up by other birds foraging within a few feet. Small fish, reptiles, and insects are also hunted in lesser quantities.

Long nuptial head plumes that develop during breeding season almost caused their demise during the late nineteenth and early twentieth centuries, when large colonies of snowy, red, and great egrets were killed for their ornamental breeding plumes. Ladies fashions in America and Europe at the time used the beautiful plumes to adorn fashionable hats. The plumes were also highly sought after as ornaments in Eastern Asian ceremonial dress. In 1901, the National Audubon Society sponsored a law prohibiting the killing of any bird except game birds, but in the Everglades where large breeding colonies existed, a labyrinth of narrow channels filled with mosquitoes and alligators made it impossible to patrol. As a result, plume hunters continued to make money as species counts dwindled. In 1903, plumes sold for $32 an ounce, slightly more than the price of gold at the time.

the unmarked sand Hawkin Road and drive 0.2 mile to the launch on your left. Parking for about ten cars is available in a small clearing on your right, about 80 feet down the road. *GPS coordinates*: 40°03.889′ N, 74°26.941′ W.

To Lake Success: From the entrance to the wildlife management area, drive straight (east) 1.0 mile to the T-junction with another sand road. Turn right and drive 2.5 miles to an informal launch. You'll find parking for about eight cars. *GPS coordinates*: 40°03.468′ N, 74°23.540′ W.

WHAT YOU'LL SEE

Remote and quiet, three lakes nestle into the landscape within the 12,000-acre Colliers Mill Wildlife Management Area. Colliers Mill was once filled with sawmills and smelters' furnaces. The name came from the prosperous charcoal burners, known as colliers. The surroundings are typical of the Pine Barrens: pine and mixed-oak hardwood forests, with cedar, sweet gum, and red maple edging the waters. Mountain laurel, sheep laurel, and fragrant sweet pepperbush comprise most of the understory shrubs. The northern pine snake, whose range is primarily in and around South Carolina and Georgia, has small, disjointed colonies within the pinelands of New Jersey. Inhabiting only flat, sandy pine barrens, their secretive burrowing behavior eludes even the most experienced snake hunter. Pickerel, smallmouth bass, and sunfish live in the tea-colored waters typical of the Pine Barrens. Goldenrod flowers splash the landscape with yellow from late summer through fall, when they are joined by bouquets of wild blue asters. The wildlife management area itself is surrounded by woods and large farms—a very remote setting.

Turn Mill Lake

Numerous coves edge Turn Mill Lake's 100 acres along the eastern shore. To the left of the launch the water is very shallow, but you can usually find water deep enough to paddle by avoiding areas of surface vegetation mats. Lots of waterfowl swim around here and wading birds stalk the shallows for prey. Butterflies and dragonflies flit about on waterlilies that literally carpet some sections by late summer. Paddle across the lake to the eastern shore and explore those areas. About a quarter-mile down there are a few small, low-lying islands tucked close to shore with just enough space to get a canoe or kayak through. In times of low water, though, the passages may be blocked by vegetation. The southern area is shallow along the shores, providing a good environment for ducks, frogs, turtles, and butterflies. The only drawback to the lake is that on some weekends local gun clubs use an established firing range for practice shooting. Though the range is not close, the sound echoes through the stillness. Should a gun club be present the day you visit, you may want to drive out to Lake Success and away from the firing range.

Lake Success

When you drive to Lake Success, keep your eyes on the road for the pheasants and quails that inhabit the area. From my experience, quails are more populous, or at least they're closer to the road and easier to spot. Because it is highly washboarded, the road to Lake Success seems much longer than it actually is. Pitch pine, cedar, and sweet gum border the lake's 40 acres along with a few small beaches for informal picnics, where you can find a pitch pine or two to sit under for shade. Cedar swamps on its western end are ideal for bird-watching. Numerous species of frogs, toads, and snakes relish this vast wilderness tract in the northern pinelands.

COLLIERS MILL WILDLIFE MANAGEMENT AREA

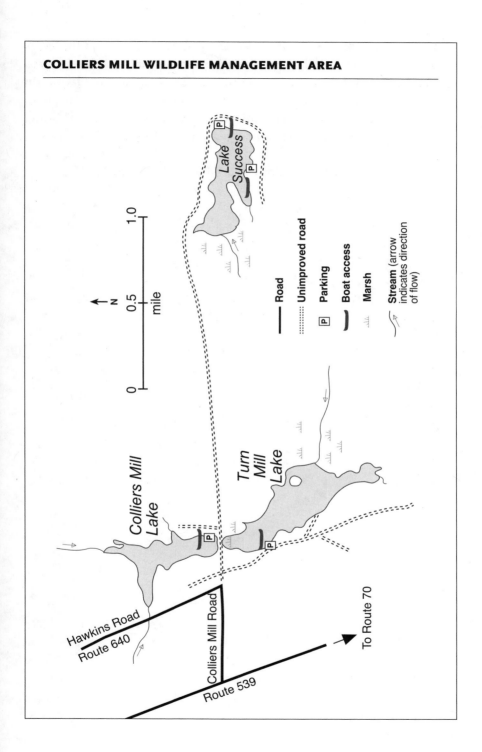

Legend:
- Road
- Unimproved road
- P Parking
- Boat access
- Marsh
- Stream (arrow indicates direction of flow)

N

0   0.5   1.0
mile

Lake Success

Turn Mill Lake

Colliers Mill Lake

Hawkins Road
Route 640

Colliers Mill Road

Route 539

To Route 70

You may have noticed the small, 17-acre Colliers Mill Lake on the left as you entered off Colliers Mill Road. The lake is shallow, but ideal if you want to introduce a young child to the joys of paddling. There's a nice sand launch on the eastern side close to the main road. An open grassy area under the trees along the lake is ideal for a picnic. Bird-watchers frequent this spot and say it's the best location within the area for kingfishers, warblers, and a large variety of songbirds.

Lakes Carasaljo and Shenandoah are 35 minutes northeast. See Trip 29.

3 | SOUTHERN NEW JERSEY

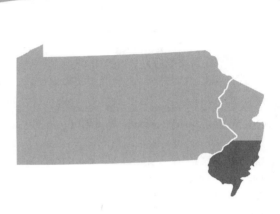

Pine Barrens. The name not only describes the environment, but is also the formal name given to this vast area that covers more than two-thirds of the land in the southern half of New Jersey. Recognized on every U.S. governmental level for its ecological importance and enormous water resources, in 1983 the United Nations Educational, Scientific and Cultural Organization (UNESCO), an agency of the United Nations, officially designated close to 1 million acres, about one-quarter of the state's total land area, as the Pinelands National Reserve. A number of sites typify this environmental area. Among them are the Mullica River (Trip 39), Batsto Lake in Wharton State Forest (Trip 38), and Lake Lenape (Trip 48).

The original Flemish settlers from Flanders, the northern region of Belgium, referred to this land as barren because traditional crops would not grow in the acidic conditions. These soils, however, provide a perfect environment for blueberry and cranberry growth, making New Jersey one of the leading producers for both products. Due to these barren lands and the numerous state forests and wildlife management areas acquired by the state over the past half-century, southern New Jersey remains the least populated region in the state.

Enormous stands of Atlantic white cedar provided wood for a large shipbuilding industry in the mid-1900s. Shipbuilders Viking Yacht, Egg Harbor

Yacht, and Ocean Yacht are still in existence today, though most of their boats now are made of fiberglass. Behind the barrier islands rimming the Atlantic Ocean, vast expanses of tidal salt marshes create one of nature's most productive nursery grounds, offering nourishment and shelter for juvenile fish, crabs, and other inhabitants of coastal waters. Two trips that will introduce you to this important habitat are Scott's Landing in Edwin B. Forsythe Refuge (Trip 49) and Manahawkin Impoundment and Bridge to Nowhere (Trip 40).

32 | Rancocas Creek

Turtles everywhere, pretty scenery, frogs, beaver, birdlife, raptors, and ducks are yours to enjoy on this quiet waterway.

Location: Pemberton, NJ
Maps: *New Jersey Atlas and Gazetteer*, Map 47; USGS Mount Holly
Area: 6.6 miles round-trip
Time: 2.5 hours
Conditions: Depth average 5 feet
Development: Suburban/rural, woodlands surrounded by small farms and county lands
Information: Burlington County Division of Parks, 6 Park Avenue, Historic Smithville Park, Eastampton, NJ 08060; 609-265-5858.
Take Note: No horsepower limit specified, but you won't encounter anything except a very rare electric motorboat
Outfitter: Clark's Canoe Rental (canoe and kayak rentals), 201 Hanover Street, Pemberton, NJ 08068; 609-894-4448; open weekends, 9 A.M. to 5 P.M.

GETTING THERE
Pemberton launch: From the junction of Routes 206 and 38/530, drive 2.7 miles on Route 530 East (it's Route 38 on the west side of Route 206 and Route 530 on the east side). It becomes Hampton Street in the town of Pemberton. Turn left onto Hanover Street and drive 0.15 mile to the access road on your left immediately before crossing the bridge. Clark's Canoe Rental is located on Hanover Street at the corner of the access road. You'll find parking for about fifteen cars. *GPS coordinates*: 39°58.210′ N, 74°41.137′ W.

RANCOCAS CREEK

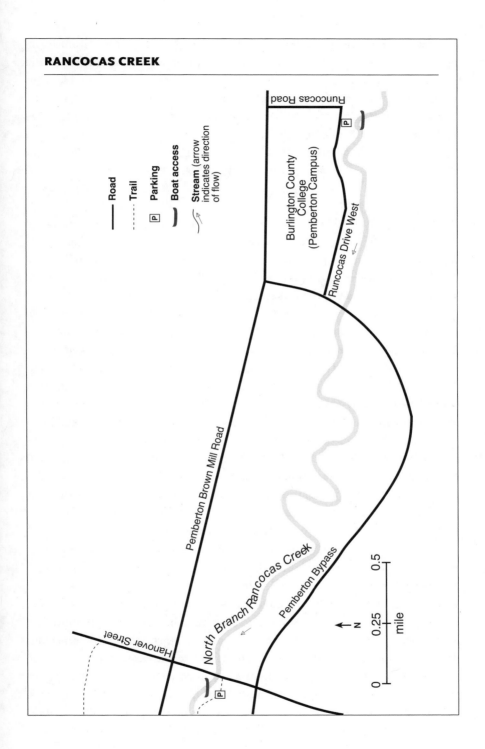

Road
Trail
P Parking
) Boat access
Stream (arrow indicates direction of flow)

Runcocas Road

Burlington County College (Pemberton Campus)

Runcocas Drive West

Pemberton Brown Mill Road

North Branch Rancocas Creek

Pemberton Bypass

Hanover Street

N

0   0.25   0.5
mile

Burlington County College launch: From the junctions of Routes 206 and 38/530, drive 2.7 miles on Route 530 East (it's Route 38 on the west side of Route 206 and Route 530 on the east side). At the junction with Hanover Street, continue straight onto Pemberton Bypass and drive 2.1 miles to the T-intersection. Turn right and drive 0.7 mile, then turn right onto Runcocas Road and drive 0.3 mile to the access road on your left. It's a 50-yard carry to the water. Portable toilets are on-site in the parking lot. You'll find parking for about twenty cars. *GPS coordinates*: 39°57.718′ N, 74°38.460′ W.

WHAT YOU'LL SEE

The Rancocas Watershed drains 350 square miles in south-central New Jersey. It comprises the Rancocas Creek Main Stem, North Branch Rancocas Creek, and the South/Southwest Branch Rancocas Creek. Although a large part of the watershed lies within the New Jersey Pinelands, it is the only Pinelands waterway that drains into the Delaware River instead of the Atlantic Ocean.

The Rancocas Creek Canoe Trail along the North Branch Rancocas Creek is 14 miles in length, beginning at Burlington County College in Pemberton and ending at Mill Dam Park in Mount Holly. A 200-yard portage is involved to bypass two dams at Smithville, and the section between Birmingham and Pemberton can only be paddled downstream because it is shallow and swift water. The prettiest section, described here, is the slow-moving waters between Pemberton and Burlington County College. It's also the least populated, with only about ten quaint riverside homes along the whole trip. While you can put in at either end, the easiest is Pemberton. The launch parking lot is located at one of the dams. You can launch into the downstream side that goes into Birmingham, but it's shallow, rocky, and has a swift enough current that it is impossible to paddle back upstream to the launch. Use the dirt launch on the upstream side of the dam and paddle upstream where current is minimal.

I've never seen so many turtles on one trip. Sliders (red-eared) on logs side-by-side with yellow-bellied and painted turtles—some as big as dinner plates. Where leaf litter catches on snags close to shore, look for frogs. The creek takes you through a variety of habitats, from lowland woods to reed clumps to swampy side channels. Bends in the creek tend to be gradual, with only a few sharp turns. Most of your adventure will be side-skirting downed limbs and ducking under overhanging branches along this scenic waterway.

Two- to three-foot steep dirt banks line most of the creek, but there are some spots with gradual slopes that lead into shallow side inlets and tiny coves. Many of those areas have very small, almost hidden, passageways into the creek. Inside you can often find egrets, mallards, and pintails seeking a more secluded

A canopy of trees will envelop you as you paddle this scenic waterway.

environment that's blanketed with pond lilies and duckweed. Along mossy embankments, look for the tiny, dark-green leaves of wild cranberry, smaller and more tart than their cultivated cousins. In the understory, you'll find wild blueberry, mulberry, mountain laurel, and sheep laurel. In a few areas, wild grape entwines its twisted vines around trees and bushes. Birdlife includes vireos, orioles, thrushes, kingfishers, tanagers, woodpeckers, and blue jays. Because of the many small farms close to the woodland edges, hawks, falcons, and vultures can be seen in the skies.

Muskrat might be spotted in areas of reeds or other dense aquatic grasses. Beaver are seen here often. On one recent trip, my buddy and I spotted several birch trees with the bark freshly gnawed off in a 2-foot area near the ground—a telltale sign of recent beaver activity. Small, narrow paths leading to the water's edge are usually deer trails, but you might also spot a fox or raccoon.

The public ramp at Burlington County College is a perfect place to stop for lunch and stretch your legs. There's a portable toilet at the top of the staired ramp in the parking lot. From here, you can paddle another 1.5 miles upstream to the next dam, but the last time I was there it was only paddleable for about a half-mile due to downed trees that spanned the creek. Since upstream from the college is not part of the water trail, passageways for canoes and kayaks aren't maintained by the county.

For information on the entire water trail, visit www.co.burlington.nj.us, click on Departments, then Resource Conservation, then Division of Parks, then Regional Trails drop-down Rancocas Creek Canoe Trail. The entire canoe trail requires two portages, the longest of which is a 200-yard portage at Smithville. The other portage, about 55 yards long, is at the dam in Pemberton. Because it is impossible to paddle upstream from Birmingham to Pemberton, you need to set up a shuttle with another paddler if you choose to do the entire trail.

The hiker can enjoy a well-marked trail that leads off from the west end of the parking lot and travels 1.25 miles into the town of Binghamton. A fork off to the right at 0.9 mile into the hike heads back into the town of Pemberton, crosses the creek along the way, and ends at the restored old Pemberton Train Station for a 1.9-mile hike. From there you can either return along the same route, or turn right onto Hanover Street and walk 0.5 mile to the launch access road.

An additional paddling trip nearby is Atsion Lake, 30 minutes south. See Trip 35.

---

33 | Cooper River Lake and Newton Lake

You'll find waterfowl, turtles, and abundant birdlife at these two lakes.

Location: Collingswood, NJ
Maps: *New Jersey Atlas and Gazetteer*, Map 54; USGS Camden
Area: Cooper River Park Lake: 150 acres; Newton Lake: 40 acres
Time: Cooper River Park Lake: 2.0–2.5 hours; Newton Lake: 1.5–2.0 hours
Conditions: Newton Lake: depth average 5 feet; Cooper River Park Lake: depth average 5 feet
Development: Cooper River Park Lake: urban with greenway; Newton Lake: urban with greenway
Information: Camden County Parks Department, 1301 Park Boulevard, Cherry Hill, NJ 08002; 856-795-7275.
Take Note: Electric motorboats only

GETTING THERE
To Cooper River Lake north shore boathouse and northeast launch: From the Routes 130/30 circle, drive north 0.6 mile on Route 130. Turn right onto

COOPER RIVER LAKE AND NEWTON LAKE

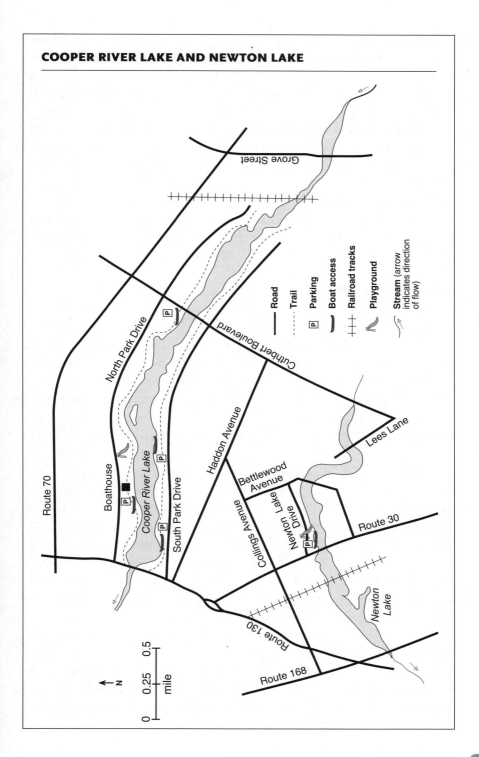

Grove Street

North Park Drive

Cuthbert Boulevard

Haddon Avenue

Lees Lane

Bettlewood Avenue

Collings Avenue

Newton Lake Drive

Route 30

Route 70

Boathouse

Cooper River Lake

South Park Drive

Route 130

Route 168

Newton Lake

Road
Trail
P **Parking**
Boat access
Railroad tracks
Playground
Stream (arrow indicates direction of flow)

N

0   0.25   0.5
mile

North Park Drive immediately after crossing over the lake and drive 0.55 mile to the boathouse parking lot on your right. You'll find parking for 30 cars. *GPS coordinates*: 39°55.597′ N, 75°04.424′ W. For the northeast launch, drive an additional 1.0 mile to the dirt entrance on your right. You'll find parking for about 60 cars. *GPS coordinates*: 39°55.555′ N, 75°03.371′ W.

To Cooper River Lake south shore launch: Drive north 0.4 mile on Route 130, turn right onto South Park Drive, and continue 0.7 mile to the boat launch parking area on your left. You'll find parking for fifteen cars. *GPS coordinates*: 39°55.467′ N, 75°04.271′ W.

To Newton Lake: From the Routes 130/30 circle, drive east 0.7 mile on Route 30, turn left onto Newton Lake Drive and make an immediate right into the boat launch parking lot and drive to the ramp. You'll find parking for about 50 cars. *GPS coordinates*: 39°54.484′ N, 75°04.896′ W.

WHAT YOU'LL SEE
Cooper River Lake

Cooper River Lake Park has come alive over the years. The city has cleaned up its waters and created a lovely park along a 2.5-mile stretch of the Cooper River where it widens to a few hundred yards—enough to call it a lake, at least by the standards of south Jersey, which is not known for having extremely large bodies of water. For those who live in the densely populated Camden area and need a place close to home, this section of the river landscaped with trees, shrubs, small garden areas, sculpture gardens, a multiuse trail, and a playground provides the perfect refuge. The best paddling is on the eastern end, where the shores become more wooded and you're farther from bustling traffic. Carp, bass, sunnies, and catfish inhabit the lake, as does a large population of turtles and frogs. Herons, egrets, ducks, and geese make their home here. Many paddlers who live in the densely populated area along the Delaware River from Gloucester City to Riverside come here after work or on weekends for a workout. It's close, convenient, and the restrooms at the boathouse are sparkling clean. The boathouse is primarily used by rowing teams and may become crowded at times, but both the restrooms and launch facilities are open to the public. The large public floating dock launches usually have a number of portable toilets on-site.

If you feel adventurous, from the far eastern end of the lake you can paddle under the railroad bridge and into Cooper River. Depending on water levels, this will add a round-trip of 2.0 to 3.0 miles to your day. Within the first three-quarter-mile, there are three islands to explore and a few open areas where waterfowl can be seen. It's a very pleasant and quiet paddle with only a few houses or businesses along the route. As the river gets narrow, dead trees across the river may block your passage.

Biking and hiking trails snake their way along both shores, and portable toilets are conveniently located all along the grounds. The total length of the trail system is 5.0 miles, but the loop from the boathouse parking lot east to East Cuthbert Boulevard and around to Route 30 and back is only 3.8 miles. For the 5-mile trail walk, continue past East Cuthbert Boulevard on the north side of the lake for an addional 1.2-mile loop. The park is open from 6 A.M. until midnight, leaving plenty of time for a moonlight paddle.

Newton Lake

Long and narrow, attractive Newton Lake sits amidst a highly populated area. A rim of the 104-acre municipal park of the same name surrounds about 60 percent of the 40-acre lake. Many improvements and amenities have been added to the park since the early 2000s, one of which is a nice boat launch with plentiful parking. Camden County has launched many ongoing programs that will one day connect multiuse trails throughout the county. The main recreation area next to the ramp features a small playground, restroom, picnic area, and a landscaped lakeside sitting areas with benches.

The lake's serpentine shape provides a long, relaxing paddle with areas of yellow pond lilies, purple pickerelweed, and yellow and white stalked hornwort. In shallow, marshy shoreline areas you'll most likely find egrets and herons fishing, their long necks stretched and focused on the task at hand. Don't just paddle past them. Sit and observe these graceful birds for a while. Turtles bask on a few limbs that stick out of the water and are most common on the northeast area of the lake, where you're also likely to find ducks, geese, and swans. One thing I like are the four bridges that cross over the lake, which add an element of interest to your paddle as you wonder what the next section of the lake will bring. It's like opening another chapter in a book. Anglers love to cast their lines from shore for carp, bass, sunnies, and catfish.

To stretch your legs after a paddle, walking paths weave their way around trees along the landscaped swath of land dotted with lakeside benches and small gardens. The total length is 2.4 miles, but you can cross over the Lees Lane bridge to shorten your walk.

Two other trips nearby are Stewart Park, 20 minutes southwest, and Rancocas Creek, 25 minutes northeast. See Trips 34 and 32.

34 | Stewart Park— Stewart Lake

Enjoy waterfowl, turtles, waterlilies, raccoons, opossums, and birdlife at this lake.

Location: Woodbury, NJ
Maps: *New Jersey Atlas and Gazetteer*, Map 54; USGS Woodbury
Area: 45 acres
Time: 1.5–2.0 hours
Conditions: Depth average 7 feet
Development: Urban
Information: Parks, Recreation & Community Forestry, City of Woodbury, 651 South Evergreen Avenue, Woodbury, NJ 08096; 856-853-0892 x208.
Camping: Timberlane Campground, 20 minutes southwest. See Appendix A.
Take Note: Electric motorboats only

GETTING THERE

From Route 45 in Woodbury (North Broad Street), drive east 0.35 mile on East Red Bank Avenue to the large brown YMCA building on your right. On the east side of the YMCA building, turn right and drive straight to the far parking lot, where you will see a sign for the boat launch at the head of a short dirt road. You'll find parking for 40 cars. *GPS coordinates*: 39°50.526′ N, 74°08.567′ W.

An alternative, but primitive, launch is at the far southeast arm of the lake. From Route 45 in Woodbury (North Broad Street), drive east 1.0 mile on Cooper Street to the stoplight at Kelly Drive. Make a U-turn (legal at the time of this writing) and drive 75 yards west on Cooper Street to the dirt road entrance to the launch area. You'll find parking for twelve cars. *GPS coordinates*: 39°49.956′ N, 75°08.185′ W.

WHAT YOU'LL SEE

Everyone simply calls this body of water Stewart Lake, but it actually interconnects Stewart Lake with a number of very small unnamed lakes. Stewart Lake itself is hugged on the northeast side by the 45-acre Stewart Park, which includes a boat launch with a floating dock, playground, portable toilets, restroom facility, and tree-studded, lakeside picnic area with tables. The lake is easily accessible and is very convenient for those living in the urban region. In some areas the woods are thin, leaving only a modest screen between you and

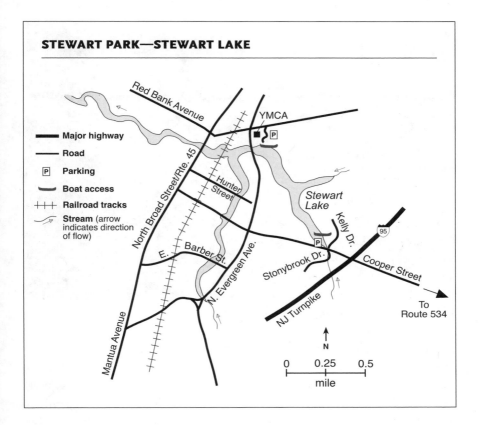

STEWART PARK—STEWART LAKE

civilization; elsewhere they provide a thick blanket of insulation. Upland woods of maple, hickory, sassafras, tulip, ash, and pine delight you with splashes of red, orange, and yellow in fall and cool greens in summer.

Wildlife is abundant here and attractive scenery is easy on the eyes. Canada geese are plentiful, blue herons are common, and kingfishers are often spotted along the wooded banks. A hawk has even been seen occasionally. Raccoons, opossums, and skunks are more likely to be spotted on the thickly wooded northeast end near the boat launch or on the west side of the east arm near the primitive dirt launch. Turtles and frogs are more prevalent in shallow areas on the eastern banks. Anglers here have good luck with largemouth bass and crappies. Sunfish are often caught by children fishing right by the launch.

Turn right as you leave the launch to go under the stone arch of the Evergreen Avenue bridge and enter the top of the western arm. Once past the bridge, the far end of that section leads down the long western arm of the lake. Before heading down there, continue west and go under the railroad bridge to the western-most section, where marshy areas will reward you with a plethora of

A family enjoys a day of canoeing and bird-watching.

birdlife. That small section is technically Broad Street Lake. A dam at the far end prevents you from going any farther. Head back out under the railroad bridge and turn right to meander down the western arm. The lake is more densely wooded on the eastern shoreline; that's where you are likely to find more birdlife and even an occasional raccoon. You can pass under the Hunter Street bridge, but there's a narrow boarded channel on the other end with some underwater pilings. Take it slow and easy to make it through into the next small section, which will end at Cooper Street. Turn around and enjoy the quiet scenery as you paddle back to the launch area. You can stop there for a picnic lunch or continue on to other stops on the east arm.

On the east side of the long east arm, about 0.35 mile from the launch, is the entrance to a short, small creek. You can paddle up there only about a quarter-mile, but there's a cute little sand landing area about 15 feet wide where you can land and enjoy a snack. The best place to stop for lunch or to stretch your legs in this arm is the very south end at the informal boat launch and fishing area site. Paddlers from a local group come here quite often on weekends or for a short paddle after work in summer. It is a great place to relax, get out on the water, and spend the day paddling.

Cooper River Park Lake is 20 minutes north. See Trip 33. Another possibility is to camp at Timberlane Campground (see this trip header for information) and visit the D.O.D. Ponds the next day. See Trip 43.

35 | Wharton State Forest— Atsion Lake

Enjoy white cedar, pine, and oak woods; waterfowl; turtles; frogs; and marsh flowers at this lake.

Location: Shamong, NJ
Maps: *New Jersey Atlas and Gazetteer*, Map 6556; USGS Jenkins
Area: 62 acres
Time: 1.5–2.0 hours
Conditions: Depth average 5 feet; bogs
Development: Remote
Information: Wharton State Forest (Atsion office), 744 Route 206, Shamong, NJ 08088; 609-268-0444. $5 weekday fee ($10 weekend) in-season. Open April 1 to December 31.
Camping: On-site; call or stop at the Atsion office for reservations.
Take Note: Electric motorboats only

GETTING THERE

From Route 30, drive north 7.3 miles on Route 206 and turn left into the park. The boat ramp is on the far side of the parking lot. *GPS coordinates for the recreation area and boat launch*: 39°44.232′ N, 74°49.637′ W. The park office is 0.3 mile north of the recreation area on the east side of the road. *GPS coordinates*: 39°44.515′ N, 74°43.552′ W. From Route 70, drive south 10.2 miles on Route 206, turn right into the entrance, and proceed as above. There's plenty of parking, more than 100 spots, because the parking lot is also used for the swimming beach and recreation area.

WHAT YOU'LL SEE

One of the larger lakes within the 110,000-acre Wharton State Forest, Atsion Lake (pronounced AT-zon by locals) is the only one that provides on-site camping facilities, many of which are lakeside. Like other Pine Barren rivers that were dammed to create a lake, it was created during the American Revolution heyday of iron forge-making because of all the bog iron in the ground. The pond furnished the village with water and powered the furnace. A paper mill and grist mill were added later. It's hard to believe that Atsion was once a thriving village with 200 residents. The old general store is now the ranger's headquarters. Next to it is the mansion built by Samuel Richards that overlooked the ironworks and

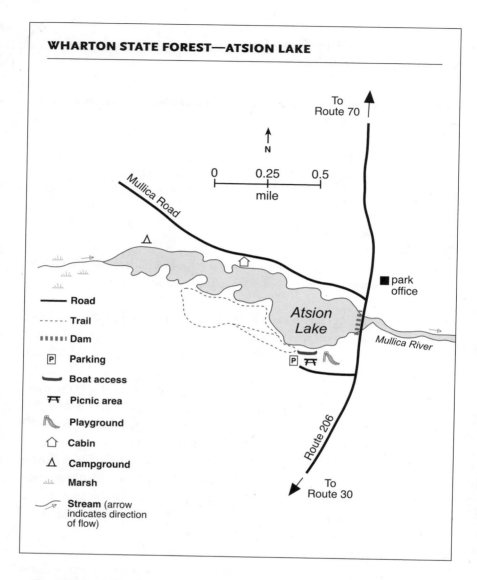

WHARTON STATE FOREST—ATSION LAKE

To
Route 70

N

| 0 | 0.25 | 0.5 |
mile

Mullica Road

Atsion
Lake

park
office

Mullica River

Route 206

To
Route 30

— Road

----- Trail

▪▪▪▪▪▪ Dam

P Parking

Boat access

🪑 Picnic area

Playground

⌂ Cabin

△ Campground

Marsh

Stream (arrow
indicates direction
of flow)

mill pond. You can walk around the site of the old Atsion village after paddling the lake. Stop in at the ranger's office to learn more about the history of the village. The public boat launch, playgrounds, showers, swimming beach, two short nature trails, and picnic facilities are at the recreation area on the south side of the lake.

This is a popular swimming and recreation spot on weekends in July and August, and the lake can be quite crowded because of the large swimming beach. But the rest of the year and during the week it's almost empty and you'll feel like you have the lake to yourself. I was there one weekday late afternoon in June and not a soul was in the park. The air was still and I was mesmerized by the soft shapes my bow wake made on mirror-smooth water as I slipped softly across the lake. Heading to the western portion of the lake, puffy white clouds in a clear blue sky contrasted sweetly with the surrounding dark cedars and tea-colored water beneath my boat.

Thick pitch pine and oak woods surround the lake, with a few stands of phragmites along shallower shores. Red maple, sweet gum, and birch trees poke their branches between dark green pine and cedar at the water's edge, creating a colorful contrast in fall. Most of the lake is fairly deep by coastal plain standards, with some spots reaching depths of 15 feet or more. Head left from the launch and paddle up the lake. Once beyond the first peninsula, any noise from the beach area quickly disappears. Take your time paddling the shoreline, wandering in and out of all the coves, observing the environment, and enjoying the quiet. In July, look for wild blueberries at the water's edge for a quick, sweet treat. Wild blueberries are much smaller than their cultivated cousins, but I think they're sweeter. Large pinkish-purple heads of joe-pye weed and yellow goldenrod add color to the wetland edges from midsummer through fall. Look for vultures and ospreys overhead.

White and yellow waterlilies carpet the shallower western end, where the headwaters of the Mullica River feed into the lake. The river is the major drainage system for the lower Pine Barrens and the only one that starts within the Pine Barrens boundaries. A number of small islands that provide bird viewing opportunities are at the entrance to the river. If water levels are high enough, you can paddle upstream about a quarter-mile and past a few small tributary inlets.

Two small trails, 0.5 and 1.0 mile in length, start from the west end of the parking lot. The 9.5-mile Mullica Trail starts from the park office parking lot across the road on Route 206.

Nine lakeside log cabins, each offering a private cartop launch, are available on the northeastern end of the lake, and a large campground on the northwestern end offers a few on-water sites. Even though I live not far from here, a small group of my paddling buddies and I will spend a kayak–camping weekend on the lake now and then, usually in fall when it's quieter and the woods around the lake come alive with color.

If you're in for another paddle, visit Batsto Lake or Mullica River, 25 minutes southeast. See Trips 38 and 39, respectively.

36 | Wharton State Forest—Lake Oswego

Look for ospreys, ducks, wild cranberries, wild blueberries, and a drowned cedar swamp at this remote lake.

Location: Jenkins, NJ
Maps: *New Jersey Atlas and Gazetteer*, Map 57; USGS Oswego Lake
Area: 92 acres
Time: 1.5 hours
Conditions: Depth average 5 feet; drowned cedar trees on the east end
Development: Remote
Information: Wharton State Forest (Batsto office), 4110 Nesco Road, Hammonton, NJ 08037; 609-561-0024.
Camping: Bodine Field primitive, 20 minutes south. Wading Pines Camping Resort, 5 minutes west. See Appendix A.
Take Note: Electric motorboats only
Outfitter: Bel Haven Canoes and Kayaks, 1227 Route 542, Green Bank, NJ 08215; 800-445-0953.

GETTING THERE

From Route 542, drive north 6.8 miles on Route 563, turn right onto Lake Oswego Road, and drive 3.4 miles to the launch site on the right, just past the guardrailed bridge going over a creek. The old blacktop portion of the road is bumpy and turns into a sand road near the end. A sign designating Penn State Forest will be on the right side of the road at the launch site. You'll find parking for about 25 cars. A portable toilet is on-site. Alternatively, from Route 532, drive south 9.6 miles on Route 563 and turn left onto Lake Oswego Road. Proceed as above. *GPS coordinates*: 39°44.062′ N, 74°29.470′ W.

WHAT YOU'LL SEE

In the heart of cranberry and blueberry farms, you will pass one of Rutgers University's Blueberry and Cranberry Field Research stations on the left as you drive to Oswego Lake. Their barn-red buildings with white trim that you see as you drive to the launch are somewhat of a landmark along roads in the area. Hawks frequent the open fields, blue jays screech through the woods, and cardinals dart through the cedars. I've seen people fish at Lake Oswego occasionally, but I've never seen anyone catch anything. There's a shaded clearing with picnic

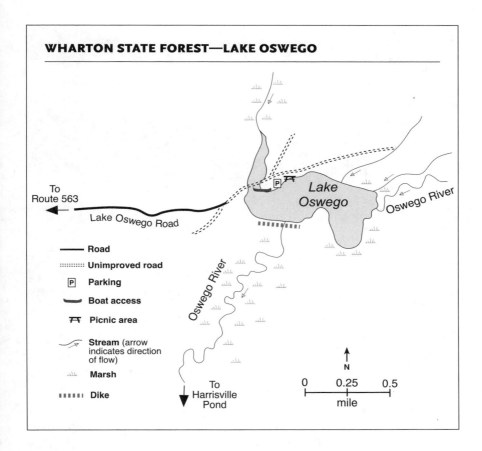

WHARTON STATE FOREST—LAKE OSWEGO

To Route 563

Lake Oswego Road

Lake Oswego

Oswego River

Oswego River

To Harrisville Pond

—— Road

:::::::: Unimproved road

P Parking

Boat access

Picnic area

Stream (arrow indicates direction of flow)

Marsh

Dike

N

0   0.25   0.5
mile

tables and swimming beach on a point of land east of the launch with a pretty view of the lake and a large portable toilet in the parking lot.

Cedar, sweet gum, and red maple line the waters within predominantly pine and oak lowland woods studded with American holly, hickory, and elder. Along the bank, look for the tiny, glossy-green leaves of the low-growing cranberry; its green fruit starts to turn red around the middle of August. If you visit in October and November, when the fruits are ripe, be aware that wild cranberries are quite tart. Ocean Spray has facilities near here to make the cranberry juice you can buy in the supermarket. The blueberries, however, are sweet and ready to eat—if you can get to them before the deer. My favorite paddle is to follow the northern shoreline to the left of the launch to look for kingfishers, and then head to the eastern end of the lake to look for woodpeckers. All the while I'm also scanning the sky for the occasional hawk. When water levels are high, you can paddle up the Oswego River for about a mile. The Oswego River enters the lake on the far eastern tip. As I paddle back along the southern

A marsh island west of the launch invites you to look for wildlife along its shores.

shore, my next stop is a small beach with a large shaded clearing and logs to sit on while I enjoy a snack and take in the scenery before heading back. That area is right by the dam.

Facing the lake from the launch, look straight across and to the left; you'll see the small dam and a few tiny clearings to the right of the dam. During paddling season, local outfitters drop off kayak and canoe groups at the launch. They paddle across the lake, portage their boats over the narrow sand dike, and launch into the Oswego River for a 3-hour paddle downstream to Harrisville Pond.

Touted as one of the prettiest rivers in the Pine Barrens, Oswego River takes you through Atlantic white cedar swamps, lowland forests, and freshwater marshes. If you want to combine biking and paddling, this is ideal. Lock your bike to a tree at the Harrisville landing, and then drive back to Oswego Lake. Paddle around the lake for a while and portage over the small sand dike to put in on the river. When you arrive at Harrisville Pond, paddle to the landing beach and picnic area at the southern end on the right. Simply unlock your bike from the tree and lock up your kayak, then bike back to your car at Oswego Lake and return to the Harrisville Pond to pick up your boat. The bike ride back to Oswego is an easy 6.0 miles, as the land is fairly flat. Since this is a prime biking location, an official bike lane has been designated along Routes 679 and 563 for safer travel. More roads in the area are slated for similar lanes in the near future. Read about Batsto Lake (Trip 38), Atsion Lake (Trip 35), and Harrisville Pond (Trip 37) for more information on Wharton State Forest and the Pine Barrens.

Harrisville Pond is 15 minutes south. See Trip 37. Batsto Lake and Mullica River are 15 minutes south. See Trips 38 and 39. Camp overnight and paddle one or both lakes or the river the next day, respectively.

37 | Wharton State Forest— Harrisville Pond

Here you will likely see wildfowl, wading birds, wild blueberries, wild cranberries, white cedar bogs, and Pine Barren marshes.

Location: Harrisville, NJ
Maps: *New Jersey Atlas and Gazetteer*, Map 65; USGS Jenkins
Area: 40 acres
Time: 1.0 hour
Conditions: Depth average 5 feet
Development: Remote
Information: Wharton State Forest (Batsto office), 4110 Nesco Road, Hammonton, NJ 08037; 609-561-0024.
Camping: Bodine Field primitive campground, 2 minutes east. Wading Pines Camping Resort, 10 minutes northeast. See Appendix A.
Take Note: Electric motorboats only
Outfitter: Bel Haven Canoes and Kayaks, 1227 Route 542, Green Bank, NJ 08215; 800-445-0953.

GETTING THERE
From Route 542, drive north 5.4 miles on Route 563. Turn right (east) onto Route 670, and drive 1.4 miles to the launch site and picnic area on your left. Launch anywhere along the beach. You'll find parking for about fifteen cars. *GPS coordinates:* 39°39.919′ N, 74°31.452′ W.

WHAT YOU'LL SEE
Wild blueberry bushes peek out among the cedar and pine dominating the shoreline of Harrisville Pond. The dark blue fruits ripen in July. Mountain and

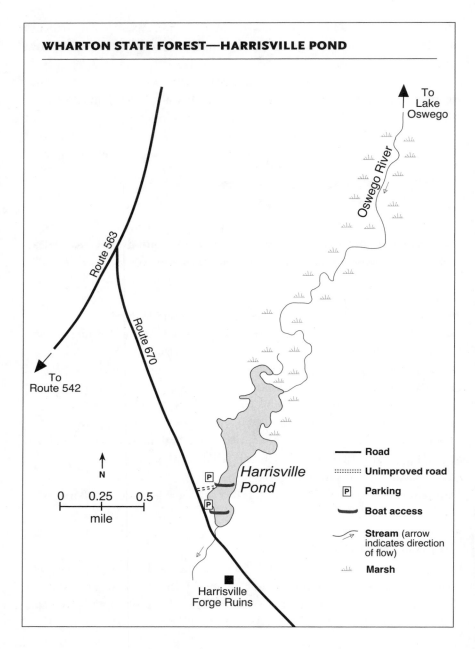

WHARTON STATE FOREST—HARRISVILLE POND

To
Lake
Oswego

Oswego River

Route 563

Route 670

To
Route 542

N

0   0.25   0.5
mile

P

P

*Harrisville
Pond*

— Road

∷∷∷∷ Unimproved road

P   Parking

━ Boat access

Stream (arrow
indicates direction
of flow)

⊥⊥⊥ Marsh

Harrisville
Forge Ruins

sheep laurel blossoms bring delicate touches of pink and white to the landscape
in early summer, along with the white flowers of the lightly scented bog magnolia. I love paddling here in midsummer, when the aroma of sweet pepperbush
fills the air with its perfumed scent as cranberries begin to grow on its moist

shores. The first large cove on the right (east) as you paddle north becomes carpeted with yellow and white pond lilies in late summer. Sneak into the cove quietly and you might spot a deer near the edge. Deer are all over the place here, and if you know what to look for, you will spot many deer trails along the edge of the lake. Their trails are small, sometimes only a foot wide. If you see a small clearing at water's edge, look closely to see if it continues into the woods even if small bushes overhang the path. If it does, it's likely a path to the water that deer, and possibly other land mammals, use. Old cedar stumps in the large cove on the northwest end of the pond are perfect basking spots for painted turtles. Ducks, often comically end-up (tails in the air), frequent this area because of the dense aquatic vegetation.

If you feel energetic, you can paddle to the pond's northeast corner, where the Oswego River enters, then paddle upstream for about 1.0 mile until the oncoming current gets too strong to navigate. It's absolutely gorgeous up there, particularly the first quarter-mile, and you'll get a good taste of what pristine and lovely rivers run through the Pine Barrens. Take a cool dip off the beach at the landing on hot days when you get back. It's so refreshing.

After paddling, walk out of the parking lot and left (east) on Route 670 and continue about 0.3 mile. Cross the road and look for a 6-foot-high cyclone fence back from the road about 20 feet. Behind it are the stately remains of the old Harrisville paper mill. The tall archways rising starkly out of the ground will give you an idea of how majestic this structure must have looked in its heyday. Fires wreaked havoc on the structure several times from its beginning around 1750 until 1914, when it was permanently abandoned. Weather and vandals have taken a toll on the remaining structures over the decades. In the late 1970s, the state erected the chain link fence around the main mill to protect it from further damage and prevent injury to visitors from falling stones and unstable ground.

Even through the fence, the mill presents a unique photographic subject, with vines creeping over the red and brown stone structure and a few small trees growing out of its 3-foot-thick walls and high arches. You can read more about the history of the mills around Harrisville on the Web at njpinebarrens.com/ghost-towns/the-rise-and-fall-of-harrisville. Walk directly across the road and look for a trail leading to the old grist mill. The remains are small, but interesting, and surrounded by a wire fence. Read about Batsto Lake (Trip 38), Atsion Lake (Trip 35), and Lake Oswego (Trip 36) for more information on Wharton State Forest and the Pine Barrens.

For an additional paddle, Batsto Lake and Mullica River, Trips 38 and 39, are 20 minutes southwest. Lake Oswego is 15 minutes north. See Trip 36.

38 | Wharton State Forest— Batsto Lake

This lake offers pine, oak, and white cedar woods; bogs; waterfowl; beaver; turtles; eagles; ospreys; and wild iris.

Location: Pleasant Mills, NJ
Maps: *New Jersey Atlas and Gazetteer*, Map 64; USGS Batsto
Area: 40 acres
Time: 1.0 hour
Conditions: Depth average 4 feet with bog and marsh areas
Development: Remote
Information: Wharton State Forest (Batsto office at Batsto Village), 4110 Nesco Road, Hammonton, NJ 08037; 609-561-0024.
Camping: Bodine Field primitive campground, 25 minutes east. Turtle Run Campground, 20 minutes east. See Appendix A.
Take Note: Electric motorboats only
Outfitter: Bel Haven Canoes and Kayaks, 1227 Route 542, Green Bank, NJ 08215; 800-445-0953.

GETTING THERE

To Batsto Lake launch: From Route 30, drive 6.5 miles on Route 542 East to where the road bends sharply to the right. At the bend you will see the wood split-rail fence that surrounds Batsto Historical Village. Drive straight into the sandy clearing to the left of the fence and follow the sand road 0.3 mile to the launch. Part of the drive parallels the wood fence. You'll find parking for about eight cars. *GPS coordinates*: 39°38.805′ N, 74°39.197′ W.

   To Batsto Village visitor center: Drive 0.6 mile past the sand road to Batsto Lake launch, turn left at the Batsto Village sign and drive 0.3 mile to the village entrance road on your left. *GPS coordinates*: 39°38.636′ N, 74°38.808′ W.

WHAT YOU'LL SEE

At more than 100,000 acres, Wharton State Forest is *huge*. If you look at a map of New Jersey, you'll notice a big green circular area with very few roads in the middle of the southern part of the state. That's Wharton State Forest. Nestled in Wharton State Forest in the heart of the Pine Barrens along Route 542, Batsto Historical Village offers a look at eighteenth- and nineteenth-century living when the village boomed with more than 200 residents. A dam was built in

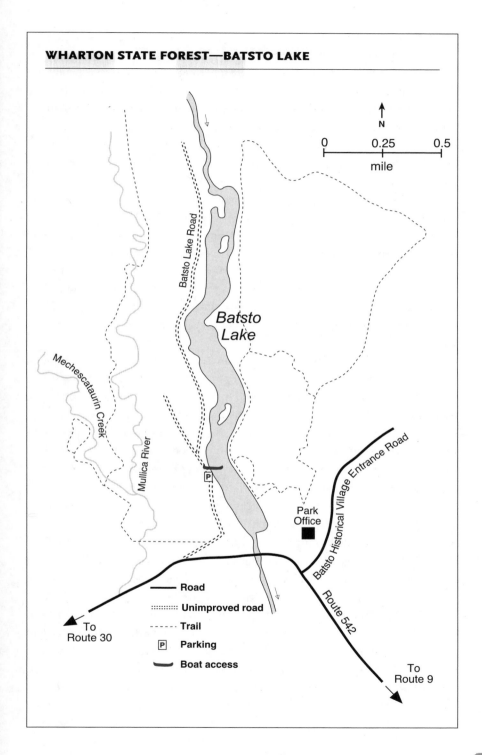

WHARTON STATE FOREST—BATSTO LAKE

Batsto Lake

Batsto Lake Road

Mechescataurin Creek

Mullica River

P

Park Office

Batsto Historical Village Entrance Road

Route 542

To Route 30

To Route 9

0   0.25   0.5
mile

N

	Road
	Unimproved road
	Trail
P	Parking
	Boat access

1765 along the Batsto River, creating the present-day lake and bogs, to provide power to operate a blast furnace for the production of iron—the first commercial operation at Batsto. Bog iron ore begins to form when vegetative matter decays and settles in soils containing high amounts of soluble iron. The ensuing chemical reaction brings the iron in solution to the surface, where it oxidizes upon contact with air. The heavier oxidized iron then settles to the bottom as a reddish-brown scum or sludge, cementing together bits of sand and gravel, and then hardening to produce ironstone, or bog iron, in a process that takes about 30 years.

Surrounding forests provided the wood that was converted to charcoal to fuel the furnaces. Those furnaces then produced the iron, which was used to make kitchenware items such as pots, stoves, and utensils. The metal was in particular demand for the production of cannons and cannonballs during the French and Indian War and American Revolution. In the mid-nineteenth century, large deposits of coal in Pennsylvania proved more efficient to burn than charcoal. The discovery of better iron ore deposits in the western United States and the depletion of local bog iron beds forced the collapse of most ironwork furnaces in New Jersey.

Furnaces such as that in Batsto were then used to produce glass, even though a number of glass factories were already operating in southern New Jersey. The plentiful sand in the state's southern region is composed primarily of silica, the basic ingredient in glass. Supposedly, the towns of Green Bank and Crowleytown produced a green glass from which the original mason jars were made. Both of these towns are located within 4.0 miles of Batsto Historical Village eastward along Route 542. A few remnants of old foundations on sandy back roads are all that remain of their furnace operations.

The launch site to Batsto Lake is on its southwestern end just outside the limits of Batsto Village. To the right of the launch will be a small dam and a few park buildings belonging to the village. You can paddle around there, but it is illegal to land on the property: signs are posted to that effect. To your left (north) it may look like the lake is very small and ends where the land juts out prominently, but paddle up the eastern edge and the larger portion of the lake will come into view. Two sandy beaches on the western shore of the northern end make great places to stop for lunch or just get out and stretch.

The first thing you may notice is the color of the water, a deep tea color typical of the Pine Barrens. Natural tannins and acids leached from cedar trees, coupled with the naturally high iron content of surrounding soils, stain the water this deep reddish-brown. It may also leave a slight stain at the waterline

Friends enjoy the scenery and wildlife on the pristine Batsto Lake.

on your boat, which is easily washed off. Lake depths generally average 3 to 6 feet, with slightly deeper waters where the river channel cuts through.

Around the lake you'll find a wide variety of dry upland and aquatic vegetation typical of the Pine Barrens. Oak and pine dominate the forest on the western and southern sides, along with a sprinkling of holly, tupelo, and sassafras. Red maple, swamp magnolia, sweet gum, and white cedar dominate in moist, low-lying areas. Swamp magnolias grace the landscape with large white blossoms that scent the air lightly from May through early July. The long, slender racemes of white flowers on sweet pepperbush release a refreshing fragrance detectable from 50 feet away. In fall, crimson leaves of red maple join the vivid yellow, orange, and red-rust of sweet gums to provide a delightful contrast to the deep green cedar and pine. Mountain and sheep laurel, huckleberry, wild blueberry, sweet pepperbush, and chokeberry fill the understory. A great treat while paddling late June through early August is to scout the shoreline for blueberry bushes, which are plentiful. Wild blueberries are smaller than their cultivated counterparts, but much sweeter. Along the banks in late summer and fall, look for the matlike growth of wild cranberries, whose yellow-green berries start turning bright red in late September.

PINE BARRENS TREE FROG

Occurring nowhere else in New Jersey outside the Pine Barrens, the tree frogs' chorus fills the air on late spring evenings during breeding season. They inhabit shallow pools in sphagnum bogs, backwater and slow-moving streams, cranberry bogs, and cedar swamps. Requiring acidic environments, the tree frog habitat is susceptible to any human infringement that raises the level of pH or decreases the water table. Listed as a threatened species, preservation of their specific wetland habitat is crucial for survival. Only a few disjunct populations have been found in the acidic bogs of the Carolinas, Georgia, and western Florida.

Lavender to plum stripes bordered by white creates a striking contrast against the rich emerald green body of this inch-and-a-half beauty. Bright yellow to orange colors the concealed surfaces of the legs. As with other tree frogs, their long webbed toes end in adhesive discs that enable them to cling to twigs and bark. Insects and other invertebrates found in moist environments constitute their main diet. Males produce the nasally *quonk-quonk-quonk* sound through vocal sacks that inflate like a balloon.

Though heard in vast numbers, they are difficult to find unless you patiently, and very quietly, follow the call to its source. Breeding and egg laying take place during May and June with the larvae metamorphosing into adults by July and early August. Due to their secretive lives, little is know about their behavior outside of the breeding season.

The northern section of the lake, particularly on the western side, becomes a shallow, swamplike environment. Here you want to paddle slowly or sit quietly, waiting for birds to come to you. Cedar becomes more prominent, requiring moist or sodden soils. Fragrant white waterlilies and yellow pond lilies carpet the lake's surface in its coves, and its blue-purple spikes of flowers poke up from the arrow-shaped leaves of the pickerelweed.

An abundant population of painted turtles, some of them quite large, sun themselves on fallen limbs and cedar stumps. Snapping turtles are common but rarely seen since they spend most of their time underwater. A number of beaver huts dot the length of Batsto River. The southernmost one can be seen from the north end of the lake.

Due to the high acidity and iron content of the water and its low nutrient level, fish and amphibian diversity is limited. Chain and redfin pickerel and yellow and brown bullheads (catfish) are about the only species fished for in this lake. The small blackbanded sunfish, with its striking black and white bands and angular body shape, is the most common species of the Pine Barrens.

If you would like to get in a little hiking, the 1.8-mile Tom's Pond Trail and the 9.5-mile Mullica River Trail start in the large sand area immediately off Route 542 on the way to the launch. Three additional trails, from 1.0 to 4.0 miles in length, start and end at the visitor center. Parts of two of those trails are also part of the 50-mile Batona Trail, which starts at Bass River State Forest and ends at Lebanon State Forest. For a larger and more detailed map, stop in at the Batsto office. Be prepared for ticks while hiking, and check yourself frequently. Read the Wildlife section in the Front Matter for more information about ticks. All trails are easy.

Mullica River is 5 minutes southeast. See Trip 39. Harrisville Pond and Lake Oswego are 30 minutes north. See Trips 37 and 36, respectively. Camp at Bodine Field and paddle Harrisville Pond and Lake Oswego the next day. Atsion Lake is 25 minutes northwest. See Trip 35.

39 | Mullica River

You'll find pine, oak, and white cedar woods; bogs; waterfowl; beaver; turtles; eagles; ospreys; and wild iris on this Pine Barrens river.

Location: Pleasant Mills, NJ
Maps: *New Jersey Atlas and Gazetteer*, Map 64; USGS Batsto
Area: Up to 7.5 miles round-trip
Time: 3.0–4.0 hours
Conditions: Depth average 6 feet
Development: Rural
Information: Wharton State Forest (Batsto office at Batsto Village), 4110 Nesco Road, Hammonton, NJ 08037; 609-561-0024.
Camping: Bodine Field primitive campground, 25 minutes east. Turtle Run Campground, 20 minutes east. See Appendix A.
Take Note: Motorboats on the first half-mile
Outfitter: Bel Haven Canoes and Kayaks, 1227 Route 542, Green Bank, NJ 08215; 800-445-0953.

GETTING THERE

The canoe- and kayak-friendly launch: From Route 30, drive 8.5 miles on Route 542 East. At that point the Mullica River will be directly in front of you. There will be a large sand parking area and informal sand beach launch. You will pass Batsto Historical Village and the entrance to Batsto Lake along the way. You'll find parking for about ten to twelve cars. *GPS coordinates*: 39°37.590′ N, 74°37.553′ W.

To Crowley's Landing launch: Crowley's Landing, another 0.4 mile east on Route 542, is another option, but it's a concrete ramp that is heavily used by personal watercraft and motorboats and thus can be very crowded on summer weekends. Restrooms located here are open seasonally. You'll find parking for about 40 cars. *GPS coordinates*: 39°37.587′ N, 74°37.160′ W.

WHAT YOU'LL SEE

This stretch of the pristine upper Mullica River is a favorite with paddlers from central and southern New Jersey as well as southeastern Pennsylvania. When paddlers talk about heading to "The Pines" to paddle a river, they're referring to the Pine Barrens of southern New Jersey, and most likely the Mullica River.

MULLICA RIVER

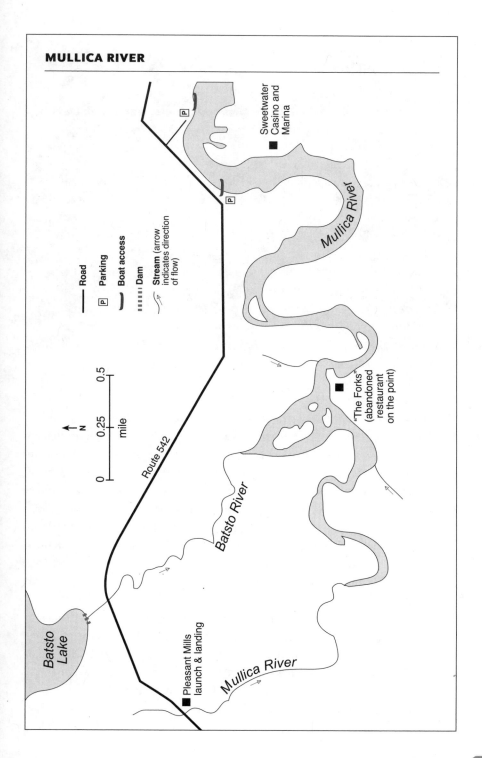

Kayakers explore coves and crannies along the gentle waters of the Mullica River.

The headwaters start in Berlin, New Jersey, 19.5 miles northwest of the launch. On its way here, a number of smaller watersheds drain into the river, including the Batsto River, Atsion River, Sleeper Branch, Nescochague Creek, and Hammonton Creek. A number of other streams drain into the river downstream, the larger of which are the Wading River, Bass River, and Nacote Creek.

A word about channel markers: Posts planted in the river with either a green square or a red triangle are channel markers and denote the deepest water. You'll want to stay close to the channel, but not in it just in case a small motorboat is going up or down the river. In some areas, the river becomes shallow quickly once outside the marked channel, but there is enough water for canoes and kayaks. Although this portion of the river is still tidal for half of the trip upstream, the flow is minimal and suitable for novices.

Paddling right (upstream) from the launch, you'll notice a large marina and restaurant a quarter-mile ahead, the Sweetwater Casino Restaurant and Marina. Beyond that point you may encounter a few small powerboats, although I paddle here frequently and have never encountered more than two or three, and most of the time I don't see any. Across from the marina is a large marsh area. Give it a 20-foot berth because it becomes shallow quickly and has numerous cedar stumps close to the surface at low tide. Marsh birds, ducks, and geese are common here and you might spot a muskrat in the water around the denser grass stands. Around the first bend, thick stands of white cedar trees interspersed with oak and pine woods give the air a nice, clean smell. Around the next bend there will be a marshy area on the right where egrets and herons are commonly seen. It's technically an island, but the channel between it and the mainland is too shallow and narrow to allow passage even at high tide.

At the next bend, you will come to an abandoned restaurant and long storage barn that sit on the peninsula-like tip. The restaurant was called The Forks because it is where the Batsto River on the right forks off from the Mullica River. The entrance to the Batsto River is wide, with a large island in the middle. This is a beautiful, pristine area to explore with abundant birdlife and colorful swamp and bog flowers. Keep an eye on the sky for eagles and ospreys, a number of which are known to have nests in the area. You can circumnavigate the island before continuing upstream on the Mullica River, or you can paddle past the island and upstream on the Batsto River to the dam at the bottom of Batsto Lake. There's a small landing on the east side of the island to stop for lunch, but a better location is a sand beach less than a quarter-mile past the island with a much larger beach and a few logs to sit on. The Batsto River is an important spawning ground for herring and hickory shad that turn a few of the small feeder streams white with frenzied spawning activity in spring.

Continuing upstream on the Mullica River from The Forks, only the left side of the river will have houses, and they will become fewer and farther between quickly. Downed trees and thick limbs jutting out of the water are prime spots for basking turtles. River otters are uncommon, but they are usually seen here at least a couple of times each year. The river will become quite twisty, with numerous downfalls and overhanging trees to paddle under or around. Since this river is well used on weekends by a local livery service, a clear passageway is always maintained.

The turnaround point for the trip will be at the boat launch at Pleasant Mills, about 200 feet south of the Route 542 bridge. It becomes tougher to paddle upstream much farther because of swifter moving water and low overhangs. If you haven't stopped for lunch yet, use this landing before heading back downstream. While many canoeists or kayakers make a round-trip from where you launched, another option is available if two or more people are paddling. Leave one car at the original launch and launch from Pleasant Mills for a leisurely one-way trip downstream. The launch is located 0.15 mile east of the junction of Route 542 and Pleasant Mills Road. Although a leisurely one-way paddle will take 2 hours, not counting a lunch stop, the launches are only a 5-minute drive from each other because the river is very serpentine. *GPS coordinates for the Pleasant Mills launch on Route 542*: 39°38.439′ N, 74°39.513′ W.

A trip up the Mullica River from the launch near Crowley's Landing to the launch at Pleasant Mills is 3.6 miles one-way. If you circumnavigate the island at the mouth of the Batsto River, add another 0.6 mile. A paddle up the Batsto River from the Mullica River is about 1.3 miles. There's so much wildlife and beautiful scenery here that it will take a few trips to see it all.

Hiking trails are available at Batsto Lake, 5 minutes northwest. See Trip 38. Both Lake Oswego and Harrisville Pond are 15 minutes north. See Trips 36 and 37, respectively.

40 | Manahawkin Impoundment and Bridge to Nowhere

Enjoy abundant birdlife, ospreys, and hawks in the salt and brackish water marshlands here.

Location: Manahawkin, NJ
Maps: *New Jersey Atlas and Gazetteer*, Map 59; USGS West Creek
Area: Manahawkin Impoundments: 45 acres; Bridge to Nowhere: 5.0–6.0 miles
Time: Manahawkin Impoundments: 1.0 hour; Bridge to Nowhere: 3.0–4.0 hours
Conditions: Manahawkin Impoundments: depth average 4 feet; Bridge to Nowhere: 8–10 feet
Development: Rural/suburban
Information: New Jersey Division of Fish and Wildlife, Southern Region (Winslow WMA), 229 Blue Anchor Road, Sicklerville, NJ 08081; 856-629-0090.
Camping: Baker's Acres Campground, 10 minutes southwest. See Appendix A.
Take Note: Manahawkin Impoundment: electric motorboats only; Bridge to Nowhere: unlimited horsepower, but unusual for most of the trip

GETTING THERE
To Manahawkin Impoundment: From Route 72, drive north 0.1 mile on Route 9 to the Bay Avenue traffic light. One hundred feet north of Bay Avenue,

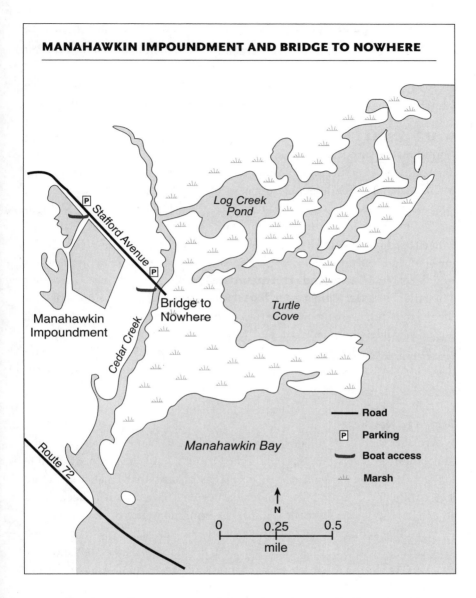

MANAHAWKIN IMPOUNDMENT AND BRIDGE TO NOWHERE

Log Creek Pond

Stafford Avenue

Bridge to Nowhere

Turtle Cove

Manahawkin Impoundment

Cedar Creek

Manahawkin Bay

Route 72

Road

P **Parking**

Boat access

Marsh

↑
N

0   0.25   0.5

mile

turn right onto Stafford Avenue and drive 2.0 miles to Hillard Boulevard. From there, Stafford Avenue continues straight as a hard-packed but rough sand road—go slow. Continue another 1.5 miles; the small launch to the impoundment will be on the right. The road widens slightly here for parking, which is casual. Park parallel to the road and close to roadside vegetation so other cars can pass easily. You'll find parking for two to three cars. *GPS coordinates*: 39°41.373′ N, 74°12.877′ W.

To the Bridge to Nowhere: Continue down Stafford Avenue another 0.6 mile to the end. A wooden bridge spans out over the channel 8 feet. Launch from the left side of the bridge, where you'll see a narrow path leading to the channel. You'll find parking for eight to ten cars. *GPS coordinates*: 39°40.997′ N, 74°12.429′ W.

WHAT YOU'LL SEE
Manahawkin Impoundment

Tall reeds and a smattering of aromatic bayberry bushes rim the shores around Manahawkin Impoundment in front of woods dominated by cedars, pines, and oaks. Marsh wrens, tough birds to spot, fill the air with their nervous, high-pitched twitter from inside dense phragmite stands. Raucous calls of the red-winged blackbird are heard throughout the marshes. Between the reeds and the lowland woods behind them, sweet gum and red maple take hold on the moist middle ground. Snowy and great white egrets often roost in trees and shrubs along the shore. Occasionally you'll see a black-crowned night heron—look for them 4 to 6 feet above the water surface in bushes. The impoundment is small, but makes a delightful side trip on the way to the Bridge to Nowhere. Swans and ducks swim on the waters, and cedar waxwings usually can be spotted on the dense clusters of cedar on the far end. If you don't visit the impoundment close to high tide, it may be too shallow to paddle.

Bridge to Nowhere

Where does the Bridge to Nowhere go? Just where its name implies; hence the funky moniker locals gave this part of the Edwin B. Forsythe National Wildlife Refuge. The bridge was built across Cedar Creek channel to the marsh, and there it ends. Situated far from inlets where tidal currents have minimal effect, this is an excellent spot to explore the salt marshes and backwaters of Barnegat Bay.

From the launch next to the bridge, paddle to your right (south) down the meandering channel leading to the bay. Keep the marshes on your left and paddle along, exploring the many small channels and coves for a variety of marsh birds and wading birds. In the sky above, look for ospreys frequently seen here. Snowy and great white egrets, ducks, geese, and sandpipers are abundant in the shallow waters along the banks, along with an occasional great blue heron. Black skimmers are a treat to see as they search for small fish by flying just above the surface of the water with their long lower bill skimming the surface.

Rounding the eastern tip, you'll enter a large cove. This is the only place where you may come in contact with motorboats, but if you stay close to the marshes, you're safe—it's too shallow for them. Continue to keep the marshes on your left as you explore more side channels and enjoy viewing wildlife. At the northwest corner of the large cove you're in, there is a channel into the next cove. Paddle through the small entrance, then around the cove to your left (west). Dip your paddle quietly so you don't alarm the wildlife and for a better chance of seeing them up close. When you're done paddling around the cove, continue to paddle through the channel into the next cove.

On the west side there will be a long, straight ditch that will take you back to the channel where you launched. Before paddling over there, take time to explore the whole cove. You'll see an exit on the east side that leads into more coves and into the bay, but if this is your first trip here, be cautious about venturing out and getting lost. After enjoying the scenery and wildlife, paddle over to the ditch on the west side. At the end of the ditch, turn left and return to the launch 0.5 mile away. If you wish to turn right and explore more of the main channel, you can follow it for about a half-mile before it becomes impassable due to the remnants of an old sand road.

No official trails are located here, but bird lovers often visit, spending most of their time along a quarter-mile stretch where the forest ends and the salt marshes begin. Park out of the way along the side of the road.For an additional trip nearby, visit Stafford Forge Ponds, 20 minutes west, or Bass River State Forest–Lake Absegami, 25 minutes southwest. See Trips 41 and 42. Visit Scott's Landing, 35 minutes south, for another paddle within the Edwin B. Forsythe National Wildlife Refuge or to learn more about the refuge. See Trip 49.

41 | Stafford Forge Wildlife Management Area— Stafford Forge Ponds

Geese, various species of duck, mute and tundra swans, migratory birds, wetland marsh birds, pheasant, muskrat, and more are yours to enjoy in these impoundments.

Location: Stafford Forge, NJ
Maps: DeLorme *New Jersey Atlas and Gazetteer*, Map 65; USGS West Creek
Area: Pond #1: 68 acres; Pond #2: 22 acres; Pond #3: 48 acres
Time: Pond #1: 1.0 hour; Pond #2: less than 1.0 hour; Pond #3: 1.0 hour
Conditions: Depth 4 feet average for all ponds

Development: Rural
Information: New Jersey Division of Fish and Wildlife, Southern Region (Winslow WMA), 229 Blue Anchor Road, Sicklerville, NJ 08081; 856-629-0090.
Camping: Sea Pirate Campground, 10 minutes south. See Appendix A.
Take Note: Electric motorboats only

GETTING THERE

From Route 72, drive south 3.7 miles on Route 9 and turn right onto Forge Road. Drive 1.9 miles and turn right onto the sand entrance road. Caution! Watch for what locals call "sugar sand"—a very soft sand known to swallow even tow trucks whole. Only a few small spots are on the main roads, but they are prevalent on other back roads, should you go exploring.

Pond #1: From the entrance, make an immediate left and drive 0.15 mile to the end. Put in anywhere on the sandy tip. You'll find parking for about fifteen cars. *GPS coordinates*: 39°40.131' N, 74°19.263' W.

Ponds #2 and #3: From the entrance, stay to your right and drive 0.1 mile, turn left and drive 0.6 mile, then turn left and drive 0.3 mile to the other end of the sand dike. Pond #3 will be on your right, pond #2 on your left. A hard-sand launch for pond #3 will be on your right. You'll find parking for about ten cars. *GPS coordinates*: 39°40.389' N, 74°19.783' W. To reach pond #2, turn left at the end of the dike, then drive 0.2 mile and launch from the sandy ramp. You'll find parking for about six cars. *GPS coordinates*: 39°40.228' N, 74°19.705' W.

WHAT YOU'LL SEE

Stafford Forge Wildlife Management Area has expanded tremendously over the years to its present size of over 17,000 acres, much of which is prime upland game bird country. There are four ponds, originally cranberry bogs, where countless herons, egrets, ducks, and other water birds inhabit the rich environment. Two of those ponds are good for paddling, and another is nice, but small. The fourth pond is usually too shallow to paddle, but is excellent for bird-watching and wildlife viewing. Electric outboards are permitted, though I've never seen one, and hunting is allowed during specific seasons.

Atlantic white cedar, sweet gum, and red maple dominate the scenery near the water, along with an occasional plush stand of phragmites and cattails. Typical pine barren forests of mixed-oak and pitch pine fill the surrounding area for miles. If you want solitude, this is it. Small coves created by inlet streams dot the southern and northern shores of pond #3, the largest and deepest of the

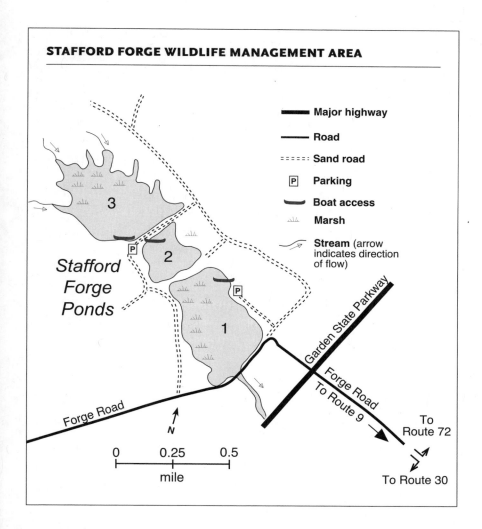

STAFFORD FORGE WILDLIFE MANAGEMENT AREA

Legend:

- ▬▬▬ **Major highway**
- ▬▬▬ **Road**
- ═════ **Sand road**
- P **Parking**
- ⌣ **Boat access**
- ⨿⨿ **Marsh**
- ↝ **Stream** (arrow indicates direction of flow)

3

2

1

Stafford Forge Ponds

Garden State Parkway

Forge Road
To Route 9

Forge Road

To Route 72

To Route 30

N

0   0.25   0.5
mile

Stafford Forge ponds. Since this is a hunting area, pay attention and you might spot quail or even pheasant.

Listen for the telltale *eep, eep* of ospreys that frequently fish these waters, especially in pond #1. If you do spot an osprey, keep an eye on it awhile—seeing one plunge into the water and come out with a fish in its talons is a rewarding experience. You may be lucky like I've been a few times and catch a photograph of one as it plunges into the water within 50 feet of you. If you have a waterproof camera, have it readily available for those opportunities. Great blue herons, great white egrets, and mallards are the more common water birds here, while blue jays, warblers, and grackles regularly inhabit the surrounding woods.

Tundra swans have been spotted here in March on their way from North Carolina and Virginia to the northern end of Alaska and Canada where they spend the summer breeding. Their snow-white bodies and distinct black bills make them easy to identify. Their call is very similar to the ubiquitous Canada geese. In contrast, mute swans are year-round residents in New Jersey and have a white body with a black face and stark orange bill. If you do hear them call, it's sort of a garbled *qwouk*. Painted and red-bellied turtles are everywhere.

Late summer and early fall are the prettiest months to visit, and the best as far as seeing migrating waterfowl. Fluffy phragmite heads laden with seed shimmer silvery-beige against a background of dark green cedar. Here and there, swamp-loving red cardinal flowers add strokes of vibrant red, and water grasses turn a deep gold to rust. Mulberry bushes become deep scarlet and sweet gum trees splash vibrant yellow, orange, and red around the ponds. Be aware that in an extreme drought year, the normally shallow 3-to-5-feet-deep waters can become nothing more than giant puddles.

For additional paddling, try Manahawkin Impoundments and Bridge to Nowhere, 20 minutes east. See Trip 40. Other sites are Bass River State Forest, 15 minutes southwest, and Scott's Landing, 25 minutes south. See Trips 42 and 49.

---

42 | Bass River State Forest— Lake Absegami

This Pinelands lake offers oak and pine woods, marshes, ospreys, waterfowl, and wading birds.

Location: New Gretna, NJ
Maps: DeLorme *New Jersey Atlas and Gazetteer*, Map 65; USGS New Gretna
Area: 63 acres
Time: 1.5 hours
Conditions: Depth average 8 feet
Development: Rural
Information: Bass River State Forest, 762 Stage Road, Tuckerton, NJ 08087; 609-296-1114; $5 weekday fee ($10 weekend) in-season.
Camping: On-site; call ahead to the park office or make reservations when you arrive.
Take Note: Electric motorboats only

BASS RIVER STATE FOREST—LAKE ABSEGAMI

Legend:
- Road
- Trail
- P Parking
- Boat access
- Picnic area
- Playground
- Cabin
- Campground
- Shelter
- Swimming beach
- Stream (arrow indicates direction of flow)
- Marsh

Lake Absegami

Boat Rental

Lake Access Road

Camping Area Access Road

To Route 654 (East Greenbush Road)

Booth ■ / ■ Park Office

Stage Road

To Tuckerton and Route 9

N

0 0.25 0.5
mile

GETTING THERE

From southbound Garden State Parkway, take Exit 52 immediately after the tollbooth. Turn right onto East Greenbush Road (Route 654) at the end of the ramp and drive 1.1 miles to the T-intersection (Stage Road, but there's no sign). Turn right and drive 0.9 mile to the entrance of Bass River State Forest on your left. After stopping at the booth (a fee is charged in summer), drive straight ahead to the sand boat launch road on your left. You'll find parking for about six cars. The park office is directly to your right after the tollbooth. From northbound Garden State Parkway, take Exit 50 (Route 9). The ramp will cross back over the parkway and place you on Route 9 north. Drive 1.9 miles, turn left onto East Greenbush Road, and drive 0.8 mile to the T-intersection. Continue as above. *GPS coordinates*: 39°37.663′ N, 74°25.688′ W.

These paddlers are having fun racing each other back to the beach.

WHAT YOU'LL SEE

This 18,000-acre forest was the first forest acquired by the state in 1905 for public use and recreation. With its proximity to the Garden State Parkway, this park is a very popular swimming and camping spot in summer. Playgrounds are located at the swimming beach and within the camping area. Weekdays are relatively quiet, but summer weekends in July and August can be hectic. The rest of the time you have the lake almost to yourself.

The 67-acre body of water offers cedar swamps, bogs, and pine and mixed-oak forests surrounding the tea-colored waters typical of the Pine Barrens. Mosey in and out of the coves as you wind your way around the lake with cedar and pine scents filling the air. Swamp magnolia lightly scents the air in late spring and early summer while sweet pepperbush found in a few small areas around the lake add a perfumed scent in midsummer. Warblers, blue jays, cardinals, kingbirds, eastern pewees, and other songbirds add to the nature experience. The raucous call of the blue jay can be heard echoing through the woods almost any time of the day.

While you're at the park, you may camp in a tent, lean-to, or trailer within the pine-scented woodlands. The park also rents rustic cabins, a few of which are lakeside. Listen for the soft hoots of owls if you camp here. Consider scheduling your trip around a full moon cycle to enjoy a pleasant moonlight paddle before retiring.

The park has eight easy walking trails from 1.0 to 3.2 miles. All trails start at the second parking lot at the beach. A trail brochure is available at the entrance booth.

Bass River State Forest is very close to the town of Leeds, where the legendary Jersey Devil is said to have been born. If you're from south or central Jersey, you grew up with the story of this creature that supposedly lives in the Pine Barrens. Although origins of the creature date back to the Lenni-Lenape people, who called the Pine Barrens "popuessing," meaning "place of the dragon," the following is the most accepted origin: According to the legend, Mother Leeds had twelve children and, after giving birth to her thirteenth child, said that if she had another, it would be the devil. In 1735, Mother Leeds was in labor on a stormy night. Gathered around her were her friends. Mother Leeds was supposedly a witch and the child's father was the devil himself. The child was born normal but then changed to a creature with hooves, a horse's head, bat wings, and a forked tail. It growled and screamed, then killed the midwife before flying up the chimney. It circled the village and headed toward the pines. In 1740 a clergy exorcised the devil for 100 years and it wasn't seen again until 1890.

For other nearby paddling opportunities, visit Harrisville Pond, 15 minutes northeast, or Scott's Landing at Forsythe Wildlife Refuge, 20 minutes south. See Trips 37 and 49.

43 | D.O.D. Ponds Wildlife Management Area

Highlights around these ponds include abundant waterfowl and song birds, lots of coves, passageways, islands, and beavers.

Location: Penns Grove, NJ
Maps: DeLorme *New Jersey Atlas and Gazetteer*, Map 53; USGS Penns Grove
Area: 120 acres
Time: 2.0–3.0 hours
Conditions: Depth average 15 feet
Development: Rural
Information: New Jersey Division of Fish and Wildlife, Southern Region (Winslow Wildlife Management Area), 220 Blue Anchor Road, Sicklerville, NJ 08081; 856-629-0090.

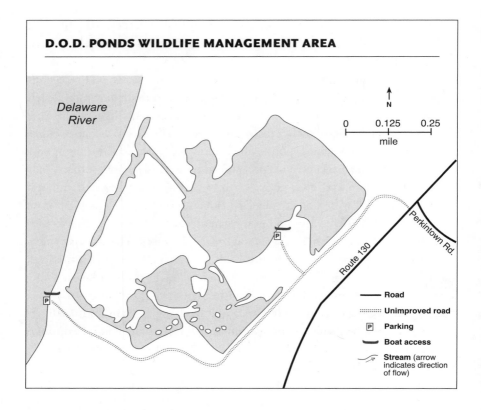

D.O.D. PONDS WILDLIFE MANAGEMENT AREA

Delaware River

N

0   0.125   0.25
mile

Road

Unimproved road

P **Parking**

Boat access

Stream (arrow indicates direction of flow)

Route 130

Perkintown Rd.

Camping: Four Season Family Campground, 25 minutes southeast. See Appendix A.

Take Note: Electric motorboats only

GETTING THERE

From the junction of Routes 130 and 48, drive 1.8 miles on Route 130 North, then turn left onto South Road into the wildlife management area. Turn left after 300 feet and follow the sand road for 0.3 mile, then turn right and drive 0.1 mile. The parking area and launch will be to your right. You'll find parking for 30 cars. *GPS coordinates*: 39°44.922′ N, 75°27.328′ W.

WHAT YOU'LL SEE

I was totally delighted to explore these quiet 120 acres that absolutely team with wildlife. They're known as the D.O.D. Ponds, formerly used by the Department of Defense and now leased by New Jersey Fish and Wildlife for management purposes. The ponds sit inside a narrow band of land separating them from

Beautiful clouds reflect off these still waters.

the Delaware River. The only downside was an unsightly heap of trash about 400 feet past the entrance. Since this is not a state or county park, there are no regular patrols to keep out those who litter. Perhaps a local group will help clean up the area soon. It's too lovely a site and too valuable a wildlife resource to let it go. With so many islands, channels, and passageways to explore, you'll think it's twice the size.

Stands of phragmites, thick in places, sway with a light breeze. Behind them, dense wetland shrubs and trees provide habitats for birds. Along the western shores is a 10-foot hill covered with trees and shrubs—a remnant of when these ponds were contained (dammed). A canal about 50 feet wide rings the perimeter on the west and south side. Beavers love it here. There's rarely a time when they are not seen or heard, especially if one paddles in early morning or before dusk when they're most active.

The launch is located on the largest of the ponds. Paddle right (north) from the launch, around the thin peninsula thick with reeds and into the cove where wrens and red-winged blackbirds are common sights. Other birds normally seen here are swans, swallows, warblers, vireos, egrets, and herons. Paddle along the north shoreline and when you get to the northeast corner and around the small peninsula directly west of the launch, there will be an interesting little cove and then a straight ditch about 20 feet in width that leads to the western canal. The canal is 0.4 mile in length, with birds to watch all along the way.

Head back out and into the main pond, paddling along the west side. A passageway leads into another pond, and this one has quite a number of islands and nooks to explore. Waterfowl are more abundant here, perhaps because it's more secluded. Turtles slide off logs into the water when you get too close. In the southwest corner, there's a small, 8-foot-wide passage into yet another pond and the southern canal. This area is where the most beaver spottings and lodges have been seen. Look for their lodges in the dense reeds lining canals and channels. To the east are a couple of islands. To the west is a passageway into the south canal, which cradles the southwest corner.

I paddled the ponds one day near dusk. As the sun started to set and birds came out for their final feeding for the day, the pond waters stilled to glass and perfectly reflected the brilliant warm yellows, oranges, and reds from the sky upon the waters. It was mesmerizing, and for a moment I couldn't tell what was sky and what was water. I headed over to the launch a few hundred feet away as an indigo sky started pulling its blanket over the land. What an amazing paddle.

Additional trips nearby include Stewart Lake, 25 minutes northeast, and Mannington Meadows, 20 minutes south. See Trips 34 and 44, respectively. If you camp at Four Seasons Campground, you can visit Mannington Meadows, 20 minutes west of the campground, the next day.

44 | Mannington Meadows

You'll enjoy watching muskrat, waterfowl, shorebirds, wading birds, bald eagles, ospreys, and turtles in these brackish waters.

Location: Pennsville, NJ
Maps: DeLorme *New Jersey Atlas and Gazetteer*, Maps 60 and 61; USGS Salem and Penns Grove
Area: 2,000-plus acres
Time: 4.0–5.0 hours
Conditions: Depth average 6 feet
Development: Rural

Information: Supawna Meadows National Wildlife Refuge, 229 Lighthouse Road, Salem, NJ 08079; 609-935-1487.

Camping: Four Season Family Campground, 30 minutes east. See Appendix A.

Take Note: Motorboats; tidal brackish water marsh

GETTING THERE

From Route 49 on the southeast end of Pennsville, drive north on Route 551 (Hook Road) for 2.0 miles. Turn right onto East Pittsfield Street, drive 0.8 mile to the boat launch, and park at the end of the road. The blacktop will stop about halfway to the end, with the rest of the road being hard-packed sand and gravel. You'll find parking for about twenty cars.

From the north, take I-295 or the New Jersey Turnpike south. The two highways come together for a short span right before the Delaware Memorial Bridge. Follow signs for the Pennsville/Salem/Last Exit Before Toll ramp. Drive 0.3 mile and turn left, following signs that read, Hook Road/40 East to Tpk and Atlantic City Expy. Drive 0.5 mile, following the signs to Hook Road. The road will bend to the right and put you onto Hook Road. Drive for 1.2 miles, turn left onto East Pittsfield Street, and continue for 0.8 mile to the launch. *GPS coordinates*: 39°38.418′ N, 75°28.818′ W.

WHAT YOU'LL SEE

Neither a lake nor a bay, Mannington Meadows' vast expanse of shallow, brackish waters can provide days of paddling enjoyment for the nature lover, especially the birder. Situated close to the Delaware River, these waters are slightly tidal but still enjoyable for the novice paddler. Although motorboats are found in the deeper channels, the majority of boats found in the shallower channels winding around the network of islands are either electric motors or low horsepower gas motors puttering around slowly seeking the elusive "best spot" for fishing. I love this paddle for its many bird-watching and photographic opportunities. The best time to paddle for optimal bird-watching is early morning or late in the afternoon, when birds tend to feed most. These are also good hours for the chorus of frogs to be heard over the waters.

A winding network of narrow channels at the mouth of the Salem River snakes its way around tiny islands and buffers most of the tidal current effect. You'll notice as the day wears on a slightly higher or lower waterline along the shores. With more than 3,000 acres in this low-lying coastal plain, you will probably need to push yourself off a sandbar or two when the tide is out, particularly in the narrower side channels. Deeper waters lie along the eastern shoreline, where the Salem River has cut a deep channel.

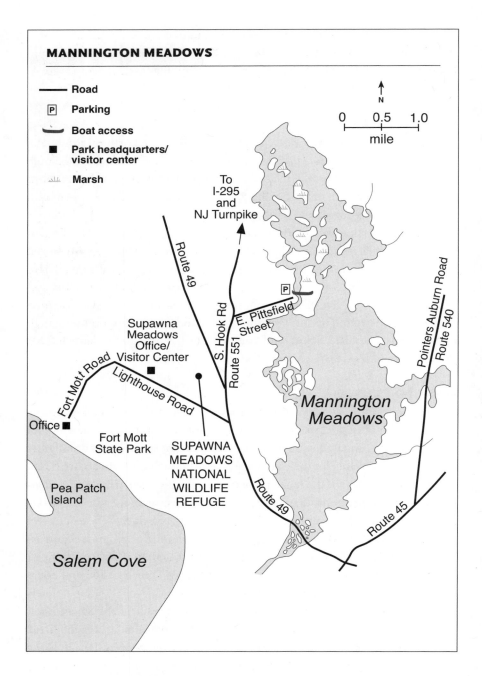

MANNINGTON MEADOWS

- ——— Road
- [P] Parking
- Boat access
- ■ Park headquarters/ visitor center
- Marsh

N

0   0.5   1.0
mile

To
I-295
and
NJ Turnpike

Route 49

Route 551

S. Hook Rd

[P]

E. Pittsfield
Street

Pointers Auburn Road

Route 540

Supawna
Meadows
Office/
Visitor Center

Fort Mott Road

Lighthouse Road

Mannington
Meadows

Office ■

Fort Mott
State Park

SUPAWNA
MEADOWS
NATIONAL
WILDLIFE
REFUGE

Route 49

Route 45

Pea Patch
Island

Salem Cove

On one of my early morning paddling trips, it seemed the different species and families of birds had staked out claims on different sections of the water. The northwestern channels were primarily occupied by herons and egrets, the

Reeds line this waterway that leads to the broad waters of Mannington Meadows.

northeastern waters were duck central, swans swam along the extreme northern edges, and the more open southwestern area was filled with gulls, sandpipers, and other shorebirds. Marsh wrens and red-winged blackbirds flitted in and out of the phragmites lining the shores while diamondback terrapins and other turtles basked on exposed logs throughout the edges of the meadows. Look overhead for ospreys, vultures, hawks, and kestrels. I'm not usually a bird counter, but one day I counted 26 species in a 3-hour span as I meandered slowly through the waters.

On another trip to the meadows, I drove into the launch area and noticed a brown animal in the low grass by the phragmites edging the water. At first I thought it might be a rat, but it was too block-shaped and didn't scurry away. I grabbed my camera, turned it on, quietly opened the car door, and slowly walked toward the animal. As I got closer, I realized it was a baby muskrat. It probably didn't move simply because it was too frightened to know what to do. I took a picture and kept stealthily moving closer to get another. The muskrat let me get to within 3 feet before it decided to scurry off into the dense cover of phragmites.

For another local paddle, head to the D.O.D. Ponds, 20 minutes north. See Trip 43.

45 | Scotland Run Park— Wilson Lake

This lake offers waterfowl, turtles, and hawks along a pleasurable paddling route.

Location: Clayton, NJ
Maps: DeLorme *New Jersey Atlas and Gazetteer*, Map 62; USGS Pitman East
Area: 58 acres
Time: 1.0 hour
Conditions: Depth average 6 feet
Development: Rural
Information: Scotland Run Park, 980 Academy Street, Clayton, NJ 08322; 856-881-0845.
Camping: Parvin State Park, 30 minutes south. Hospitality Creek Campground, 20 minutes southeast. See Appendix A.
Take Note: Electric motorboats only

GETTING THERE

From Route 322 and Delsea Drive in Glassboro, drive east 2.9 miles on Route 322, turn right onto Fries Mill Road, and drive 2.35 miles to the entrance for the boat launch on your left. The sign is small and the road is easy to miss; keep alert as you near. Follow the signs to the boat launch. Portable toilets are located at the boat launch parking lot. You'll find parking for about 40 cars. *GPS coordinates for the entrance road to the launch*: 39°39.653′ N, 75°03.274′ W.

To Wilson Lake Recreation Area: Drive 0.3 mile south on Fries Mill Road from the boat launch entrance and turn left on Academy Street. The park entrance will be on your left. You'll find parking for 50 cars. *GPS coordinates*: 39°39.367′ N, 75°03.132′ W.

WHAT YOU'LL SEE

Scotland Run Park on the southeast side of Clayton contains 940 acres of natural woodlands, a nature center, and Wilson Lake. A small swimming beach with shaded picnic tables, a playground, and restrooms occupies 300 feet of shoreline near the dam on the southwest end. Next to the concrete boat ramp, a fishing pier juts into the lake about 25 feet. Only electric motorboats are allowed, which makes for a quiet paddle. The majority of anglers cast their lines into the deeper waters near the dam for pickerel and smallmouth bass.

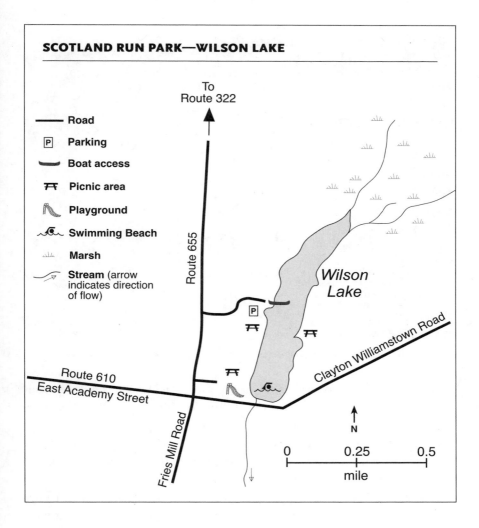

SCOTLAND RUN PARK—WILSON LAKE

To
Route 322

Route 655

Wilson
Lake

— **Road**

P **Parking**

⌣ **Boat access**

🏓 **Picnic area**

🛝 **Playground**

🏊 **Swimming Beach**

⌖ **Marsh**

↘ **Stream** (arrow
indicates direction
of flow)

Clayton Williamstown Road

Route 610
East Academy Street

Fries Mill Road

N

0   0.25   0.5
mile

Most of the waters are shallow, averaging 4 feet, with deeper waters in the channel closer to the southern shore. Oak, pine, maple, and beech comprise the upland woods with cedar and red maple along the water's edge. Where aquatic vegetation approaches the surface, juvenile fish and a few species of turtles can be observed darting in and out of their protective environment. From the boat launch, paddle across the lake before turning left (north) if lake levels are low. The water is deepest on that side because of the channel created by Scotland Run, a small creek that feeds into the lake. On the northern end of the lake, where conditions are more swamplike, cedar, magnolia, sweet gum, pickerelweed, and other water-loving flora dominate the landscape. This area is shared with the lake's turtle and frog population. Boglike coves and stump-

A killdeer struts casually along the coarse sand beach near a preening Canada goose.

strewn inlets create a perfect habitat for birds, deer, and raccoons. An abundant hawk population almost guarantees you'll see one while paddling. The most likely is the broad-winged hawk.

On one visit to the lake I decided to stretch my legs and take a little walk on the beach since the park was fairly empty. A killdeer was feeding along the edge of the beach at the waterline. What a treat!

There's no official trail map yet (they're working on it) but a narrow hiking trail starts at the boat ramp along the north shore of the lakes and continues for 0.5 mile. The longer trail lies along the southern shore and is accessible by foot or by landing on the park's small beach.

For another paddle the same day, try Malaga Lake, 20 minutes south, or Parvin State Park, 35 minutes south. See Trips 46 and 47.

46 | Malaga Lake

Swans, waterfowl, abundant songbirds, freshwater cedar bogs, and marshes make this lake an enjoyable paddle.

Location: Malaga, NJ
Maps: DeLorme *New Jersey Atlas and Gazetteer*, Map 62; USGS Newfield
Area: 105 acres
Time: 2.0–2.5 hours
Conditions: Depth average 5 feet
Development: Suburban
Information: Franklin Township, 1571 Delsea Drive, Franklinville, NJ 08322; 856-694-1234.
Camping: Parvin State Park, 25 minutes southwest. See Appendix A.
Take Note: Electric motorboats only

GETTING THERE

From Route 55 south, take Exit 39A and merge onto Route 40 East/Harding Highway. Drive 0.6 mile, then make a sharp left onto Oak Avenue and drive 0.3 mile. Turn right onto Malaga Lake Boulevard and drive 0.2 mile to the parking area and launch at the south end. You'll find parking for twenty cars. *GPS coordinates*: 39°34.827′ N, 75°03.615′ W.

From Route 55 north, take Exit 39B and continue as above.

WHAT YOU'LL SEE

This tea-colored cedar lake is fairly shallow, but abundant wildlife and unusual plant life make this a rewarding paddle. From the launch, paddle right (south) into the body of the lake. The wide border of woods is interesting and good for fishing. If you fish, cast your line for pickerel, smallmouth bass, carp, and perch. I've never failed to see swans on the lake here, and they seem to prefer this side of the lake in addition to the northern end. You won't find many houses until you get to the southern end, which can be noisy because busy Route 40 borders the lake. Pass around the south end and paddle up the east shoreline, where you'll find a nice cove dotted with an island in the center.

A little beyond the cove is a swimming beach and recreation area, which can be noisy on hot summer weekends. The facilities are posted "for township

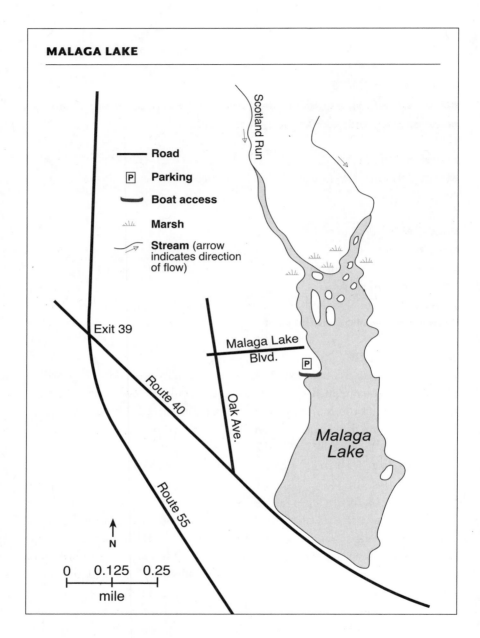

MALAGA LAKE

Road
P Parking
Boat access
Marsh
Stream (arrow indicates direction of flow)

Scotland Run

Exit 39

Malaga Lake Blvd.

Route 40

Oak Ave.

Malaga Lake

Route 55

N

0   0.125   0.25
mile

residents only." North of the recreation area is the best part of the trip, in my opinion, because it's where I've always seen abundant wildlife. The lake narrows and forks into streamlets that wind their way around cedar hammocks and tiny sand islands where grasses and small marsh bushes gain a foothold. Explore the

Morning mist rises off the waters of Malaga Lake near Scotland Run.

northeast corner, where you might spot great white and snowy egrets stalking the shallow waters around a number of islands. Great blue herons are usually seen closer to the northwestern edges where tall trees along the shore provide more background camouflage. The raucous calls of red-winged blackbirds are heard throughout this area. Dense cedar stands make paddling in fall and early spring a "green" experience while deciduous trees are bare. Turtles are very abundant, occupying many stumps and logs sticking out of the water. Bullfrogs often bellow back and forth in the early morning and just after sunset.

If you're paddling casually, you'll only experience a little bump and shift of your boat a few inches one way or the other when you encounter an underwater cedar stump. Look for the open channel in the northeast corner. That's the entrance to Scotland Run, a creek that you can follow upstream for a half-mile or longer, depending on water levels. Along the way you'll see a variety of wetland and lowland birds, cedars woods, mountain and sheep laurels, swamp magnolia, wild irises, and a variety of wetland wildflowers. Look for telltale signs of beaver activity—tree stumps about a foot above ground with conical tops. Although I've never seen a lodge, I have seen the stumps indicative of their presence.

For additional paddling nearby, visit Parvin State Park, 25 minutes southwest, or Wilson Lake, 20 minutes north. See Trips 47 and 45, respectively.

PITCHER PLANT

The common name of this carnivorous plant is derived from the unusual shape of the leaf and its capacity to hold water. Sandy wetland soils are high in iron but low in essential nitrogen and other essential nutrients. Unusual plants such as pitchers and sundews have developed insect-eating adaptations to augment the inadequate supply of nitrogen in poor soil conditions. The hollow leaves of pitcher plants retain water and digestive juices that first lure, then kill and slowly absorb unwary insects. Internal hairs point downward to hinder the insect's escape. The plant's diet consists of flies, moths, gnats, ants, bees, small butterflies, and even an occasional tiny frog. Leaves vary from yellow-green to deep purple with striking dark red-purple veins.

While they can grow to 17 inches, most plants you find will range between 6 and 12 inches. Leaves develop each year from stems that emerge from underground rhizomes and remain evergreen, making them easier to find during winter months. Reproduction is typically by seed with bees as the main pollinators but may also be accomplished by fragmentation of rhizomes.

Pitcher plants thrive in the acidic soils of savannas, flat woods near lakeshores, sphagnum moss and cedar bogs, and swamps—of which we have plenty in south and central New Jersey. Spiders take advantage of the plant by spinning webs inside the pitcher to catch insects. American Indians used the plant's root to treat tuberculosis and kidney ailments.

Other carnivorous plants to look for in moist poor soils are the tiny sundews. They emit a sticky fluid that clings like dewdrops to catch and hold insects. Hairs press the victim down onto the surface of the blade, where it is then digested.

Opportunities for finding these and other unusual plants can be found at Harrisville Pond, Trip 37; Batsto Lake, Trip 38; and Malaga Lake, Trip 46.

47 | Parvin State Park— Parvin Lake

You'll enjoy hardwood forest, swamps, turtles, waterfowl, shore birds, and wading birds at these two lakes.

Location: Centerton, NJ
Maps: DeLorme *New Jersey Atlas and Gazetteer*, Maps 60 and 61; USGS Salem and Penns Grove
Area: Parvin: 95 acres; Thundergust: 21 acres
Time: 1.5 hours
Conditions: Average depth in both lakes is 5 feet; numerous shallow marshy areas
Development: Rural
Information: Parvin State Park, 701 Almond Road, Pittsgrove, NJ 08318; 856-358-8616. The public boat launch is free, but the entrance to the park and recreation facilities is $5 in-season.
Camping: On-site; call the park office for reservations.
Take Note: Electric motorboats only; marshy areas

GETTING THERE

To the park office: From Route 77, drive east 6.0 miles on Route 540 to the entrance and the park office on your right. Signs are posted prominently along Route 540. *GPS coordinates*: 39°30.618′ N, 75°07.952′ W.

To the public launch on Parvin Lake: From Route 77, drive east 6.3 miles on Route 540, then turn right onto Parvin Mill Road and drive 0.15 mile to the launch site on your right. You'll find parking for about 25 cars. Restrooms are on-site. *GPS coordinates*: 39°30.369′ N, 75°07.770′ W.

WHAT YOU'LL SEE

With a reputation as the best-kept secret of southern New Jersey, almost 2,000 acres of Parvin State Park are yours to enjoy for paddling, swimming, camping, fishing, and hiking. It's one of those parks that many people return to year after year, thanks to amenities that offer activities for the whole family, while not diminishing the sense that you've escaped. Picnic tables and grills are located throughout the park. Parvin has a carry-in/carry-out program and bags are provided throughout the park. Stop in at the park office for trail guides and current trail conditions and take the opportunity to view the interpretive nature

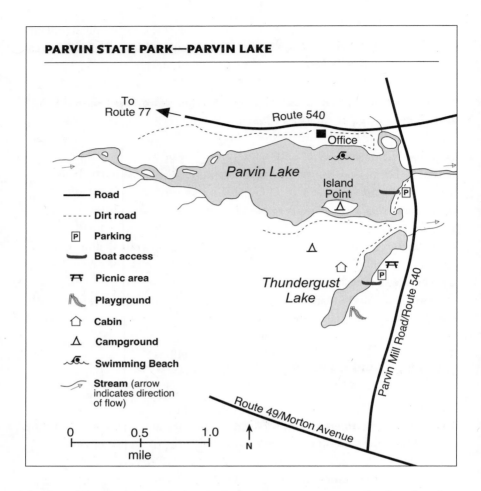

PARVIN STATE PARK—PARVIN LAKE

To Route 77

Route 540

Office

Parvin Lake

Island Point

Road

Dirt road

P Parking

Boat access

Picnic area

Playground

Cabin

Campground

Swimming Beach

Stream (arrow indicates direction of flow)

Thundergust Lake

Parvin Mill Road/Route 540

Route 49/Morton Avenue

0   0.5   1.0
mile

N

displays. The remains of American Indian encampments can be found within the park, but as with any site of historical importance, please do not disturb. Report any potential artifact found to the park office, but leave it in place. Canoe and kayak rentals are available on-site through a private concession.

Mountain laurel and dogwood lend a light perfumed scent to the air in late spring as their blossoms open wide to splash the landscape with pinks and whites. My personal favorite is the swamp magnolia with its very delicate scent and yellow-centered white blossoms. The park is home to the state-threatened barred owl and the endangered swamp pink, whose pink blossoms in late spring stand atop 2-foot stalks. An "endangered" species is one that is in danger of extinction throughout all or a significant portion of its range. A "threatened" species is one that is likely to become endangered in the foreseeable future. When you explore the swamp area, also search for the carnivorous pitcher plant, which thrives in this moist, acidic environment. See the essay on pitcher plants on page 170 to find out more about these small, cupped-leaved plants that eat crawling and flying insects by attracting them with nectar.

Parvin State Park is noted as a hot spot for the spring migration of neo-tropical songbirds and is frequently visited by bird-watcher groups. Muddy Run Creek, which feeds Parvin Lake in the northwest tip, is a particularly good area to spot bog and painted turtles, kingfishers, and a diverse assortment of song-birds in the many small coves and fingers. Have your camera and binoculars ready when you paddle into that area. Stop and listen for different birds, then scan for them with binoculars. Sit quietly in your boat and you will often have birds come quite close. In times of decent water, you can paddle more than a mile upstream in Muddy Run Creek. Ospreys hunting for fish will be more often sighted gliding over open areas of both lakes, while ducks and swans are often in the shallower southwestern and northwestern areas of Parvin Lake.

Thundergust Lake is a small, 14-acre lake within the park that has lakeside cabins to rent. Visit or call the park office for details.

---

48 | Lake Lenape Park and Great Egg Harbor River

Look for eagles, hawks, waterfowl, wading birds, more eagles, ospreys, muskrat, cedar swamps, and islands at this lake.

Location: Mays Landing, NJ
Maps: DeLorme *New Jersey Atlas and Gazetteer*, Map 70; USGS Mays Landing
Area: 350 acres
Time: Lake Lenape: 2.5–3.5 hours; Great Egg Harbor River: 1.5–2.0 hours
Conditions: Lake Lenape: depth average 12 feet; Great Egg Harbor River: depth average 4 feet
Development: Lake Lenape: suburban; Great Egg Harbor River: remote
Information: Lake Lenape Park Recreation Center, 303 Old Harding Highway, Mays Landing, NJ, 08330; 609-625-8219.
Camping: On-site at the lake with eighteen tent-only sites. Call the park for reservations. Pleasant Valley Family Campground is 10 minutes south. See Appendix A.
Take Note: Motorboats are limited to 10 horsepower

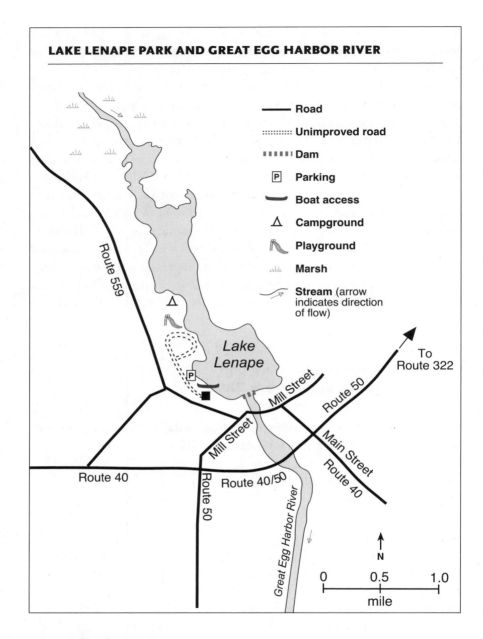

LAKE LENAPE PARK AND GREAT EGG HARBOR RIVER

——— Road

:::::::::: Unimproved road

ıııııı Dam

P Parking

Boat access

△ Campground

Playground

Marsh

Stream (arrow indicates direction of flow)

Route 559

△

Lake Lenape

P

To Route 322

Mill Street

Route 50

Mill Street

Main Street

Route 40

Route 40

Route 40/50

Route 50

Great Egg Harbor River

N

0   0.5   1.0
mile

GETTING THERE

From Route 322 (Black Horse Pike), drive south 1.8 miles on Route 50. Turn right onto Main Street (Route 40) and drive 0.3 mile to the T-junction. Turn left onto Mill Street (Route 50) for 0.1 mile, and then right onto Old Harding Highway (Route 559) for 0.2 mile to the park entrance on your right. Follow

This pooch loves to spend time on the water with his owner.

the park road for 0.3 mile to the recreation center. A concrete boat ramp is on the north side of the recreation center building. You must sign in (provide your name and an emergency contact name) at the boathouse prior to launching and sign out once you're off the water. You'll find parking for 40 cars. Access to Great Egg Harbor River is from the north end of the lake. *GPS coordinates*: 39°27.404′ N, 74°44.313′ W.

WHAT YOU'LL SEE
Lake Lenape
On its way to the Atlantic Ocean, the scenic Great Egg Harbor River was dammed to create Lake Lenape, most of which lies within the confines of the county-owned Lake Lenape Park. Private property and the park's recreational facilities (swimming beach and playground) rim the southern end of the lake, but escape to wilder waters is an easy paddle away. The 1,900-acre park protects the lake and major portions of the river. Campsites are available within the park. An extra camping bonus is that this is one of the few tent-only campgrounds in New Jersey. In addition to the concrete boat launch, there is a large sandy beach in front of the gravel parking lots that many people use to launch their boats, even though it is a small portage down a grassy slope from the parking lot.

You may spot an eagle here; this is one of the best locations in southern New Jersey to observe them. Try the northern half of the lake, where the lake becomes wider and suburban houses on the east shore thin dramatically. From the boat ramp, turn left and paddle up the heavily tree-lined west side, where you'll find big and little coves and fingers galore to explore. Deep green cedar trees line the shores in front of mixed-oak and pine forests. Blueberry, sheep laurel, and mulberry bushes fill the understory, while stands of phragmites and cattails grow in open shallows. After passing through the somewhat narrower central portion, the lake opens wide and beautiful. Islands, lots of them, dot the far northern end and are a delight to paddle around. Lots of small sweet gum trees add a spectacular array of colors in the fall.

Birds and waterfowl are abundant, especially around islands, coves, marshes, and small inlets that provide good nesting and feeding environments. Keep your eyes open for the occasional otter; they have been spotted in the area. Colorful painted and red-bellied turtles abound on swollen cedar logs jutting from swampy shallows. Hawks, falcons, vultures, ospreys, and eagles are common in the skies while kingfishers, blue jays, crows, and songbirds flit about the shoreline. In shallow areas and marshy shorelines, you'll find blue herons, egrets, gulls, and abundant waterfowl.

After the paddle, cool off in the water by the beach. A large public beach with lifeguards on duty in-season is located on the opposite side of the lake from the launch if you choose to go there.

Great Egg Harbor River

The Great Egg Harbor River enters Lake Lenape in the northwest corner of the lake. A Dutch explorer, Cornelius Jacobsen Mey, named it in 1614 when he came into the inlet of the river and saw the meadows covered with shorebird and waterfowl eggs and called it "Eyren Haven" (Egg Harbor). In 1992, the United States Congress designated the river and its tributaries as the Great Egg Harbor Scenic and Recreational River as part of the National Wild and Scenic River system.

You can paddle upstream 2 to 3 miles, depending on the water level and flow rate, before the oncoming current becomes too difficult. The best part is that you will pass only a few modest riverside residences along the way—the rest is pristine wilderness. As you depart the lake and enter the river, numerous islands and wetland marshes invite you to drink in the wide variety of wetland shrubs and flowers. This is a bird-watcher's heaven and botanist's delight. You'll find numerous fingers and small inlets in the first 1.5 miles that will keep you busy exploring every crevice. Blue jays, pine warblers, blackbirds, vireos, and other woodland birds will be heard and seen along the way. In the more open marsh areas and larger inlets, waterfowl and wading birds are common. In early summer, wild blue iris can be found at the edge of low marshes and the white blossoms of swamp magnolia lightly scent the air. By late summer, joe-pye weed develops large mauve flowerheads and the vibrant red cardinal flower comes into bloom.

Atlantic white cedars, oaks, and pines are the dominant trees. River birch, white birch, red maple, and white gum are sprinkled along the river's edge with sumac, huckleberry, and sheep laurel filling in the understory. Fallen and overhanging trees create interest, and sometimes a challenge, as you meander along the sinuous river. In some sections there are riverside bluffs 3 to 5 feet high. Kingfishers make their nests in bluffs 2 to 3 feet above the surface of the water. Pure sand bluffs are too soft for them, but where the bluffs are a darker sandy loam, listen and watch for these crest-headed birds and look for their nests. Enjoy this beautiful river as far up as you can paddle.

For those who wish to add some hiking or biking to the day, the lake offers a 2-mile hiking and biking trail that skirts lakefront properties and wildlife observation points. A number of local bird-watchers walk the sand road that leads to the camping area and the campground launch for a rewarding experience.

Another paddling trip nearby is Corbin City Impoundments, 20 minutes south. See Trip 51.

49 | Edwin B. Forsythe National Wildlife Refuge—Scott's Landing

Enjoy salt marshes, raptors, wading birds, shore birds, and abundant migrating birds at this refuge.

Location: Smithville, NJ
Maps: DeLorme *New Jersey Atlas and Gazetteer*, Map 65; USGS Oceanville
Area: 5.0-plus miles of meandering brackish water channels
Time: 2.0–4.0 hours
Conditions: Saltwater marsh, tidal
Development: Rural
Information: Edwin B. Forsythe National Wildlife Refuge Headquarters, Great Creek Road, Box 72, Oceanville, NJ 08231; 609-652-1665.
Camping: Bass River State Forest, 25 minutes north. Red Wings Lakes Campground, 20 minutes northwest. Evergreen Woods Lakefront Resort, 20 minutes west. See Appendix A.

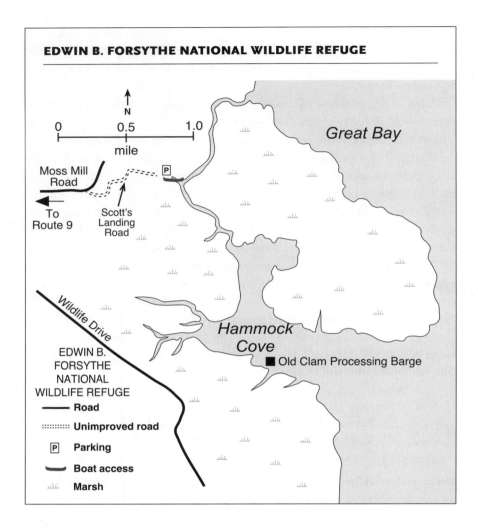

EDWIN B. FORSYTHE NATIONAL WILDLIFE REFUGE

Great Bay

0   0.5   1.0
mile
N

Moss Mill
Road

To
Route 9

Scott's
Landing
Road

P

Wildlife Drive

EDWIN B.
FORSYTHE
NATIONAL
WILDLIFE REFUGE

Hammock
Cove

■ Old Clam Processing Barge

—— **Road**

········· **Unimproved road**

P **Parking**

⌣ **Boat access**

⏞ **Marsh**

Take Note: Motorboats on a small portion of the trip can be noisy on summer weekends; best season is spring and fall during bird migration; best time to launch is 2 to 3 hours before low tide, although the current is on the weak side in the back bay. Check tides at saltwatertides.com for Main Marsh Thorofare under the bolded heading Main Marsh Thorofare to Cape May about halfway down the page and add 45 minutes.

GETTING THERE

From the south, drive north on Route 9 for 3.2 miles from Route 30, turn right (east) onto Route 561 (Moss Mill Road), and drive 1.5 miles. The road turns to the left here. Drive around the bend and take the next right, about 100 feet

The black and white plumage and bright orange bill make the oystercatcher quite striking.

away. Follow that dirt road 0.4 mile. The parking area will be on your left; the concrete boat ramp will be about 100 feet straight ahead. You'll find parking for about twenty cars.

From the north, take Garden State Parkway Exit 48, which puts you onto Route 9 south. Drive 6.7 miles and turn left onto Route 561. Continue as above. *GPS coordinates*: 39°29.631′ N, 74°25.243′ W.

To Edwin B. Forsythe Refuge: From Routes 9 and 561, drive 1.7 miles south on Route 9 and turn left onto East Great Creek Road and drive 0.6 mile. There's a large sign on Route 9 for the refuge. *GPS coordinates*: 39°27.833′ N, 74°27.034′ W.

WHAT YOU'LL SEE

This coastal bay area offers prodigious bird species that can be observed year-round. Edwin B. Forsythe National Wildlife Refuge is one of the major stop-overs along the Atlantic flyway for migratory birds. You will paddle out through the salt marshes and on to the back side of Great Bay along Hammock Cove. Spring and fall migrations bring large numbers of shore birds, waterfowl, and wading birds to rest and feed before continuing their journey. Some remain for the entire summer. Diamondback terrapins, with their decorative concentric whorls, are found frequently in and around the marshes. Look skyward for bald eagles, ospreys, peregrine falcons, and hawks.

Mid-May to early June, when migrating birds feast on horseshoe crab eggs in the Chesapeake and Delaware Bay estuaries, this refuge provides their next major stopover along the Atlantic flyway. One of my favorite early summer migratory species is the Arctic tern, travelers from South America that stop here for a few weeks prior to continuing their journey to the Arctic. That's a total distance of at least 10,000 miles. In mid-October, the sky is filled with large flocks of snow geese, large white birds with black-tipped wings. In winter, black ducks, Atlantic brants, and Canada geese dominate the ponds. On the nearby barrier islands, beaches and dunes provide nesting habitat for piping plovers, black skimmers, and least terns. Watch for posted signs if you decide to explore these islands; a few are primary nesting sites for the piping plover, an endangered species in New Jersey, and are off-limits during nesting season.

Head right from the launch and make an immediate left. Along the 1.0-mile paddle from the launch to Hammock Cove, you'll be winding your way through a narrow salt marsh channel where egrets, herons, and red-winged blackbirds are plentiful. Hug the western edge of Hammock Cove to your right and continue another 0.7 mile. There will be two channels in front of you. Take the left channel. After a half-mile you'll see a straight-line channel on your left that will take you close to the refuge dike. You will probably see a car or two driving down the north dike of the refuge. Returning the way you came, the trip is a little less than 5 miles. But, on your way back, once out in Hammock Cove, look to your right for the abandoned derelict wind-powered clam processing barge less than a half-mile away.

More than 43,000 acres of southern New Jersey coastal land, most of which is tidal salt marsh, are under the auspices of the Edwin B. Forsythe Refuge. Open from dawn until dusk, an 8-mile vehicle loop takes you past upland fields and woodlands, coastal salt meadows and marshes, open bays, channels, and impoundments. Two observation towers are located along the drive, the second of which is closest to the large, human-made peregrine nesting house.

The visitor center, open 8 A.M. to 4 P.M. weekdays and weekends, displays numerous wildlife exhibits. Bring lots of insect repellent July through September; the greenheads and mosquitoes are cannibalistic! A $5 entrance fee is charged to enter the drive loop, which operates under an honor system after hours. The best time for the drive and associated hiking is early morning and late afternoon when the birds are most active.

Another paddling opportunity nearby is Bass River State Forest, 20 minutes north. See Trip 42.

50 | Union Lake

You'll find large islands, waterfowl, and raptors at Union Lake.

Location: Millville, NJ

Maps: DeLorme *New Jersey Atlas and Gazetteer*, Map 68; USGS Millville

Area: 898 acres

Time: 3.0–4.0 hours

Conditions: Depth average 14 feet

Development: Urban, but mostly surrounded by a large and quiet wildlife management area

Information: New Jersey Division of Fish and Wildlife, Southern Region (Winslow Wildlife Management Area), 220 Blue Anchor Road, Sicklerville, NJ 08081; 856-629-0090.

Camping: Parvin State Park, 25 minutes north. Lazy River Campground, 25 minutes east. See Appendix A.

Take Note: 10 horsepower motor limit; large dam

GETTING THERE

From Route 55 near Millville, take Exit 29 (Sherman Avenue) and turn west onto Sherman Avenue. Drive 2.5 miles, turn left onto Route 608 (Carmel Road), and drive 3.4 miles to Union Lake Wildlife Management Area on the left. Drive 0.2 mile to the parking area and concrete ramp. You'll find parking for about 60 cars. *GPS coordinates*: 39°24.484' N, 75°04.036' W. If you come by way of Route 49 (Main Street), Carmel Avenue veers off Route 49 about 1.2 miles west of Route 47. Drive 2.0 miles west on Carmel Avenue to the lake entrance on the right. Portable toilets are available in-season.

WHAT YOU'LL SEE

Located in the southeast corner of Cumberland County on the western out-skirts of Millville, Union Lake was created by the damming of the Maurice and Mill rivers. This oblong lake covers 898 acres and is 4.0 miles long and 1.2 miles at its widest point—a big lake. The state acquired it in the early 1990s, and it is now a 5,000-acre fish and wildlife management area. As at many other waterways in the state, American Indian artifacts have been found here. The Vineland Historical and Antiquarian Society, at Seventh and Elmer streets in

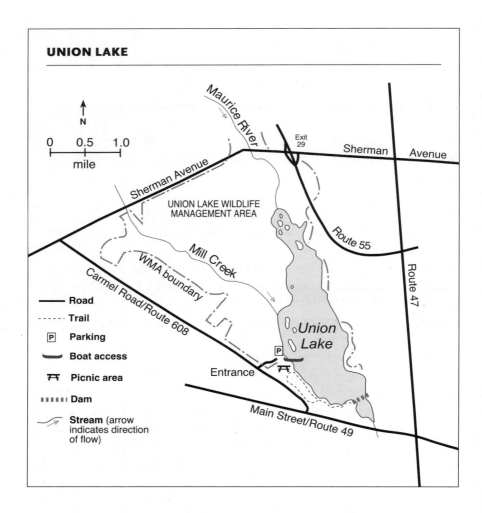

UNION LAKE

Maurice River

Exit 29

Sherman Avenue

Sherman Avenue

N

0   0.5   1.0
mile

UNION LAKE WILDLIFE
MANAGEMENT AREA

Route 55

Mill Creek

WMA boundary

Carmel Road/Route 608

Route 47

Union Lake

P

Entrance

Picnic area

Main Street/Route 49

Road

Trail

P **Parking**

Boat access

Picnic area

Dam

Stream (arrow indicates direction of flow)

Vineland, display many of the artifacts uncovered over the years. If you do find an artifact while at the lake, take notes on its location and notify the historical society. Don't move or remove the item, since archaeologists reconstruct the history of an area based on the exact location of various artifacts. Because this is state-owned property, keeping artifacts is illegal.

Pollution in the form of various chemicals, by-products from a now defunct paint production company in North Vineland, once plagued this waterway all the way to the Delaware Bay. Dumping stopped in the early 1980s, largely due to pressure from surrounding communities and local environmental groups. With the river and lake cleaned up, you'll find not only some of the best fishing in southeastern New Jersey, but also some of its cleanest and clearest waters for swimming and paddling.

An angler comes in from an afternoon of fishing around the large islands in Union Lake.

Consider a moonlight paddle here, when the full moon peeks through tree-tops before spraying a radiant glow across the water. Seventy feet in front of the dam is a line of buoys warning of danger. Be very careful here, especially after a heavy rain when water flow increases. The drop over the dam is 45 feet. Most coves along the lakeshore have shallow margins that are only 2 to 4 feet deep, which is perfect for a refreshing swim. Along the shoreline you'll find red maple, birch, swamp magnolia, cedar, and mountain laurel. In late spring and early summer, dainty, pale pink mountain laurel and white sheep laurel blos-soms sprinkle the landscape like pixie dust against a background of dark green cedar and evergreen laurel leaves.

Three islands, within 1.0 mile of the put-in off its southwest shore, each have one or two landing sites with small clearings for a picnic lunch and short walk-ing trails to stretch your legs. The largest of these islands is Rattlesnake Island, named for the reptile once found in abundance there. Never fear—rattlesnakes have not been seen on the island for more than 10 years. Largemouth bass, colorful sunfish, catfish, pickerel, and yellow perch are caught by local anglers under the watchful eye of ospreys, which nest along the lake's western shore.

The lake is also stocked with a hybrid fish, a cross between a striped bass and largemouth bass. Numerous species of ducks and geese frequent the lake. On a few occasions I've even seen a bald eagle scouting the clear water. Watch carefully and you might spot wood ducks or hooded mergansers in fall, particularly in the coves. At dawn you're likely to see white-tailed deer and raccoons sauntering along the shore. Short cliffs, about 0.75 mile down from the landing, host a few kingfisher nest holes. Look for their cavities about 2 feet above the waterline.

Miles of unmarked sand roads and hiking trails meander along the western and northern lakeshores and the interior of the wildlife management area. One unmarked trail from the top of the launch ramp leads south along the shoreline. The last time I was there I came across a bright yellow iris right on the trail. What tickled me most about it was that no one had picked it, but left it in the wild for others to enjoy. Another trail leads off from the north corner of the parking lot and follows the lake for about a half-mile before turning left away from the lake.

While outboards are permitted, there is a 10-horsepower limit. Most outboard traffic I have encountered, and there isn't much, has been on the deeper, southeastern end of the lake close to the dam. The best and least-crowded paddling is along the lake's western and northern shores where you can meander around islands and quiet coves enjoying the scenery and looking for birds, including bald eagles that nest here.

Another paddle nearby is Corbin City Impoundments, 35 minutes east. See Trip 51. Parvin State Park is 25 minutes north. See Trip 47. Malaga Lake is 20 minutes north. See Trip 46.

51 | Tuckahoe Wildlife Management Area— Corbin City Impoundments

Enjoy an expansive saltwater marsh and see marsh birds, swans, wading birds, and ospreys at these unique impoundments.

Location: Tuckahoe, NJ
Maps: DeLorme *New Jersey Atlas and Gazetteer*, Map 70; USGS Marmora
Area: Impoundment #1: 104 acres; Impoundment #2: 243 acres; Impoundment #3: 284 acres
Time: Impoundment #1: 1.0–1.5 hours; Impoundments #2 and #3: 1.5–2.0 hours total
Conditions: Depth average 5 feet at high tide, 3 feet at low tide; shallow saltwater impoundments
Development: Rural

Information: New Jersey Division of Fish and Wildlife, Southern Region (Winslow Wildlife Management Area), 220 Blue Anchor Road, Sicklerville, NJ 08081; 856-629-0090.

Camping: Scenic Riverview Campground, 10 minutes southeast. Belleplain State Forest, 30 minutes southwest. Lake Lenape, 25 minutes north. See Appendix A.

Take Note: Electric motorboats only; slightly tidal

GETTING THERE

The main roads to the impoundments off Route 50 form a rough semicircle around the eastern side of the impoundments. The north and south entrances are 3.5 miles apart.

To reach the south entrance of Griscom Mill Road from Route 50 in Corbin City, at the junction with Route 611 (Aetna Road), drive west 0.7 mile on Route 50 and turn right onto Griscom Mill Road. A sign for the wildlife management area is on Route 50, but it is placed parallel to Route 50 and thus is hard to see. After turning onto Griscom Mill Road, drive 0.4 mile to where the blacktop ends and a sand road begins. Continue another 0.3 mile and turn right at the T-intersection, continuing to follow the main sand road for another 0.8 mile to the southern end of the south impoundment. The road continues around the impoundments and exits onto Route 50. Because there are no specific launches, only the coordinates for the entrance to Griscom Mill Road from Route 50 are provided. *GPS coordinates*: 39°18.340′ N, 74°45.504′ W.

To launch into the northern impoundment or into the salt marsh channels that lead to Great Egg Harbor River, drive to the northeast tip of the north impoundment. You'll find a sand parking area for about five cars. *GPS coordinates*: 39°21.025′ N, 74°45.420′ W.

WHAT YOU'LL SEE

Get ready for fantastic birding and remote, peaceful paddling in a safe, brackish water environment. Impoundments, similar to shallow reservoirs, are large dammed areas creating basins to collect and confine waters. Three large impoundments, ranging from 104 to 284 acres, lie within the Tuckahoe Wildlife Management Area not far from the Great Egg Harbor River. Parking and launching are informal. A few openings here and there through the narrow border of shrubs and trees rimming the road around the impoundments provide access to the waters where the road widens enough for two to four cars to park parallel to the road. Hug the edge when you park so as not to block other cars.

Any place there's an outlet pipe between the marsh and the impoundments, the road widens enough to park and there will be an opportunity to launch, although at some spots it can be a little steep. Anglers often use the areas at the outlet pipes, and the constant use keeps the ground clear of vegetation.

All three impoundments offer spectacular scenery typical of lands bordering brackish marshes, where lowland woods stand behind the water-loving plants that frame creeks and ponds. Here you will find a mix of flora and fauna from freshwater and saltwater environments: hawks, muskrats, deer, foxes, shorebirds, ospreys, egrets, kingfishers, warblers, and numerous species of songbirds. Bird-watching is always best in early morning and late afternoon; during the heat of the day, many birds seek cover.

To me, the southern two impoundments offer a more scenic and rewarding trip as you wind your way around numerous islands and into large coves. The sounds you'll hear most while paddling are the *tjeet, tjeet* of the red-winged blackbird. They are all over the place. I've found kingfishers to be most abundant in the second impoundment, where slightly steeper banks provide a better nesting habitat. Their trademark white throat and collar makes them easy to spot even though they are small. They hover, much like a hummingbird, over the water before plunging in to catch a fish. Swans add a peaceful elegance, their snowy bodies contrasting against dark waters. I always see swans in at least two of the impoundments. Egrets and herons stalk the shallows everywhere, their long necks stretched out, searching for small fish swimming just beneath the surface. Little green herons are usually spotted closer to wooded areas, like the south shore of Impoundment #3 and along the dike areas lined with trees that separate the impoundments.

Pay attention to any breeze, no matter how light, and set yourself up to let the wind carry you to the birds feeding in the shallows. Have your camera out and ready to click. Listen for the deep, hoarse croak, *gwaawk gwaawk*, of the great blue heron as it flaps long and gracefully over the water. If you have a digital camera, make sure it's fully charged. One of my favorite birds to see here and in the little channel next to the impoundments is the black skimmer, a bird whose black and vibrant orange-red beak is longer on the bottom. They fly just above the water and drop their long lower beak to skim the surface for small fish.

If you want to paddle around the channels leading off the Great Egg Harbor River that feed into the impoundments, be mindful that they are tidal, although the current is relatively slow. To launch, use the parking area for the launch site at the north end of the north impoundment. There's a small area riverside

TUCKAHOE WILDLIFE MANAGEMENT AREA

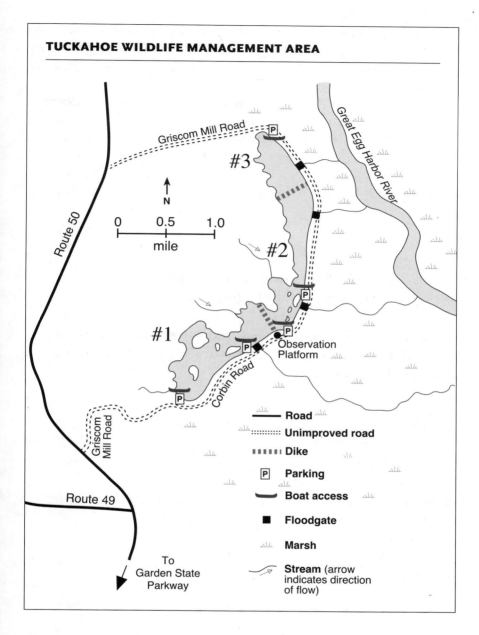

where you can launch into the channel and paddle right or left for a mile before you get to the river and turn around. You could paddle into the river, but boat traffic can be heavy with large motorboats zipping up and down between Great Bay and Mays Landing. If you do decide to venture into the river, make sure you mark the channel on your GPS before entering the river so you can get yourself back—and make sure you have enough battery left. In addition, bring plenty of insect repellent in summer. The greenheads (big, nasty, biting green flies) are voracious feeders.

For tide information, go to saltwatertides.com and look for River Bend Marina, Great Egg Harbor River. It will be listed under the bolded heading Main Marsh Thorofare to Cape May about halfway down the page. That marina is on the river directly across from the northern impoundment.

Other paddling destinations nearby are Lake Lenape, 20 minutes north, and Belleplain State Forest, 25 minutes southwest. Both have on-site camping. See Trips 48 and 52.

52 | Belleplain State Forest—Lake Nummy and East Creek Pond

This state park offers raptors galore, magnificent bird-watching, 40 miles of hiking trails, pine and oak forest with white cedars, and a remote and quiet setting.

Location: Woodbine, NJ
Maps: DeLorme *New Jersey Atlas and Gazetteer*, Maps 69 and 72; USGS Woodbine and Heislerville
Area: Lake Nummy: 26 acres; East Creek Pond: 62 acres; Pickle Factory Pond (aka Paper Mill Pond): 67 acres
Time: Lake Nummy: less than 1.0 hour; East Creek and Pickle Factory Ponds: 1.0–1.5 hours total
Conditions: Depth average 6 feet for each
Development: Rural
Information: Belleplain State Forest, County Route 550, PO Box 450, Woodbine, NJ 08270; 609-861-2404; $5 weekday fee ($10 weekend) in-season to enter the park via the visitor center to Lake Nummy. There is no fee to launch at East Creek or Pickle Factory ponds.
Camping: Three large camping areas surround Lake Nummy. A lake front group cabin is located at East Creek Pond. For reservations call the park office or visit state.nj.us/dep/parksandforests/parks/campreserv.html.
Take Note: Electric motorboats only; best season is spring and fall during bird migration

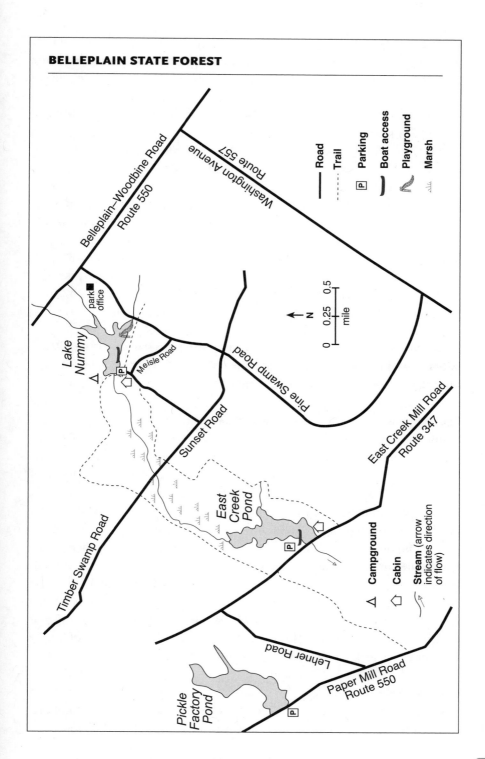

BELLEPLAIN STATE FOREST

Legend:

— Road
····· Trail
Ⓟ Parking
⟩ Boat access
⚘ Playground
⩟ Marsh

△ Campground
⬠ Cabin
∿ Stream (arrow indicates direction of flow)

N
0   0.25   0.5
mile

park office

Lake Nummy

Belleplain–Woodbine Road
Route 550

Washington Avenue
Route 557

Meisle Road

Pine Swamp Road

Sunset Road

Timber Swamp Road

East Creek Pond

East Creek Mill Road
Route 347

Lehner Road

Paper Mill Road
Route 550

Pickle Factory Pond

GETTING THERE

To the park office: From Route 47 on the south side of Woodbine, drive north 3.1 miles on Route 557, turn left (west) onto Route 550, and drive 1.4 miles to the park entrance on your left. The visitor center will be on your right, 100 feet inside the park. *GPS coordinates*: 39°14.907′ N, 74°50.550′ W.

To Lake Nummy: Continue past the visitor center 0.35 mile, turn right onto Meisle Road, and drive 0.4 mile to the dock at Lake Nummy. You'll find parking for six cars. *GPS coordinates*: 39°147.731′ N, 74°51.446′ W.

To East Creek Pond: From Route 557, drive north 0.7 mile on Route 47. The road forks here, with Route 47 going to the left and Route 347 to the right. Take the right fork onto Route 347 and drive 2.0 miles. Turn right into the boat ramp area on your right at the end of the guardrail. If you're inside the park at Lake Nummy, turn onto Savage Bridge Road directly across from the dock, drive 0.8 mile to the T-intersection and turn right onto Sunset Road and drive 1.7 miles to Hands Mill Road. Turn left and drive 0.8 mile to Route 347. Turn left onto Route 347 and drive 1.5 miles to the launch site on your left. You'll find parking for about fifteen cars. *GPS coordinates*: 39°13.347′ N, 74°53.138′ W.

WHAT YOU'LL SEE

Belleplain State Forest is one of my favorite destinations. Forty-two miles of hiking and multiuse trails meander through more than 20,000 acres of upland oak and pine forests, hardwood forests, Atlantic white cedar swamps, and bogs within the forest. Situated on the outskirts of the Pine Barrens, the soil conditions here are better than they are in the Pine Barrens and allow for a wider variety of trees and shrubs, including hickory, beech, and ash. You can literally spend several camping weekends paddling the lakes and hiking all the trails. The crisp, clean pine-scented air will grab your attention as you drive into the park on a road lined with tall trees bordering dense woods.

Two bodies of water, East Creek Pond and Lake Nummy, lie completely within the park's boundaries. The smaller of the two, Lake Nummy, is in the center of the park's campground, swimming beach, and recreational area on the northwest shore and can become quite crowded in summer. It was named after the last Lenni-Lenape chief in Cape May County, where Belleplain is situated. He lived during the mid to late 1600s. Only the northeast portion of a third body of water, Pickle Factory Pond, lies within the park's boundary.

Lake Nummy

After launching from the floating dock, paddle right along the southern shoreline that will lead to a marshy, narrow cove where you will likely find turtles,

This view of Pickle Factory Pond is from the launch. Look for ospreys that are commonly seen here.

ducks, and wading birds. Continue along the shoreline and pass under the footbridge in the northwest corner. I love paddling under bridges. It's the happy anticipation of what lies on the other side, almost like I'm about to discover a secret hideaway. In summer, large numbers of tanagers, warblers, finches, and songbirds can be seen flitting about the trees. Why does this site attract so many species? As the saying goes in real estate, "Location. Location. Location." Belleplain is situated just north of the Cape May Peninsula, part of a major migratory route known as the Atlantic flyway. The diverse habitats within the park further enhance its desirability as both a stopover site for spring and fall migrations, as well as for summertime residents that nest and reproduce. Sit quietly and observe. Let the wildlife come to you. Although this lake is small, it offers a peaceful setting and makes an ideal paddle for novices or parents taking their children out for the first time.

East Creek Pond

East Creek Pond is perfect for eagle and hawk sightings and it's rare to not spot at least one. The launch area can be a little noisy with road traffic, particularly on summer weekends, but once you start paddling north the noise seems to disappear. Numerous coves and inlets house large populations of painted and bog turtles that bask in the sun on picturesque logs and cedar stumps set against a background of dense forest. In summer, sweet pepperbush develops thin, elongated clusters of white flowers, which fill the air with a sweet aroma detectable for more than 50 feet. For a sweet snack in July and August, look for blueberry bushes that peek out along the edge of the lake. Arrow weed, pickerelweed, and waterlily along the shallower shores provide a protective environment for young pickerel, smallmouth bass, catfish, sunfish, and crappie that are found in the lake. Eagles abound here throughout the year.

My favorite areas are two northern coves that become a little marshy. It's there where you're likely to encounter little green and blue herons flitting about on branches just above the water looking for a meal. You're also out of sight of any roads, giving you a better wilderness experience. Sometimes I like to paddle into a cozy cove and sit quietly in my boat. I'll listen to all the different sounds of various wildlife and the breeze rustling through the trees, and look for treats such as an eagle or osprey soaring overhead looking for dinner. With all the dense woods, there are always going to be a few dead or dying trees. Listen for woodpeckers drilling holes into them, and then try to locate the bird. In fall, the dark evergreen foliage of pines, cedars, and mountain laurel create a stunning contrast to the bright colors of deciduous trees and bushes. A group cabin sits on the opposite shoreline of the lake along Route 347, but only once have I ever seen a group there and even then it was a small group. This would be a great place to rent with a bunch of friends in late spring or early fall when migrations are at a peak.

Belleplain State Forest offers 42 miles of trails to choose from to round out your stay with an invigorating hike. East Creek Trail is one of the more popular trails, taking you through hardwood forests, skirting white cedar swamps and tall pine stands. Be sure to ask for the trail map, which is more detailed than the general park map.

Tent, lean-to, and trailer campsites are available year-round at Lake Nummy, but only one site, a group cabin at East Creek Pond, is on the water.

For another nearby paddle, visit Corbin City Impoundments, 25 minutes northeast. See Trip 51.

4 | EASTERN PENNSYLVANIA

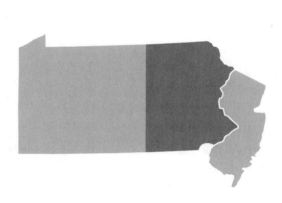

The Appalachian Highlands covers a wide swath of land from Maine through Louisiana and is an official geographic province defined by the United States Geologic Survey. In Pennsylvania, it covers most of the state except for a narrow sliver of the Atlantic Coastal Plain along the southeast edge and a sliver of the Central Lowlands along the northwest edge. It is further separated into smaller provinces that have a general northeast-southwest trend: the Piedmont, or rolling foothills of the Appalachian Mountains, borders the coastal plain in the southeast; the Ridge and Valley, with its steep-sided ridges and narrow valleys, lays west of the Piedmont starting roughly from Chambersburg and continuing in an arc to Stroudsburg; and the Appalachian Plateau, where the topography starts to flatten, covers western and north-central Pennsylvania.

With such diverse topography, Pennsylvania offers a wide variety of scenic paddling opportunities for you to explore and enjoy. Bodies of water in lowland rolling hills, wetlands, and tucked in the mountains provide a rich diversity of habitats and wildlife. Most trips are within the Pennsylvania Highlands, where the Appalachian Mountain Club maintains a large effort in protecting large tracts of natural lands. Further information on AMC's involvement can be found in the Critical Treasures of the Highlands and AMC and the Highlands Conservation Act essays, on pages 232 and 24, respectively.

A number of lakes, like Marsh Creek State Park and Beltzville State Park, are popular paddling spots where local groups paddle regularly and have skills practice days—a great way to find other paddlers and increase or maintain your skills.

To start you off, four trips within the Pennsylvania Highlands that will give you a taste of this unique area are: Nockamixon State Park, Trip 61; Middle Creek Wildlife Management Area, Trip 64; French Creek State Park, Trip 66; and Gifford Pinchot State Park, Trip 72. Outside of the Highlands, Beltzville State Park, Trip 57, and Ricketts Glen, Trip 53, will delight you with even more of what the state has to offer.

53 | Ricketts Glen State Park—Lake Jean

Waterfalls, mountains, steep gorges, birds, centuries-old hemlock forests, islands, and even more waterfalls are yours to enjoy at this magnificent park.

Location: Benton, PA
Maps: DeLorme *Pennsylvania Atlas and Gazetteer*, Map 51; USGS Red Rock
Area: 245 acres
Time: 2.0–2.5 hours
Conditions: Depth average 8 feet
Development: Rural
Information: Ricketts Glen State Park, 695 State Route 487, Benton, PA 17814; 570-477-5675.
Camping: On-site. Call the park, or for online reservations, go to www. visitPAparks.com. Goods Campground, 5 minutes south. See Appendix A.
Take Note: Electric motorboats only; Pennsylvania boating regulations apply. See Appendix D.

GETTING THERE
From the intersection of Routes 118 and 487, drive 3.6 miles north on Route 487 to the park entrance. Turn right into the park. The park office and the first boat launch are 0.1 miles from the entrance; the second boat launch is about 1.1 miles past the park office. You'll find parking for about fifteen cars at the park office and both boat launches. *GPS coordinates*: 41°20.172′ N, 76°18.159′ W.

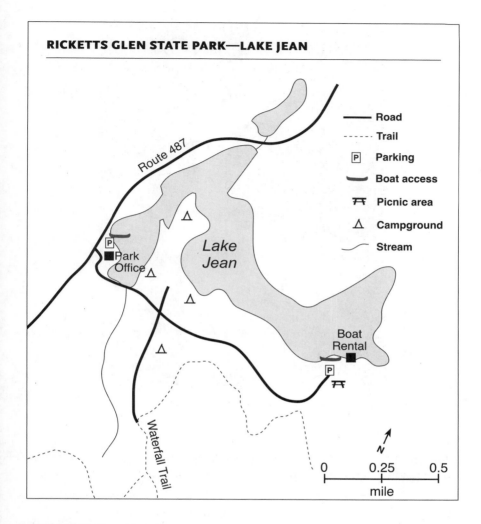

RICKETTS GLEN STATE PARK—LAKE JEAN

Legend:
- Road
- Trail
- P Parking
- Boat access
- Picnic area
- Campground
- Stream

Route 487

Lake Jean

Park Office

Boat Rental

Waterfall Trail

N

0   0.25   0.5
mile

WHAT YOU'LL SEE

There's no question about it; this is a wonderland of nature. A fascinating geologic history helped carve a magnificent mountain landscape with steep gorges and mesmerizing waterfalls. People then created miles of breathtaking hiking trails and built a dam to expand Lake Jean to its current 235 acres within this 13,000-acre park. I recommend this destination for a two-day stay.

Unless you're from a mountainous area, the first thing that will hit you is the seemingly never-ending drive up Route 487. I kept thinking, "Does this mountain have a top? Will I get there before my transmission rebels?" Next I wondered if they had any bumper stickers similar to the ones that say, "This car climbed Mt. Washington," because it certainly earned the distinction: You

A paddler rests at the top of the 36-foot Adam's waterfall to admire the view.

climb almost 1,200 feet in under 2 miles. Finally there's a sign on the road that says, "Red Rock Mountain: Elevation 2,447." I came here for an overnight stay with two friends, and although the day was windy, we enjoyed the lake until evening and arose early the next day to hike part of the waterfall trail.

Lake Jean actually comprises two natural lakes, Lake Jean and Mud Pond, which were combined by damming the Ganoga Branch of Kitchen Creek to raise the levels of both lakes. You can spend hours paddling around the lake, exploring all the coves and crannies, looking into clear water along shallower edges, watching fish swim by, scanning the skies for raptors, and watching the woods' edge for warblers, songbirds, woodpeckers, kingfishers, and a host of other avian species. Because of the diverse number of species here, the park was added to the official Audubon Susquehanna River Birding and Wildlife Trail that lists the finest birding and wildlife sites across Pennsylvania. You won't wonder why as your ears fill with melodious sounds coming from all directions.

Numerous small islands scattered around the lake add interest and provide extra areas to investigate. In the east end of the lake, Cherry Ridge is the high peak you see toward the northeast. The 600-foot beach on the southeast side of the lake can be noisy on hot summer days, but that's such a small part of the lake that you can quickly paddle out of earshot. Swimming is allowed only within the buoyed area of the beach. Under the surface, largemouth bass, yellow perch, white and black crappies, brown and brook trout, yellow and brown bullheads, and sunnies make their home.

If you are here for two full days, you might want to head out from the west launch near the visitor center and explore the west arm of the lake and around the peninsula in the morning, then pick a hike to do in the afternoon. The next day, head out from the east launch near the beach to paddle the eastern half of the lake and do another hike in the afternoon.

As for hiking, there are 26 miles of trails from which to choose. Eleven trails range from 0.8 to 7.2 miles in length and from easy to very difficult. The longest and most difficult is Falls Trail, which features 22 named waterfalls. Ganoga Falls, 94 feet high, is the highest waterfall in the park and the second highest in Pennsylvania.

I hope you will make this trip. Tip 1: If you want to rent a cabin, reserve early as they are often booked months in advance. Tip 2: The parking lots near the Falls Trail fill quickly, especially on weekends. Hike there early morning and paddle in the afternoon.

54 | Faylor Lake and C. F. Walker Lake

These lakes offer raptors, waterfowl, freshwater marshes, and islands.

Location: Troxelville, PA
Maps: DeLorme *Pennsylvania Atlas and Gazetteer*, Map 63; USGS Beavertown
Area: Faylor Lake: 140 acres; C. F. Walker Lake: 239 acres
Time: Faylor Lake: 1.5 hours; C. F. Walker Lake: 2.0–2.5 hours
Conditions: Faylor Lake: depth average 8 feet; C. F. Walker Lake: depth average 25 feet
Development: Rural

Information: Pennsylvania Fish and Boat Commission, Southcentral Regional Office, 1704 Pine Road, Newville, PA 17241; 717-486-7087.
Camping: Gray Squirrel Campsites is 10 minutes south and Penn's Creek Campground is 10 minutes north. See Appendix A.
Take Note: Electric motorboats only; Pennsylvania boating regulations apply. See Appendix D.

GETTING THERE

To Faylor Lake: From Routes 22/322 and 333, drive north 3.7 miles on Route 333. Turn left onto Route 235 north and drive 13.3 miles, then make a slight left onto Lake Road. A small, white sign for Faylor Lake marks the turnoff. Drive 0.7 mile on Lake Road to the launch and parking lot. You'll find parking for about twenty cars. *GPS coordinates*: 40°45.657′ N, 77°12.941′ W.

To C. F. Walker Lake: From the turnoff to Faylor Lake, continue north on Route 235 for an additional 4.3 miles, then continue straight on Troxlerville Road for 1.1 miles. There will be a large, brown wood sign for Walker Lake at the junction of a no-name road. Turn right and drive 0.7 mile to the launch parking lot. You'll find parking for about 40 cars. *GPS coordinates*: 40°48.313′ N, 77°10.771′ W.

WHAT YOU'LL SEE
Faylor Lake

Yes, Virginia, there is a Santa Claus. Well, not exactly, but Pennsylvania Game Commission's Faylor Lake is one of the very few lakes in Pennsylvania that allow *only* manually powered boats on the water. It might not seem like much when you drive up to it because it's not surrounded by wooded hills, but stop and look. A low wooded hill borders the northeast quarter, short trees and shrubs line the northwest corner, and short trees with shrubs surround most of the rest of the lake. Numerous tiny islands, prime for fishing, bird-watching, and general sightseeing, and shoreline irregularities make it very interesting. Look across the lake to the northwest to see the groomed stripes of a large farm typical in rural areas. After you explore the shoreline and numerous islands in the main lake, work your way over to the southwest corner to the long, thin arm.

Depending on water levels and recent rains, you can paddle up Middle Creek almost a mile until the terrain steepens and the oncoming current becomes difficult to paddle. White and black crappies, brown and yellow bullheads, bluegills, and pumpkinseed are common fish here. The lake teems with birds: swan geese, wood ducks, pintails, teals, mergansers, warblers, kingfish-

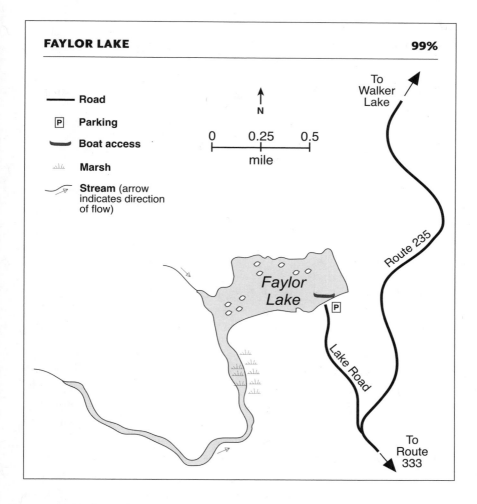

ers, songbirds, and more. Turtles and frogs are all over the place, along with dragonflies and darners.

C. F. Walker Lake

C. F. Walker Lake, operated by the Pennsylvania Fish and Boat Commission, is a short 12-minute drive to the northeast of Faylor Lake and is fed primarily by North Branch Middle Creek on its east end. Walker Lake's elongated shape is nestled between two broken mountain ridges, higher on the north side, which makes a spectacular backdrop as you paddle west along the north shore. There were about a dozen electric motorboats on the water the day I visited, but they were all drifting silently around their favorite fishing spots and it was hard to

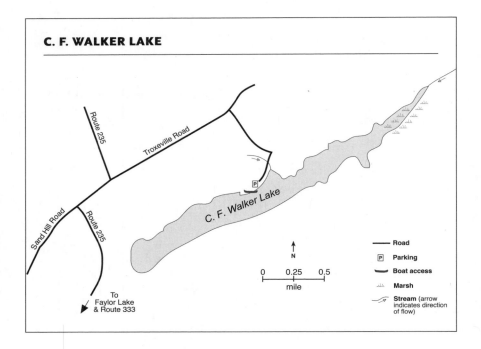

C. F. WALKER LAKE

Route 235

Troxeville Road

Sand Hill Road

Route 235

C. F. Walker Lake

P

To
Faylor Lake
& Route 333

N

0   0.25   0.5
mile

——— Road

P Parking

Boat access

Marsh

Stream (arrow indicates direction of flow)

tell there was anyone else on the lake. Northern pike, largemouth bass, walleye, black crappie, and bluegill are the primary species. Lots of vultures, two osprey, and a few hawks soared above throughout the day. A few small areas of sloping dirt bank along the lake are convenient to get out and stretch your legs.

The east end of the lake, where it narrows into the feeder creek, becomes shallow with dense carpets of pond lilies like giant green area rugs with a defined narrow and clear waterway between. Interspersed within the lilies, during my recent visit, were pickerelweed and various aquatic grasses in different stages of bloom. Frogs were numerous and rather raucous that day. Even though the rest of the lake is big, wide, and very scenic, I had the most enjoyable time here because of all the butterflies, herons, and ducks that preferred this section of the lake. A few tiny, 2-inch diameter turtles were basking on larger lily pads. A short nature trail is on the north side of the entrance road to the launch about 0.2 mile east of the parking area; it has a large trailhead sign. No other marked formal trails exist, but a well-used narrow dirt road leads off the northwest corner of the parking lot and follows the edge of the lake for about a third of a mile before heading up the hill toward the top for about another half-mile.

You can camp overnight at Little Buffalo State Park, 1 hour south, and paddle that lake the next day. See Trip 59.

55 | Tuscarora State Park— Tuscarora Lake

Tall shoreline hills, raptors, and waterfowl are all found around both lakes.

Location: Barnesville, PA
Maps: DeLorme *Pennsylvania Atlas and Gazetteer*, Map 56; USGS Delano
Area: Tuscarora Lake: 96 acres; Locust Lake: 52 acres
Time: Tuscarora Lake: 2.0–2.5 hours; Locust Lake: 1.5 hours
Conditions: Tuscarora Lake: depth average 35 feet; Locust Lake: depth average 20 feet
Development: Rural
Information: Tuscarora State Park and Locust Lake State Park, 687 Tuscarora Park Road, Barnesville, PA 18214; 570-467-2404.
Camping: Tuscarora State Park: Six camping cottages on-site; Locust Lake State Park: 282 tent and trailer sites. For online reservations, go to www.visitPAparks.com, or call the park office or 888-727-2757.
Take Note: Electric motorboats only; Pennsylvania boating regulations apply. See Appendix D.

GETTING THERE

Tuscarora park office and launch: From I-81 Exit 131, drive 4.2 miles on Route 54 East, then turn right onto Golf Club Road and drive 0.5 mile. At the Y-junction, make a slight left onto Tuscarora Park Road and drive 0.3 mile. Turn right onto Tuscarora State Park Road and drive 0.2 mile. The entrance to the park office and visitor center will be on your right. *GPS coordinates*: 40°48.549′ N, 76°01.245′ W. To get to the launch, return to Tuscarora State Park Road, cross the road and drive 0.2 mile to the boat launch entrance road on your right. Turn right and drive 0.3 mile to the parking lot and launch. You'll find parking for 25 cars. *GPS coordinates*: 40°48.383′ N, 76°00.927′ W.

WHAT YOU'LL SEE

Looking across Tuscarora Lake from the launch, densely wooded mountains rise almost 400 feet above the lake surface. Paddle out and head east (left) along the shoreline and past the dam on the east end. As you travel along the south shoreline, hikers might be seen on part of the Lake View Trail that follows

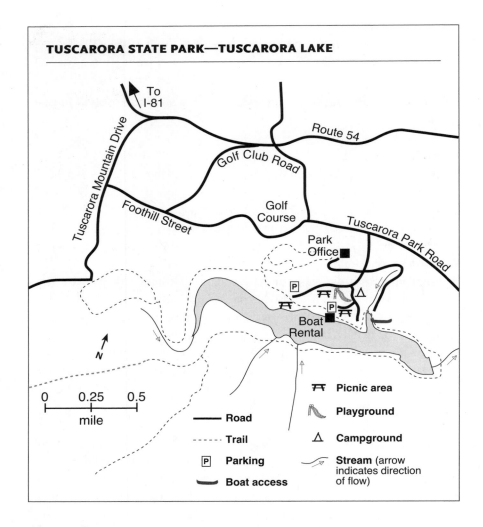

TUSCARORA STATE PARK—TUSCARORA LAKE

To I-81

Tuscarora Mountain Drive

Route 54

Golf Club Road

Foothill Street

Golf Course

Tuscarora Park Road

Park Office

P

P

Boat Rental

N

| 0 | 0.25 | 0.5 |
mile

🎋 Road

----- Trail

P Parking

⌣ Boat access

🎋 Picnic area

🎋 Playground

△ Campground

⌒ Stream (arrow indicates direction of flow)

the lakeshore for part of its length. Woodpeckers can be heard, and possibly seen, in an area with a few dead trees close to shore about halfway down the south shoreline. A number of small coves are prime spots for kingfishers. At the southwest end you can paddle up a narrow arm of the lake and into Locust Creek, which feeds the lake, for about 0.3 mile. A few beaches and gravel bars there make good spots to get out and stretch your legs or stop for a snack.

On the western and northwest areas, mountains rise steeply for 120 feet and the view down the lake is spectacular. A little less than halfway down the north side is the swimming beach, which may be crowded on hot summer days. Hawks and vultures are the primary species you'll see in the skies, while

Heading around the bend, this kayaker enjoys exploring the coves of Tuscarora Lake.

warblers and woodland birds will be found flitting about in the trees lakeside. Ducks and geese will be seen more in the grassy area west of the dam and in the southwest arm of the lake. Do look into the clear waters on occasion, especially in shallow areas, to see sunfish, minnows, or even a bass. Muskellunge, pickerel, catfish, and yellow perch also inhabit the lake.

After your paddle, you may consider taking the 0.1-mile hiking trail that leads west from the restrooms to a shady picnic area. You can also head to the east side of the launch and walk the 0.6-mile Lake View Trail for a lakeside hike around the dam and along the southern shoreline. Raccoons, deer, skunks, pheasants, grouse, and foxes are some of the wildlife you might find along the trail. Tuscarora State Park offers seven trails for a total of 9.8 miles of hiking. Trails range from 0.3 to 1.4 miles. Pick up a detailed map at the park office.

Locust Lake is a short 10-minute drive west. There you will find a large campground with many sites close to the lake. Pick up a brochure with travel directions from the Tuscarora park office and make camping arrangements if you intend to stay overnight.

For another nearby paddle, visit Mauch Chunk Lake, 30 minutes east. See Trip 56.

56 | Mauch Chunk Lake Park

A backdrop of a long mountain range, birds of prey, waterfowl, and the nearby historic town of Jim Thorpe are yours to enjoy when you visit this lake.

Location: Jim Thorpe, PA
Maps: DeLorme *Pennsylvania Atlas and Gazetteer*, Maps 66 and 67; USGS Nesquehoning
Area: 330 acres
Time: 2.5–3.0 hours
Conditions: Depth average 15 feet
Development: Rural
Information: Mauch Chunk Lake Park, 625 Lentz Trail, Jim Thorpe, PA 18229; 570-325-3669.
Camping: On-site. Call the park for reservations. Jim Thorpe Camping Resort is 5 minutes east. See Appendix A.
Take Note: Electric motorboats only; Pennsylvania boating regulations apply. See Appendix D.

GETTING THERE

From the intersection of Route 209 and the PA Turnpike NE Extension, drive 2.2 miles west on Route 209 to Bankway Street/Route 209. Turn right on Bankway Street/Route 209 and continue to drive 3.9 miles to Race Street. Turn left on Race Street and drive 0.2 miles to West Broadway Street. Turn left on West Broadway Street and drive 1.2 miles. West Broadway Street will then change name to Lentz Trail/White Bear Drive. Continue on Lentz Trail/White Bear Drive for 2.5 miles. Turn left into the park office. The boat ramp is about 200 yards past the park office. Parking is available for about 40 cars. *GPS coordinates*: 40°50.629′ N, 75°48.335′ W.

WHAT YOU'LL SEE

Approximately 2,500 acres in size, Mauch Chunk Lake Park offers a 300-acre lake, camping, swimming, and 30 miles of trails. Around the park office on the northeast side, you'll find a small camp store, picnic area, boat launch, and a 400-foot swimming beach. Mauch Chunk Ridge rises more than 200 feet above the lake on the south side to provide a beautiful sloping forest backdrop. A long

MAUCH CHUNK LAKE PARK

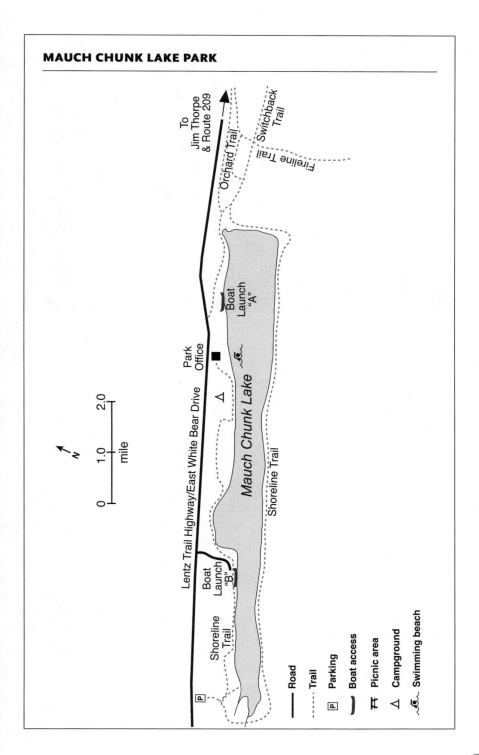

Mauch Chunk Ridge creates a scenic backdrop all along the southern shore of the lake.

ridge also rises more than 200 feet on the north side, and although it's a steeper incline, the rise starts farther back from the lake.

The long, thin lake is rather straight along its southern shore, but has enough little irregularities for an interesting and scenic paddle. On my first trip here, I spent at least half an hour simply paddling along without looking where I was going—I could not take my eyes off the beautiful long mountain range rising directly up from the south shore. Many birds dart in and out of the trees along the lake. In the sky, watch for eagles, hawks, and vultures. White Bear Creek enters the lake on the western end. The water here gets very shallow, which means it's the first area to warm up in early summer. You'll also find more patches of water grasses and plants that provide good foraging for ducks and geese. The marshy wetlands literally teem with birds. Look for the observer's shack in the northwest corner. It's part of the bird sanctuary along the Fitness Trail that you might want to hike later. Fish commonly found throughout the lake are walleye, which are stocked each year, yellow perch, yellow bullhead, largemouth bass, pickerel, black crappie, pumpkinseed, and bluegill. Fish habitat structures have been placed in the lake over the years to provide improved environmental conditions for local species.

On the north side of the lake, the western half has a few areas of open fields and a large boat launch primarily used for boats on trailers. Once past that launch, the lakeshore is once again forested and very pretty. A large cove west of the launch is shallow along the shoreline and has a lot of picturesque fallen trees and weathered stumps. Look on the stumps for turtles basking in the sun, and peer into the clear water for fish, especially sunfish. Deer, foxes, groundhogs, and raccoons inhabit the park and might be sighted close at the edge of the lake.

Almost 30 miles of trails will keep the hiker happy. The longest, Switchback Trail, is 18 miles long. This out-and-back trail guides you from the east end of the lake along an old gravity railroad bed and into the quaint historic town of Jim Thorpe. Pick up a park map at the office and ask about current trail conditions and specifics before starting out.

The camping area is primarily for tents. The bathroom and shower facilities were clean during my recent visit, but the shower valve only remained on while I held it. One tip I found online was to bring an 8-foot string, tie it to the valve, and stand on it to provide continuous water while you lather up and again to rinse off.

Take a drive through the town of Jim Thorpe after your paddle and stroll the streets and quaint shops. The town was named Mauch Chunk until 1954, when the widow of Olympic athlete Jim Thorpe, who never set foot in the town, offered her husband's name in exchange for a memorial. The town had been looking for a way to attract business. A 20-ton monument marks his burial place on the east side of town.

Nearby trips include Tuscarora State Park, 30 minutes west, and Beltzville State Park, 30 minutes east. See Trips 55 and 57, respectively.

---

57 | Beltzville State Park— Beltzville Lake

Enjoy steeply wooded cliffs, rock faces, crystal clear water, a hike to a waterfall, and abundant wildlife at this lake.

Location: Lehighton, PA
Maps: DeLorme *Pennsylvania Atlas and Gazetteer*, Map 67; USGS Lehighton
Area: 949 acres
Time: 4.0–4.5 hours
Conditions: Depth average 40 feet

Development: Rural

Information: Beltzville State Park, 2950 Pohopoco Drive, Lehighton, PA 18235; 610-377-0045.

Camping: Mauch Chunk State Park, 20 minutes west; Don Laine Family Campground, 10 minutes east. See Appendix A.

Take Note: Two no-wake zones; unlimited horsepower motorboats; winds; Pennsylvania boating regulations apply. See Appendix D.

GETTING THERE

To the park office: From the intersection of Route 209 and Harrity Road (the PA Turnpike NE Extension overpass is next to and nearly above this intersection), drive north on Harrity Road for 0.1 mile. Turn right onto Pohopoco Drive and go 2.1 miles to the entrance road and park office on your right. *GPS coordinates*: 40°51.832′ N, 75°37.630′ W.

To Preacher's Camp boat ramp: From the intersection of Route 209 and the PA Turnpike NE Extension, drive 5.7 miles north on Route 209 to Preacher's Camp Road. Make a very sharp left onto Preacher's Camp Road and drive 1.0 mile to the launch entrance on your left. You'll find parking for about 40 cars. *GPS coordinates*: 40°52.371′ N, 75°34.439′ W.

WHAT YOU'LL SEE

Wait until you see this 949-acre long and narrow lake that sits within a 3,000-acre state park. Motorboats are limited to a maximum speed of 45 MPH, which can produce quite a wake, but close to 12 of the nearly 20 miles of shoreline lay within a strictly enforced "no wake zone."

From the quiet boat launch at the end of Preacher's Camp Road within the no wake zone, you can paddle left (west) for 0.5 mile before the zone ends at the beginning of the first long and narrow cove on the north side. Many paddlers simply head northeast across the lake to enter Wild Creek Cove, the long northeast arm of the lake. On my last trip there, my friend and I spotted a river otter about a half-mile up from the cove's entrance. That cove is only 1.0 mile long, but it will take some time to paddle to the northeast tip as you look at wildlife, investigate the thinly layered rocks and numerous rock faces, and make "wow" sounds around every corner at the beautiful scenery of steep, wooded cliffs. Along the paddle, particularly in the upper reaches of the cove, peer beneath the surface at the huge boulders, some of which come within 2 to 3 feet of the surface. The water is so clear that you can sometimes see 20 feet down. I always enjoy seeing how many different fish species I can spot.

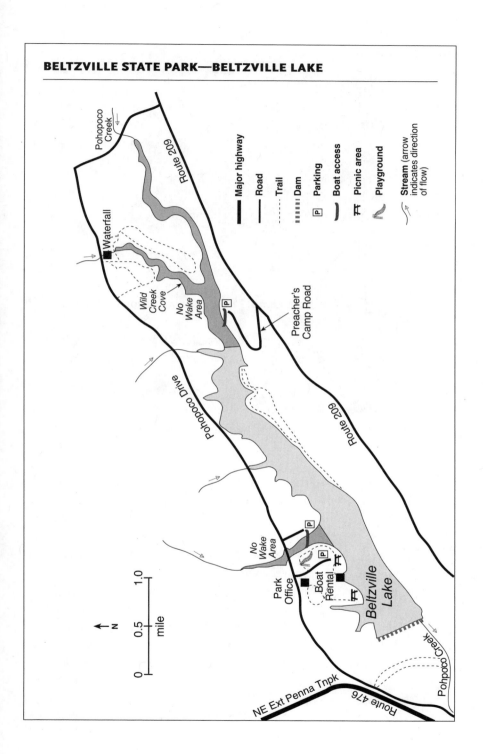

BELTZVILLE STATE PARK—BELTZVILLE LAKE

Legend:
- Major highway
- Road
- Trail
- Dam
- P Parking
- Boat access
- Picnic area
- Playground
- Stream (arrow indicates direction of flow)

Pohopoco Creek

Route 209

Waterfall

Wild Creek Cove

No Wake Area

Preacher's Camp Road

Pohopoco Drive

Route 209

No Wake Area

Park Office

Boat Rental

Beltzville Lake

Pohpoco Creek

N

0   0.5   1.0
mile

NE Ext Penna Tnpk

Route 476

This paddler taking out the tip of Wild Creek Cove is about to take a short hike.

The best treat in this arm is the waterfall at the end. At the very tip of the arm, look for gravel bars on your right where Wild Creek enters the lake. You'll see a wooden bridge ahead of you where the Falls Trail crosses the creek about 50 feet north of the gravel bars. The size of the bars will depend upon water levels, but there's always room for at least six to eight boats. A bonus is that because there are shallow gravel areas and sunken tree trunks along the last hundred feet or so, even small motorboats don't make it up this far—you'll find only canoes and kayaks. Exit your boat, grab your lunch, and look for a small trail that leads to the east side of the bridge and continues to the waterfall about 150 feet farther north. The path meanders through a primarily pine and hemlock forest with a needle-strewn understory and lots of mountain laurel. A huge boulder on the side of the waterfall offers a terrific spot to have lunch to the music of water cascading over rocks. It's not a large waterfall, perhaps only about 10 feet high, but the setting is gorgeous and the walk through the shady forest is a welcome respite on a hot day.

After lunch, head back out Wild Creek Cove and turn left to enter Pohopoco Creek Cove on the southeast side of the lake. This cove is 2.0 miles long from its entrance to the Trachsville Hill bridge. Picturesque rock faces along the steep sides of the lake present numerous photo opportunities. If you have a fishing rod, cast your line for striped bass, largemouth and smallmouth bass, muskellunge, trout, walleye, perch, and pan fish. Beyond the bridge, the right side of the creek hosts an area of cattails, pickerelweed, and waterlilies where you'll likely find Canada geese and assorted ducks. If water levels are low, a gravel bar may extend too far across the creek to allow easy passage farther upstream into Pohopoco Creek.

Seven trails ranging from 0.4 to 2.5 miles in length for a total of 15 miles are located around the lake. Stop at the visitor center and pick up a brochure on hiking trails. For fossil hunters, Beltzville has Devonian period fossils of brachiopods, clams, bryozoans, crinoids, coral, cephalopods, snails, and trilobites.

Mauch Chunk Lake is 30 minutes west. See Trip 56. Consider paddling Beltzville, then heading to Mauch Chunk to camp overnight and paddle there the next day.

---

58 | Minsi Lake

Unique wetlands, marble salamanders, scarlet tanager breeding grounds, plentiful wildlife, and a view of the Kittatinny Ridge are yours to enjoy here.

Location: North Bangor, PA
Maps: DeLorme *Pennsylvania Atlas and Gazetteer*, Map 58; USGS Stroudsburg
Area: 117 acres
Time: 1.5–2.0 hours
Conditions: Depth average 12 feet
Development: Rural
Information: Northampton County Parks and Recreation Division, 669 Washington Street, Easton, PA 18042; 610-746-1975.
Camping: Hickory Lake Campground, 10 minutes northwest. See Appendix A.
Take Note: Electric motorboats only; Pennsylvania boating regulations apply. See Appendix D.

GETTING THERE
To the west launch: From the intersection of Routes 191 and 512 in Bangor, drive 450 feet east on Market Street, then turn left onto North Main Street and drive 1.0 mile. Stay right to make a slight right onto Creek Road and drive 2.1 miles, then stay right to make a slight right onto Lake Minsi Drive and drive 1.0 mile. Turn left onto Blue Mountain Drive and drive 300 feet. The parking lot entrance will be on your right. You'll find parking for 80 cars. *GPS coordinates*: 40°54.829′ N, 75°10.698′ W.

To the east launch: Follow as above, but stay right to stay on Lake Minsi Drive and drive an additional 0.4 mile, then turn left onto East Shore Drive and drive 0.4 mile to the parking lot entrance on your left. You'll find parking for 80 cars. *GPS coordinates*: 40°54.814′ N, 75°09.892′ W.

WHAT YOU'LL SEE
This lake lies within the 300-acre Minsi Lake Wilderness Area, which also includes hiking trails and a unique vernal pond wilderness, in the shadow of the striking Kittatinny Mountain escarpment 3 miles north. An escarpment is an abrupt change in elevation defining two physiographic provinces. In this case, the escarpment defines the edge between the Ridge and Valley province to the northwest and the Great Valley and Piedmont provinces to the southeast. It is a spellbinding geographic landscape that will keep you turning your head throughout your paddle.

From above, it looks like two lakes connected by a narrow strip of water on the southern edge. Two boat launches, one on each side of the lake, have surfaced ramps. Two streams on the northwest arm and one stream on the northeast arm provide the majority of the water for the lake. If you look at a satellite image, the area north of the lake for more than a half-mile is pockmarked with vernal ponds that average 30 to 50 feet in diameter. These temporary pools of water are created by snow melt and spring rains, and usually dry up in summer. These ponds are ecologically important because they provide a perfect habitat for salamanders that can grow without becoming prey to fish. Numerous species of smaller birds find water in these ponds and cover to nest and reproduce.

The west half of the lake sports two narrow berms that jut into the lake for people to fish, bird-watch, or simply enjoy the feeling of being out in the lake a bit. Anglers cast their lines here for walleye, rainbow trout, catfish, pickerel, white perch, and largemouth bass. Kayak fishing is becoming very popular.

There is an informal trail in the park around the southern end of the lake. However, that awesome mountain you've been looking at offers spectacular

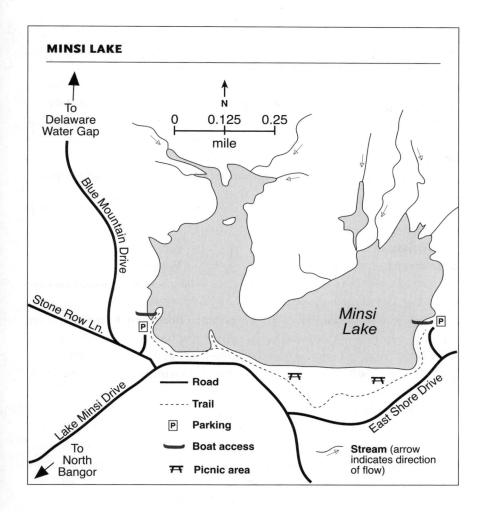

MINSI LAKE

To
Delaware
Water Gap

N

0   0.125   0.25
mile

Blue Mountain Drive

Stone Row Ln.

Lake Minsi Drive

P

P

Minsi
Lake

East Shore Drive

To
North
Bangor

————— **Road**

- - - - - **Trail**

P **Parking**

⌣ **Boat access**

🏓 **Picnic area**

↝ **Stream** (arrow
indicates direction
of flow)

hiking within a 20-minute drive. Many hikers want to climb Mount Tammany on the New Jersey side, but the best view is from Mount Minsi on the Pennsylvania side. To reach the trail heads in the town of Delaware Water Gap, turn right out of the west launch parking lot, make an immediate right onto Blue Mountain Drive, and drive 2.4 miles. Continue straight on National Park Road (an unimproved, but well-maintained road) and drive 2.5 miles, then turn right onto the paved National Park Road for 0.8 mile. Turn left onto Route 611 and drive 3.3 miles, then turn left onto Mountain Road for 0.1 mile, and then left onto Lake Road for 0.1 mile. A large kiosk with trails and descriptions is at the east end of the parking lot.

For an additional paddle the same day, visit Columbia Lake in New Jersey, 20 minutes northeast. See Trip 14.

59 | Little Buffalo State Park—
Holman Lake

Raptors, aquatic mammals, woodland birds, and a historic grist mill are the highlights of this park.

Location: Newport, PA
Maps: DeLorme *Pennsylvania Atlas and Gazetteer*, Map 77; USGS Newport
Area: 88 acres
Time: 1.5 hours
Conditions: Depth average 8 feet
Development: Rural
Information: Little Buffalo State Park, 1579 State Park Road, Newport, PA 17074; 717-567-9255.
Camping: On-site, call the office. For online reservations, go to www. visitPAparks.com or call 888-727-2757. Riverfront Campground is 25 minutes southeast. See Appendix A.
Take Note: Electric motorboats only; Pennsylvania boating regulations apply. See Appendix D.

GETTING THERE
To the park office and main launch: From the junction of Routes 22/322 and Route 34, drive west on Route 34/Red Hill Road 1.9 miles to South Fourth Street/Route 34/Route 849. Turn left onto South Fourth Street/Route 34/Route 849 and drive 0.2 mile to Route 34/Route 849. Turn right onto Route 34/Route 849 and drive 0.4 mile to Route 34/Route 849. Turn right to stay on Route 34/ Route 849 and continue driving on Route 34 for 0.4 mile to Little Buffalo Road. Turn right onto Little Buffalo Road and drive 1.8 miles to State Park Road. Turn left and the park office will be on your left in 300 feet. *GPS coordinates:* 40°27.494′ N, 77°10.143′ W.

    To the east launch: Continue past the park office on State Park Road and drive 0.14 miles to the entrance road to the boat launch and drive 0.4 mile to the launch parking lot. You'll find parking for about 40 cars. *GPS coordinates:* 40°27.382′ N, 77°10.128′ W.

WHAT YOU'LL SEE
Nobody seems to know the origin of the name of this 923-acre park, but the best guess from locals is that buffalo once roamed the area more than a hundred

LITTLE BUFFALO STATE PARK—HOLMAN LAKE

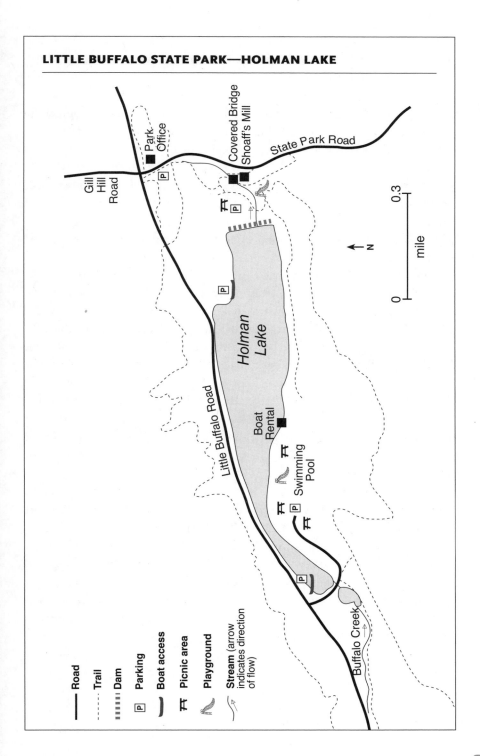

Gill Hill Road

Park Office

Covered Bridge
Shoaff's Mill

State Park Road

N

0.3

0

mile

Holman Lake

Little Buffalo Road

Boat Rental

Swimming Pool

Buffalo Creek

Road

Trail

Dam

P **Parking**

Boat access

开 **Picnic area**

Playground

Stream (arrow indicates direction of flow)

years ago. Most of the waters to the west and north of Harrisburg are either fast-flowing and often shallow, rocky creeks or the large Susquehanna River, which attracts large motorboats. Fortunately there are a few quiet water areas for you to paddle within an hour's drive, and Holman Lake is one of them.

The north shoreline is rimmed by a swath of relatively barren land about 20 feet wide. Only a few scrubby bushes are found along the edge, except for a small area of trees around the northwest launch and another one near the far northeast spillway. Directly behind that edge is Little Buffalo Road, which is backed by low wooded hills. Small areas of aquatic grasses and plants such as waterlilies and arrow weed grow in the southern side of the narrow western third of the lake, where I got a quick glimpse of either a mink or muskrat along a low embankment. I watched for a while, but the critter never showed again. Mink are nocturnal feeders, so my guess is that it was a muskrat.

The large eastern part of the lake can be quite noisy on hot summer weekends because of the huge pool, playground, boat rental, and picnic facilities. Once past that area, the rest of the wooded southern shoreline is fairly quiet and pleasant to paddle. Most of the trees are oak, maple, ash, hemlock, and pine. For a picnic lunch, my advice would be to finish your paddle, drive back toward the park office, turn right on State Park Road, cross over the creek, and make the first right turn into a large parking lot. Beyond the east edge of the lot behind the restroom building is a trail that leads to rustic Clay's Covered Bridge, with its huge, long arches and then on to historic Shoaff's Mill. Between the parking lot and the covered bridge are numerous small, shady clearings with a picnic table in each. After lunch, follow the trail to the covered bridge and on to the mill for a walk back into history.

The park offers seven trails that cover 8.0 miles. Trails range from 0.25 mile to 2.5 miles in length and from easy to difficult. Muskrat, mink, and beaver are usually spotted in and around the Little Buffalo Creek Trail on the west that follows alongside Little Buffalo Creek for about a half-mile. On many of the trails you might spot wild turkeys, grouse, and large colonies of biting Allegheny mound-builder ants. Stay clear of the mounds!

You can camp overnight here and visit Faylor and Walker lakes, 1 hour north, the next day. Or drive to the campground near Walker and Faylor lakes, stay there, and paddle those lakes the next day. See Trip 54.

60 | Memorial Lake
State Park

Enjoy bluebirds, waterfowl, butterflies, and more at this lovely park.

Location: Grantville, PA

Maps: DeLorme *Pennsylvania Atlas and Gazetteer*, Map 79; USGS Indiantown Gap

Area: 85 acres

Time: 2.0 hours

Conditions: Depth average 10 feet

Development: Rural

Information: Memorial Lake State Park, 18 Boundary Road, Grantville, PA 17028; 717-865-6470.

Camping: Lickdale Campground, 15 minutes east, and Twin Grove Campground, 25 minutes northeast. See Appendix A.

Take Note: Electric motorboats only; Pennsylvania boating regulations apply. See Appendix D.

GETTING THERE

To the northeast launch: From I-81, take Exit 85 toward Fort Indiantown Gap. Merge onto Route 934 North/Fisher Avenue and drive 0.3 mile to Asher Miner Road. Turn left onto Asher Miner Road and drive 0.3 mile to Boundary Road. Turn left at Boundary Road and drive 0.8 mile to the entrance for the boat launch on your left. Parking is available for about 70 cars. *GPS coordinates*: 40°25.444' N, 76°35.800' W.

To the park office: Continue past the entrance to the northeast launch for 0.1 mile to the park office on your left. *GPS coordinates*: 40°25.406' N, 76°35.917' W.

To the northwest launch: Continue past the park office for 0.25 mile to the entrance for the northwest launch area on your left. Parking is available for 40 cars. *GPS coordinates*: 40°25.433' N, 76°36.195' W.

WHAT YOU'LL SEE

As I drove along Boundary Road to the park office, I wondered if all the bluebird houses I saw would yield a sighting of that beautiful bird. In less than half an hour I'd have my answer: Yes. Less than 20 miles east-northeast of Harrisburg, Memorial Lake State Park comprises 230 acres of woodlands, open fields,

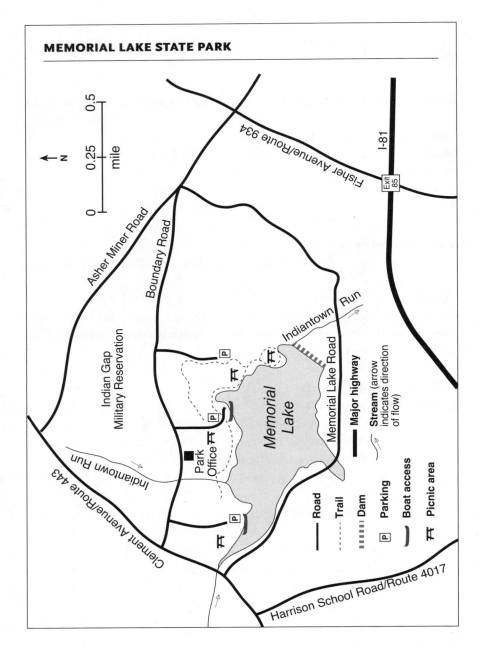

MEMORIAL LAKE STATE PARK

and an 85-acre lake. The park is surrounded by Fort Indiantown Gap, a U.S. Army National Guard Training Center and headquarters for the Pennsylvania Department of Military and Veterans Affairs and the Pennsylvania National Guard.

The beautiful vista from Memorial Lake is very inviting.

Both launch areas have ramps, floating docks, restrooms, and picnic areas with a few grills. The northeast launch has seasonal canoe and kayak rentals. Of the two launches, I prefer the northwest one because it is in a wooded and more secluded area of the park. The small arm of the lake west of the west launch harbors ducks, geese, kingfishers, blue jays, warblers, vireos, and numerous songbirds. Paddling counterclockwise around the lake, there's a small arm in the southwest corner that you can paddle into by going under the Memorial Lake Road bridge. The tunnel is corrugated metal, not picturesque in the least, but when you come out on the other side you may be surprised by the wildlife in that more secluded spot, including little green herons, butterflies and darners, ducks, and a variety of birds. Return to the main lake body and pause at little alcoves to look for birds. More than 100 species have been identified on and around the lake. In late spring and early fall, migrating waterfowl stop on the lake for a respite on their journey. Continue your paddle along the north side, where you may spot some hikers and joggers along the trails.

Look to the sky for red-tailed hawks and vultures. The area is noted for hawks. Second Mountain Hawk Watch, a place where people watch and count hawks, is located at the top of Second Mountain, north of the lake. Signs on the road point to the watch area. Volunteer hawk counters are on duty from

August through December. In the northeast corner, keep your eyes peeled for bluebirds. The open habitat and nearby bluebird houses contribute to this prime bluebird nesting territory. It's there where I spotted three of them, two while I was investigating the boat rental concession and one while paddling. Bluebirds are unbelievably gorgeous with their vivid blue head, neck, wings, and tail, with contrasting blood-rust throat and chest. Males are more vividly colored than females, the latter having a gray head and muted rust throat and chest. When they're in shade, the blue, though vivid, is quite dark, which makes them tough to spot. If you think you've spotted one that has flown into a tree, scan the tree and look for the blood-rust color of the neck and chest.

Continue past Middle Road launch and boat rental area and meander into the large cove. There's a small inlet where Indiantown Run enters the lake. You can't paddle up far, but it's a nice shaded area worth exploring before winding your way to the launch around the corner. Beneath the surface, largemouth bass, muskellunge, pike, perch, crappie, catfish, carp, sunfish, and trout make their home. The lake, in fact, is a designated Big Bass Area, so bring your fishing pole.

The short 0.6-mile Woodland Trail snakes through the hardwood forest on the north side of the lake. A 0.9-mile Exercise Trail on the northeast side of the lake has stations along a path that leads you across open grassland meadows and woodland stands.

Head an hour south to Gifford Pinchot State Park to camp overnight and paddle that magnificent lake the next day. See Trip 72.

---

61 | Nockamixon State Park

Ospreys, waterfowl, a natural rock waterfall, and miles of hiking are attractions of this large lake nestled on the east side of a pretty mountain range.

Location: Quakertown, PA
Maps: DeLorme *Pennsylvania Atlas and Gazetteer*, Map 82; USGS Bedminster
Area: 1,450 acres
Time: 4.0–4.5 hours

Conditions: Depth average 40 feet

Development: Rural

Information: Nockamixon State Park, 1542 Mountain View Drive, Quakertown, PA 18951; 215-529-7300.

Camping: Ten cabins are available on-site. Call the park office, or for online reservations, go to www.visitPAparks.com. Colonial Woods Family Camping Resort is 10 minutes north and Tohickon Campground is 10 minutes west. See Appendix A.

Take Note: 20 horsepower motorboats except in the no-wake zones; winds; Pennsylvania boating regulations apply. See Appendix D.

GETTING THERE

To the park office: From the intersection of Route 563/Mountain View Drive and Route 313/Dublin Pike, take Route 563/Mountain View Drive north. Drive 3.5 miles to the park office on your right. Parking for about ten cars. *GPS coordinates*: 40°27.787′ N, 75°14.526′ W.

To the fishing pier launch: From the intersection of Route 563 (Mountain View Drive) and Route 313 (Dublin Pike), take Route 563 (Mountain View Drive) north. Drive 3.3 miles to Deerwood Lane on your right, turn right and drive 0.5 miles to the parking lot at the fishing pier. Parking for about eight cars. *GPS coordinates*: 40°27.391′ N, 75°14.224′ W.

To Haycock Boat Ramp: Follow the directions to the park office. Pass the park office and continue driving 3.3 miles to the entrance for the Haycock Boat Ramp on your right. Parking for more than 50 cars. *GPS coordinates*: 40°29.368′ N, 75°11.640′ W.

WHAT YOU'LL SEE

Set in the beautiful rolling hills and farmland of northern Bucks County, the 15,283-acre Nockamixon State Park houses a 1,450-acre lake fed by three major streams and a number of small feeder streams. The park is bordered all along its north side by a 2-mile swath of largely uninhabited forested hills, including Maycock and Haycock mountains on the northwest corner, which rise more than 400 feet from the lake's surface, and Rock Hill off the southwestern tip that also rises more than 400 feet. The name Nockamixon comes from the American Indian phrase "nocha-miska-ing" which is Lenni-Lenape for "at the place of soft soil." Of the lake's approximately 24 miles of shoreline, about 13.5 miles lie within no-wake zones. That's a lot of water waiting to be paddled. Off-season and during the week, the rest of the lake is quiet enough that you can explore it in peace and quiet. A plus is that the park's recreational day-use area, centrally located on the north side, is set back from the lake behind a thick cover of trees away from the no-wake zones. The day-use area sports a large swimming pool and most of the designated picnic areas. A large marina is located on the east edge of the activity area.

Haycock boat launch is within the lake's northeast no-wake zone. Lakeside picnic tables under cool pine trees offer a lovely picnic setting. From the launch, paddle left and head under the Route 563 bridge. You'll have road noise for a while, but will soon be beyond it. Explore the nooks, crannies, and shallow coves on both sides of the lake. It gets shallow, with gravel bars and areas of lily pads, as you near where Haycock Creek enters the lake, but most of the time there's a water path to the creek's entrance. You can't paddle up far at all, but it's nice to see one of the input streams. Turn around and paddle back underneath the bridge and head down the east (left) side where there are two large, narrow coves, the first of which has a small feeder stream at its tip. Paddle out of the second cove and head southwest along the shore and rock dam. Haycock Mountain dominates the landscape to the north.

On the far side of the dam, a solid line of white buoys slightly above the surface warns of the spillway 170 feet beyond. I've always seen ospreys here, hunting for fish both in the lake and at the small pond at the bottom of the spillway. If water levels are high, you can hear the magnificent rush of water cascading over the natural stone steps of the 300-foot-wide spillway. You can canvass the spillway from a viewing area off South Park Road after your paddle. You may see many anglers on the lake and fishing from shore; the lake is highly noted for its largemouth bass population. On the far end of the spillway buoys there's a bit of a beach and another about 0.15 mile farther where you can land and take a break while you enjoy the scenery, watch ospreys, hawks, and vultures fly aloft, and watch fish jump in the water. Deer and rabbits are often spotted along the shores, as well as kingfishers, warblers, and a variety of other songbirds.

Continue paddling a little farther and round the point, where you'll have another 0.8 mile before coming to the end of the no-wake zone that ends at the tip of the peninsula to your right (north). You'll be able to see the park's marina a mile ahead of you. If boat traffic is low, consider rounding the peninsula and paddling into the half-mile-long arm. The shallow area at the end is usually filled with waterfowl, frogs, butterflies, darners, and possibly some water snakes. At the Tohickon launch, you can either continue into the large, wide central body of the lake or head back to the launch. On windy days, the center of the lake can whip up quite a chop. Take heed of the wind direction before you decide to venture out.

NOCKAMIXON STATE PARK

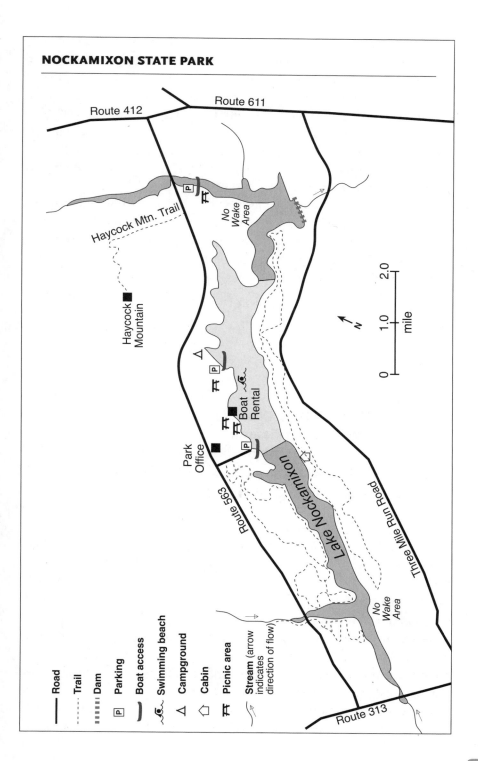

Route 412

Route 611

Haycock Mtn. Trail

No Wake Area

Haycock Mountain

Boat Rental

Park Office

Route 563

Lake Nockamixon

Three Mile Run Road

No Wake Area

Route 313

N

0   1.0   2.0

mile

— Road

---- Trail

▪▪▪ Dam

P Parking

) Boat access

Swimming beach

△ Campground

⬠ Cabin

Picnic area

Stream (arrow indicates direction of flow)

To launch into the other no-wake zone, drive to the fishing pier on Deer-wood Lane, south of the main recreation area. Turn right just before the road heads to the pier and there will be a grass-and-dirt launch immediately to your left. This is the other area where a lot of paddlers launch. You'll have 2.0 miles of paddling south, not counting all the coves, before reaching the end of the no-wake zone. A beautiful large cove, about 0.3 mile long, will be on your right, 0.3 mile south of the launch on the same side. This is where another small feeder stream enters the lake. Raccoons, skunks, rabbits, and deer might be spotted along this quieter area of the lake.

Once you come to a short peninsula where the lake narrows and you see a large inn a few hundred yards across the lake, you're at the end of the no-wake zone. If conditions and boat traffic permit, paddle around the peninsula and into the long cove where Tohickon Creek enters the lake.

If you have time, head to the overlook at the dam. From the junction of Route 611 and South Park Road, drive west on South Park Road 1.35 miles to the pullover area on your right. Don't forget to take your camera.

Lake Galena, 25 minutes south, offers another opportunity to paddle. See Trip 62.

---

62 | Peace Valley County Park—Lake Galena

Here you'll find waterfowl and pleasant pastoral landscapes interspersed with wooded hillsides.

Location: New Britain Township, PA
Maps: DeLorme *Pennsylvania Atlas and Gazetteer*, Map 82; USGS Doylestown
Area: 365 acres
Time: 2.0–2.5 hours
Conditions: Depth average 25 feet
Development: Suburban
Information: County of Bucks Parks and Recreation Department, 230 Creek Road, New Britain, PA 18901; 215-489-5132.
Camping: Homestead Family Campground, 20 minutes west. Tohickon Campground, 20 minutes northwest. See Appendix A.
Take Note: Electric motorboats only. Because this is a county park, you must have a county launch permit. Permits are available at the office or from any

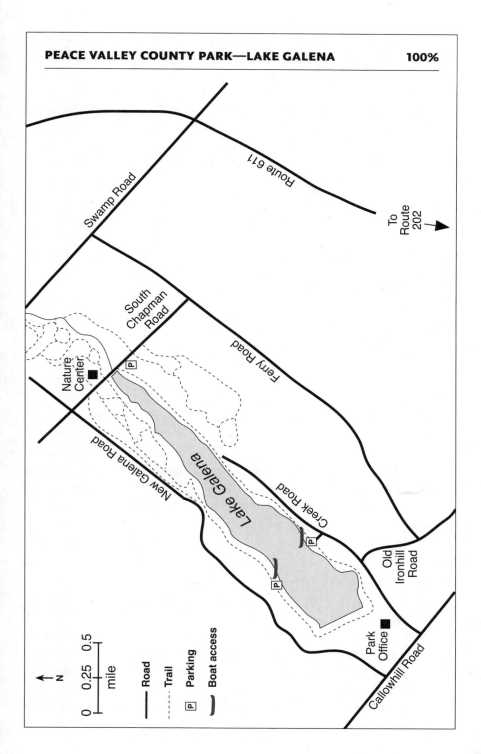

ranger in the park: $20 for non-county residents, $10 for county residents. This permit is also valid for Core Creek Park (Trip 68).

GETTING THERE

To the park office: From the intersection of Route 611 and Route 202, drive south on West State Street/US 202 for 2.2 miles to Keeley Avenue. Turn right onto Keeley Avenue. After 0.5 mile Keeley Avenue will change names to Old Ironhill Road. Continue on Old Ironhill Road and drive 0.9 mile to Creek Road. Turn left onto Creek Road and drive 0.5 mile to the park office on your right. *GPS coordinates*: 40°18.772′ N, 75°12.186′ W.

To the southwest boat launch: From the intersection of Old Ironhill Road and Creek Road above, turn right onto Creek Road and drive 0.3 mile to Creek Court. Turn left onto Creek Court to the boat launch, parking area, and park office. Parking is available for about 50 cars. *GPS coordinates*: 40°19.140′ N, 75°11.518′ W.

WHAT YOU'LL SEE

Set in a rural landscape of rolling hills covered with alternating forests and farmlands, Peace Valley Park's 1,500 acres offer a nature center, duck blinds for viewing wildlife, picnic areas, hiking and multiuse trails, and the 365-acre Lake Galena. The lake's name is derived from the mineral galena, a lead ore, which was mined in this area from the 1860s until the mid-1920s. Don't worry though; ongoing extensive testing by the Department of Environmental Resources reveals absolutely no lead content in these waters. Of the three launches, the southwest launch is oriented more to small boats because it doesn't have the long concrete block ramps for trailered boats found on the two north ramps. This park is quite popular and can become very crowded on weekends and late afternoons with hikers, bikers, and joggers. Out on the lake it's much more peaceful.

Launch your boat and travel along the south shore to enjoy the country views and observe the abundant waterfowl. For the fishing enthusiast, channel catfish, brown bullhead, white perch, largemouth bass, white crappie, gizzard shad, bluegill and pumpkinseed sunfish, and walleye can be caught in the lake. Halfway up the lake you'll notice more woods and less open areas. Here's where you are likely to see belted kingfishers, cardinals, and warblers flitting among the trees along the edge of the lake. Listen for the coarse squawk of the blue heron, a popular bird known to have many nesting colonies in the surrounding countryside. Their long-winged, graceful flight is something I never tire of seeing. Although you'll find ducks, herons, ospreys, gulls, cormorants, and a host of other birds all over the lake, the best bird-watching is here in the eastern half of the lake away from the heavier day-use areas. More than 250 bird species have been sighted in the park, including the long-eared owl.

Painted and red-bellied turtles bask on logs, and rabbits, groundhogs, and deer frequent the shorelines. Cheerful yellow black-eyed Susans, bright red cardinal flowers, and blue asters are among the wildflowers that add bouquets of color along grassy lowland shores. The woods are primarily elms, maples, oaks, ashes, and tulip trees, with enough pines to make a lovely contrast in autumn, and I understand from local paddlers that the display is magnificent. As you near the narrow east side where Branch Neshami enters the lake, you'll start seeing a few hemlocks and cedars. A row of white buoys across the lake marks the protected, human-free wildlife area. Although paddling farther is prohibited, you can visit the shore of that area by foot later. Head back to the launch and explore the tiny coves and little nooks the north shore offers.

It would be worth your time to stop at the nature center on North Chapman Road at the east end of the lake, pick up a detailed hiking map, and find out about current bird sightings. You can also download a map from www.peacevalleynaturecenter.org/pdf/map.pdf. More than 14 miles of trails, with numerous blinds for bird-watching, traverse through lowland forests and wetlands. The center's restrooms are open in the off-season after the other restrooms in the park have closed.

For an additional paddle the same day, visit Lake Nockamixon, 25 minutes north. See Trip 61.

63 | Blue Marsh Lake

Steeply wooded hillsides, scenic views, and abundant wildlife provide hours of paddling pleasure on this large lake.

Location: Leesport, PA
Maps: DeLorme *Pennsylvania Atlas and Gazetteer*, Map 80; USGS Bernville
Area: 1,150 acres in summer, 961 acres in winter
Time: 2.0–10.0 hours
Conditions: Depth average 25 feet
Development: Rural

Information: U.S. Army Corps of Engineers, 1268 Palisades Drive, Leesport, PA, 19533; 610-376-6337.

Camping: Adventure Bound Camping Resort at Eagle's Peak is 20 minutes southwest and Appalachian Campsites is 25 minutes northwest. See Appendix A.

Take Note: Winds; Pennsylvania boating regulations apply (see Appendix D); unlimited horsepower motorboats except in the no-wake zones; both Sheidy boat launch and Pleasant Valley boat launch are within the no-wake zones.

GETTING THERE

To the visitor center: From Route 222, take the exit for Spring Ridge Drive. Turn left onto Spring Ridge and drive 0.1 mile, then turn right onto Papermill Road and drive 0.2 mile. Turn right to stay on Papermill Road and drive 0.2 mile, then turn left to stay on Papermill Road and drive 1.1 miles. Turn right at Rebers Bridge Road and drive 0.6 mile to Palisades Drive, then turn left and drive 1.3 miles to the entrance to the visitor center on your left. *GPS coordinates*: 40°22.852′ N, 76°01.570′ W.

To Sheidy boat launch: From Route 222, take the exit for Route 183/Bernville Road. Turn left on Bernville Road and drive 6.1 miles to the parking area and boat launch on the left. There's parking for more than 100 cars. *GPS coordinates*: 40°24.774′ N, 76°05.128′ W.

To Pleasant Valley boat launch: From Route 222, take the exit for Route 183/Bernville Road. Turn left on Bernville Road and drive 4.5 miles to the parking area and boat launch on the right. Caution: The turnoff for the launch is on your right immediately after crossing a 150-foot bridge that spans one of the lake's small arms. There's parking for about fifteen cars. *GPS coordinates*: 40°24.152′ N, 76°03.679′ W.

WHAT YOU'LL SEE

This 1,150-acre serpentine lake lies within 6,100 acres of Pennsylvania Fish and Boat Commission property and additional State Game Lands acreage. Facilities include the Dry Brooks Day Use Area with swimming beach, showers, food concession, and picnic areas. Picnic facilities are also available at the Old Church Road launch. Of the 35 miles of shoreline, about 20 miles are within the northern no-wake zone, which fortunately is also the prettiest and most interesting part of the lake. If you want to fish, bring appropriate bait for trout, largemouth and smallmouth bass, striped bass hybrid, muskies, walleye, crappie, perch, catfish, carp, and sunfish. Because of the great shoreline mileage, I've broken it into three sections.

BLUE MARSH LAKE

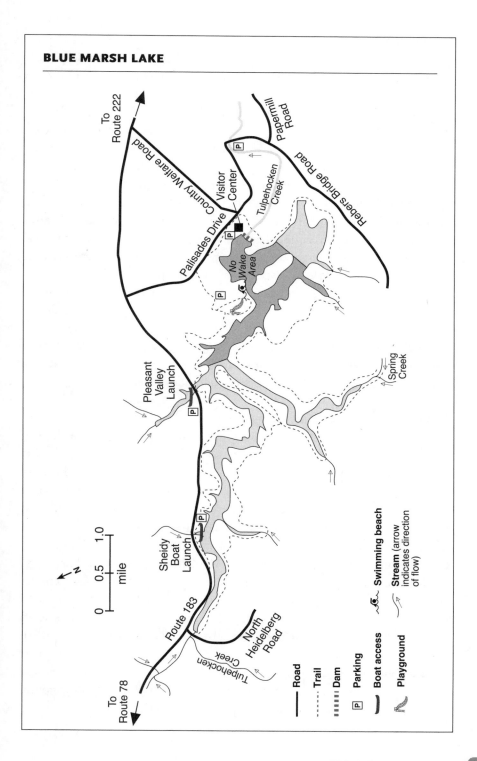

To Route 222

Country Welfare Road

Palisades Drive

Visitor Center

No Wake Area

Tulpehocken Creek

Papermill Road

Rebers Bridge Road

Spring Creek

Pleasant Valley Launch

Sheidy Boat Launch

Route 183

North Heidelberg Road

Tulpehocken Creek

To Route 78

N

0   0.5   1.0
        mile

—— Road
······ Trail
▪▪▪▪ Dam
P Parking
) Boat access
≈ Swimming beach
↗ Stream (arrow indicates direction of flow)
Playground

Sheidy Launch and North

This leg is 4.0 miles round-trip to Robeson Road bridge and 7.0 miles round-trip if you paddle north of the bridge and into the left creek up to the old broken dam.

From the launch, paddle north along the east (launch) side a short way to an inlet where you can paddle under two bridges to explore that little hideaway. Continuing north, you'll pass a point with a nice island at the tip; waterfowl usually hang out between the island and the point. From there, you will have varying amounts of road noise from Route 183 in summer, especially on weekends. Feast your eyes on the high wooded hills to your left to forget about the noise. Once at the tip, where Robesonia Road crosses the lake, Route 183 veers away from the lake. Once under the bridge, you can paddle up the right (east) fork, Little Northkill Creek, for about 0.3 mile until it gets too shallow and rocky.

Return and enter the left (west) fork, Tulpehocken Creek, where egrets and herons share the water with ducks and geese. Low shrubs and a few trees make this is a good habitat for the brilliant blue indigo bunting. Depending on downfalls, you can paddle up a half-mile or more. Lots of wildlife can be found here, including deer, rabbits, waterfowl, and songbirds. Return along the densely wooded west shore to the launch area. Look for cardinals, wrens, kingfishers, flickers, woodpeckers, towhees, and kingbirds along these shores.

Sheidy Launch to Pleasant Valley

This leg is 6.0 miles round-trip and 7.5 miles round-trip if you include the arm across the lake from the launch. Paddle south, investigating coves along the way and admiring the steep, wooded hillside on your right (west). On the other side of Old Church Road bridge, you can ramble around numerous coves and shallow inlets as you snake your way around the highly serpentine waterway. It's so squiggly, you may think you're in an Oriental garden maze—on water, of course. If you see a bird with a forked tail and boomerang-shaped wings that flies with quick, flicking actions, that's a swift. The next wide inlet leads off to your left (north) and passes under a bridge where Licking Creek enters the lake. Turn around here and paddle the other side of the lake back to the launch. Right before the launch, a half-mile arm is tucked between hills of forests and farmland where paddlers often see deer, rabbits, and groundhogs.

Pleasant Valley and South

This leg is 7.0 miles round-trip and 8.5 miles round-trip if you paddle up the Licking Creek arm. Paddle left from the launch to paddle up the arm where

Paddlers head out to explore a narrow passage between the mainland on the right and the island on the left.

Licking Creek enters. Lots of small coves and inlets provide ample opportunity to spot numerous species of birds, including waterfowl, hawks, and kestrels. When you pass under the bridge, stay left and paddle around the point until you see the inlet across the lake. Head directly for the inlet: The no-wake zone is somewhat nebulous in the center of the lake here, but the entire inlet is a no-wake zone. Enter the inlet, where the scenery and quiet are great. After about 1.5 miles, you'll come to a fork. The right side is a little less than a mile round-trip, with wooded hills on the north side and terraced farmland on the south side. Watch for hawks and kestrels that fly over the farmland looking for small rodents. The left side is about 1.8 miles round-trip, mostly dense woodlands with some farmland. There are two small islands to play around that usually have waterfowl. Keep left as it gets narrower to stay in the deeper channel and you can paddle up the creek about 250 yards if water levels are good. Turn around and paddle back to the launch.

Trails include a 30-mile, multiuse trail that circles the lake, and five additional trails totaling 7.5 miles in length. To download trail information and a trail guide map, go to www.berksweb.com/marsh.html, click Army Corps of

CRITICAL TREASURES OF THE HIGHLANDS

The Appalachian Mountain Club has made conservation in the Mid-Atlantic Highlands a priority (see "AMC and the Highlands Conservation Act" on page 24). Within the four-state region of Pennsylvania, New Jersey, New York, and Connecticut, more than ninety priority natural areas threatened by urban sprawl and development have been identified as Highlands Critical Treasures by conservationists. These Critical Treasures provide habitat for plants and wildlife, protection for watersheds, and gateways for nature lovers from nearby cities. However, they are not fully safeguarded and are in need of further protection. And by most accounts, residents living near this greenbelt don't even know these treasures exist.

Highlands Critical Treasures were selected by the state committees of the Highlands Coalition, a conservation project of the Appalachian Mountain Club that fosters collaboration among 200 member organizations to protect the Highlands' natural resources. The coalition successfully advocated for national recognition of this region through the federal Highlands Conservation Act, signed by President George W. Bush in 2004.

The Appalachian Mountain Club's Delaware Valley Chapter leads hikes through many of the Critical Treasures. These hidden gems provide essential habitat for more than 200 species of birds, 300 plant species, and a number of am-phibians, reptiles, and mammals. Some of those species require very specific environments in order to live, reproduce, and roam. A number of them are rare or endangered, while others are threatened in some way.

Middle Creek Wildlife Management Area, Trip 64, is one of Pennsylvania's Critical Treasures and provides an essential refuge for migrating waterfowl. Haycock Mountain, another designated treasure, can be seen from Nocka-mixon Lake, Trip 61. The parking area for the trailhead is a short 5-minute drive from Haycock launch on the northeast side of the lake.

The AMC has produced resources to help guide people toward the Critical Treasures, including the *Pennsylvania Highlands Regional Recreation Map* and Guide and *Hike the Highlands* hiking cards. Visit www.outdoors.org/hikethe-highlands to order the map, view the cards, see a list of all the Critical Treasures, and find out what you can do to help protect these hidden gems.

Engineers info on Blue Marsh Lake, and then click Trail System under Recreational Opportunities.

You may camp at Adventure Bound Camping Resort at Eagle's Peak and paddle Middle Creek Wildlife Management Area or Speedwell Forge Lake the next day. See Trips 64 and 65. The campground is 25 minutes southwest of Blue Marsh Lake and both paddling sites for the next day are within a half hour.

64 | Middle Creek Wildlife Management Area

This lake and surrounding grounds are premier spots for birding and wildlife observation.

Location: Kleinfeltersville, PA
Maps: DeLorme *Pennsylvania Atlas and Gazetteer*, Map 80; USGS Womelsdorf
Area: 400 acres
Time: 3.0–3.5 hours
Conditions: Depth average 8 feet
Development: Rural
Information: Middle Creek Wildlife Management Area, PO Box 110, Kleinfeltersville, PA 17039; Visitor's Center at 717-733-1512.
Camping: Starlite Camping Resort is 10 minutes south and Hickory Run Family Campground Resort is 15 minutes east. See Appendix A.
Take Note: Unpowered boats only; Pennsylvania boating regulations apply (see Appendix D); open from May 16 through September 14.

GETTING THERE
To the visitor center: From the intersection of Routes 501 and 897 in Schaefferstown, drive east on Route 897 for 2.4 miles to Hopeland Road. Turn right on Hopeland Road and drive 1.5 miles, and then continue straight onto Kleinfeltersville Road for 0.8 mile. Turn right onto Museum Road and drive 0.1 mile to the museum and visitor center. *GPS coordinates*: 40°16.234′ N, 76°14.860′ W.

To the boat launch from the visitor center: Exit Museum Road and turn right onto Kleinfeltersville Road. Drive 0.8 mile and turn left onto Millstone

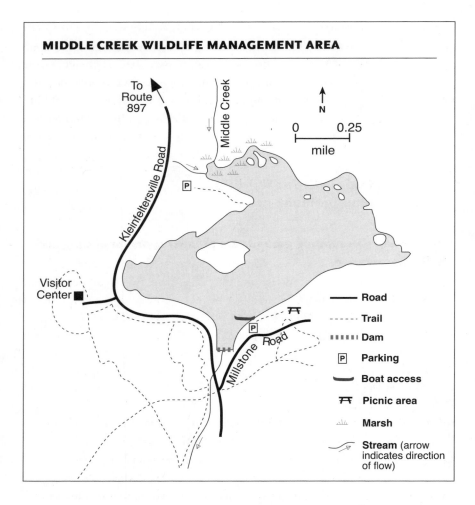

MIDDLE CREEK WILDLIFE MANAGEMENT AREA

To Route 897

Middle Creek

Kleinfeltersville Road

N

0   0.25
mile

Visitor Center

Millstone Road

Road
Trail
Dam
P   Parking
Boat access
Picnic area
Marsh
Stream (arrow indicates direction of flow)

Road. Drive 0.3 mile to the entrance for the launch on your left. You'll find parking for about fifteen cars. *GPS coordinates*: 40°16.057′ N, 76°14.108′ W.

WHAT YOU'LL SEE

Pack binoculars (waterproof ones if you have them), camera, and bird identification guides. Load the boat and gear, then drive on out to Middle Creek for a most intense feathered wildlife show. This 6,254-acre area set aside for protection and propagation is a bird-watcher's dream. The lake is open only from May 16 through September 14, but if you love bird-watching you'll be here often before and after the lake's paddling season. In addition to a regular brochure, hiking trail guide, and driving tour guide, the visitor center offers numerous environmental displays including dozens of nests with eggs of different birds, duck display, binoculars at the viewing area windows, and much more. Up to 100,000 snow geese and 3,000 tundra swans have been on the lake at the same time. The sight must be magnificent, particularly when they flock together near sunset. While the lake is noted as being shallow, it has an average depth of 3 feet and a maximum depth of 12 feet.

Head east (right) from the launch area and paddle quietly along the lake's southern forested hillside. Listen to melodious sounds of woodland birds and look at all the waterfowl floating or flying around the lake from spot to spot. Near the southeast corner, a number of dead trees stick out of the water, providing a good habitat for fish species that prefer to swim around structures. Bald eagles are more likely observed in this area. There's at least one active eagle nest within the forests here and a park ranger told me there are likely three or four nests within the grounds. Limbs sticking out of the water are prime spots for turtles to bask: I saw five on one log, all lined up perfectly by size, although I'm not sure they planned it that way. An interesting cove, two small peninsulas, and a number of very small islands along the east shore harbor a multitude of ducks, geese, swans, egrets, and herons.

At openings in the shrubs and trees at the water's edge, you might catch sight of a pheasant or quail in the tall grasses. Listen for the distinct, and loud, *conk-la-ree* of the male red-winged blackbird. It's a classic sound heard in reeds, tall grasses, and cattail marshes around the continent. Their distinctive patch of red shoulder underlined with yellow against the otherwise all-black bird make them easy to spot. A large cove on the wooded north side can be quite shallow at times of low water, especially in the northeast area where numerous small islands dot the shoreline. Middle Creek, after which the area was named, enters the lake on the northwest corner of this cove. A word of caution, which applies to the whole perimeter of the lake: If a bird acts funny and starts chasing after you, *don't* go closer. Paddle away slowly and quietly. It's quite possibly a mother guarding her nest close to the water's edge.

The northwest side of the lake has a large island to circumnavigate. Do not land on the island as you will most likely disturb courting or nesting birds. There are two other islands, quite small, to venture around, and then you paddle to the southern side, where forested hillsides begin again. Don't be surprised to see a number of deer along your way; they seem to know they're protected here and are not shy about venturing to the lake. Continue around into the cove, where a line of bright orange buoys warns of the dam 80 feet away. Pass well in front of it and around the corner to the launch.

A few picnic tables are located on the west side of the parking lot. Additionally, White Oak Picnic Area, only 0.3 mile north on Millstone Road from the parking lot, has a spectacular view of the lake and permits propane camp stoves so you can heat up hot chocolate or soup in cooler weather. A description of all trails can be found in the wildlife management area's brochure at the visitor center. Eight trails within the park cover 8.0 miles. Trails range from easy to rigorous and from 0.5 to 1.4 miles in length. Additionally, 9.0 miles of the 130-plus miles of Horse-Shoe Trail, which begins at Valley Forge National Park and ends at the Appalachian Trail north of Hershey, crosses Middle Creek.

Speedwell Forge Lake is a 20-minute drive southwest. See Trip 65. You can also camp at Adventure Bound Camping Resort at Eagle's Peak, 30 minutes north-northeast, and paddle Blue Marsh Lake the next day. See Appendix A and Trip 63.

---

65 | Speedwell Forge Lake

Enjoy abundant birds and wildlife in this quiet gem.

Location: Lititz, PA
Maps: DeLorme *Pennsylvania Atlas and Gazetteer*, Map 79; USGS Lititz
Area: 106 acres
Time: 2.0–2.5 hours
Conditions: Depth average 12 feet
Development: Rural
Information: Pennsylvania Fish and Boat Commission Southeast Regional Office, 304 W. Brubaker Valley Road, Lititz, PA 17543
Camping: Starlite Camping Resort is 20 minutes northeast and Pinch Pond Campgrounds is 25 minutes west. See Appendix A.
Take Note: Electric motorboats only; Pennsylvania boating regulations apply. See Appendix D.

GETTING THERE
To the Pennsylvania Fish and Boat Commission office and south boat launch: From the intersection of Route 501 and Route 322, drive 0.1 mile south on Route 501/Furnace Hills Pike. Turn right onto Crest Road and drive 0.8 mile to Blantz Road, then turn left and drive 0.5 miles to West Brubaker Valley Road. Turn right onto West Brubaker Valley Road and drive 0.2 mile to Lakeview Drive. Turn left onto Lakeview Drive into the parking area and boat

launch. To get to the PFBC office, drive 0.1 miles past Lakeview Drive and turn left into the parking lot. Parking is available for about 60 cars. *GPS coordinates*: 40°12.539′ N, 76°19.111′ W.

To the more remote north launch: From the intersection of Route 501 and Route 322, drive 0.1 mile south on Route 501/Furnace Hills Pike to Crest Road. Turn right on Route T476/Crest Road and drive 0.8 mile to Route T582/Blantz Road. Turn left onto Route T582/Blantz Road and drive 0.5 mile to West Brubaker Valley Road. Turn right onto West Brubaker Valley Road and drive 0.2 mile to Lakeview Drive. Turn right onto Lakeview Drive and drive 0.2 mile to the entrance to the parking lot and boat launch on your right. Parking is available for about 30 cars. *GPS coordinates*: 40°12.691′ N, 76°19.256′ W.

WHAT YOU'LL SEE

As you might suspect, the lake was named after an iron forge, which operated between 1760 and 1854. The exact location of any remains of the original forge is not known, but artifacts are believed to be underwater in the lake. The ironmaster's stone mansion is located on a 120-acre farm between the lake and the county park. It was fully restored in 2005 and converted into a bed-and-breakfast. Seasonal canoe and kayak rentals are available at the two northern launches, and a viewing platform is accessible from the south end of the parking lot at the middle launch. A few paddlers I spoke with said that the southern launch by the dam is primarily used by people fishing with trailered electric motorboats because of the deep water there. Portable restrooms are seasonal, but kept well into fall. There are plenty of shaded grassy areas at all launches to enjoy a lakeside lunch.

Launching from the north ramp, paddle left into the north end of the lake. A few shallow areas should allow you to see bait fish beneath the clear waters and sunfish under shrubby overhangs. This area of the lake is where to look for egret nests. Up ahead to the north are a few islands. Paddle to the left side of them where a quiet cove is visited by hungry herons, egrets, and ducks. Fallen branches provide sunning spots for turtles that usually allow you to get quite close if you paddle softly.

Near the entrance to that cove, there's a narrow passageway on the north side where Hammer Creek enters the lake. As long as the water level isn't too low, you can paddle up the creek 0.4 mile or better, depending on downed trees and branches. Paddle back out and around, or through, the islands where you can then explore the small cove. If you think you hear wolves howling, you're correct. There's a wolf preserve very close, part of the 120-acre Darlington farm mentioned above. Information about the preserve is at the end of the text.

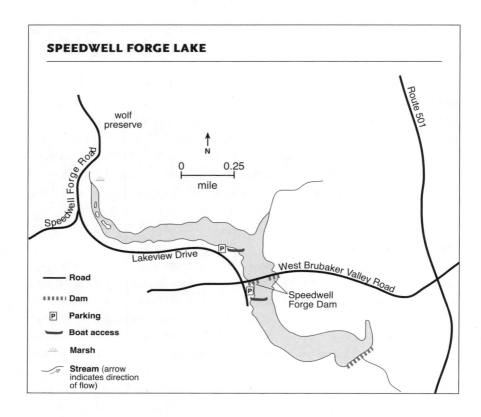

SPEEDWELL FORGE LAKE

wolf preserve

Route 501

Speedwell Forge Road

0   0.25
mile

N

Lakeview Drive

P

West Brubaker Valley Road

P

Speedwell Forge Dam

—— Road

▮▮▮▮▮ Dam

P Parking

╰── Boat access

⸝⸝⸜ Marsh

⤳ Stream (arrow indicates direction of flow)

Paddle along the north shore, keeping your eyes peeled for white egret nesting colonies high in the trees. Egret and heron nesting colonies are built in trees at heights above ground in succession according to their size. In other words, the smaller snowy egret's nests are closer to the ground and the larger great white egret's nests are higher up in the trees. Abundant birdlife, including cardinals, blue jays, warblers, hawks, and many species of waterfowl, are found on and around the lake. There's a neat little cut in the north bank, a little more than halfway back to the launch, where I surprised a raccoon—or rather, it surprised me. Almost directly across from the launch is a refreshing narrow cove with steep sides, about 350 feet in length, where an unnamed creek enters the lake.

Continue paddling around and pass under the West Brubaker Valley Road bridge into the southern half of the lake. This section is more open, with a large farm on the east side. Paddle down the east side toward the dam, following the shoreline, and you'll come to a small arm with a steep north side where you'll likely find belted kingfishers. Largemouth bass, white crappie, carp, channel catfish, and bluegill are sought after species that dwell in the lake. Continue paddling north, go under the bridge, and back to the launch.

A few kayakers head to the southern end of the lake while another enjoys the scenery and waits for her husband to unload his boat.

The preserve will be on your right. Its website is www.wolfsancpa.com.

A veritable birding hotspot is Middle Creek Wildlife Management Area, 20 minutes northeast. See Trip 64. Another option is to camp at Muddy Run Park, an hour south, and paddle that lake the next day. See Trip 78.

---

66 | French Creek State Park— Hopewell Lake

Enjoy waterfowl, raptors, islands, and beaver at this lovely park.

Location: Elverson, PA
Maps: DeLorme *Pennsylvania Atlas and Gazetteer*, Map 81; USGS Elverson
Area: Hopewell Lake: 68 acres; Scott's Run Lake: 22 acres
Time: Hopewell Lake: 1.5–2.0 hours; Scott's Run Lake: 1.0 hour
Conditions: Hopewell Lake: depth average 20 feet; Scott's Run Lake: depth average 8 feet

Development: Rural

Information: French Creek State Park, 843 Park Road, Elverson, PA 19520; 610-582-9680.

Camping: On-site; call the park office. For online reservations, go to www.visitPAparks.com, or call 888-727-2757.

Take Note: Electric motorboats only; Pennsylvania boating regulations apply. See Appendix D.

GETTING THERE

To the park office: From the Pennsylvania Turnpike, take Exit 298 to merge onto I-176 North toward Morgantown/Route 10/Reading. Drive 0.4 mile, then take Exit 1A and drive 0.5 mile to merge onto Morgantown Road/Route 10. Drive 0.5 mile, turn right on Joanna Road and drive 0.9 mile to the T-intersection. Turn right on Elverson Road and drive 0.6 mile, then slight left onto Hopewell Road at the Y-intersection. Drive 2.4 miles to where Hopewell Road becomes Park Road and continue on Park Road 1.4 miles to the park office on the right. *GPS coordinates*: 40°11.903′ N, 75°47.641′ W.

To Hopewell Lake from the park office: Continue past the park office 0.15 mile on Park Road, turn right and then take the first left to the parking lot and launch. Parking is available for 40 cars. *GPS coordinates*: 40°12.002′ N, 75°47.359′ W.

WHAT YOU'LL SEE

This charming lake is nestled within 7,500 acres of magnificent forests at French Creek State Park. Absorbed by the beauty, I almost drove off the road during my first visit as I wound my way down an avenue lined with tall, stately trees on densely wooded hills studded with large rocks and flowering mountain laurel. Most of the park's lands were once part of the Hopewell Furnace landholdings. The furnace's historical site of 848 acres sits within French Creek State Park in the southeast quadrant and houses a museum and several restored buildings. The park is so vast and beautiful that it's no wonder French Creek is a popular summer destination. Make sure to visit the park in the off-season for a more remote adventure.

Two exquisite Lilliputian islands, 50 yards off the beach, filled my vision when I drove down to the launch. As I prepared to paddle, a graceful mute swan glided from behind one of the islands, accompanied right behind by a male mallard, called a drake, with its telltale iridescent green neck and head glistening in the dappled sunlight. When islands are involved, the first thing I do is paddle around them, inspect the types of vegetation, and look for poten-

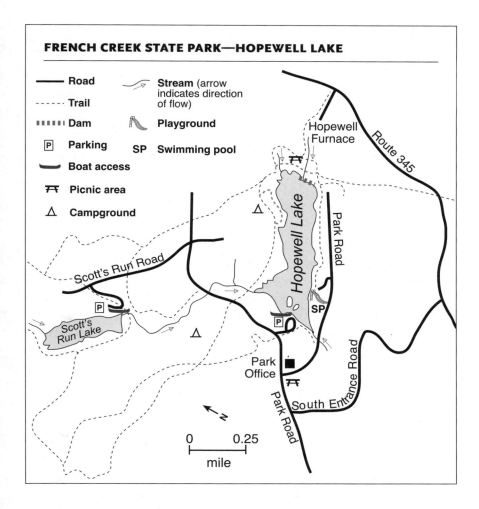

FRENCH CREEK STATE PARK—HOPEWELL LAKE

Road

Trail

Dam

P Parking

Boat access

Picnic area

Campground

Stream (arrow indicates direction of flow)

Playground

SP Swimming pool

Hopewell Furnace

Route 345

Hopewell Lake

Park Road

Scott's Run Road

Scott's Run Lake

SP

Park Office

South Entrance Road

Park Road

N

0   0.25
mile

tial landing sites. Even though there were numerous potential landing areas, I decided that will be an option for a less crowded weekday or the off-season. There's something about having lunch on an island, no matter how close to shore it is, that that makes me feel like I'm in a special hideaway.

Start your paddle counterclockwise from the launch and head into the large cove, where ducks, geese, and swan glide and graze among waterlilies and freshwater grasses. A small creek, Scott's Run, enters the lake near the northern tip of that cove. A small island in front of the creek's entrance makes it somewhat hidden.

The southeast shoreline is much straighter and the southwest half has quite a bit of the park's land-based activities. Beyond that is a long pier for fishing or simply a scenic overlook. A boat rental concession sits on the edge of the entrance to the southwestern cove. The cove is narrow, but quite interesting. This is where there have been large beaver lodges in the past. Downed trees blocked the entrance to the cove when I was there, but I later hiked around the edge and spotted a few remnants of a beaver lodge in the water. Also, look around the path and you will see numerous conical ends of tree stumps that signify beaver activity. I'm not sure if the park will clear the downed trees from that cove area, but if they do and you can paddle in there, listen for the telltale whomping splash of a beaver's tail as it slaps the surface or look for furry heads gliding across the surface.

Scott's Run Lake is a smaller lake within the park and is only a short, well-marked drive from Hopewell Lake. Pick up a map at the office when you enter the park.

A hiker's paradise, the park offers almost 40 miles of trails. Deer, pheasants, turkeys, raccoons, rabbits, and groundhogs inhabit the surrounding woods and are often seen on hikes. Trail lengths range from 1.0 to 8.0 miles, and from easy to difficult. Eight miles of the 130-mile Horse-Shoe Trail, which begins at Valley Forge National Historic Park and ends at the Appalachian Trail near Harrisburg, pass through the park. Pick up a detailed map at the park office or download a park map at dcnr.state.pa.us/stateparks/parks/frenchcreek/frenchcreek_mini.pdf.

If you're camping here or nearby, Marsh Creek State Park is 40 minutes south and Hibernia County Park is 45 minutes south-southwest. See Trips 70 and 71, respectively.

67 | Schuylkill River and the Schuylkill Canal

Historic Lock 60, a locktender's house, a historic canal, wildlife, and a section of the Schuylkill River make this a great destination.

Location: Oaks, PA
Maps: DeLorme *Pennsylvania Atlas and Gazetteer*, Map 85; USGS Phoenixville
Area: 2.5 miles in length, 5.0 miles round-trip
Time: 2.0–2.5 hours
Conditions: Schuylkill River depth average: varies from 1 to 6 feet depending on water levels; Schuylkill Canal: depth average 12 feet
Development: Suburban and open

Information: Schuylkill Canal Association, PO Box 966, Oaks, PA 19456; 610-917-0021.

Take Note: Short portage; Pennsylvania boating regulations apply. See Appendix D.

GETTING THERE

From the intersection of Route 422 and Route 29, drive 2.3 miles on Route 29 South to the entrance for Lock 60. Turn right into the entrance and drive 1.0 mile to the boat launch parking lot on your left. You'll find parking for 50 cars. *GPS coordinates*: 40°08.680′ N, 75°30.529′ W.

WHAT YOU'LL SEE

This paddling trip includes the Schuylkill River and part of the Schuylkill River Canal system that was used to transport coal to the port of Philadelphia from the early 1800s until the 1920s. This is one of the longest sections of the canal and by far the best preserved and restored. The nice thing about paddling here is that if there have been recent heavy rains making the river too dangerous to paddle, you still have a scenic 5-mile round-trip paddle down and back on the flat and calm canal.

Defining a few terms: River-left and river-right are terms used to define river sides—river-left defines the left side of the river when facing downstream, and river-right defines the right side of the river when facing downstream. Hence, if people are paddling upstream, one might say, "Look at the heron river-left," meaning on their right.

Most paddlers launch into the river and take advantage of the downstream flow to carry them along. A word of caution: If the river is muddy and running fast, do not enter it. Launch into the canal and plan your paddle down and back on the canal. Do not paddle upstream to the dam. It looks pretty, but it's dangerous water at the bottom of the dam. On the river, the 2.5-mile paddle downstream offers numerous islands to explore and quite a variety of wildlife. Deer, rabbits, and squirrels are often seen along the shores and there is a wide variety of birds that live along the banks. The first bridge you'll encounter is a railroad bridge about a half-mile downstream, followed thereafter by the Route 29 bridge. Be cautious when passing under stream bridges and pass as centrally as you can between abutments. Strainers, places where limbs and debris collect, will sometimes be found around abutments after a storm. Remember too that a storm 20 miles upstream can affect the waters you paddle here.

After passing under the Route 29 bridge, there will be a few islands on your right you might be able to explore around if the river isn't running too

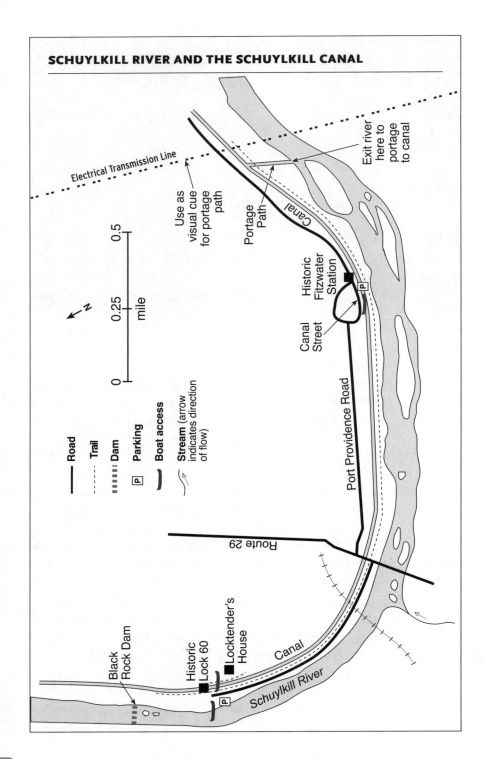

SCHUYLKILL RIVER AND THE SCHUYLKILL CANAL

Exit river here to portage to canal

Electrical Transmission Line

Use as visual cue for portage path

Portage Path

Canal

Historic Fitzwater Station

Canal Street

Port Providence Road

Route 29

0   0.25   0.5
mile

N

Road
Trail
Dam
P Parking
Boat access
Stream (arrow indicates direction of flow)

Black Rock Dam

Historic Lock 60

Locktender's House

Canal

Schuylkill River

Paddlers enjoy a slow, scenic trip on the historic Schuylkill Canal.

fast. You'll find some areas of riffles here, but nothing a novice needs to worry about in normal conditions. Beyond the riffles will be three large islands to enjoy. Look for an abundance of birdlife here that nest on these secluded pieces of land. As you get to a bend in the river where power lines cross, that's your signal to stay river-left and hug the shore. The cleared swath of land where the power lines cross is the portage path over to the canal. A "Portage to Canal" sign is usually visible, but may be temporarily down after a storm. The portage is about 400 feet long, relatively flat, grassy, and easy.

Put in on the canal and begin your paddle upstream. Dense trees overhang and hug both shores, sometimes creating a tunnel effect—a welcome respite on hot summer days. A half-mile up the canal will be Fitzwater Station, a historic tavern still in operation. The food here is excellent. Enjoy a lunch break or come after your paddle for food and refreshments. They are kayak-friendly and provide a small concrete dock on the north side of the parking lot to exit and enter the canal. The restaurant comes complete with an accompaniment of ducks, geese, and swans that have taken up permanent residence here. The outside deck offers a scenic view of the canal that's particularly enjoyable in the sweet light of late afternoon.

From there back to the launch is a very relaxing and pleasant 2-mile paddle with plenty of birdlife to enjoy along the way. If you fish, cast your line for carp, smallmouth bass, crappies, catfish, and blue gills. The exit from the canal can be a little tricky. There's a floating dock that's attached to an area of land with three to four wood-rimmed dirt steps. Just take your time and be careful and you'll be fine; dozens of novice paddlers do this most weekends in summer.

From the launch parking lot, the hiker can enjoy walking along the towpath alongside the canal. A truss bridge crosses Lock 60 and leads south to the Locktender's House across the canal, and north to the natural towpath under a dense canopy of trees that begins above Black Rock Dam and extends 2.7 miles north to Upper Schuylkill Valley Park. Head south from the parking lot and you can walk the towpath to Port Providence, where you portaged from the river to the canal.

An additional paddle nearby is Marsh Creek State Park, 35 minutes southwest. See Trip 70.

68 | Core Creek Park— Lake Luxembourg

Enjoy waterfowl and pleasant paddling at this county park.

Location: Newtown, PA
Maps: DeLorme *Pennsylvania Atlas and Gazetteer*, Map 82; USGS Langhorne
Area: 166 acres
Time: 2.0–2.5 hours
Conditions: Depth average 10 feet
Development: Suburban
Information: Core Creek County Park, Middletown Township, south of Newtown, east of Rt. 413 on Tollgate Road; 215-757-0571. Bucks County launch permit (annual): $10 for county residents; $20 for non-county residents. This permit is available at the park office or from any park ranger. It is also valid for Lake Galena in Peace Valley County Park (Trip 62).
Take Note: Electric motorboats; Bucks County boat permit required; Pennsylvania boating regulations apply. See Appendix D.

GETTING THERE
To the park office and the south launch: From Route 1 north in Langhorne, take Exit 213 S toward Langhorne. At the end of the exit ramp, continue straight

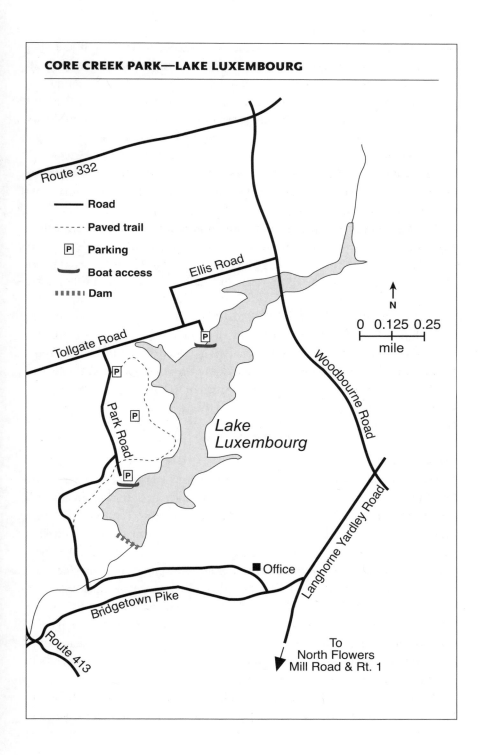

CORE CREEK PARK—LAKE LUXEMBOURG

Route 332

— Road
----- Paved trail
P Parking
⏝ Boat access
⠿ Dam

Ellis Road

Tollgate Road

Park Road

Lake Luxembourg

Woodbourne Road

0   0.125 0.25
━━━━━━━━━━
mile
N

Langhorne Yardley Road

■ Office

Bridgetown Pike

Route 413

To
North Flowers
Mill Road & Rt. 1

on North Flowers Mill Road and drive 0.5 mile. Turn right on Winchester Avenue and drive 0.6 mile (it becomes Langhorne Yardley Road after the railroad tracks), then turn left on Bridgetown Pike and drive 0.2 mile to Park Road on your right, the entrance to the park. Turn right on Park Road and drive 0.1 mile to the park office. If you do not stop at the park office, continue on Park Road 1.4 miles, then turn right and drive to the boat launch straight ahead. You'll find parking for 35 cars. *GPS coordinates*: 40°11.997′ N, 74°55.152′ W.

From Route 1 south in Langhorne: Take exit 213 S toward Langhorne and stay right to turn onto East Maple Avenue. Drive 0.1 mile and turn right on North Flowers Mill Road. Continue as above.

To the quieter and more scenic north launch: From Route 1 north in Langhorne, take Exit 213 S toward Langhorne. At the end of the exit ramp, continue straight on North Flowers Mill Road and drive 0.5 mile. Turn right on Winchester Avenue and drive 1.6 miles (it becomes Langhorne Yardley Road after you cross over the railroad tracks), then turn left on Woodbourne Road and drive 1.0 mile. Turn left on Ellis Road and drive 0.4 mile, then turn left on Fulling Mill Road and drive 0.2 mile to the T-intersection. Turn left onto an unimproved road, make an immediate right, and drive to the launch. You'll find parking for about twenty cars. From Route 1 south in Langhorne, take Exit 213 S toward Langhorne and stay right to turn onto East Maple Avenue. Drive 0.1 mile and turn right on North Flowers Mill Road. Continue as above. *GPS coordinates*: 40°12.538′ N, 74°54.823′ W.

WHAT YOU'LL SEE

Lake Luxembourg is located in the 1,200-acre Core Creek Park near Newtown. The park is the center of recreational activities for a large suburban area, which means it can be crowded on weekends in summer. However, I visited over a major holiday weekend, and while there were family picnics galore, as well as people using the tennis courts, ball field, and playgrounds, the lake itself was fairly quiet. Restrooms and portable toilets are available throughout the park, as are small and large picnic areas and playgrounds. A portable toilet is located at the main launch on the southwest side. A canoe and kayak rental concession is located next to the boat ramp and operates on a first-come, first-served basis. The northwest launch has no facilities, but it's a much prettier place to put in because motorboats can't launch from the dirt launch area and because it's in the more remote area of the lake away from the park's other activities.

From the northwest launch, turn left and paddle northeast along the shoreline, which is lined with hardwood species such as maple, sycamore, oak, and willow. Continue under the Woodbourne Road bridge into the uppermost northeast corner of the lake. Shallow areas such as this usually attract waterfowl. Most of the lake's wildlife congregates here, including turtles, ducks, and geese. You can even paddle into Core Creek, which feeds into the lake, for more than a half-mile and enjoy the cool shade of the canopy. In times of drought, the creek can become quite shallow, so be careful you don't get stuck; otherwise your paddle may turn into a biathlon. Return back to the main part of the lake and venture down the eastern and southern shores lined with sugar maple, willow, beech, and oak. It is spectacular here in October when the trees are dressed in autumnal colors.

The southwest and western shoreline is open and has few trees. That area contains the main launch, a concrete boat ramp suitable for motorboats, plus a number of open group picnic areas. Bass, catfish, sunfish, and white perch inhabit the lake. There is good fishing here and you may see many anglers along the banks. A man fishing from a kayak told me that fishing is better in the center of the lake than along the edges. You'll occasionally see members of Temple University's rowing team in their long skinny boats, called shells, practicing on the lake. Don't get too close; their oars stick out quite far from their boats.

An easy 1.5-mile bike trail is located on the western part of the park. A nearby trip is Silver Lake Park and Magnolia Lake, 10 minutes south. See Trip 69.

69 | Silver Lake Park

You'll find an abundance of waterfowl, wading birds, songbirds, turtles, and wetland wildflowers and vegetation along these lakes.

Location: Bristol, PA
Maps: *Pennsylvania Atlas and Gazetteer*, Map 83; USGS Langhorne
Area: Silver Lake: 50 acres; Magnolia Lake: 35 acres
Time: 1.0–1.5 hours
Conditions: Silver Lake: depth average 4 feet; Magnolia Lake: depth average 10 feet
Development: Urban
Information: Silver Lake Park, Bath Road, Bristol Township, PA 19007; 215-757-0571. Silver Lake Nature Center, 1306 Bath Road, Bristol, PA 19007; 215-785-1177.
Take Note: Electric motorboats only (rare)

GETTING THERE

To Silver Lake Park: From Route 13 in Bristol, drive 0.5 mile north on Bath Road. The entrance to the boat launch will be on your right. You'll find parking for 50 cars. *GPS coordinates*: 40°06.528′ N, 74°51.743′ W.

To Silver Lake Nature Center: Follow directions to Silver Lake Park and drive another 0.4 mile north on Bath Road to the nature center entrance on your right. *GPS coordinates*: 40°06.847′ N, 74°51.827′ W.

WHAT YOU'LL SEE

Silver Lake

Silver Lake Nature Center is a 235-acre complex within the 460-acre Silver Lake Park and bordered by Black Ditch Park on the north end. Mill Creek enters Magnolia Lake from Black Ditch Park, then flows south through the nature center into Silver Lake. This is one of those surprise little gems found in the midst of an urban area, readily accessible for local residents who would like to get in a paddle after work or take a nice hike through the preserve. Restrooms, lakeside benches, a playground, and a picnic area are on the south side of the launch in Silver Lake Park.

Paddle to your right after launching and down the western shoreline to the south end of the lake. Road noise at this end of the lake from Route 13 traffic is partially drowned by a modest buffer of trees and honks from Canada geese that live on the lake. Swinging around the southern tip of the lake you'll probably spot walkers and bikers on the trail that runs very close to the water here. As you meander up along the eastern shoreline, road noise dims. Butterflies, dragonflies, and myriad songbirds become more frequent toward the northern half of the lake, where it starts to narrow. Marsh areas on both shorelines come alive with bright white waterlilies, arrowhead weed, cardinal flower, and a host of other bog plants. Stay river-right for the deepest water as the lake narrows to a creek.

Once in the creek, you are now in the Silver Lake Nature Center. The nature center is involved in ongoing projects to enhance and increase the diversity of plant, insect, and bird species at the preserve. The center also offers guided kayak tours. The area you are now paddling through is an unglaciated bog. Most bogs were formed when ancient glaciers scraped pond-sized depressions into the earth and typically lack good drainage. Unglaciated bogs can form when a nonporous rock layer lies close to the surface and the rock layer itself has a depression, creating an environment conducive to the growth of sphagnum, also known as peat moss.

SILVER LAKE PARK

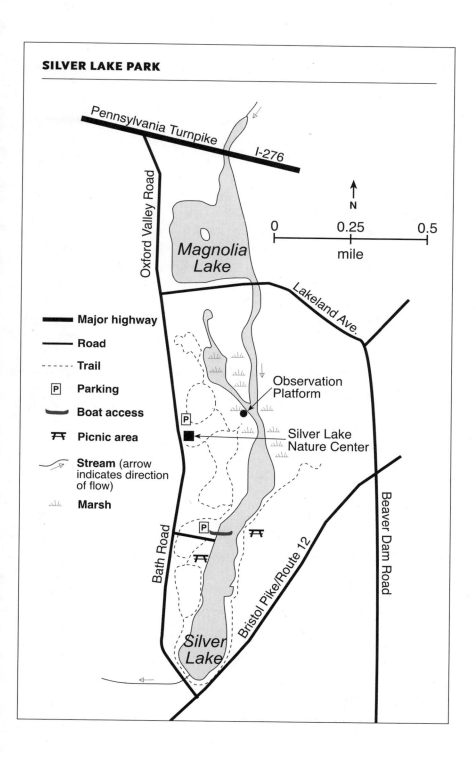

Pennsylvania Turnpike

I-276

Oxford Valley Road

Magnolia Lake

Lakeland Ave.

N

0   0.25   0.5
mile

Major highway

Road

Trail

P   **Parking**

Boat access

⊼   **Picnic area**

⤳   **Stream** (arrow indicates direction of flow)

Marsh

Observation Platform

Silver Lake Nature Center

P

P

Bath Road

Bristol Pike/Route 12

Beaver Dam Road

Silver Lake

Many butterflies landed, or wanted to land, on my boat as I passed through the preserve. Most of the trees are comprised of red maple, red oak, white oak, sweet gum, and sassafras. Now and then a swamp magnolia or holly peeks out from the woods. Painted and red-bellied turtles bask on logs and frog croaks are interspersed with bird chirps. The preserve is home to the coastal plain leopard frog (*Rana sphenocephala*), whose sound is the classic *ribbet, ribbet, ribbet*. Keep your ears attuned. If you see a frog with a white throat and two distinctive yellow stripes down its side, you have found the source of that sound. Along the creek you'll notice an observation platform on the west side. You can get there from one of the trails in the nature center—a walk I recommend.

To enter Magnolia Lake from Spring Lake, keep heading north in the creek and paddle under the Lakeland Avenue bridge and into the block-shaped Magnolia Lake. In times of severe drought, this passage may be difficult or perhaps impossible. Once in the lake, you'll notice a very small island smack-dab in the middle.

For the hiker, the nature center grounds have approximately 4.5 miles of interconnecting trails that link to a few walking paths in the more open Silver Lake Park. One trail leads across the street into Delhaas Woods, a remnant of the Atlantic coastal plain when the shore of the Atlantic Ocean was much farther inland about 10,000 years ago.

Another lake to paddle is Lake Luxembourg, Core Creek Park, 10 minutes north. See Trip 68.

---

70 | Marsh Creek State Park

Enjoy eagles, waterfowl, hardwood forests, and hills at this lake.

Location: Downingtown, PA
Maps: DeLorme *Pennsylvania Atlas and Gazetteer*, Map 81; USGS Downingtown
Area: 535 acres
Time: 3.5–4.0 hours
Conditions: Depth average 15 feet
Development: Suburban
Information: Marsh Creek State Park, 675 Park Road, Downingtown, PA 19335; 610-458-5119.

Camping: Brandywine Creek Campground is 10 minutes west. See Appendix A.

Take Note: Electric motorboats only; winds; Pennsylvania boating regulations apply. See Appendix D.

GETTING THERE

To the park office and main (east) launch: Take Exit 312 off I-76 to Route 100 north toward Pottstown. Drive 2.0 miles to Park Road on your left (it is Station Boulevard on your right), turn left and drive 2.0 miles to the parking lot at the marina. The park office is on your left a few hundred feet before the parking lot. Parking is available for about 100 cars. *GPS coordinates:* 40°03.980′ N, 75°43.258′ W.

To the west launch: Take Exit 312 off I-76 to Route 100 north toward Pottstown. Drive 2.0 miles to Park Road on your left (it is Station Boulevard on your right), turn left and drive 0.1 mile. Turn right on Little Conestoga Road and drive 2.6 miles, then turn left to stay on Little Conestoga Road and drive 0.4 mile. Continue straight on Marshall Road for 0.7 mile, then turn left on Creek Road/Route 282 and drive 1.6 miles. Turn left on Lyndell Road and drive 0.9 mile to the launch. You'll find parking for about 100 cars. *GPS coordinates:* 40°03.893′ N, 75°43.762′ W.

WHAT YOU'LL SEE

Marsh Creek State Park sports 1,705 acres of woods, fields, and a 535-acre lake frequented by paddlers throughout the year. The lake was created in the early 1970s when the small farming community of Milford Mills was vacated and a dam built to flood the valley. Yes, under those deep waters are the remains of a town. Remnants of an old road leading to the town can be seen on the southwest shoreline. If you didn't know what it was, you'd think it was simply a dirt road leading to the lake, but it actually continues into the lake. In summer, the lake is popular for windsurfing and sailing.

I paddle here often with my friends, and our usual plan from the main launch area is to head across the lake to the north arm, pass under the Little Conestoga Road bridge and into the shallow area adjacent to the Pennsylvania Turnpike. Amazingly enough, you won't hear as much road noise from the turnpike as you might think, especially if you focus on observing wildlife. Because a large portion of this section is fairly shallow and has abundant aquatic vegetation, it's perfect for various ducks as well as wading birds and snapping turtles—*huge* snapping turtles big enough to chomp off half your paddle blade. Lots of sunken logs and water plants create an ideal environment for fish fry.

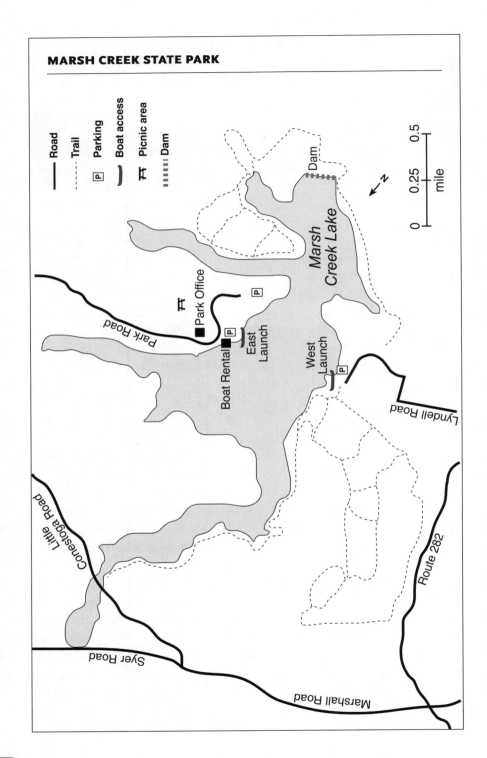

MARSH CREEK STATE PARK

Legend:
- —— Road
- ······ Trail
- Ⓟ Parking
-) Boat access
- 🛉 Picnic area
- ▦ Dam

Marsh Creek Lake

Dam

Park Road

Park Office

Boat Rental

East Launch

West Launch

Lyndell Road

Little Conestoga Road

Syer Road

Marshall Road

Route 282

N

0   0.25   0.5
mile

Marsh Creek Lake is very popular with local paddlers and makes for an ideal place to meet others.

If water levels are high enough, paddle to the northwest corner, where you can go under the double-arched stone Styer Road bridge and enter Marsh Creek. The stream bed gets rocky and you'll find some current. You can't paddle far upstream, but it is a neat side venture in late spring and early summer while the waters are high. By mid-July, that northwest corner may become so weed-choked that you can't paddle beyond the Little Conestoga Road bridge.

Return to the main lake body and head south along the western shoreline, winding your way to the dam while scanning the skies for osprey, frequent visitors of the lake. Once past the dam, the land rises more steeply from the lake. The first arm is short and usually chock-full of waterfowl and wading birds. Cast your eyes into the water next to your boat and notice the good visibility. Continue on to the long, narrow eastern arm, populated by painted turtles and wading birds. By late summer that arm becomes pretty weed-choked, but the wildlife is still present. You may have to clean your blades often of what I call mermaid's hair, long strands of freshwater algae.

Continue to paddle north along the shoreline back to the launch, enjoying the vista and wooded hillside. That last leg, less than a half-mile, can be tough if the winds have come up. Before heading out for the day, check the local weather. If you like to fish, cast your line for largemouth bass, crappie, walleye, tiger mus-kellunge, and channel catfish. The lake is a designated "big bass" lake, which means only bass 15 inches and greater may be kept. The weedy, shallow areas in a couple of lake arms serve as hatcheries for the fish that inhabit the lake.

Six miles of trails ramble throughout the lovely park. Hikes are usually moderate due to the hilly landscape, but they are well worth the effort, particularly for the trails that overlook the lake.

Hibernia County Park is 30 minutes west. See Trip 71. You may wish to consider camping at lovely French Creek State Park, 40 minutes north, and paddle those lakes the next day. See Trip 66.

71 | Hibernia County Park, Chambers Lake

Waterfowl, deer, raptors, frogs, and turtles are part of the wildlife found at this lake.

Location: Wagontown, PA
Maps: DeLorme *Pennsylvania Atlas and Gazetteer*, Map 80; USGS Chambers Lake
Area: 90 acres
Time: 1.0–1.5 hours
Conditions: Depth average 20 feet
Development: Rural, quiet
Information: Hibernia County Park, 1 Park Road, Wagontown, PA 19376; 610-383-3812.
Camping: On-site primitive camping is available Friday and Saturday nights only, from mid-April through late October. No advanced reservation system, although the campground never fills, or so the park ranger told me. Check in at the office to reserve a site before paddling if you plan to camp here. Brandywine Meadows Campground is 15 minutes north. See Appendix A.
Take Note: Electric motorboats only; Pennsylvania boating regulations apply. See Appendix D.

GETTING THERE
To the park office: From Route 30 in Coatesville, drive north 3.2 miles on Route 82 miles to Cedar Knoll Road. Turn left and drive 1.3 miles to Park Road and the park entrance on your left. Turn left on Park Road and drive 0.4 mile to the park office on your right. *GPS coordinates*: 40°01.835′ N, 75°50.484′ W.

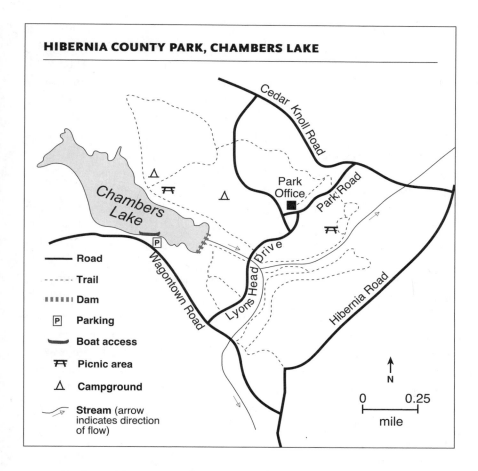

HIBERNIA COUNTY PARK, CHAMBERS LAKE

Cedar Knoll Road

Park Office

Park Road

Chambers Lake

Wagontown Road

Lyons Head Drive

Hibernia Road

—— Road

----- Trail

ııııı Dam

P Parking

⌣ Boat access

⛱ Picnic area

△ Campground

⤳ Stream (arrow indicates direction of flow)

N

0   0.25

mile

To the launch from park office: Drive back out of the park to Cedar Knoll, turn right and drive 0.5 mile to Hibernia Road, then turn right and drive 1.4 miles to the stop sign, which will be Wagontown Road on your right. As of this writing, there was no street sign designating Wagontown Road. Turn right and drive 1.0 mile to the gravel-and-dirt parking lot on your right. Parking is available for about 30 cars. *GPS coordinates*: 40°01.716′ N, 75°51.212′ W.

WHAT YOU'LL SEE

More than 900 acres of Hibernia County Park's woodlands and meadows are set within the steeply rolling Pennsylvania countryside north of Coatesville. Here you can enjoy remote primitive camping, paddle Chambers Lake, and hike along 6 miles of trails. Rock-strewn hills covered with dense woods surround you on your drive to the visitor center. On my visit, a large hawk swooped down about 50 feet in front of the car to snatch something off the road. It was too brief a sighting to accurately identify the species, but a thrilling encounter nonetheless. The restored Hibernia Mansion, an eighteenth-century ironmaster's home, is a short 500-foot walk from the park office and worth a visit. It is open for public tours on Sunday afternoons from Memorial Day through Labor Day.

Chambers Lake's launch facility, located at the opposite side of the park from the visitor center, is open 24 hours a day. It sounds like a great place for a full-moon paddle. The launch area is dirt and gravel with a floating dock and a portable toilet. The hilly north and northwest shorelines are heavily tree-lined with pines, sycamore, maples, and oaks. Some areas have dense understory, while other areas are open and carpeted with pine needles. Parts of the northern shoreline are stabilized with large rocks along the edge that add interest to your paddling and provide a good environment to see fish darting about in the clear water. The small cove area on the western tip is shallow and becomes quite marshy in summer. It's there where you're likely to find ducks, geese, and other waterfowl and wading birds. Healthy populations of dragonflies and darners add sparkles of iridescent blues and greens as they dart around marsh grasses and lily pads. Small clusters of trees, open fields, and grassy knolls share the rest of the shoreline around the lake. Vultures, eagles, blue herons, cardinals, wrens, blue jays, and warblers are commonly sighted. The primary fish species are channel catfish, chain pickerel, bluegills, trout, and smallmouth and largemouth bass. The lake is not large, but the pleasant scenery and quiet surroundings make this an enjoyable paddle.

Almost 6.0 miles of trails meander through woodlands, floodplains, and a mix of gently sloping and steep hillsides. Five trails range from 0.7 to 2.4 miles, and from easy to steep (difficult). Forge Trail traverses through the historic Hibernia Forge area, where the surface is still black with charcoal dust.

The campsites are large with dense understory for privacy. The one drawback is that the campground is open only on weekends. Camp here and paddle from Marsh Creek State Park, 30 minutes east, the next day. See Trip 70. Marsh Creek is also within a 25-minute drive of Brandywine Meadows Campground, mentioned in the trip header in this section.

72 | Gifford Pinchot State Park

Enjoy rocky shorelines and forested hillsides at this state park.

Location: Lewisberry, PA
Maps: DeLorme *Pennsylvania Atlas and Gazetteer*, Map 78; USGS Dover
Area: 340 acres
Time: 4.0–4.5 hours
Conditions: Depth average 10 feet
Development: Rural
Information: Gifford Pinchot State Park, 2200 Rosstown Road, Lewisberry, PA 17339; 717-432-5011.
Camping: On-site. Call the park office, or for online reservations, go to www.visitPAparks.com. Park Away Park Family Campground, 15 minutes northeast. See Appendix A.
Take Note: Electric motorboats only; Pennsylvania boating regulations apply. See Appendix D.

GETTING THERE

To the park office: From I-83, take Exit 32 for Route 382 toward Newberrytown. Drive 3.7 miles on Route 382 to Route 177/Rosstown Road, then turn left and drive 3.7 miles to the park office on your left (Gifford Pinchot State Park Road). *GPS coordinates*: 40°5.226′ N, 76°53.303′ W.

To launch #1: From the park office, continue south on Route 177/Rosstown Road 1.6 miles to the boat launch on your right, immediately after the bridge. You'll find parking for about ten cars. *GPS coordinates*: 40°4.097′ N, 76°54.512′ W.

To launch #2: From the park office, continue south on Gifford Pinchot State Park Road for 0.4 miles to the boat launch on your right. You'll find parking for about twenty cars. *GPS coordinates*: 40°4.994′ N, 76°53.027′ W.

To launch #3: From the intersection of Route 177 and Alpine Road, drive south on Alpine Road 1.6 miles to the launch road entrance on your right. There will be a sign on Alpine Road. You'll find parking for 30 cars. *GPS coordinates*: 40°04.636′ N, 76°52.512′ W.

WHAT YOU'LL SEE

Pinchot Lake sits within the 2,338-acre Gifford Pinchot State Park, named after the first chief of the U.S. Forest Service and former Governor of Pennsylvania.

GIFFORD PINCHOT STATE PARK

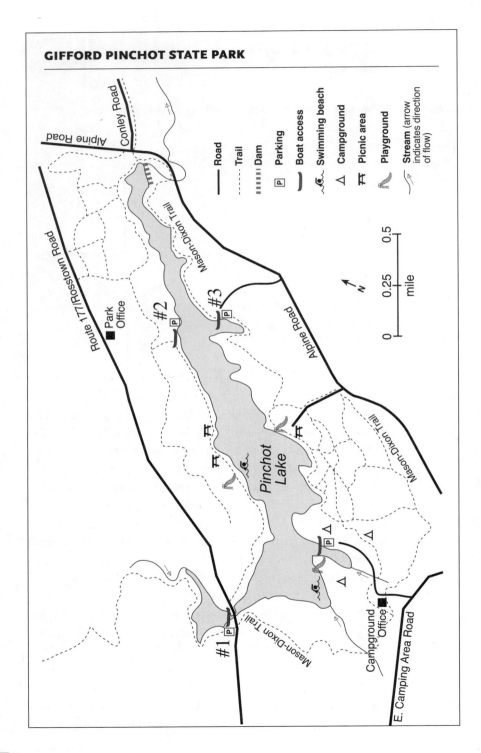

Conley Road

Alpine Road

Route 177/Rosstown Road

Park Office

#2

#3

Mason-Dixon Trail

Alpine Road

Mason-Dixon Trail

Pinchot Lake

#1

Mason-Dixon Trail

Campground Office

E. Camping Area Road

Legend
- Road
- Trail
- Dam
- Ⓟ Parking
- Boat access
- Swimming beach
- △ Campground
- Picnic area
- Playground
- Stream (arrow indicates direction of flow)

0   0.25   0.5
mile

N

A couple head over to Boulder Point, which has interesting rocks called diabase, a rock formed by the cooling of molten lava.

Shortly after I arrived at launch #2, a frequent local visitor remarked, "It's our overlooked gem." Diabase rock underlying most of the park was created when molten rock intruded into the sandstone and melted it into a new kind of rock. Unique cracks formed as the rocks slowly cooled. Large diabase boulders can be found throughout the park, along the shoreline, and at Rock Creek in the northeast corner of the lake. One of the more picturesque spots where diabase boulders are abundant is Boulder Point, the tip of the peninsula, directly across the lake from launch #2. An interesting formation on the point is Balanced Rock, where environmental processes rounded the top and eroded the boulder around the base, leaving a gap between the boulder and the underlying rock. The result looks like a giant rock mushroom. It can be seen on Lake Side Trail, a short walk from launch #3 on the east side of the lake.

I recommend launch #2 or #3 for your first trip here. They're both fairly close to the middle of the lake, giving you the option of a short or long paddle. The park's sailing club center operates from the south side of launch #2. Sailboat activities are generally more active in the afternoon when the winds are up.

From either ramp, paddle to Boulder Point for a close-up look at the diabase boulders. Then head into the northeast end of the lake to explore the many coves, observe wildlife, and enjoy the solitude of the day and sounds of birds, frogs, and breezes rustling leaves. Mountains rise 120 feet on the north side and up to around 40 feet on the south side, giving you a snuggled-by-the-mountains feeling. This park is noted for having at least seven species of woodpeckers. I also spotted quite a few vireos in the trees along the south shoreline, including blue-headed and red-eyed vireos. I love their snowball-shaped nests, when I can find them.

Spring and fall are the best seasons to observe migrating forest birds, warblers, vireos, thrushes, and many more that stop to rest and eat before flying on. The large size of the lake invites thousands of waterfowl such as mergansers, mallards, loons, teals, and geese. Spring also shows the beauty of redbud trees that burst into dusky pink and lavender flowers. Fall is a feast for the eyes with deep green pine and cedars popping out in contrast to the yellows, oranges, and reds of deciduous trees. When you reach the tip of the lake, a row of solid red buoys warns of a spillway. The little cove in the northwest tip is where Rock Creek enters the lake. Paddle into the cove to study the rock steps of this ephemeral stream. Water levels are usually conducive to land and saunter up the natural rock steps for a closer inspection.

Paddle back toward Balance Point and continue toward the more open area of the lake. Large scenic coves on the south side have shallow areas where you're likely to spot fish swimming beneath the surface. Largemouth bass, walleye, muskellunge, crappies, sunfish, carp, catfish, and hybrid striped bass are species sought after by anglers around the lake.

The next lake section, which contains the large beach area on the north side and the day-use playground area on the south side, might be a just-get-past-it paddle if there's heavy activity. It's the only downside of paddling this lake, but fortunately there are still a lot of quiet areas to paddle. On days with strong northeast or southwest winds, this part of the lake can have short choppy wind-waves. Activity areas on the south side are a little back from the shoreline and will be the quieter passage. The far southeast tip becomes carpeted with waterlilies by midsummer. Their bright green leaves and yellow and white flowers provide a pretty change of scenery. Meander over and paddle under the bridge to your north where Route 177 crosses over a very narrow neck of the lake. Immediately to the left you'll see launch #1, another access to the lake you can launch from at a later date. This area is rather shallow, with waterlilies and aquatic grasses taking over the edges as summer wears on. Ducks, geese, egrets, and herons are common visitors here. On the right (northeast) side is the channel where Beaver Creek enters the lake.

More than 18 miles of marked trails and a total of ten trails are located within the park. Most trails interconnect to create longer or shorter hikes. Trails range from 0.4 to 8.5 miles in length, and from easy to difficult. Additionally, 8.5 miles of the 193-mile Mason-Dixon Trail pass through the park. A downloadable version of the park map can be found at www.dcnr.state.pa.us. In the top left search box, type Gifford Pinchot trail. The first result is a guide that gives a brief description of each trail.

Camp overnight here and visit either Williams or Redman lakes, 45 minutes southeast, or Speedwell Forge Lake, an hour northeast, the next day. See Trips 76 and 65, respectively.

73 | Long Pine Run Reservoir

Waterfowl, mountains, raptors, clean clear water, and a nearby historic forge make this trip a delight.

Location: Fayetteville, PA
Maps: *Pennsylvania Atlas and Gazetteer*, Map 91; USGS Caledonia Park
Area: 150 acres
Time: 2.0–2.5 hours
Conditions: Depth average 25 feet
Development: Rural
Information: Michaux State Forest, 10099 Route 30, Fayetteville, PA 17222; 717-352-2211.
Camping: Caledonia State Park, 10 minutes south. See Appendix A.
Take Note: Electric motorboats only; Pennsylvania boating regulations apply. See Appendix D.

GETTING THERE

From the junction of Routes 30 and 81, drive east on Route 30 for 8.6 miles. Turn left onto Route 233 north and drive 1.6 miles, then turn left onto Milesburg Road and drive 1.4 miles to the parking lot entrance on your right. Caution: The turn onto Milesburg Road is a hairpin turn. Also, the wood-carved sign on the road can be confusing as it states three roads: Milesburg Road/Long Pine Dam, Birch Run Road, and Stillhouse Hollow Road. Only Birch Run Road has the grooves filled in with white paint to make it stand out. There's parking for about 30 cars. *GPS coordinates*: 39°56.079′ N, 77°27.140′ W.

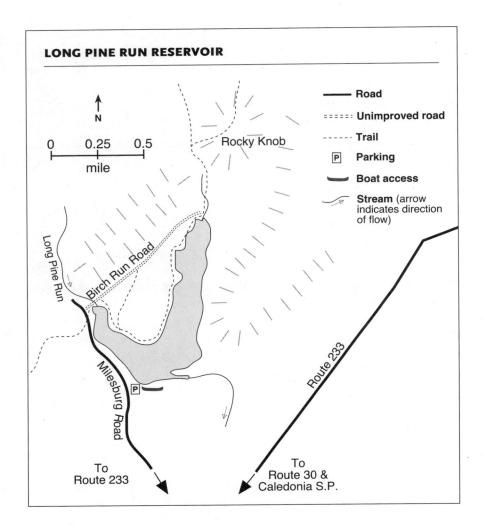

LONG PINE RUN RESERVOIR

N

0   0.25   0.5
mile

Rocky Knob

Long Pine Run

Birch Run Road

Milesburg Road

Route 233

P

To
Route 233

To
Route 30 &
Caledonia S.P.

Road
Unimproved road
Trail
P Parking
Boat access
Stream (arrow
indicates direction
of flow)

WHAT YOU'LL SEE

This 150-acre reservoir is a gem snuggled deep within the 85,000-acre Michaux State Forest. The first thing you may wish to do when you turn onto Route 233 from Route 30 is to stop in the large parking lot on the northeast corner of the junction. There you will see a bronze plaque on the stone wall remnants of Thaddeus Stevens' 1830 forge. Plan a hike here after your paddle to view the lake and surrounding forest from the top of Rocky Knob, the tall mountain on the north side of the lake. As you continue your drive to the launch, you will pass woods that are thick with beautiful wild rhododendron. A vista of mountains, 300 to 400 feet high, surrounds the clear lake. From left to right are Wigwam

Tucked into the mountains, the Long Pine Reservoir is a little-used gem that invites paddlers to explore it.

Hill, long Wolf Hill, high and narrow Rocky Knob, and Strasbaugh Hill. Because there are no amenities here, few people other than the occasional angler or paddler visit, making this an ideal place for a day of peace and quiet.

A forest of mixed hardwood, hemlock, and pines embraces almost 4 miles of craggy shoreline strewn with large boulders. Pines, pines, and more pines line much of the east arm of the lake, giving the air a fresh, clean outdoors scent and pleasing scenery. In late spring and early summer, small groves of pink and white wild rhododendron peek out of the forest edge. Here and there, tall light-colored rock faces add a rugged and picturesque tone to the landscape. Eagles, hawks, and vultures soar high in the sky while kingfishers abound at lake level. Numerous songbirds and wood thrush can be seen among deciduous trees, particularly in areas with more open understory. Wild blueberries and huckleberries abound and make a tasty treat—if you get to them before the animals do.

Along marshy edges, stop and examine the prolific diversity of mosses, tiny colorful mushrooms, and wetland flowers. Ducks and geese are mostly found around the southern area by the launch and along the northern tips of the two arms. There's no shortage of small dirt and rock landing areas around the lake to accommodate a couple of boats for a lakeside lunch break. Perch, pike, muskellunge, crappies, and smallmouth and largemouth bass are sought after by anglers. Definitely visit here in late September to soak in the fall array of colors. In fall and winter, ducks, mergansers, loons, and buffleheads frequent the lake.

For the hiker, Beaver Trail is an unmarked 1.25-mile trail that connects with the orange-blazed Rocky Knob Trail. You can either circle the knob on the loop trail or take the right fork and hike about 0.4 mile to interpretive marker 11, where you will find a steep, short spur trail that leads to the summit for a magnificent view of the lake. You may find large Allegheny mound-building ant mounds when hiking here. I understand their bites are nasty. Look, but do not disturb the mounds. You can download a trail map for all of Michaux State Forest from www.dcnr.state.pa.us/Forestry/stateforests/maps/fd01_map.pdf. Another great trail map and guide is at midatlantichikes.com/rockyknob-quarrygap.htm.

Hiking and camping can be found at Caledonia State Park, which lies within the Michaux State Forest but operates under its own administration. The 1,200-acre park has eleven hiking trails, including a part of the Appalachian Trail. Alternatively, camp at Caledonia State Park and paddle Gifford Pinchot State Park, about an hour northeast, the next day. See Trip 72.

---

74 | Lawrence Baker Sheppard Reservoir

This reservoir features waterfowl and plentiful lakeside wildlife in a very quiet, rural setting.

Location: Hanover, PA
Maps: DeLorme *Pennsylvania Atlas and Gazetteer*, Map 82; USGS Hanover
Area: 225 acres
Time: 2.0–2.5 hours
Conditions: Depth average 25 feet
Development: Rural
Information: Hanover Municipal Waterworks, Borough of Hanover, 44 Frederick Street, Hanover, PA 17331; 717-637-3877.
Camping: Cordurus State Park, 15 minutes northeast. See Appendix A.
Take Note: Electric motorboats only; Pennsylvania boating regulations apply. See Appendix D.

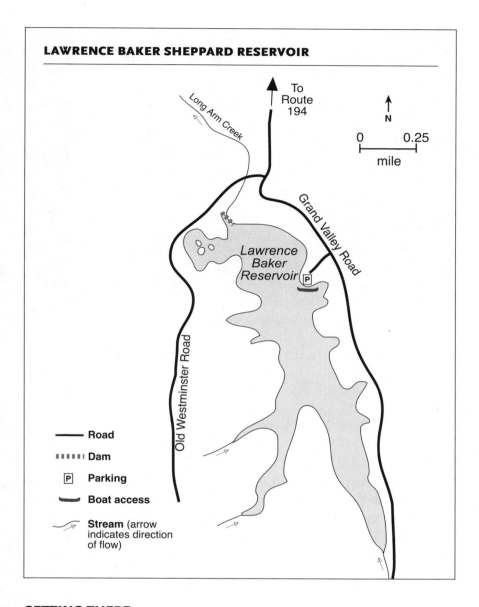

LAWRENCE BAKER SHEPPARD RESERVOIR

To Route 194

Long Arm Creek

N

0   0.25
mile

Grand Valley Road

Lawrence
Baker
Reservoir P

Old Westminster Road

— Road

∎∎∎∎∎ Dam

P Parking

⌣ Boat access

↗ **Stream** (arrow indicates direction of flow)

GETTING THERE

From the intersection of 94 and 194 in Hanover, drive west on Route 194 for 0.7 mile to Westminster Avenue. Turn left onto Westminster Avenue and drive 2.5 miles. Westminster Avenue changes to Grand Valley Road. Continue driving on Grand Valley Road 0.5 mile to the park and boat launch entrance on the right. Parking is available for about 35 cars. *GPS coordinates*: 39°45.117′ N, 76°59.346′ W.

It is quite a treat to find wildlife like this deer at the water's edge.

WHAT YOU'LL SEE

Lawrence Baker Sheppard Reservoir is also known as Long Arm Creek Reservoir because it's fed by Long Arm Creek. Don't confuse it with the much smaller Sheppard-Meyers Reservoir, fed by the same creek, a little over a mile southeast. The highly convoluted shoreline of the 225-acre reservoir provides peaceful and quiet paddling in the midst of low-rolling hills and farmland just north of the Maryland border.

Head northeast (right) from the launch and paddle to the cove on the northwest tip. It's a quiet area with a few small islands that provides a beckoning environment for song birds and waterfowl. Meander south along the western shoreline, exploring the many inlets. Most of the inlets range from 200 to 500 feet in length, but there's a half-mile long one on the southwest side of the lake you'll really enjoy exploring. Tucked between farmlands rimmed with dense woods, this inlet itself has a few coves and plentiful birdlife. Don't be surprised if you spot a deer taking a drink at the lake.

More woodland birds are found on this side due to the wide swaths of woods and dense understory shrubs along the lakeshore. Look for kingfishers, blue jays, woodpeckers, flickers, vireos, and warblers, to name a few. Because fish are plentiful here, look to the sky for ospreys and perhaps the occasional eagle that scout the waters for prey.

The western shore at the southern tip, where Long Arm Creek enters the reservoir, offers the opportunity to land for a stretch or snack. Because it is shallow, this is the area you're more likely to find egrets and herons stalking along the shallow shores and ducks foraging on submerged vegetation. Heading back to the launch on the east side, open fields and farms provide the opportunity to spot vultures, hawks, kestrels, bluebirds, songbirds, and swifts. Anglers come here mostly for smallmouth and largemouth bass, but they also cast their lines for pike, crappies, catfish, perch, and panfish.

A nearby additional paddle is Codorus State Park, 20 minutes northeast. See Trip 75.

75 | Codorus State Park— Lake Marburg

Highlights of this lake are two large islands, bald eagles, a wide variety of waterfowl, and hours of paddling to enjoy.

Location: Hanover, PA

Maps: DeLorme *Pennsylvania Atlas and Gazetteer*, Map 82; USGS Hanover

Area: 1,275 acres

Time: Variable up to 8.0 hours

Conditions: Depth average 20 feet

Development: Suburban/rural

Information: Cordorus State Park, 2600 Smith Station Road, Hanover PA 17331; 717-637-2816.

Camping: On-site; call the park office. For online reservations, go to www.visitPAparks.com or call 888-727-2757. Conewago Isle Campground is 25 minutes north. See Appendix A.

Take Note: Motorboats to 20 horsepower; winds; Pennsylvania boating regulations apply. See Appendix D.

GETTING THERE

To the park office: From the junction of Routes 30 and 94, drive south 5.4 miles on Route 94 to Route 194. Turn left and drive 200 feet to Route 116/York Street, then turn right and drive 1.5 miles to Route 216/Blooming Grove Road. Turn right and drive 2.1 miles to Smith Station Road and turn left. The entrance to the park office will be 300 feet ahead on your left. *GPS coordinates*: 39°47.425′ N, 76°55.063′ W.

To Smith Station launch: Proceed as above to the park office, but after turning onto Smith Station Road, drive 0.35 mile to the parking area and launch on your right. You'll find parking for about 25 cars. *GPS coordinates*: 39°47.656′ N, 76°53.713′ W.

To Black Rock launch: From the intersection of Route 30 and Route 94, drive 6.9 miles on Route 94 South to Black Rock Road. Bear left onto Black Rock Road and drive 1.8 miles to the boat launch on your left. You'll find parking for ten cars. *GPS coordinates*: 39°46.483′ N, 76°56.090′ W.

WHAT YOU'LL SEE

The large 1,272-acre Lake Marburg is 3.5 miles long with a 1.75-mile arm off the south shore close to the middle of the lake. It has 26 miles of shoreline, not including the two islands. The park's recreation areas on the south side flank both sides of Blooming Grove Road, which crosses the western half of the lake. Amenities include a large marina, nature center, several play fields, picnic areas, and a large swimming pool with shower facilities. Six launches are positioned around the lake. An additional launch is within the camping area and available only to registered campers. The lake would be more suited for quiet water paddling all the time if they had a large section restricted to a no-wake zone. Still, it's a very nice place and large enough to provide hours—or even days—of paddling enjoyment. During the summer, the least boat traffic will be weekdays, particularly early morning and early evening.

Three bridges, two islands, and close to two dozen coves and inlets will provide many interesting escapades around the lake. Three-quarters of the lake's area lay north of Blooming Grove Road and houses the park's marina and five of the six launches, making it the more active on-water part of the lake. Woodlands of elm, hickory, ash, oak, tulip, and maple create spectacular fall vistas. Miles of lakeshore that has wide borders of dense woods provides habitats for deer, rabbits, squirrels, and opossums. Look for muskrats in areas with cattails and reeds.

Shorebirds share the water with waterfowl on the main body of the lake. Grebes, wood ducks, coots, yellowlegs, egrets, herons, and wading birds forage along shallow edges of coves. Turtles tan on logs jutting from shore while frogs create quite a symphony in areas where aquatic grasses and pond lilies abound. During spring and fall migrations, large flotillas of ruddy ducks and mergansers can be spotted in the middle of the lake. Woodland birds like blue jays, wrens, warblers, kingfishers, thrushes, gnat-catchers, tanagers, and rufous-

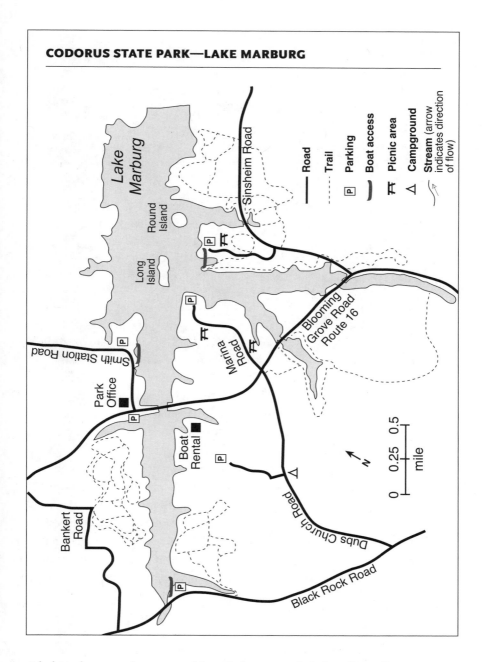

CODORUS STATE PARK—LAKE MARBURG

sided towhees can be seen and heard along wooded shorelines. In open areas sprinkled sparsely with trees, look for the beautiful bluebird.

People who enjoy fishing cast their lines for perch, pike, largemouth bass, muskies, catfish, crappies, and bluegill sunfish. Some fish become dinner for

MUSKRAT

Semi-aquatic rodents, muskrats live in and around lakes, ponds, freshwater and saltwater marshes, and slow-moving streams throughout North America. Their common name is derived from their musk glands, predominant beneath the skin on the lower abdomen of males, which produce a strong scent. Averaging two feet in length, their dark gray to brown fur fools many people into thinking they've spotted a beaver. Adaptations for movement in water include partially webbed hind feet that act as paddles and a long scaly, hairless tail, flattened sideways, that acts as a rudder. Mainly nocturnal, the best time to see them is dawn and dusk when they leave their burrow to feed on aquatic plants. Although primarily vegetarians preferring cattails, arrowhead, pond weed, bulbs, and tubers, they will occasionally dine on snails, crayfish, frogs, and carrion when plants are scarce; all their food is cleaned and washed before consumption.

In marshlands, muskrats build dome-shaped houses as large as 6 to 8 feet across and 2 feet high using reeds and mud. Check channel corners as you paddle by for chewed-off reeds, the telltale sign that a muskrat lives nearby—probably within 150 feet. Houses are located near the water where an extensive tunnel system leads to several underwater entrances. In tidal waters, lakes, and slow-moving streams with steep banks, they will sometimes make their home by burrowing into the bank and only a small dome is built for a surface entrance. Reeds and grasses line the main room above the high-water line and tunnels lead to underwater entrances. Special "food huts" are constructed near the main hut to store vegetative roots and grasses for use during times of nursing or bad weather

Breeding takes place from late March through July, producing an average of four litters of 5 to 7 young each year. Although they do not mate for life, they are thought to have only one mate during rearing seasons. The gestation period lasts about a month and the young are weaned by two months of age. As self-regulating animals, population density, habitat quality, and food availability reflect the number and size of litters in a given year. Usually a solitary animal except when mating, they often share a communal den during the winter. Muskrats provide prey food for fox, hawks, raccoons, coyotes, and owls.

High population density can be deleterious to aquatic vegetation necessary for other wildlife and their burrowing activities weaken dikes and earthen dams. On a commercial scale, they are valued for their fur, often referred to as "river mink."

ospreys and eagles. Watch where they fly after catching a fish—they might be taking it back to a nest. If you plan to paddle around the islands, you may want to schedule your lunch stop on one of the large sandy beaches that can be found on both islands. Here are two trip suggestions among many creative possibilities on this large lake.

Put in at the more secluded Black Rock launch. Far from the lake's centers of activities, this tends to be the quieter and more serene part of the lake. A loop paddle along the southern shore, across Blooming Grove Road, and back along the north shore is approximately 6 miles. Immediately to the right of the launch is a long cove a little over a quarter-mile in length. It becomes shallow halfway down, but there's where you'll find sandpipers, herons, egrets, and other wading birds. The south shoreline takes you past dense woods, open woodlands, and an open area with a scattering of trees at the swimming pool center close to the bridge. The long coves on either side of the bridge are no-wake zones, although the passageway underneath the bridge is not—take heed when crossing that area. This is quite a nice paddle packed with an abundance of wildlife.

Smith Station Launch, north of the park office, is a perfect location for a paddle around the large upper portion of the lake. The north shoreline is primarily dense woods with a variety of coves to explore. Along the south side, dense woods, open habitats, and two islands create many possibilities. A counterclockwise paddle along the north shore, across the dam, then down the south shore to the islands and circumnavigating them before heading back to the launch is 8 to 9 miles. In addition to wildlife, this trip offers the adventure of visiting two islands. If you decide to paddle the long arm of the lake that leads south from the marina, the trip will be 15 to 16 miles.

There are 20 miles of trails in the park, two of which are hiking only. The hiking trails are 1.5 and 4.5 miles long and lead you through a variety of habitats from dense woods to freshwater marshes and open spaces. Trails are easy with only a few very short areas of slightly rugged terrain.

Lawrence Baker Sheppard Reservoir is 20 minutes southwest. See Trip 74.

76 | William H. Kain County Park— Lake Williams and Lake Redman

Enjoy waterfowl, raptors, song birds, and scenic wooded hillsides on these quiet waters.

Location: York, PA
Maps: DeLorme *Pennsylvania Atlas and Gazetteer*, Map 92; USGS York
Area: Lake Williams: 220 acres; Lake Redman: 290 acres
Time: Lake Williams: 1.5–2.0 hours; Lake Redman: 2.5 hours
Conditions: Depth average 25 feet for both lakes
Development: Suburban
Information: William H. Kain County Park, 400 Mundis Race Road, York, PA 17402; 717-428-1961.
Camping: Indian Rock Campgrounds, 15 minutes northwest. See Appendix A.
Take Note: Electric motorboats; Pennsylvania boating regulations apply. See Appendix D.

GETTING THERE
To Lake Williams: From I-83 take Exit 14 for Route 182/Leaders Heights Road and drive 0.2 mile to Leaders Heights Road. Turn right and drive 0.2 mile to

Joppa Road. Turn left and drive 0.5 mile to Route 892/South George Street. Turn left and drive 1.5 miles to West Water Street, then turn right and drive 0.3 mile to the boat launch entrance road on the right. You'll find parking for about 30 cars. *GPS coordinates for the entrance road*: 39°53.252'N, 76°43.034'W.

To Lake Redman's main launch: From I-83, take Exit 14 for Route 182/ Leaders Heights Road. Turn right onto Leaders Heights Road and drive 0.2 mile to Joppa Road. Turn left and drive 0.5 mile to Route 892/South George Street, turn left and drive 1.4 miles to Church Street. Turn left and drive 0.5 mile (Church Street will change names to Salem Church Road in the middle) to the parking area and boat launch on the left. You'll find parking for more than 100 cars. *GPS coordinates*: 39°53.275' N, 76°42.031' W.

To Lake Redman's east launch: From I-83, take Exit 16A for Route 74/ South Queen Street. Merge onto Route 74/South Queen Street and drive 2.1 miles to Route 2087/Ironstone Hill Road, then turn right and drive 0.8 miles to Sparton Road. Turn right and drive 0.9 mile to the boat launch on the left. You'll find parking for about twenty cars. *GPS coordinates*: 39°53.254' N, 76°41.260' W.

WHAT YOU'LL SEE

Surrounded by forested hills and a few farms, this attractive 1,637-acre park contains two lakes separated by a short, narrow dam. The western body of water, Lake Williams, has one launch for cartop boats only and two shaded picnic tables. It is open from 8 A.M. until dusk. Lake Redman has two launches and three picnic areas. The east launch is for cartop boats only and is open 24 hours. The main launch has modest recreation facilities, including a playground, pavilions, and a seasonal canoe and kayak rental concession. Restrooms or portable toilets are located at all launch sites and at most picnic areas throughout the park.

Lake Williams

Large swaths of pine trees weave through deciduous woods on tall hillsides surrounding Lake Williams. A protected waterfowl sanctuary involving 30 acres of the lake at the north end is off-limits to boating, but that still leaves 3.5 miles of shoreline and lots of wildlife and scenery to enjoy. The sanctuary ensures a safe area for nesting and reproduction for a variety of waterfowl and other birds. Ospreys, vultures, and hawks ride thermals above the lake. The densely wooded shores are home to deer, foxes, pheasants, and rabbits on the ground and a variety of woodland birds in the trees. Sit, listen, and look. Tuck yourself

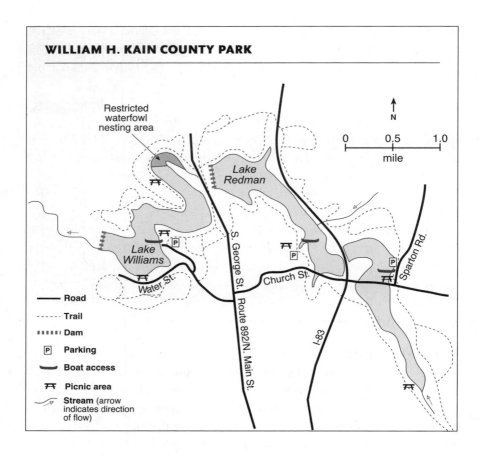

WILLIAM H. KAIN COUNTY PARK

Restricted waterfowl nesting area

Lake Redman

Lake Williams

S. George St.

Route 892/N. Main St.

Church St.

I-83

Sparton Rd.

Water St.

N

0   0.5   1.0
mile

— Road
----- Trail
▪▪▪▪▪ Dam
P Parking
⌣ Boat access
⊼ Picnic area
⤳ Stream (arrow indicates direction of flow)

close to the tree line and simply savor the fresh air and scenery. Hills on the north side rise more steeply from the lake.

Beneath you, crappie, sunfish, catfish, largemouth bass, pike, muskie, and striper swim in clean water. Along the shoreline there are plenty of small niches to explore and observe woodland birds and other lakeside wildlife. All boats are required to stay 100 feet away from the dam. Two large white buoys mark the 100-foot line. While there are good locations to land around the lake, choose carefully because the bottom drops off quickly in a few areas. Otherwise, you may be making an unplanned wet-exit.

Lake Redman

Lake Redman has a section bordering I-83 where you'll experience road noise when you are close to it, but it dissipates quickly as you paddle past it. The rest of the lake is quiet and enjoyable. The lake is bordered primarily by wide

These kayakers happily paddle out to explore Lake Williams and look for wildlife.

swaths of wooded hills tucked in a valley. Small sections of farmland and open fields constitute the remaining landscape. Most paddlers launch from the quiet Sparton Road parking area, which is cartop launching only and away from the main launch and recreation grounds. Paddle to your right from the launch along the steep, sheer hills. I love that kind of topography; it gives me a cuddled "protected by nature" feeling as I nestle against the shoreline. As you approach the I-83 bridge, you'll pick up road noise. Once under the bridge and around the corner, the noise abates quite a bit, but you might want to cross the lake and paddle up the western side to get even farther away.

As with Lake Williams, all boats are required to stay 100 feet away from the dam. Pass under the I-83 bridge and around to the next bridge, which is Hess Farm Drive. Beyond that bridge, dense trees on both sides narrow to shallow freshwater marshlands where Inners Creek and East Branch Barshinger Creek enter the lake. Waterfowl, wading birds, and songbirds of every description are frequent visitors. Muskrat might be spotted along the shores near the long wildlife observation platform on the east side.

More than 12 miles of marked trails are located throughout the park around both lakes. Trails range from 1.4 to 2.7 miles in length and from easy to moderate. Trail #5 on the southeast tip of Lake Redman has a 350-foot observation deck that is spectacular for bird-watching.

Gifford Pinchot State Park is 45 minutes northwest. Consider camping there and paddling that lake the next day. See Trip 72.

77 | Susquehanna River—Conowingo Reservoir and Lake Aldred

On this trip you'll paddle through a wonderland of rock islands on Conowingo Reservoir and view petroglyphs on rocks in Lake Aldred with abundant birdlife, including eagles and osprey, at both sites.

Location: Slab and Pequea, NJ

Maps: DeLorme *Pennsylvania Atlas and Gazetteer*, Map 83; USGS Holtwood and Conowingo Dam

Area: Conowingo Reservoir: 15,875 acres, but only about 10,000 acres are in Pennsylvania; Lake Aldred: 2,400 acres

Time: Conowingo Reservoir: 4.0–5.0 hours; Lake Aldred: 3.0–4.0 hours

Conditions: Conowingo Reservoir: depth average 15 feet; Lake Aldred: depth average 20 feet

Development: Rural

Information: Conowingo Reservoir: Managed by Exelon Corporation, Exelon Power Generation, 300 Exelon Way, Kennett Square, PA 19348; 800-483-3220.

Lake Aldred: Managed by Pennsylvania Power and Light, Holtwood Preserve, 9 New Village Road, Holtwood, PA 17532; 800-354-8383.

Camping: Tucquan Park Family Campground, 10 minutes southeast of Lake Aldred and 13 minutes north of Conowingo Reservoir. See Appendix A.

Take Note: Unlimited motorboat horsepower; winds; dam releases (with warning); Pennsylvania boating regulations apply. See Appendix D. Conowingo Reservoir is unlimited horsepower, but within the described trip you'll only encounter them for 0.5 mile, if that.

GETTING THERE

To Conowingo Reservoir from Lake Aldred: Turn right out of the parking lot at Lake Aldred and drive 2.0 miles on Bridge Valle Road. Turn right onto Westview Road and drive 0.4 mile, then slight left at Delta Road and drive 0.2 mile. Turn right onto River Road and drive 4.0 miles, then turn right onto Route 372/Holtwood Road and drive 2.3 miles. Turn left onto River Road and drive

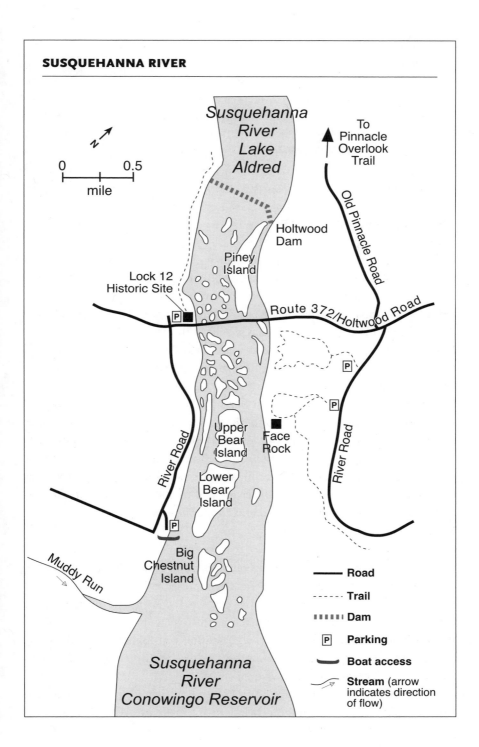

SUSQUEHANNA RIVER

Susquehanna River Lake Aldred

To Pinnacle Overlook Trail

Old Pinnacle Road

0   0.5
mile

Holtwood Dam

Piney Island

Lock 12 Historic Site

Route 372/Holtwood Road

River Road

Upper Bear Island

Face Rock

Lower Bear Island

River Road

Muddy Run

Big Chestnut Island

Susquehanna River Conowingo Reservoir

Road

Trail

Dam

Parking

Boat access

Stream (arrow indicates direction of flow)

1.4 miles to the Muddy Creek boat launch entrance on your left. You'll find parking for about 80 cars. *GPS coordinates*: 39°47.913′ N, 76°18.362′ W.

To Lake Aldred: From Route 30 just west of Lancaster, take the exit for Route 741 toward Rohrerstown/Millersville. Turn right onto Route 741 South/Rohrerstown Road and drive 6.9 miles, then continue straight onto Route 324/Marticville Road/Pequea Boulevard and drive 8.3 miles. Turn right onto Duck Hill Road/Route 324 and drive 0.2 mile, then turn left onto River Hill Road/Route 324 and drive 0.5 mile to the parking lot on your right. You'll find parking for about 40 cars. *GPS coordinates*: 39°53.282′ N, 76°21.987′ W.

WHAT YOU'LL SEE

Conowingo Reservoir and Lake Aldred are dammed sections of the Susquehanna River. Lake Aldred is bordered by Safe Harbor Dam on the north and Holtwood Dam on the south; Conowingo Reservoir is bordered by Holtwood Dam on the north and Conowingo Dam on the south (in Maryland). These dammed sections are called "lakes" or "reservoirs" because they're generally quiet, except when there's been heavy rainfall that causes the waters to run fast—or if there's a dam release (rare). As part of a river, there is current to contend with, of course, but it is minimal and suitable for novices. Like any large lake, winds can whip up the surface any time, particularly on Lake Aldred, which is more open. Check the local weather forecast before heading out.

Fishing is bountiful with largemouth and smallmouth bass, northern pike, walleye, muskellunge and tiger muskellunge, pickerel, striped bass, shad, herring, sunfish, crappies, carp, catfish, and yellow perch commonly caught by anglers. In the river, you can't help but stare in awe at the gorge this river has carved over millions of years. Cliffs rising 300 to 400 feet, too steep for residences, are covered with hardwood and conifer forests.

Conowingo Reservoir

A paradise of islands to weave through and phenomenal bird-watching provide hours of exploration and wildlife observation pleasure. The area is amazing. I couldn't keep my eyes off it when I drove across the Route 372 bridge—and I couldn't wait to get my boat in the water. With so many rock islands off and to the north of the launch, motorboats won't bother you—where you'll paddle is so rock-strewn that power boaters stay away. This is definitely at the top of the list for author's choices in Pennsylvania.

From the launch, paddle across to Lower Bear Island, the closest to the launch, and hug the shore as you travel north (upstream). There's a long line of rocks barely underwater that lead out from the western shore about 400 feet

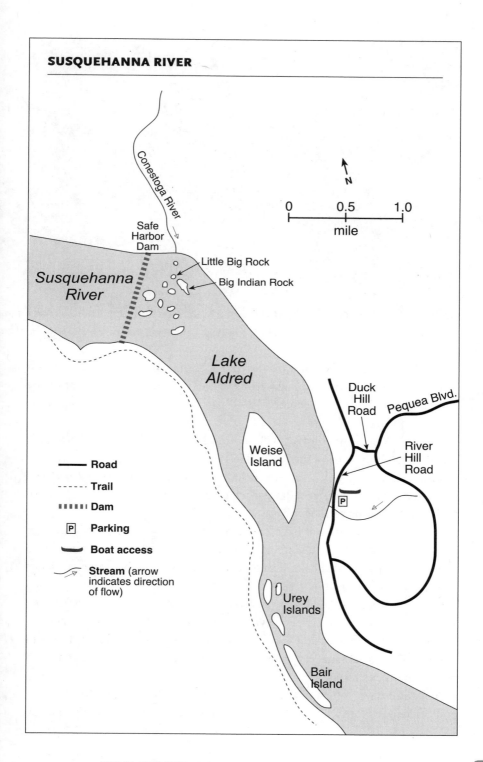

SUSQUEHANNA RIVER

Conestoga River

Safe Harbor Dam

Little Big Rock

Big Indian Rock

Susquehanna River

Lake Aldred

Weise Island

Duck Hill Road

Pequea Blvd.

River Hill Road

P

Urey Islands

Bair Island

0   0.5   1.0
mile

N

Road

Trail

Dam

P **Parking**

Boat access

Stream (arrow indicates direction of flow)

The unique rocky islands and striking formations make Conowingo Reservoir a wonderland.

north of the launch that you want to avoid. Continue north along Upper Bear Island and about halfway up, numerous islands with narrow passageways are laid out in front of you to explore. Wind your way in and out, looking at the awesome formations.

One type of formation that will pop out is perfectly cylindrical, sculpted holes carved into some of the rocks. These are a result of nature at work over thousands of years. When the Susquehanna River was engorged with glacial meltwaters, tons of abrasive sediment acted like hundreds of drills, swirling and sculpting the forms you see today.

Some small islands will have barely a tuft of grass on them, while larger islands have collected dirt, silt, and other debris over thousands of years and support wildflowers, shrubs, and large stands of trees. A few of the larger islands have cabins on plots of land leased from the state. Remember, even though these are summer weekend getaway cabins, they are private property. You can spend hours here and not explore every nook, cranny, and passageway. The day I visited, my two friends and I spotted four great blue herons, an eagle, about half a dozen scarlet tanagers, a number of kingfishers, great white egrets, and dozens of other species.

On calm days, return to the launch from the eastern edge of the islands, and perhaps explore a few of the islands immediately southeast of the launch.

Travel through passageways of time in and among the islands, marveling at the wildlife and the geographic features. When you return to the launch, hug the islands as much as you can if there's motorboat traffic around to avoid their wakes. They slow down as they approach the launch because there are logs and rocks beneath the surface that could wreak havoc on propellers. You'll come back time and again to explore more of this wonderland of rock islands.

Caution: Do not paddle north of the Route 372 bridge. You are permitted to do it, but if there is a dam release, that area can become squirrelly while the waters are running swiftly. Within the safe harbor of islands south of the bridge, even if you do experience the rare occasion of a release, you're out of the main channel, which is river-left, and in a very protected area. You might find the waters rise about a foot, and the current will increase some, but it's primarily a safe haven to wait while the waters subside.

Lake Aldred

The closest launch for access to Indian Rock Island is from the town of Pequea, 2.5 miles south of the Safe Harbor Dam and 5 miles north of the Holtwood Dam. Weise Island, in the middle of the lake offshore from Pequea, is the first thing that fills your eyes. It's almost a mile long and a third of a mile wide at its widest point. From the launch, head north (upstream) for the 2.5-mile paddle to an area of small islands about five hundred yards in front of the Safe Harbor Dam. As you cruise by Weise Island, look for bald eagles usually seen flying over and around the island. At least three known eagle nests are in this section of the lake alone.

This upper section of the lake is at most 20 feet deep. For that reason, most anglers and large pleasure boats will be in deeper areas to the south. To find the petroglyphs, it's best to either have a GPS or paddle with someone who knows where they are. Paddle north along the eastern shore toward the dam. When you near Indian Rock Island, 600 yards downstream from the dam, check your GPS. GPS coordinates for the larger island are 39°54.966′ N, 76°22.972′ W. There's a smaller island, dubbed Little Indian Rock, about 80 yards upstream that has many more petroglyphs. Once you've located them, you'll be able to find them again easily. The large island is rounded with a few petroglyphs. According to research, there are petroglyphs on other rocks directly out from the mouth of the Conestoga River, which feeds into Lake Aldred on the eastern shore right below the dam. Do not ever get closer than a few hundred yards from the dam. Boaters are warned to stay at least 100 yards downstream; paddlers should stay farther away.

Numerous small rocks and small rock islands in this area are fun to explore. Along the eastern shoreline, keep your eyes open for the numerous woodland bird species found here. A few nice beaches on Weise Island are perfect places to stop for lunch, including the large sand beach at the southern tip of the island that you can see from the launch. If you do stop for lunch there, remember that the trip over to the launch is slightly upstream. When you paddle back, aim for a point a few hundred feet north of the launch; it's far easier to get back to the launch by drifting downstream at the end of a paddle.

Caution: It is rare, but if you should hear the siren sound at Safe Harbor Dam, paddle to river-right (western side of the lake) because the main channel, where the increases in water flow will be, is river-left (eastern side of the lake). Depending on the length of the release, time to calm waters will be anywhere from 10 minutes to maybe a half-hour. Even those modestly experienced will have no problem, but novices should wait perhaps an additional 5 minutes after they think the waters are back to normal.

For additional paddles nearby, visit Muddy Run Recreation Park, 15 minutes east of Lake Aldred. See Trip 78.

78 | Muddy Run Park

This lovely park features waterfowl, shore birds, wading birds, and a large island.

Location: Holtwood, PA
Maps: DeLorme *Pennsylvania Atlas and Gazetteer*, Map 83; USGS Holtwood
Area: 100 acres
Time: 2.0–2.5 hours
Conditions: Depth average 25 feet
Development: Rural
Information: Muddy Run Park, 172 Bethesda Church Road West, Holtwood, PA 17532; 717-284-5869; $4 boat launch fee if not staying at the campground.
Camping: On-site; call 717-284-5850. Tucquan Park, 10 minutes northwest. See Appendix A.
Take Note: Electric motorboats only; no inflatable boats; Pennsylvania boating regulations apply. See Appendix D.

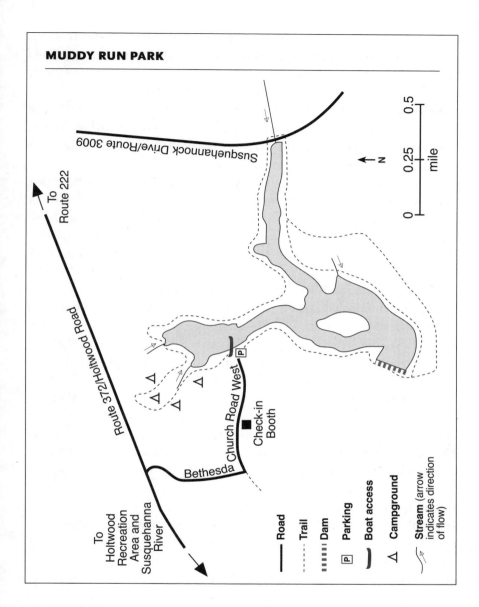

MUDDY RUN PARK

Susquehannock Drive/Route 3009

To
Route 222

Route 372/Holtwood Road

To
Holtwood
Recreation
Area and
Susquehanna
River

Bethesda Church Road West

Check-in
Booth

N

0   0.25   0.5
mile

— Road
····· Trail
▪▪▪▪▪ Dam
Ⓟ Parking
❩ Boat access
△ Campground
〰 Stream (arrow
   indicates direction
   of flow)

GETTING THERE

From the junction of Routes 222 and 372 in Quarryville, drive 7.2 miles on Route 372 West/West State Street (State Street becomes Buck Road almost immediately and then becomes Holtwood Road after crossing Route 272). Turn left onto Bethesda Church Road West and drive 0.4 mile, then turn left to stay on Bethesda Church Road West and drive 0.1 mile to the park entrance. *GPS coordinates*: 39°50.892′ N, 76°17.265′ W. The boat launch is straight ahead, 0.3 mile past the park entrance. You'll find parking for about 50 cars. *GPS coordinates*: 39°50.889′ N, 76°16.905′ W.

WHAT YOU'LL SEE

Filling the valleys between rolling hills of woodlands and open fields less than 3 miles from the Susquehanna River, Muddy Run Park offers 700 acres filled with wildlife, wonderful campgrounds, and a lovely 100-acre lake with a large island. The lake's shape reminds me of a rabbit head. You'll want to camp here just to watch the setting sun cast its light over the lake and hillsides from your boat or lakeside camp. With its proximity to the Susquehanna River, feathered species that use the migration corridor spill over into the waters here. In addition to resident species, you're likely to find a much wider variety of migratory birds in early summer and fall.

Cast your lines and fish for trout, largemouth and smallmouth bass, crappies, carp, and sunfish. From the launch, head right (south) past the tree-lined shore toward the central part of the lake. As you round the bend, a picturesque island comes into view. Head to the island and soak in the serenity of the landscape as you watch for ospreys and eagles above. The dam is hidden in the southwest corner, but you'll see it as you near the end of the island. The forested hill that rises a little over 80 feet on the south side of the dam is a great area to look for deer and rabbits. Search the trees for cardinals, blue jays, and vireos. Enjoy the pretty forested hills as you glide into a little cove on the east side of the lake, or travel back and forth between island and shore.

Stop on a landing-friendly spot simply to soak in the view or enjoy a snack before wandering up the east arm. Entering the east arm, steep, wooded hills edge the south side where kingfishers, flickers, woodpeckers, and blue jays make their home in oak, ash, hickory, and other deciduous trees. Near the tip of the arm, a power line path offers another opportunity to land. Head back to the central part of the lake along the north shore where a wooded but more open landscape offers the opportunity to spot kingbirds, kestrels, kingbirds, chickadees, finches, and other birds that prefer a slightly more open environment. Round the point and head back toward the launch. Paddle up the right side past an area of open fields that offer an opportunity to spot bluebirds, kestrels, hawks, tanagers, goldfinches, and warblers.

Informal trails meander throughout the park, including a 3-mile trail that circles the lake. For spectacular views of Lake Aldred (see Trip 77) on the Susquehanna River, drive to Holtwood Recreation Area, 6 minutes from this trip, where you'll find the trailhead for Kellys Run–Pinnacle Trail, a 3.5-mile strenuous loop that connects to a 1.5-mile spur of the Conestoga Trail to Pinnacle Overlook. The view is incredible! For details, see www.midatlantichikes.com/id96.html. *GPS coordinates for the parking lot at Holtwood Recreation Area*: 39°50.434′ N, 76°18.990′ W.

For another paddle nearby, visit Lake Aldred, 15 minutes west. See Trip 77.

79 | Octoraro Lake

Bald eagles, waterfowl, and other birds, as well as rock cliffs, are attractions at this large lake.

Location: Spruce Grove, PA
Maps: DeLorme *Pennsylvania Atlas and Gazetteer*, Map 94; USGS Kirkwood
Area: 670 acres
Time: 3.5–4.5 hours
Conditions: Depth average 20 feet
Development: Rural
Information: Fishing Headquarters, 212 Spruce Grove Road, Kirkwood, PA 17536; 717-529-2488; $4 launch fee; open April 1 through October 31.
Camping: D&J Shady Rest Campground, 10 minutes north. See Appendix A.
Take Note: Electric motorboats only; you must sign in at the fishing center and receive a flag to display on your boat; best season is spring and fall during bird migration.

GETTING THERE
From Route 1 in Oxford, take the Route 472 North Exit toward Quarryville. Drive 3.4 miles and turn left on Spruce Grove Road. Drive 1.0 mile to the fishing center entrance and boat launch on your left. Stop at the bait shop next to the house to purchase a launch permit. Parking is available for 40 cars. *GPS coordinates*: 39°48.689′ N, 76°03.578′ W.

WHAT YOU'LL SEE
As I drove up and down the hills past large farms and tiny hamlets on my way to the lake, twice I had to slow down considerably when I came upon Amish horse-drawn carriages, common in this countryside. You're bound to encounter at least one of them on the road. This is Lancaster County, also known as

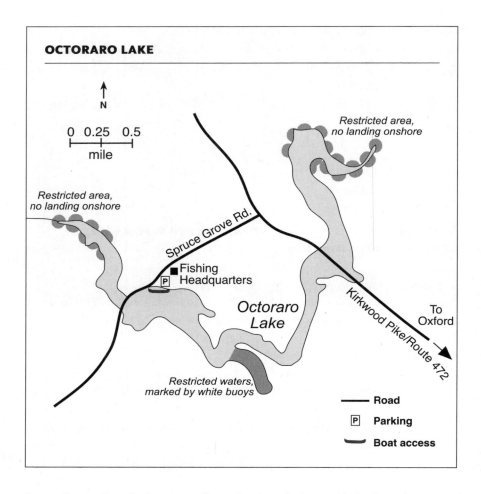

OCTORARO LAKE

N

0   0.25   0.5
mile

Restricted area,
no landing onshore

Restricted area,
no landing onshore

Spruce Grove Rd.

■ Fishing
P Headquarters

*Octoraro
Lake*

Kirkwood Pike/Route 472

To
Oxford

*Restricted waters,
marked by white buoys*

——— Road

P   Parking

⌣   Boat access

Pennsylvania Dutch Country, where the Amish first settled when they came to America around 1730.

Owned by the Chester Water Authority, the reservoir grounds encompass 1,150 acres, 650 acres of which are the lake. Stop at the small Fishing Headquarters building to pay the launch fee and obtain a little flag to attach to your boat to indicate that you may legally be on the lake. Rubber-footed spring clamps for kayaks allay any concerns of scratching your boat. If you live close to the lake and plan to paddle here often, consider a season pass. The headquarters also rents canoes and kayaks. Pit toilets and a grassy picnic area are located between the headquarters and the launch. On the map you'll be given when you sign in, be aware of three restricted areas. Two are restricted waterfowl nesting areas and one is an arm of the lake leading to the dam and marked with a very obvious line of white buoys.

A paddler admires rock faces about a half-mile west of the launch.

Large stands of white pines and hemlocks are the primary woodland cover on steep slopes around the lake. Oak, hickory, ash, and maple are the more populous deciduous species that create magnificent colors in fall. Octoraro Lake ("Octoraro" means "muddy river" in the original Lenni-Lenape language) is listed by the Pennsylvania Audubon Society as an important bird area, so it's no wonder there are restricted waterfowl nesting areas on the lake. Spring and fall bring the migration of shore birds, wading birds, ducks, geese, and songbirds. Loons and northern pintails are common late fall through winter. Egrets, swans, Canada geese, and ducks are usually seen along the lake, particularly in shallow areas. Be on the lookout for eagles nesting around the lake. If you like to fish, Octoraro is particularly noted for its population of large channel catfish. Largemouth bass abound in areas of murky water. The rip rap (rocks) around bridges provides an environment conducive for fishing because of the protective nooks and crannies. Perch, crappies, smallmouth bass, and sunnies inhabit the lake.

My first visit here was on a holiday weekend, and I was amazed by how few boats were on the lake, which is spectacular but underutilized. I was fortunate to run into a fellow kayaker who offered to show me a few of his favorite spots. I recommend that you follow the route he took me on.

Head left from the launch and paddle along the shoreline for about a half-mile, where there will be a small cove with interesting rock cliffs. Continue paddling along that shoreline for another area of rock cliffs, larger than the first, that are even more interesting. Beyond that the lake doglegs (makes a sort of N-shaped zigzag) northeast past the restricted buoyed area that leads to the dam and around Camp Tweedle peninsula, a Girl Scout retreat and camp. Now you'll feel as if you're really in the middle of the wilderness. Continue your trip through the wide dogleg. Where the lake opens up, you'll see the Route 472 bridge, which you may have taken from Route 1.

Along your trip, numerous opportunities will present themselves to land for a break or snack. Be sure to avoid landing on a beach in the restricted waterfowl nesting areas. When you are near the launch area again, venture under the Spruce Grove Road bridge. As you pass to the other side, a vista opens with a steep hillside on your left. Straight ahead the lake becomes quite shallow, with patches of waterlilies and aquatic plants resting atop the water. This is a great area for wading birds, ducks, swan, and geese.

Talk to an attendant at the Fishing Headquarters to learn about hiking opportunities. About a half-mile from the headquarters, a 1.5-mile ridge trail offers a spectacular view of the lake. Another hiking opportunity is a fire-break trail that starts behind the pit toilet building. I took a short hike along the trail and was delighted as I entered the tunneled hemlock canopy. The variety of sounds made it difficult for me to focus on just one to try to locate the birds. A footpath trail leads away from the southern part of the picnic area and follows the lake for about a half-mile. At a few spots, you can connect to the fire-break trail.

Muddy Run park, which offers on-site camping, is 40 minutes west-northwest. Consider camping there and paddling that 100-acre lake the next day. See Trip 78.

80 | Schuylkill River

You'll find fantastic views of Boathouse Row and the Philadelphia Art Museum along this scenic stretch of the Schuylkill River.

Location: Philadelphia, PA
Maps: *Pennsylvania Atlas and Gazetteer*, Map 86; USGS Philadelphia
Area: 4.6-mile round-trip downstream, 6.0-mile round-trip upstream
Time: 2.0–4.0 hours
Conditions: Depth average 7 feet

Development: Urban

Information: Fairmount Park Commission Office, One Parkway, 10th Floor, 1515 Arch Street, Philadelphia, PA 19102; 215-683-0200.

Take Note: Unlimited horsepower motorboats, but it's rare to see anything over 15 horsepower; winds; Pennsylvania boating regulations apply. See Appendix D.

GETTING THERE

From the intersection of Route 1/City Line Avenue and Kelly Drive: Coming off I-76/Schuylkill Expressway, take the ramp exit for Kelly Drive. Drive south on Kelly Drive for about 400 feet. Keep left at the fork on the off-ramp to stay on Kelly Drive, then keep right to stay on Kelly Drive/East River Drive and drive 1.8 miles to the parking lot entrance and boat ramp on the right. You'll find parking for about 100 cars. *GPS coordinates for the parking lot entrance:* 39°59.569′ N, 75°116.636′ W. See notes at the end of this text for Kelly Drive closures and rules of the road for this section of the Schuylkill River.

WHAT YOU'LL SEE

The Schuylkill River (pronounced SKOO kuhl) accounts for one-third of the Delaware River's total flow as the latter winds its way to Delaware Bay and into the Atlantic Ocean. It starts its 128-mile journey a little north of Tamaqua in Schuylkill County, about 10 miles south of Route 80, and drains 2,000 square miles within 5 counties. This is why water levels in Philadelphia can be affected by rainstorms as far away as 75 miles to the northwest a day later. Coach's launches (for rowing crews) are primarily the new wakeless motorboats—they don't leave even a 2-inch wake—and relatively few small electric motor fishing boats can be seen on the river. Please read the Special Notes section at the end of the text prior to planning a paddle here.

Defining a few terms: River-left and river-right are terms used to define river sides; river-left refers to the left side of the river when facing downstream, and river-right defines the right side of the river when facing downstream. Hence, if people are paddling upstream, one might say, "Look at the heron river-left," meaning on their right.

From the launch, the bridge immediately upstream is the Strawberry Mansion Bridge. It's beautiful at dusk when the colored lights rimming the arches are turned on. Head downstream (left) from the launch, staying river-left the whole way. In about a half-mile, you'll pass Peter's Island on your right. Near the end of the island you'll see the grandstands and announcement center for rowing regattas held frequently on the river, the most notable of which is the Dad Vail

Regatta, held every year in early May. Beyond that, the river turns and you'll pass under a railroad bridge. Farther down, right past the long floating docks, look over at the bank to the Three Angels statues—one of the many examples of art in the park. The river will narrow some as you pass under a railroad bridge followed by the Girard Avenue Bridge.

Beyond the last bridge, you'll see a few concrete statues on the greenway and the lighthouse (Philadelphia Girls Rowing Club) at the start of Boathouse Row. Be cautious when you round the corner, watching for sleek rowing shells returning or leaving the docks. On the hill to your left is the magnificent Philadelphia Art Museum with its quasi-Greek Revival architectural design. The four-acre Azalea Garden on the west side is stunning in May when blooms show their bold colors. Don't get too distracted here, as there's a dangerous dam ahead. Fortunately, there's a thick, white wire line across the river 400 feet before the dam. Check for rowing traffic and cross over to the west bank (river-right) and snuggle tightly into the shoreline to drink in the view before heading upstream.

The trip upstream won't have the variety of sculptures that you saw on the way down. There's a large statue of Saint George and the Dragon midway between the two train bridges, but it sits back from the river, and unless the trees are bare, you won't see it. As you get close to the launch below Strawberry Mansion Bridge, decide whether you want to continue upstream or return to the launch. If you decide to return to the launch, do not cut diagonally across the river if there are any boats on the water. Instead, the normal procedure is to go upstream beyond the bridge by about 200 feet, then cut directly across the river to the east bank and come back down to the launch.

If you choose to do the upstream leg of the trip, you'll be rewarded by two lovely stone railroad bridges, the old and unique Falls Bridge, and a view into the outfall of the Manayunk Canal. The two stone railroad bridges are upriver three-quarters of a mile from the Strawberry Mansion Bridge. The two modern bridges there are called the Twin Bridges, the northbound and southbound bridges for Route 1 North/Roosevelt Boulevard. A quarter-mile farther is the unique metal Falls Bridge, beyond which you need to be on the lookout for a few rocks in the middle of the river. They stick out of the water, but a few rocks surrounding them are just below the surface. Rowers don't go upstream beyond that bridge because of those rocks in the water.

A magnificent greenway borders both sides of the river from the Art Museum to the Falls Bridge. Kelly Drive (a.k.a. East River Drive) borders the river on the east, and M. L. King Drive (a.k.a. West River Drive) borders the west side. An 8.5-mile multiuse loop trail weaves its way through this scenic section

SCHUYLKILL RIVER

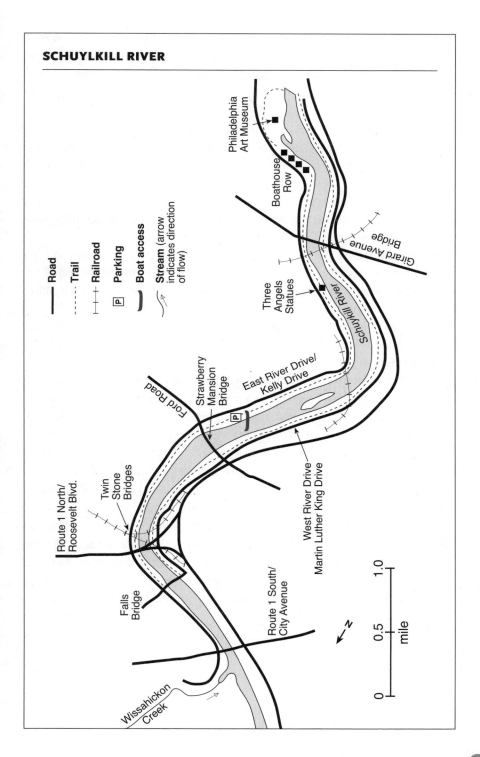

Legend:
- —— Road
- ····· Trail
- +–+ Railroad
- P Parking
- ❱ Boat access
- Stream (arrow indicates direction of flow)

Philadelphia Art Museum

Boathouse Row

Girard Avenue Bridge

Three Angels Statues

Schuylkill River

Ford Road

Strawberry Mansion Bridge

East River Drive/ Kelly Drive

West River Drive/ Martin Luther King Drive

Route 1 North/ Roosevelt Blvd.

Twin Stone Bridges

Falls Bridge

Route 1 South/ City Avenue

Wissahickon Creek

N

0   0.5   1.0
mile

of the river. Along the way there are art sculptures, drinking fountains, riverside benches, landscaped gardens, and restrooms.

For an additional paddle the same day, head to Cooper River Park Lake, 20 minutes southeast, in New Jersey. See Trip 33.

SPECIAL NOTES

Kelly Drive closures: Spring through summer regattas are often held on the river, which may involve the closure of Kelly Drive where the public boat launch is located. Visit http://www.fairmountpark.org/mlk_closure.asp for updates on events in the area and detour information.

Rules of the road for the Schuylkill River: The Schuylkill Navy (no relation to the United States Navy) is the overall governing body for all the boathouses and regattas. It governs the rules of the road on the Schuylkill River from Boathouse Row upstream to the Falls Bridge. All boaters in this section of the river must follow the rules. Boats traveling upstream must stay river-right (of center); boats traveling downstream must stay river-left (of center). Rowers have right of way because they are the least-maneuverable craft. The Schuylkill Navy's website is www.boathouserow.org.

River flow: If the river is muddy looking and running fast, postpone your paddle. Logs floating on or just under the surface, strainers around bridge abutments, and fast-flowing waters are dangerous. The average discharge is 4,650 cu ft/s (cubic feet per second), but in summer months it's closer to 2,500 cu ft/s. When discharge levels approach 5,000, it can be challenging for the novice. As levels approach 6,000 cu ft/s, the river may be flowing too swiftly for safety. At 7,000 cu ft/s and above, visit your favorite eatery, or head across the river to Cooper River Park Lake, 20 minutes southeast (Trip 33). Visit http://waterdata. usgs.gov/pa/nwis/rt and select gauge number 01474500 for Schuylkill River at Philadelphia, PA. Halfway down the next Web page you will see a table labeled Discharge, cubic feet per second. This table shows the instantaneous value at the top and a graph of the past 7 days, which you can change at the top for a longer period of time. If discharge is increasing, it means the watershed is still draining from recent rains. Slight fluctuations on a daily basis are normal, but take heed if the chart starts spiking.

Appendix A: Campgrounds

Campground	Address	Reservations	Delorme Atlas and Gazetteer
NEW JERSEY			
Albocondo Campground	1480 Whitesville Road Toms River, NJ 08755	732-349-4079	NJ pg 50: K6
Allaire State Park	4265 Atlantic Avenue Farmingdale, NJ 07727	732-938-2371	NJ pg 50: B9
AMC's Mohican Outdoor Center	50 Camp Road Blairstown, NJ 07825	908-362-5670	NJ pg 23: E15
Atsion Lake	744 Route 206 Shamong, NJ 08088	609-268-0444	NJ pg 56: M3
Baker's Acres Campground	230 Willets Avenue Little Egg Harbor, NJ 08087	609-296-2664	NJ pg 65: E28
Bass River State Forest	762 Stage Road Tuckerton, NJ 08087	609-296-1114	NJ pg 65: F21
Beaver Hill Campground	120 Big Spring Road Hardyston, NJ 07419	973-827-0670	NJ pg 19: M23
Belleplain State Forest	County Route 550 Woodbine, NJ 08270	609-861-2404	NJ pg 72: A8
Bodine Field	4110 Nesco Road Hammonton, NJ 08037	609-561-0024	NJ pg 65: D15
Camp Taylor Campground	85 Mt. Pleasant Road Columbia, NJ 07832	908-496-4333	NJ pg 22: J10

Campground	Address	Reservations	Delorme Atlas and Gazetteer
Columbia Valley Campground	3 Ghost Pony Road Andover, NJ 07821	973-691-0596	NJ pg 24: I4
Delaware River Family Campground	100 Route 46 Delaware, NJ 07833	800-543-0271	NJ pg 22: N11
Evergreen Woods Lakefront Resort	106 East Moss Mill Road Pomona, NJ 08240	609-652-1577	NJ pg 65: M16
Four Seasons Family Campground	158 Woodstown-Daretown Road Pilesgrove, NJ 08098	856-769-3635	NJ pg 35: F26
High Point State Park	1480 Route 23 Sussex, NJ 07461	973-875-4800	NJ pg 19: C20
Hospitality Creek Campground	117 Coles Mill Road Williamstown, NJ 08094	856-629-5140	NJ pg 63: F19
Indian Rock Campground	920 W. Veteran's Highway Jackson, NJ 08527	732-928-0034	NJ pg 49: E22
Lake Lenape Park	303 Old Harding Highway Mays Landing, NJ 08330	609-625-8219	NJ pg 70: A2
Lazy River Campground	103 Cumberland Avenue Estell Manor, NJ 08319	609-476-2540	NJ pg 69: G23
Mahlon Dickerson Reservation	995 Weldon Road Lake Hopatcong, NJ 07849	973-697-3140	NJ pg 24: H11
Mountainview Campground	131 Goritz Road Little York, NJ 08848	908-996-2953	NJ pg 34: C11
Panther Lake Camping Resort	6 Panther Lane Road Andover, NJ 07821	800-543-2056	NJ pg 24: J2
Parvin State Park	701 Almond Road Pittsgrove, NJ 08318	856-358-8616	NJ pg 62: M7
Pine Cone Resort	340 Georgia Road Freehold, NJ 07728	732-462-2230	NJ pg 50: A2
Pleasant Acres Farm Campground	61 Dewitt Road Sussex, NJ 07461	973-875-4166	NJ pg 19: E22
Pleasant Valley Family Campground	60 South River Road Estell Manor, NJ 08319	609-625-1238	NJ pg 70: D2
Red Wings Lakes Campground	317 Sooys Landing Road Port Republic, NJ 08241	609-748-1948	NJ pg 65: K16

Campground	Address	Reservations	Delorme Atlas and Gazetteer
Round Valley State Park	Lebanon Stanton Road Lebanon, NJ 08833	908-236-6355	NJ pg 35: B23
Scenic Riverview Campground	465 Route 49 Box 184 Tuckahoe, NJ 08250	609-628-4566	NJ pg 69: K27
Sea Pirate Campground	Route 9 West Creek, NJ 08092	609-296-7400	NJ pg 65: F28
Spruce Run State Park	One Van Syckel's Corner Road Clinton, NJ 08809	908-638-8572	NJ pg 29: N18
Swartswood State Park	PO Box 123 Swartswood, NJ 07887	973-383-5230	NJ pg 23: C25
Timberland Lake Campground	1335 Reed Road Cream Ridge, NJ 08514	732-928-0500	NJ pg 49: D19
Timberlane Campground	117 Timberlane Road Clarksboro, NJ 08020	856-423-6677	NJ pg 53: I28
Triplebrook Family Camping Resort	58 Honey Run Road Hope NJ, 07844	908-459-4079	NJ pg 22: M13
Turtle Run Campground	3 Cedar Lane Wading River, NJ 08215	800-894-8854	NJ pg 65: G16
Wading Pines Camping Resort	85 Godfrey Bridge Road Chatsworth, NJ 08019	888-726-1313	NJ pg 64: B14
Wawayanda State Park	885 Warwick Turnpike Hewitt, NJ 07421	973-853-4468	NJ pg 20: J8

PENNSYLVANIA

Campground	Address	Reservations	Delorme Atlas and Gazetteer
Adventure Bound Camping Resort	397 Eagles Peak Road Robesonia, PA 19551	800-336-0889	PA pg 70: E2
Appalachian Campsites	60 Motel Drive Shartlesville, PA 19554	610-488-6319	PA pg 70: B2
Brandywine Creek Campground	1091 Creek Road Downingtown, PA 19335	610-942-9950	PA pg 85: B5
Brandywine Meadows Campground	429 Icedale Road Honey Brook, PA 19344	610-273-9753	PA pg 84: B4
Caledonia State Park	101 Pine Grove Road Fayetteville, PA 17222	717-352-2161	PA pg 81: D5

Campground	Address	Reservations	Delorme Atlas and Gazetteer
Codorus State Park	2600 Smith Station Road Hanover PA, 17331	888-727-2757	PA pg 82: F3
Colonial Woods Family Camping Resort	545 Lonely Cottage Road Upper Black Eddy, PA 18972	610-847-5808 800-887-2267	PA pg 72: B3
Conewago Isle Campground	6220 Big Mount Road Dover, PA 17315	717-292-1461	PA pg 82: D2
D&J Shady Rest Campground	2085 Kirkwood Pike Kirkwood, PA, 17536	717-529-2020	PA pg 84: E2
Don Laine Family Campground	790 57 Drive Palmerton, PA 18071	800-635-0152	PA pg 57: D7
French Creek State Park	843 Park Road Elverson, PA 19520	610-582-9680	PA pg 71: G5
Gifford Pinchot State Park	2200 Rosstown Road Lewisberry, PA 17339	717-432-5011	PA pg 83: B3
Goods Campground	288 State Route 118 Benton, PA 17814	570-477-5361	PA pg 41: E8
Gray Squirrel Campsites	507 Gray Squirrel Road Beavertown, PA 17813	570-837-0333	PA pg 53: E8
Hibernia County Park	1 Park Road Wagontown, PA 19376	610-383-3812	PA pg 84: C4
Hickory Lake Campground	264 Laurel Hill Road Bangor, PA 18013	570-897-5811	PA pg 58: C3
Hickory Run Family Campground Resort	285 Greenville Road Denver, PA 17517	800-458-0612	PA pg 70: F2
Homestead Family Campground	1150 Allentown Road Green Lane, PA 18054	215-257-3445	PA pg 72: D1
Indian Rock Campground	436 Indian Rock Dam Road York, PA 17403	717-741-1764	PA pg 82: D4
Jim Thorpe Camping Resort	129 Lentz Trail Jim Thorpe, PA 18229	570-325-2644	PA pg 57: D5
Lickdale Campground	11 Lickdale Road Jonestown, PA 17038	877-865-6411	PA pg 69: C6
Little Buffalo State Park	1579 State Park Road Newport, PA 17074	717-567-9255	PA pg 67: C8

Campground	Address	Reservations	Delorme Atlas and Gazetteer
Mauch Chunk Lake Park	65 Lentz Trail Jim Thorpe, PA 18229	570-325-3669	PA pg 57: D5
Muddy Run Park	172 Bethesda Church Road West Holtwood, PA 17532	717-284-5869	PA pg 83: D8
Park Away Park Family Campground	1300 Old Trail Road Etters, PA 17319	717-938-1686	PA pg 82: A4
Penn's Creek Campground	7300 Creek Road Millmont, PA 17845	570-922-1371	PA pg 53: D8
Pinch Pond Campgrounds	3075 Pinch Road Manheim, PA 17545	800-659-7640	PA pg 69: G7
Ricketts Glen State Park	695 State Route 487 Benton, PA 17814	570-477-5675	PA pg 41: D8
Riverfront Campground	9 Newport Road Duncannon, PA. 17020	717-439-3016	PA pg 68: D2
Starlite Camping Resort	1500 Furnace Hill Road Stevens, PA 17578	717-733-9655	PA pg 70: F1
Tohickon Campground	8308 Covered Bridge Road Quakertown, PA 1895	215-536-7951	PA pg 72: C2
Tucquan Park	917 River Road Holtwood, PA 17532	717-284-2156	PA pg 83: E8
Tuscarora State Park	687 Tuscarora Park Road Barnesville, PA 18214	570-467-2404	PA pg 56: E3
Twin Grove Campground	1445 Suedberg Road Pine Grove, PA 17963	800-562-5471	PA pg 69: C6

Appendix B: Further Reading

PADDLING EQUIPMENT AND TECHNIQUE

Gullion, Laurie. *The Canoeing and Kayaking Instruction Manual*. Springfield, VA: American Canoe Association, 1993.

Harrison, David. *Canoeing: The Complete Guide to Equipment and Technique*. Mechanicsburg, PA: Stackpole Books, 1988.

Hutchinson, Derek C. *The Complete Book of Sea Kayaking*. Guilford, CT: Globe Pequot Press, 2004.

Killen, Ray. *Simple Kayak Navigation; Practical Piloting for the Passionate Paddler*. Columbus, OH: McGraw Hill Publishers, 2006.

Knapp, Andy. *The Optimum Kayak: How to Chose, Maintain, Repair, and Customize the Right Boat for You*. Camden, ME: Ragged Mountain Press, 2000.

PROTECTING THE ENVIRONMENT

Hampton, Bruce, and David Cole. *Soft Paths*. Third Edition. Mechanicsburg, PA: Stackpole Books, 2003.

McGiveny, Annette. *Leave No Trace: A Practical Guide to the New Wilderness Ethic*. Second Edition. Seattle, WA: Mountaineers Books, 2003.

CAMPING/CAMPGROUNDS

Web source campground locator: *www.gocampingamerica.com*

Daniel, Linda. *Kayak Cookery*. Guilford, CT: Globe Pequot Press, 1986.

Getchell, Annie. *The Essential Outdoor Gear Manual*. Camden, ME: Ragged Mountain Press, 1995.

Harrison, David. *Kayak Camping*. New York, NY: Hearst Books, 1995.

Kuhne, Cecil. *Kayak Touring and Camping*. Mechanicsburg, PA: Stackpole Books, 1999.

HIKING

Case, Dan. *AMC's Best Day Hikes near New York City*. Boston, MA: Appalachian Mountain Club Books, 2010.

Charkes, Susan. *AMC's Best Day Hikes near Philadelphia*. Boston, MA: Appalachian Mountain Club Books, 2010.

Hike the Highlands cards. Appalachian Mountain Club, 2009. Download the cards at www.outdoors.org/conservation/wherewework/highlands/hikehighlands/.

Pennsylvania Highlands Regional Recreation Map and Guide. Appalachian Mountain Club, 2009.

Scherer, Glenn. *Nature Walks in New Jersey*, 2nd. Boston, MA: Appalachian Mountain Club Books, 2003.

TAKING THE KIDS ALONG

Lessels, Bruce, and Blom, Karen. *Paddling with Kids: AMC Essential Guide for Fun and Safe Paddling*. Boston, MA: Appalachian Mountain Club Books, 2002.

Woodson, Roger and Kimberley. *The Parent's Guide to Camping with Children*. Cincinnati, OH: Betterway Books, 1995.

Appendix C: Resources

LOCAL PADDLING CLUBS AND ORGANIZATIONS

AMC Delaware Valley Chapter
www.amcdv.org
Paddling Committee website:
www.paddlenow.com

AMC New York/North Jersey Chapter
www.amc-ny.org
Canoe and Kayak Committee
www.amc-ny.org/recreational-activities/
canoe/

Delmarva Paddlers; groups.yahoo.com/
group/DelmarvaPaddlers.
Hackensack River Canoe & Kayak Club
PO Box 369, Bogota, NJ, 07603
www.hrckc.org.

Jersey Shore Sea Kayaking Association
www.jsska.org.

Pennsylvania Kayaking and Canoeing
Group
groups.yahoo.com/group/
penn_kayaking

OUTFITTERS

Bel Haven Canoe and Kayaks
1227 Route 542
Green Bank, NJ 08215
800-445-0953
www.belhavencanoe.com

Blue Mountain Outfitters
103 South State Road
Marysville, PA 17053
717-957-2413
www.bluemountainoutfitters.net

Hidden River Outfitters
57 East Schuylkill Avenue #2
Pottstown, PA 19465
www.hiddenriveroutfitters.com

Jersey Paddler
1756 Route 88
Brick, NJ 08724
888-22-KAYAK
www.jerseypaddler.com

Kayak East
PO Box 77
Columbia, NJ 07832
866-529-2532
www.kayakeast.com

Nature's Way Canoe & Kayak
Routes 563 & 412
Quakertown, PA 18951
215-536-8964
www.naturecanoe.com

New Jersey Kayak
409 East Bay Avenue
Barnegat, NJ 08005
609-698-4440
www.newjerseykayak.com

Paddle Shack
5045 Mays Landing-Somers Point Road
Mays Landing, NJ 08330
609-909-5250
www.paddleshack.com

Princeton Canoe and Kayak
Carnegie Lake location:
    483 Alexander Street
    Princeton, NJ 08540
    609-452-2403
*Griggstown on the Delaware and Raritan
Canal location*:
    1076 Canal Road
    Princeton, NJ 08540
    908-359-5970
    www.canoenj.com

Shark River Kayak Company
Belmar Marina, Belmar, NJ 07719
732-749-0490
www.sharkriverkayaks.com
www.nynjtc.org

USEFUL ADDRESSES AND PHONE NUMBERS

Appalachian Mountain Club
Mid-Atlantic Office
520 Long Street
Bethlehem, PA 18018
610-868-6903
www.outdoors.org

New Jersey Audubon Society
Headquarters
9 Hardscrabble Road
PO Box 126
Bernardsville, NJ 07924
908-204-8998
www.njaudubon.oerg

The Nature Conservancy
New Jersey Field Office
Elizabeth D. Kay Environmental Center
200 Pottersville Road
Chester, NJ 07930
908-879-7262
www.nature.org/newjersey

Sierra Club
57 Mountain Avenue
Princeton, NJ 08540
609-924-3141
newjersey.sierraclub.org

New Jersey Recreation and Parks
Association
4 Griggstown Causeway
Princeton, NJ 08540
908-281-9212
www.njrpa.org

Pennsylvania Fish and Boat Commission
(PFBC)
1601 Elmerton Avenue
PO Box 67000
Harrisburg, PA 17106-7000
717-705-7800
www.fish.state.pa.us

Division of Conservation and Natural
Resources (DCNR)
Rachel Carson State Office Building
400 Market Street
Harrisburg, PA 17105
888-727-2757
www.dcnr.state.pa.us

Appendix D:
Launch Permits by State

NEW JERSEY WILDLIFE MANAGEMENT AREA LAUNCH PERMITS
You must have either a Boat Ramp Maintenance Permit or a photocopy of a valid hunting, fishing or trapping license showing the Conservation ID Number (CID#). Permits may be purchased for a fee of $15.00 from any license agent (visit www.njfishandwildlife.com/agentlst.htm) or online at the Divisions license website at *www.njfishandwildlife.com/licenses.htm*. For further assistance, call 908-637-4125 or e-mail njfishandwildlife@dep.state.nj.us.

PENNSYLVANIA BOAT LAUNCH PERMIT
For most lakes and reservoirs in Pennslyvania, canoes, kayaks, and non-powered boats must display one of the following: boat registration from any state; launching permit or mooring permit from Pennsylvania State Parks, available at most state park offices; or a launching permit from the Pennsylvania Fish and Boat Commission.

State Parks are governed by the Department of Conservation and Natural Resources (DCNR). Their launch permits are $10 per year for residents and $15 for non-residents, with discounts available for two-year permits. Permits can be obtained from any state park office or online at www.theoutdoorshop. state.pa.us.

Many other reservoirs and lakes are governed by the Pennsylvania Fish and Boat Commission (PFBC). You can purchase a launching permit by printing out and mailing the form from www.fish.state.pa.us.

Occasionally, county parks will have their own permits, like Bucks County for Peace Valley County Park, Trip 62, and Core Creek Park, Trip 68. Bucks County launch permits are conveniently obtained from the park offices or from any park ranger at each of those locations.

List of Waterways

About the Author

Kathy Kenley is a retired marine biologist with additional degrees in geology and creative writing. She started kayaking in 1966, and since then has explored and kayaked lakes, rivers, coastal marshlands, open bays, and near-shore ocean waters along the East Coast and as far away as Thailand and Tahiti. She has competed on the national level in many kayak races, and occasionally leads tours for a local outfitter within the Pine Barrens of New Jersey. Her current focus is to help introduce older men and women into the world of paddling for fun, exploration, and physical fitness.

Kenley, an avid scuba diver and snorkeler, owned and operated her own charter dive boat for more than ten years and held a U.S. Coast Guard captain's license. Her numerous eclectic interests range from paleontology to art and anthropology. She is committed to protecting the environment, participating in waterway cleanups, and carrying a trash bag in her boat to pick up discarded refuse.

About the AMC Delaware Valley Chapter

The AMC Delaware Valley Chapter offers a wide variety of hiking, backpacking, climbing, paddling, bicycling, snowshoeing, and skiing trips each year, as well as social, family, and young member programs and instructional workshops. The chapter is also maintains a 15 mile section of the Appalachian Trail between Wind Gap and Little Gap, as well as trails at Valley Forge National Park.

To view a list of AMC activities in Pennsylvania, central and southern New Jersey, northern Delaware, and other parts of the Northeast, visit trips.outdoors. org.

AMC Books Updates

AMC Books strives to keep our guidebooks as up-to-date as possible to help you plan safe and enjoyable adventures. If we learn after publishing a book that trails are relocated or that route or contact information has changed, we will post the updated information online. Before you hit the trail, check for updates at www.outdoors.org/publications/books/updates.

If you notice discrepancies in the descriptions or maps while hiking or pad-dling, or if you find other errors in the book, please let us know by submit-ting them to amcbookupdates@outdoors.org or in writing to Books Editor, c/o AMC, 5 Joy Street, Boston, MA 02108. We will verify all submissions and post key updates each month.

AMC Books is dedicated to being a recognized leader in outdoor publishing. Thank you for your participation.

AMC BOOKS & MAPS

EXPLORE THE POSSIBILITIES

Appalachian Mountain Club

Founded in 1876, the AMC is the nation's oldest outdoor recreation and conservation organization. The AMC promotes the protection, enjoyment, and stewardship of the mountains, forests, waters, and trails of the Appalachian region.

People
We are more than 100,000 members, advocates, and supporters; 16,000 volunteers; and more than 450 full-time and seasonal staff. Our 12 chapters reach from Maine to Washington, D.C.

Outdoor Adventure and Fun
We offer more than 8,000 trips each year, from local chapter activities to major excursions worldwide, for every ability level and outdoor interest— from hiking and climbing to paddling, snowshoeing, and skiing.

Great Places to Stay
We host more than 140,000 guests each year at our lodges, huts, camps, shelters, and campgrounds. Each AMC destination is a model for environmental education and stewardship.

Opportunities for Learning
We teach people the skills to be safe outdoors and to care for the natural world around us through programs for children, teens, and adults, as well as outdoor leadership training.

Caring for Trails
We maintain more than 1,500 miles of trails throughout the Northeast, including nearly 350 miles of the Appalachian Trail in five states.

Protecting Wild Places
We advocate for land and riverway conservation, monitor air quality and climate change, and work to protect alpine and forest ecosystems throughout the Northern Forest and Mid-Atlantic Highlands regions.

Engaging the Public
We seek to educate and inform our own members and an additional 2 million people annually through AMC Books, our website, our White Mountain visitor centers, and AMC destinations.

Join Us!
Members support our mission while enjoying great AMC programs, our award-winning *AMC Outdoors* magazine, and special discounts. Visit www.outdoors.org or call 800-372-1758 for more information.

Appalachian Mountain Club
Recreation • Education • Conservation
www.outdoors.org

More Books from the Outdoor Experts

AMC's Best Day Hikes near New York City

BY DANIEL CASE

You don't have to travel far from New York City to find some of the best day hikes in the Northeast. This guidebook takes you to 50 of the best excursions in New York, Connecticut, and northern New Jersey.

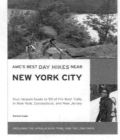

ISBN: 978-1-934028-38-4
$18.95

AMC's Best Day Hikes near Philadelphia

BY SUSAN CHARKES

Ideal for families, tourists, and local residents, this easy-to-use guide will help you explore eastern Pennsylvania, New Jersey, and Delaware year-round, from lesser-known excursions to area favorites, including several hikes on the Appalachian Trail.

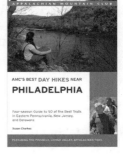

ISBN: 978-1-934028-33-9
$18.95

Quiet Water New York, 2nd Edition

BY JOHN HAYES AND ALEX WILSON

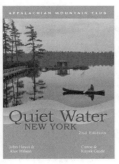

From clear and quick-flowing waterways to picturesque ponds surrounded by mountain peaks, this guide allows paddlers to explore the great variety of water adventures New York has to offer with 90 spectacular quiet-water destinations.

ISBN: 978-1-929173-73-0
$19.95

AMC's Best Day Hikes in the Berkshires

BY RENÉ LAUBACH

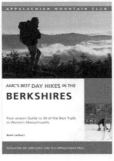

Discover 50 of the most impressive trails in the Berkshires, from short nature walks to long day hikes. Each trip description includes a detailed map, trip time, distance, and difficulty. You'll also find tips on area snowshoeing, cross-country skiing, and nature notes.

ISBN: 978-1-934028-21-6
$18.95